STOP!

This is the back of the book. You wouldn't want to spoil a great ending!

This book is printed "manga-style," in the authentic Japanese right-to-left format. Since none of the artwork has been flipped or altered, readers get to experience the story just as the creator intended. You've been asking for it, so TOKYOPOP® delivered: authentic, hot-off-the-press, and far more fun!

DIRECTIONS

If this is your first time reading manga-style, here's a quick guide to help you understand how it works.

It's easy... just start in the top right panel and follow the numbers. Have fun, and look for more 100% authentic manga from TOKYOPOP®!

1
2
3
4
5
6
7
8
9
10

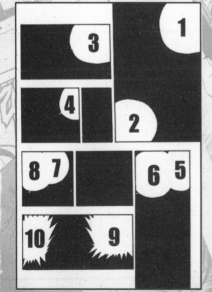

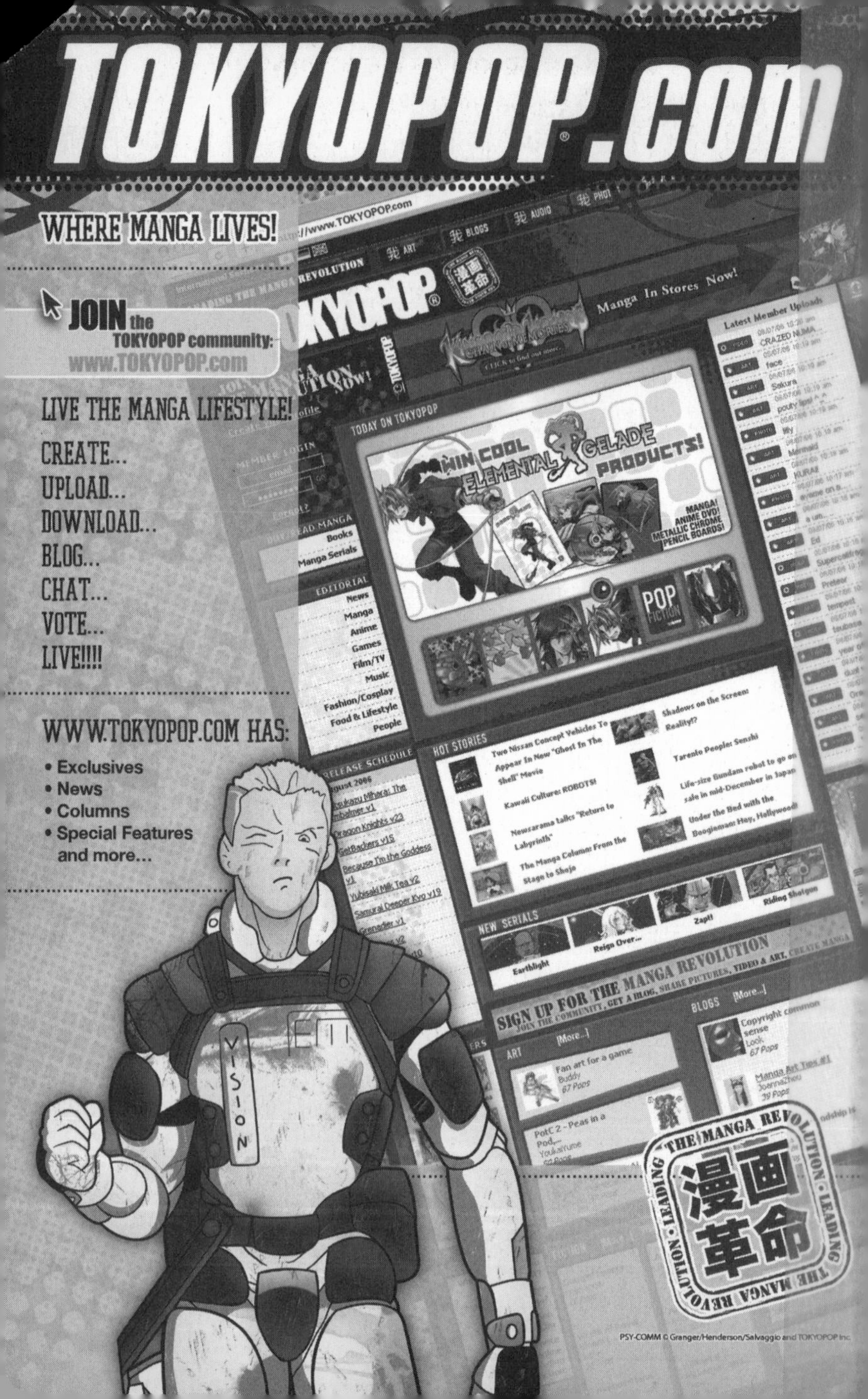
TOKYOPOP.com
WHERE MANGA LIVES!
JOIN the TOKYOPOP community:
www.TOKYOPOP.com
LIVE THE MANGA LIFESTYLE!
CREATE...
UPLOAD...
DOWNLOAD...
BLOG...
CHAT...
VOTE...
LIVE!!!!
WWW.TOKYOPOP.COM HAS:
• Exclusives
• News
• Columns
• Special Features and more...
THE MANGA REVOLUTION • LEADING THE MANGA REVOLUTION • LEADING
漫画革命
PSY-COMM © Granger/Henderson/Salvaggio and TOKYOPOP Inc.

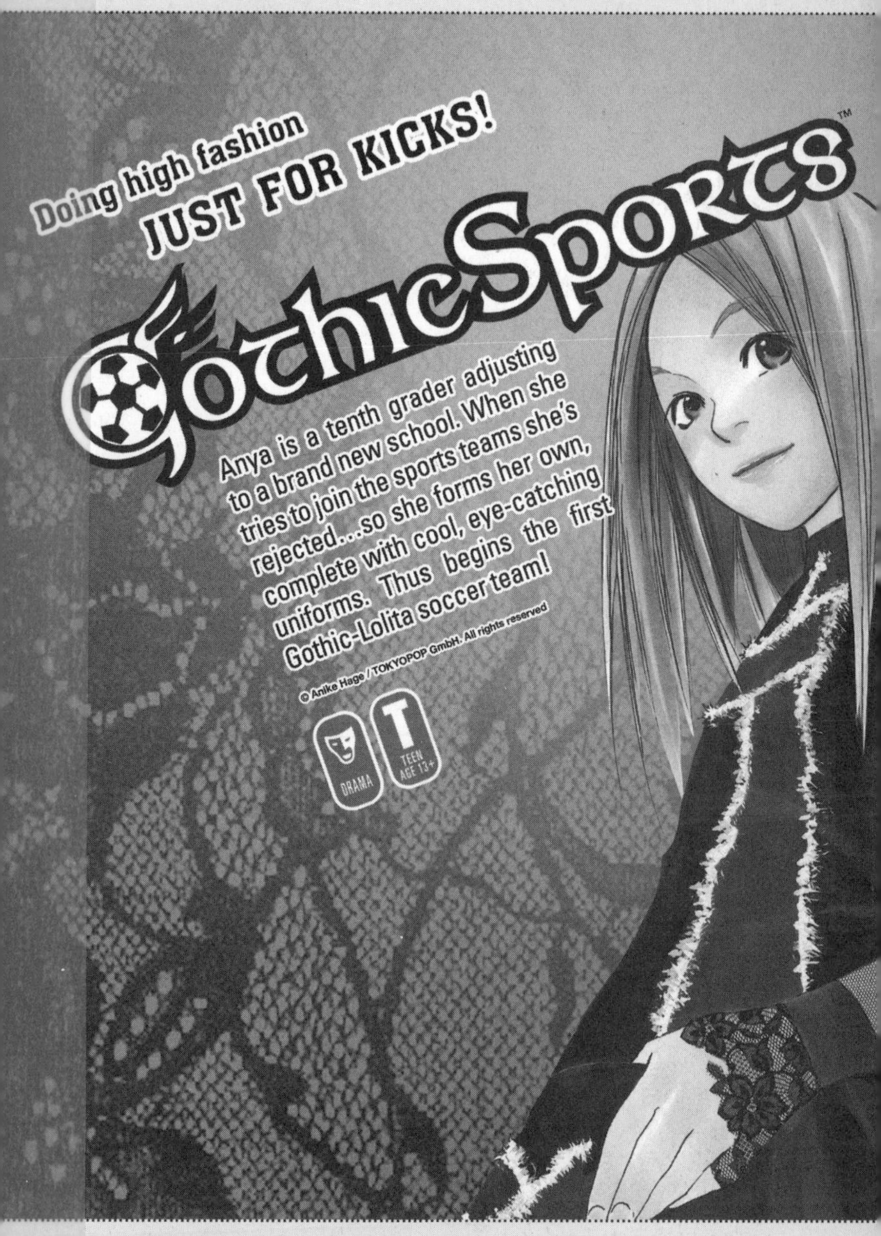
Doing high fashion
JUST FOR KICKS!
GothicSports™
Anya is a tenth grader adjusting to a brand new school. When she tries to join the sports teams she's rejected...so she forms her own, complete with cool, eye-catching uniforms. Thus begins the first Gothic-Lolita soccer team!
© Anike Hage / TOKYOPOP GmbH. All rights reserved
DRAMA
T
TEEN AGE 13+

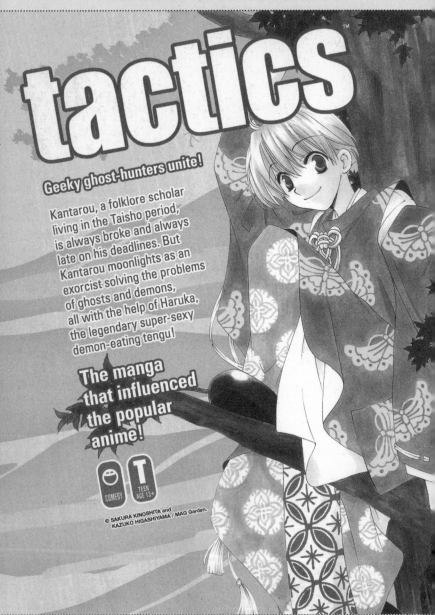

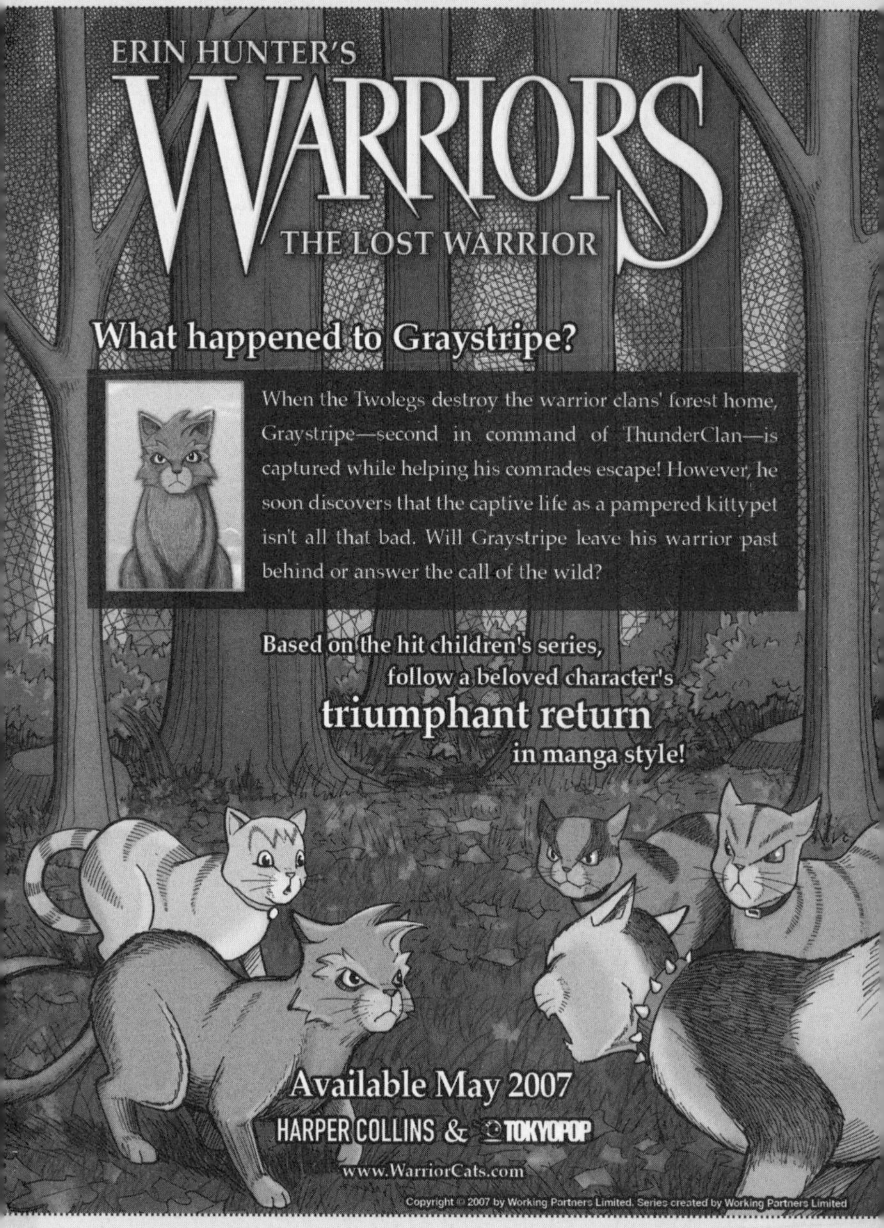
ERIN HUNTER'S
WARRIORS
THE LOST WARRIOR
What happened to Graystripe?
When the Twolegs destroy the warrior clans' forest home, Graystripe—second in command of ThunderClan—is captured while helping his comrades escape! However, he soon discovers that the captive life as a pampered kittypet isn't all that bad. Will Graystripe leave his warrior past behind or answer the call of the wild?
Based on the hit children's series, follow a beloved character's triumphant return in manga style!
Available May 2007
HARPER COLLINS & TOKYOPOP
www.WarriorCats.com
Copyright © 2007 by Working Partners Limited. Series created by Working Partners Limited

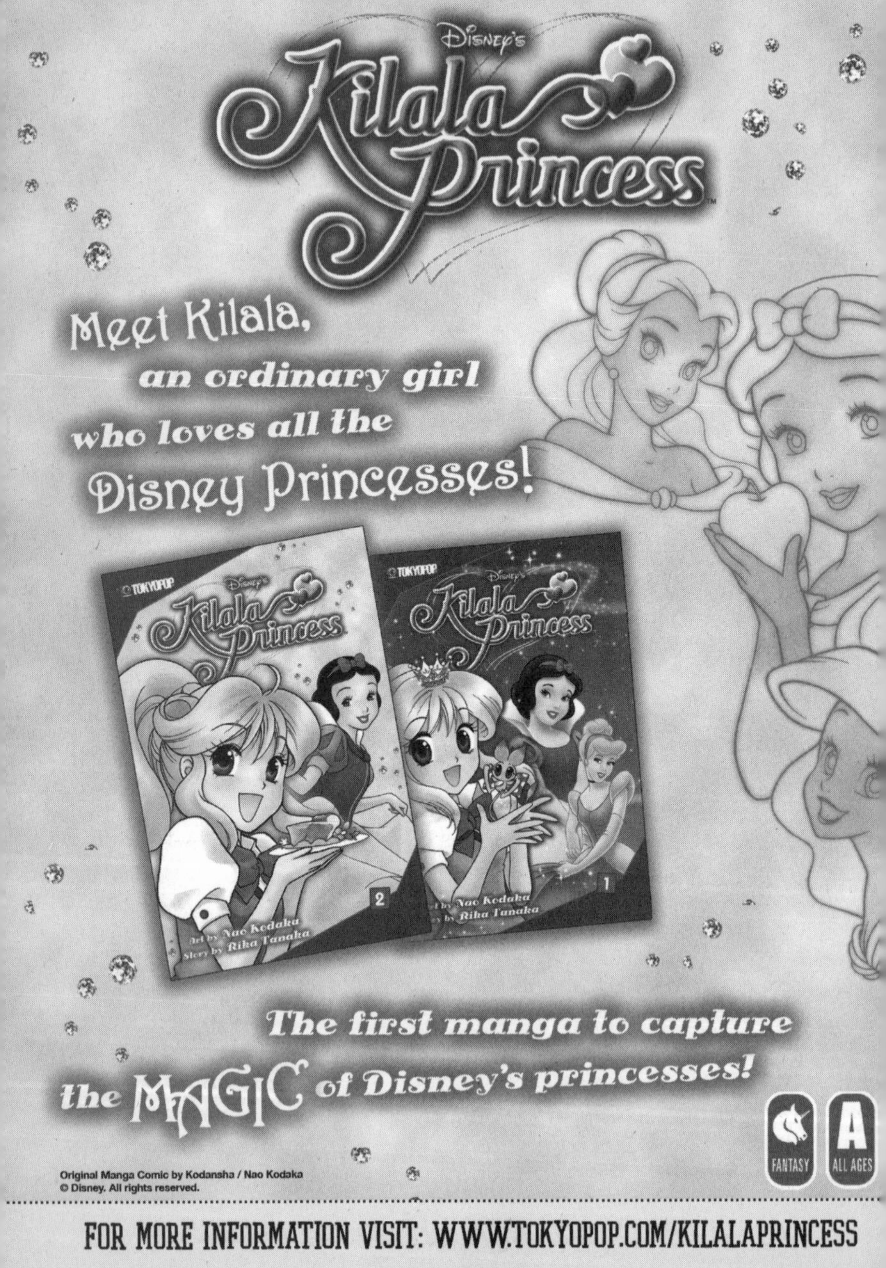
Disney's
Kilala Princess
Meet Kilala,
an ordinary girl
who loves all the
Disney Princesses!
TOKYOPOP
Disney's Kilala Princess
2
Art by Nao Kodaka
Story by Rika Tanaka
TOKYOPOP
Disney's Kilala Princess
1
Nao Kodaka
Rika Tanaka
The first manga to capture
the MAGIC of Disney's princesses!
FANTASY
A
ALL AGES
Original Manga Comic by Kodansha / Nao Kodaka
© Disney. All rights reserved.

FOR MORE INFORMATION VISIT: WWW.TOKYOPOP.COM/KILALAPRINCESS

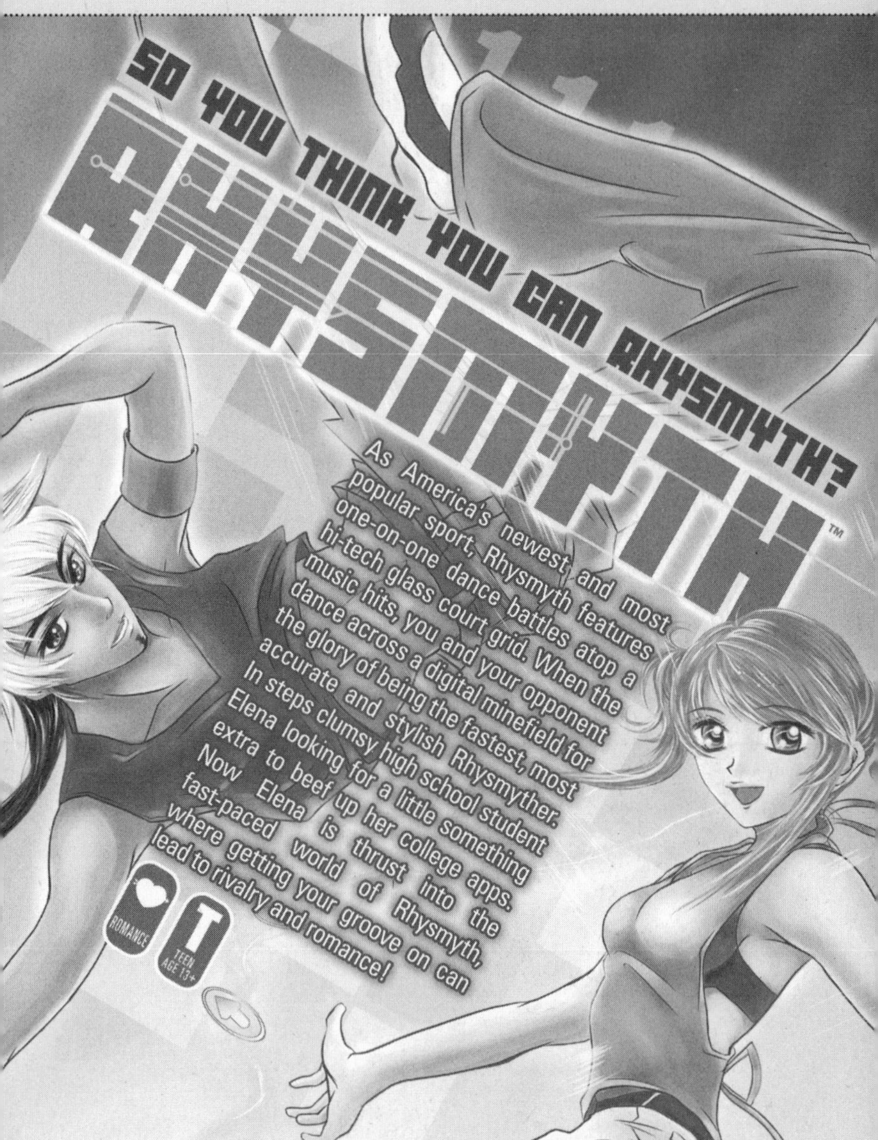
SO YOU THINK YOU CAN RHYSMYTH?
RHYSMYTH™
As America's newest and most popular sport, Rhysmyth features one-on-one dance battles atop a hi-tech glass court grid. When the music hits, you and your opponent dance across a digital minefield for the glory of being the fastest, most accurate and stylish Rhysmyther. In steps clumsy high school student Elena looking for a little something extra to beef up her college apps. Now Elena is thrust into the fast-paced world of Rhysmyth, where getting your groove on can lead to rivalry and romance!
ROMANCE
T
TEEN AGE 13+
Rhysmyth © Anthony Andora, Lincy Chan and TOKYOPOP Inc.

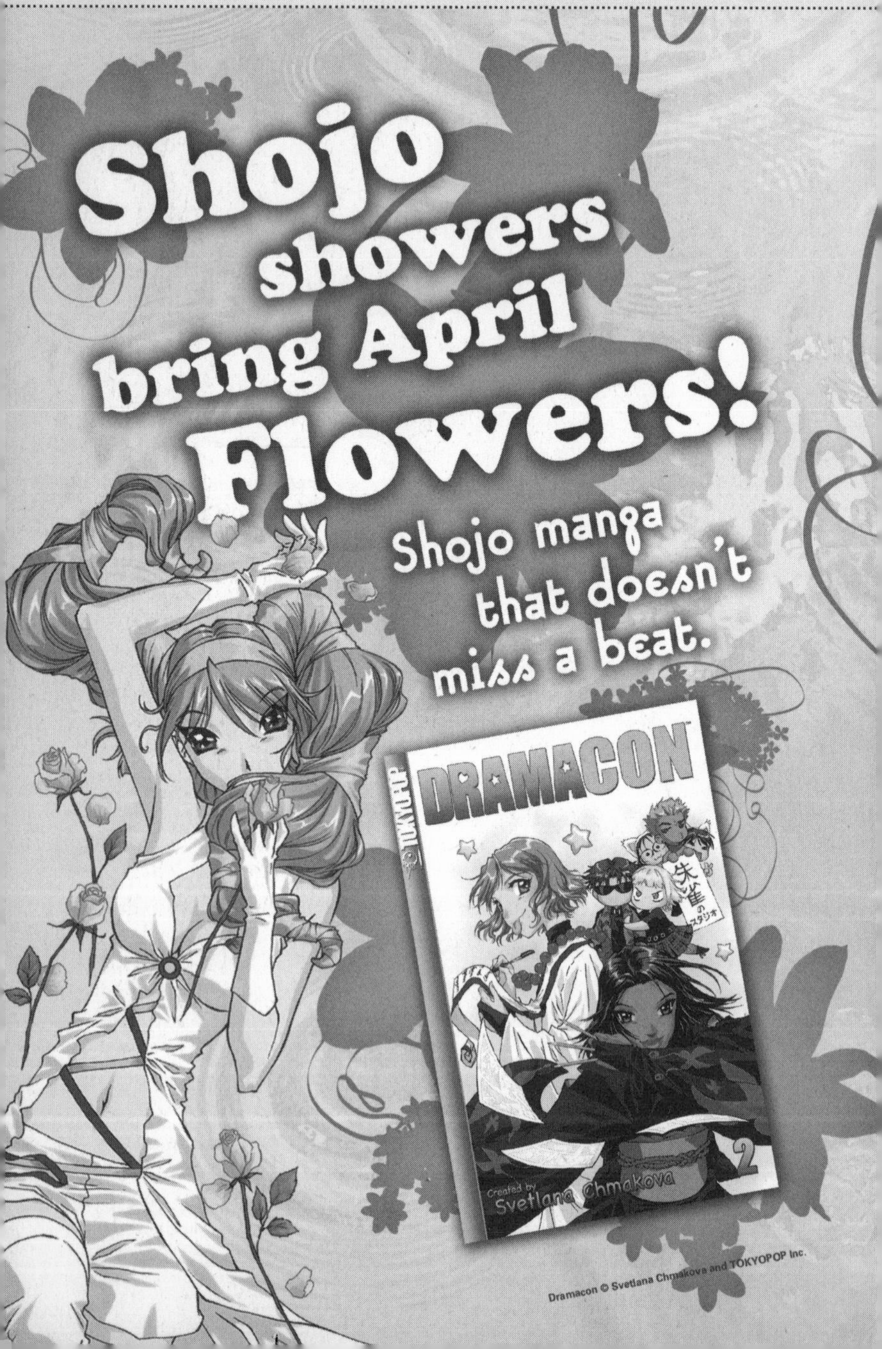
Shojo showers bring April Flowers!
Shojo manga that doesn't miss a beat.
DRAMACON
TOKYOPOP
2
Created by Svetlana Chmakova
Dramacon © Svetlana Chmakova and TOKYOPOP Inc.

Genju no Seiza

TABLE OF CONTENTS

H

Genju no Seiza™

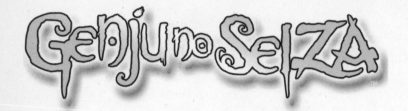

Volume 3

Created by
Matsuri Akino

TOKYOPOP®

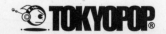

MBURG // LONDON // LOS ANGELES // TOKYO

STORY SO FAR

An empty throne...

Not in the literal sense (but I'll get to that in a moment), but for the past forty years, that is in truth what Dhalashar has had. For forty years, we've been without a king. But that has all changed now. We have found our heir to the throne. He is the half-Sherpa son of a world-famous photographer, and his name is Fuuto Kamishina. Currently living in Japan with his mother, young Fuuto has already begun to exhibit some of the powers of our king, and although he is unaware of this, his use of them has affirmed to me that he will be a good king. However, he is also a tad stubborn, and to this he refuses to accept his role as our new sovereign and religious leader.

There are further complications as well. While the people of Dhalashar have been without their TRUE king for quite some time, they have not been without a king. The Snake-God, Naga, a treacherous and deceitful deity, recently sensed opportunity upon our vacant throne. He has instilled an impostor king—little more than a puppet to Naga's ambitions—to rule Dhalashar. And much to my chagrin, many people of my nation have accepted this false sovereign as our next heir to the throne. However, Naga knows his king is false and that the emergence of the true sovereign will prove that to the people of Dhalashar. He fears young Fuuto Kamishina, and will do what he can to ensure he never ascends to the throne. He has already dispatched several assassins, and I fear more may be on the way.

—Garuda, Guardian Beast of the true King of Dhalashar

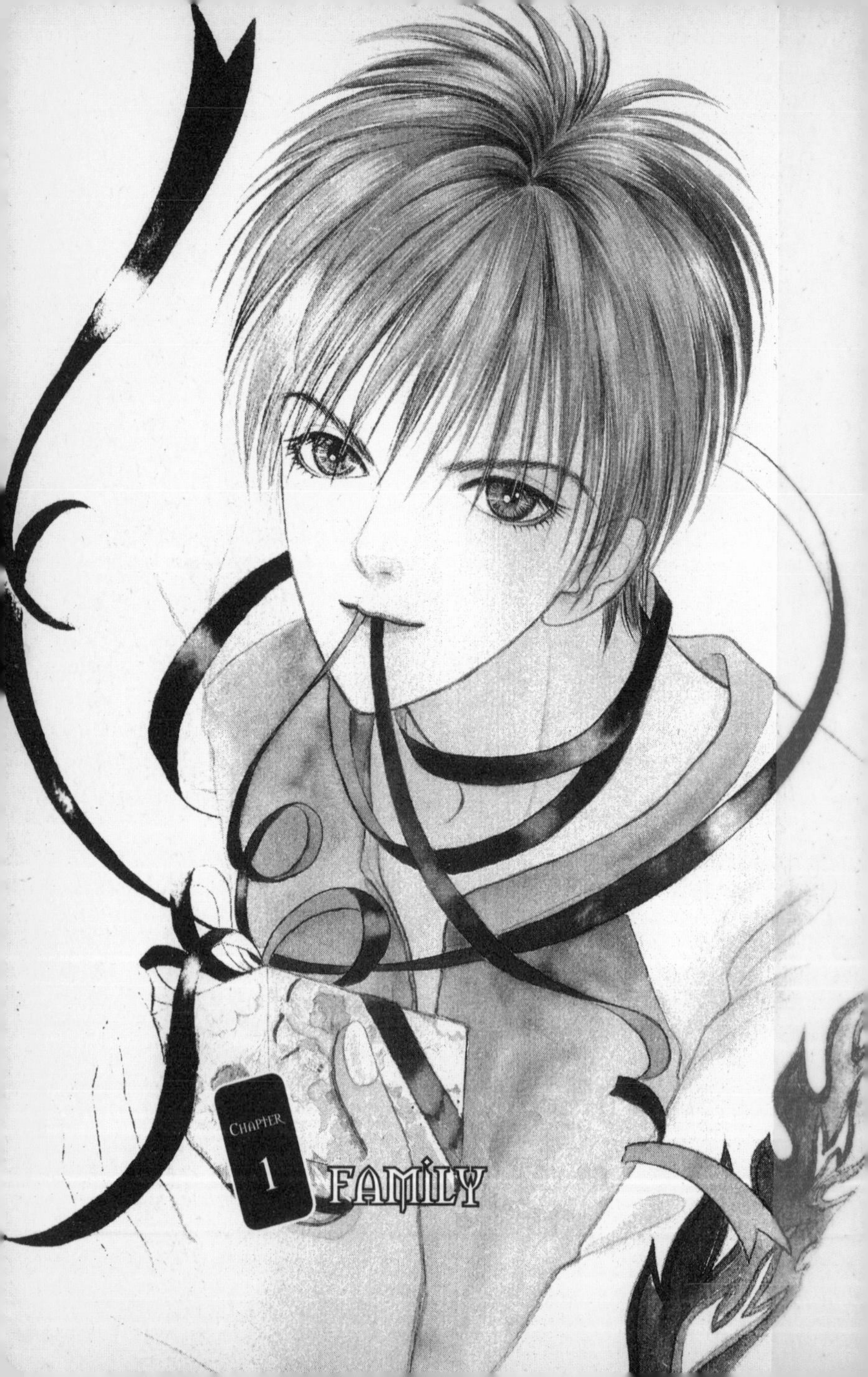
CHAPTER
1
FAMILY

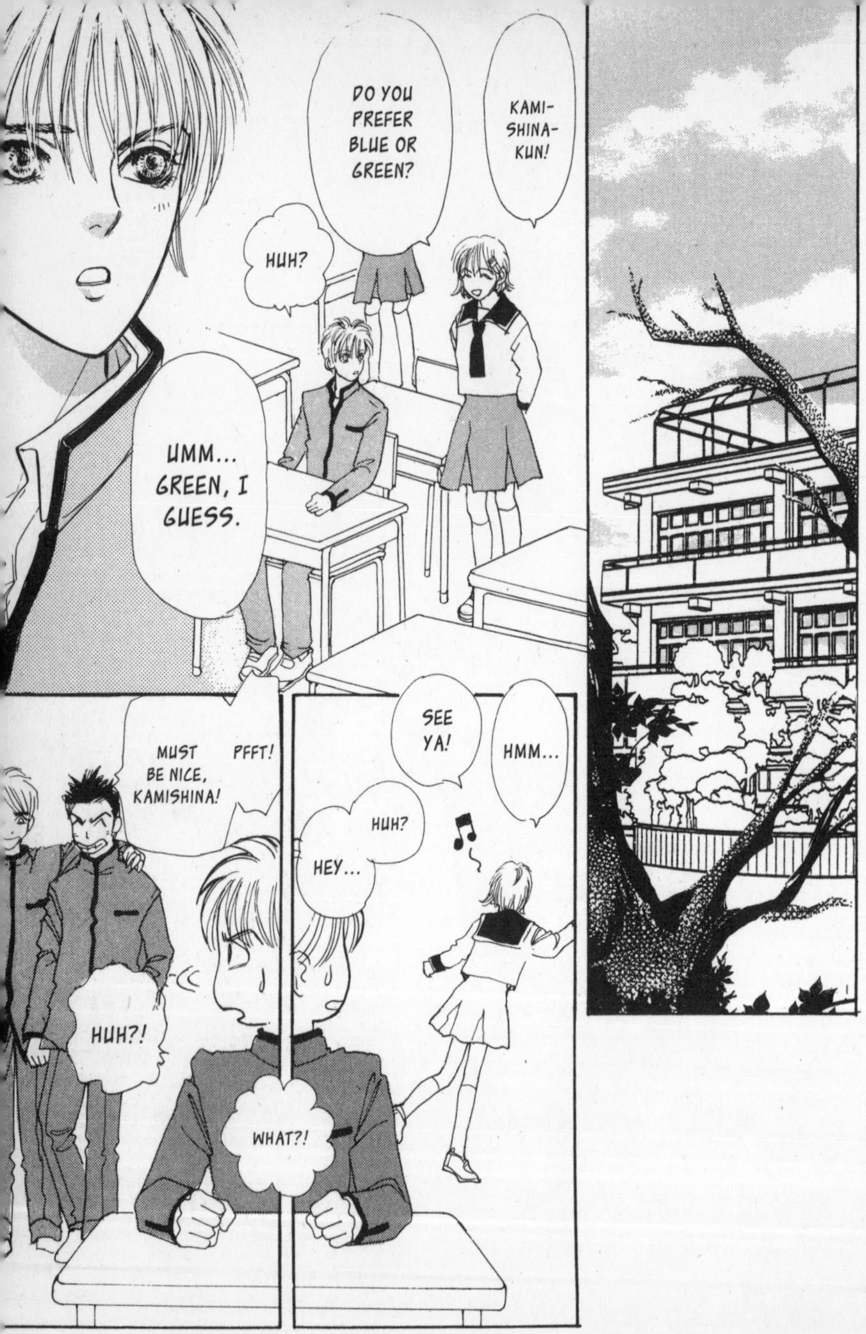
KAMI-SHINA-KUN!
DO YOU PREFER BLUE OR GREEN?
HUH?
UMM... GREEN, I GUESS.
HMM...
SEE YA!
HUH?
HEY...
WHAT?!
PFFT!
MUST BE NICE, KAMISHINA!
HUH?!

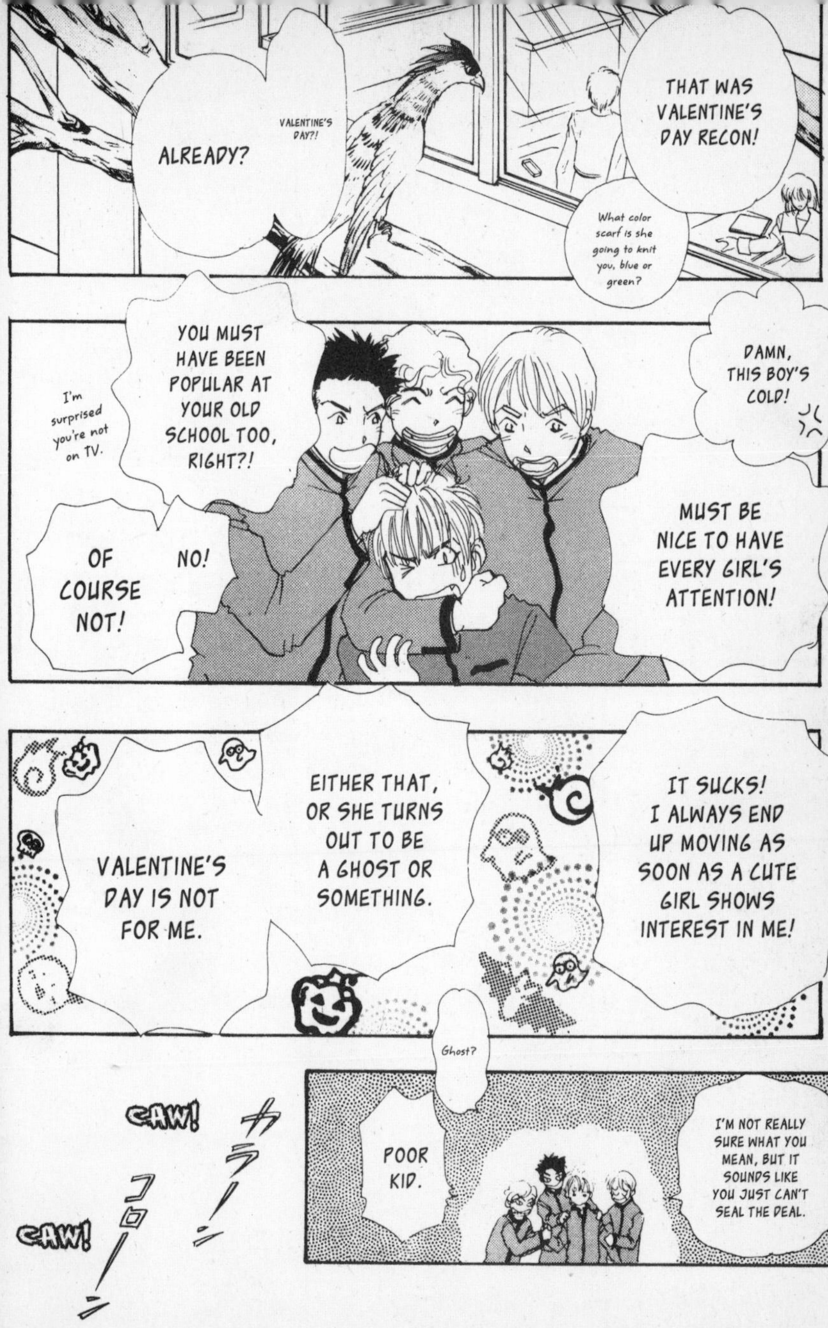
THAT WAS VALENTINE'S DAY RECON!
What color scarf is she going to knit you, blue or green?
VALENTINE'S DAY?!
ALREADY?
DAMN, THIS BOY'S COLD!
YOU MUST HAVE BEEN POPULAR AT YOUR OLD SCHOOL TOO, RIGHT?!
I'm surprised you're not on TV.
MUST BE NICE TO HAVE EVERY GIRL'S ATTENTION!
NO!
OF COURSE NOT!
IT SUCKS! I ALWAYS END UP MOVING AS SOON AS A CUTE GIRL SHOWS INTEREST IN ME!
EITHER THAT, OR SHE TURNS OUT TO BE A GHOST OR SOMETHING.
VALENTINE'S DAY IS NOT FOR ME.
Ghost?
I'M NOT REALLY SURE WHAT YOU MEAN, BUT IT SOUNDS LIKE YOU JUST CAN'T SEAL THE DEAL.
POOR KID.
CAW!
CAW!

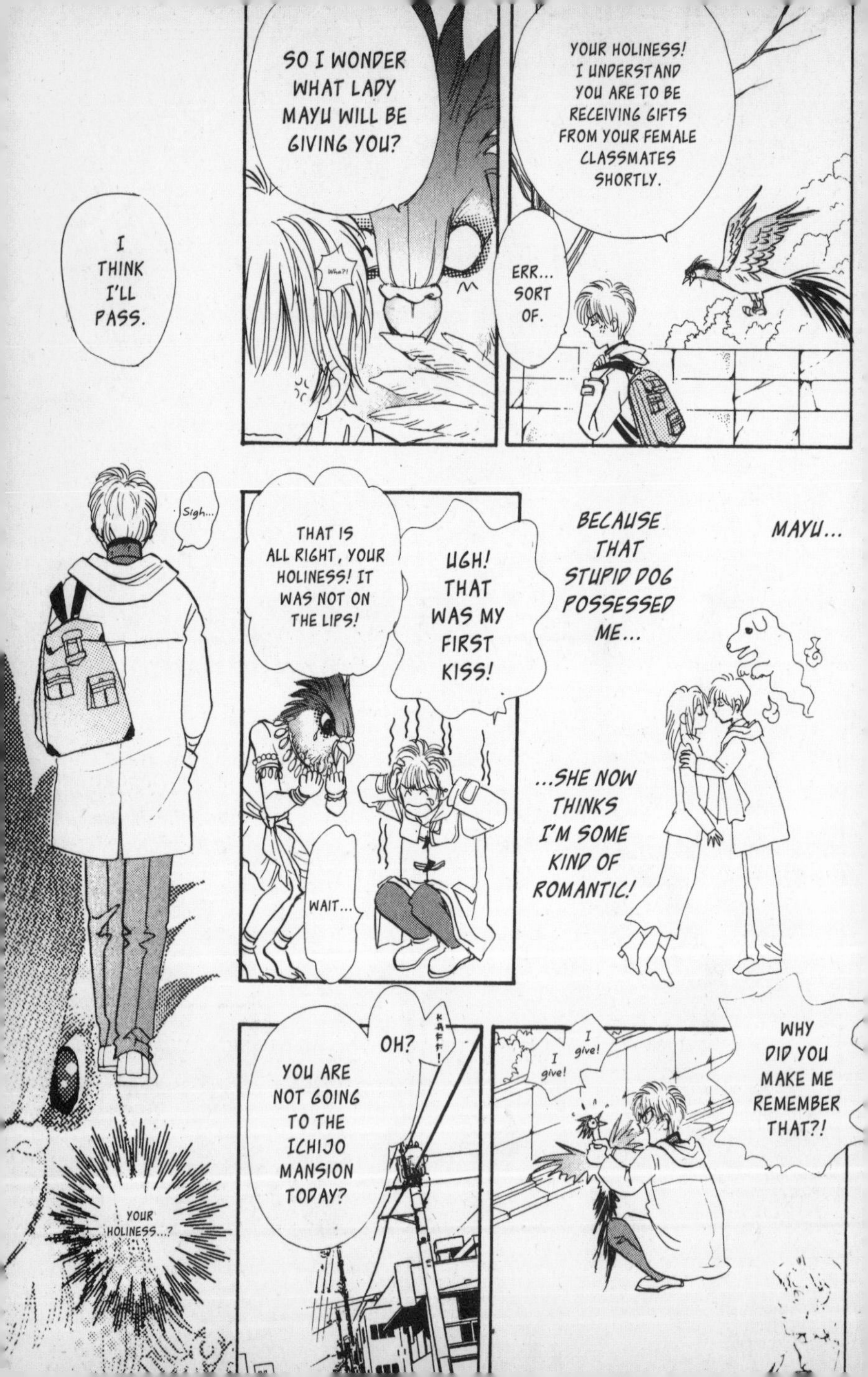
YOUR HOLINESS! I UNDERSTAND YOU ARE TO BE RECEIVING GIFTS FROM YOUR FEMALE CLASSMATES SHORTLY.
ERR... SORT OF.
SO I WONDER WHAT LADY MAYU WILL BE GIVING YOU?
What?!
I THINK I'LL PASS.
MAYU...
BECAUSE THAT STUPID DOG POSSESSED ME...
...SHE NOW THINKS I'M SOME KIND OF ROMANTIC!
UGH! THAT WAS MY FIRST KISS!
THAT IS ALL RIGHT, YOUR HOLINESS! IT WAS NOT ON THE LIPS!
WAIT...
WHY DID YOU MAKE ME REMEMBER THAT?!
I give!
I give!
OH?
KAFF!
YOU ARE NOT GOING TO THE ICHIJO MANSION TODAY?
Sigh...
YOUR HOLINESS...?

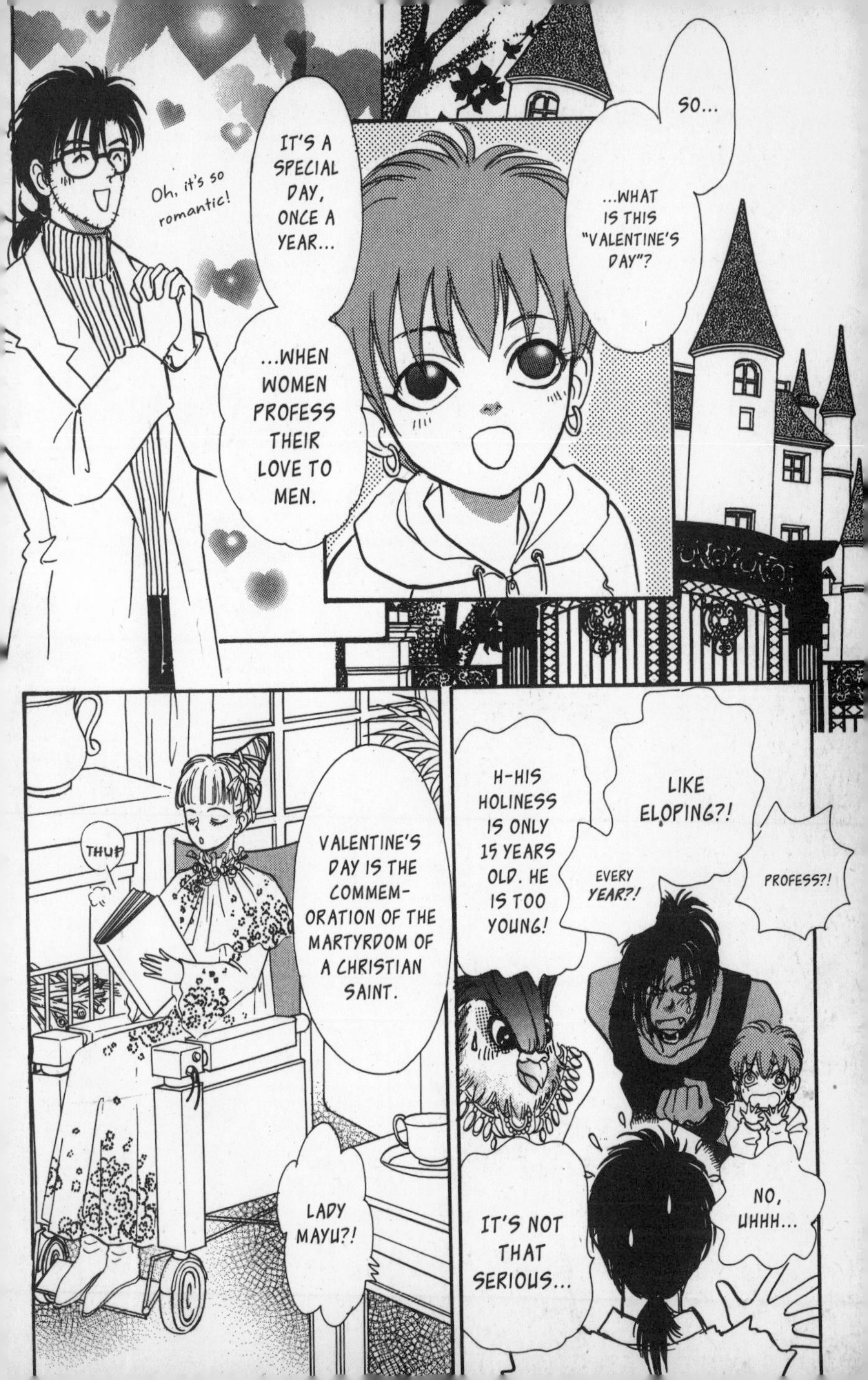
Oh, it's so romantic!
IT'S A SPECIAL DAY, ONCE A YEAR...
...WHEN WOMEN PROFESS THEIR LOVE TO MEN.
SO...
...WHAT IS THIS "VALENTINE'S DAY"?
THUP
VALENTINE'S DAY IS THE COMMEM-ORATION OF THE MARTYRDOM OF A CHRISTIAN SAINT.
LADY MAYU?!
H-HIS HOLINESS IS ONLY 15 YEARS OLD. HE IS TOO YOUNG!
EVERY YEAR?!
LIKE ELOPING?!
PROFESS?!
IT'S NOT THAT SERIOUS...
NO, UHHH...

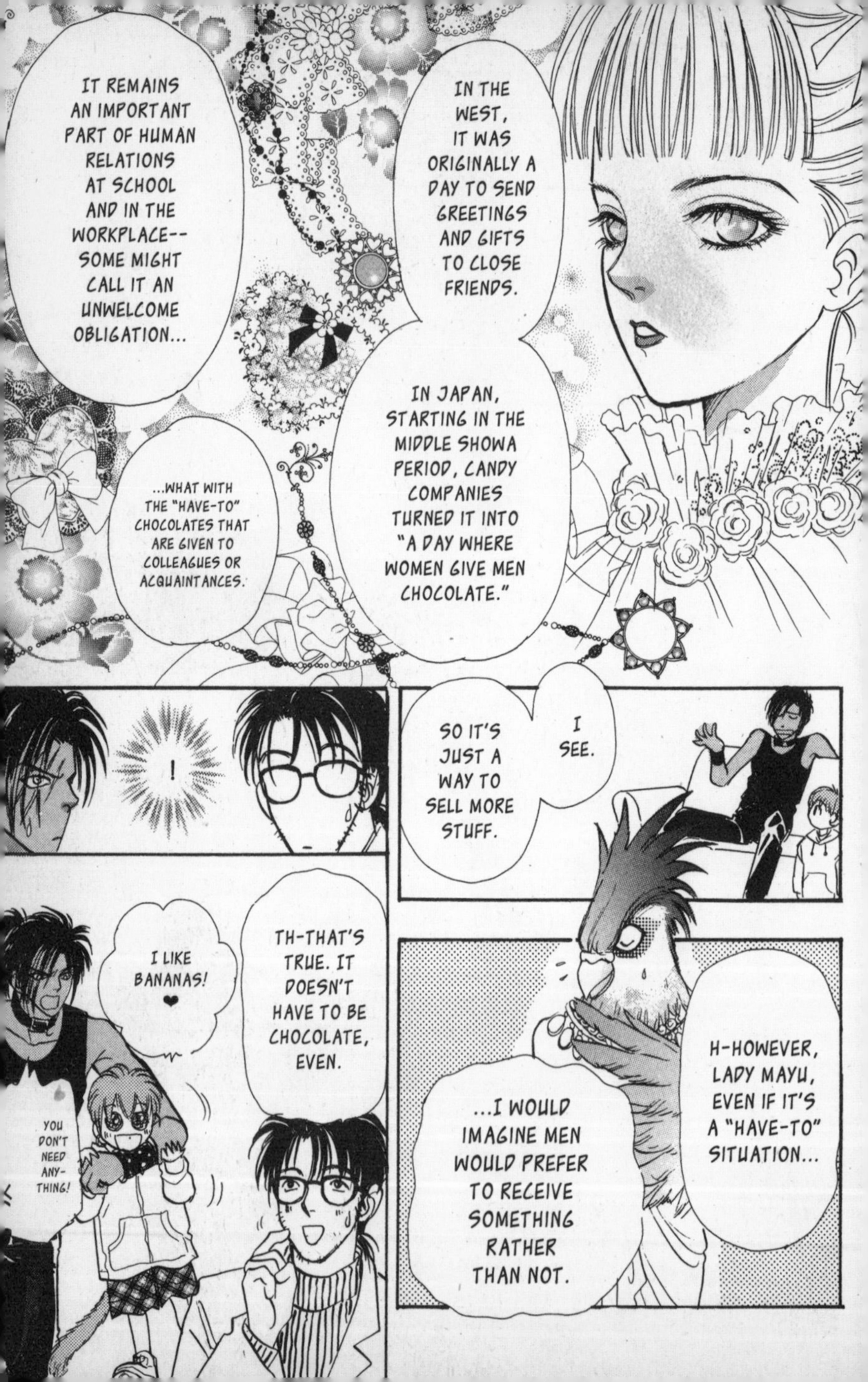
IN THE WEST, IT WAS ORIGINALLY A DAY TO SEND GREETINGS AND GIFTS TO CLOSE FRIENDS.
IN JAPAN, STARTING IN THE MIDDLE SHOWA PERIOD, CANDY COMPANIES TURNED IT INTO "A DAY WHERE WOMEN GIVE MEN CHOCOLATE."
IT REMAINS AN IMPORTANT PART OF HUMAN RELATIONS AT SCHOOL AND IN THE WORKPLACE-- SOME MIGHT CALL IT AN UNWELCOME OBLIGATION...
...WHAT WITH THE "HAVE-TO" CHOCOLATES THAT ARE GIVEN TO COLLEAGUES OR ACQUAINTANCES.
I SEE.
SO IT'S JUST A WAY TO SELL MORE STUFF.
!
H-HOWEVER, LADY MAYU, EVEN IF IT'S A "HAVE-TO" SITUATION...
...I WOULD IMAGINE MEN WOULD PREFER TO RECEIVE SOMETHING RATHER THAN NOT.
TH-THAT'S TRUE. IT DOESN'T HAVE TO BE CHOCOLATE, EVEN.
I LIKE BANANAS! ❤
YOU DON'T NEED ANYTHING!

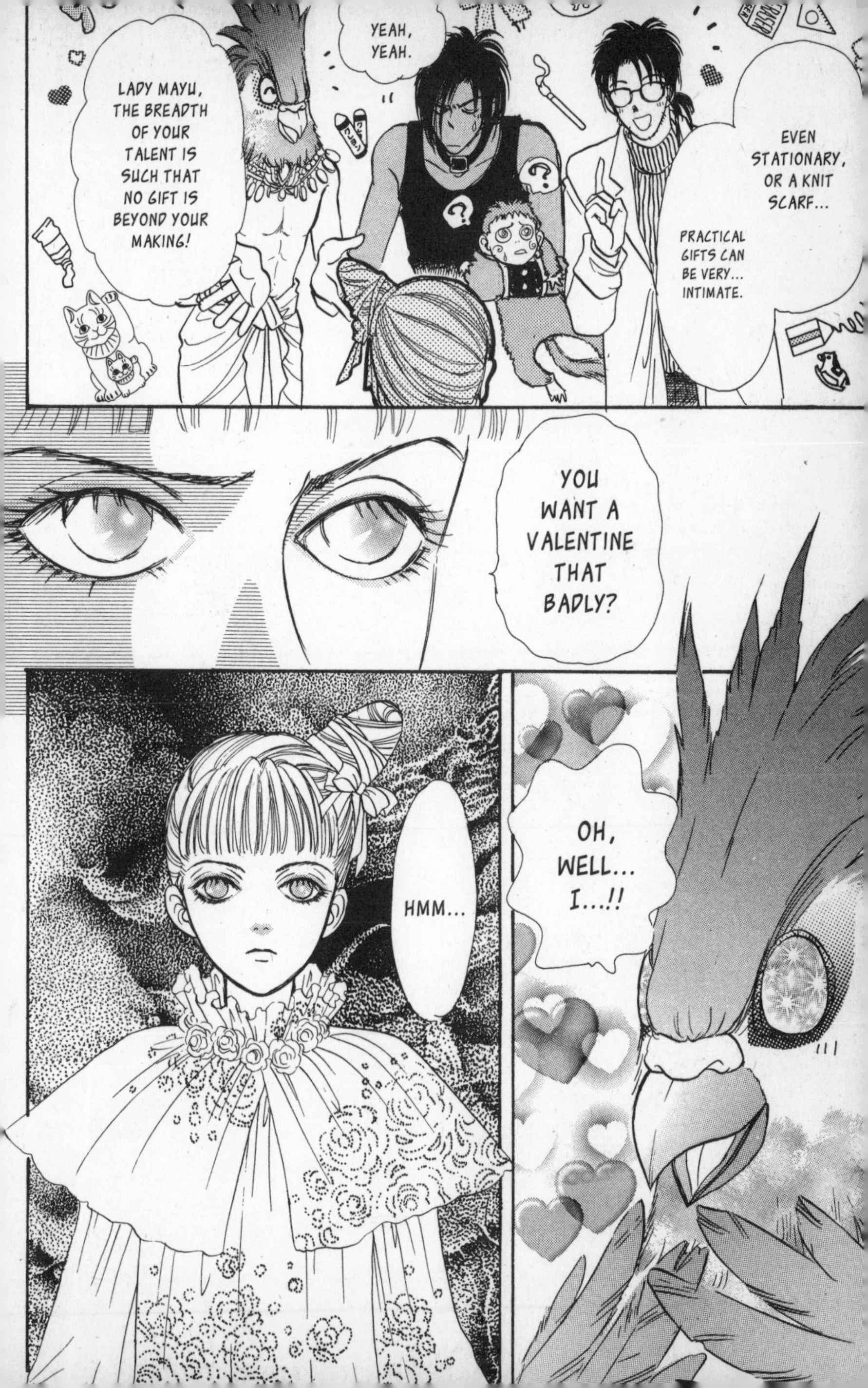
EVEN STATIONARY, OR A KNIT SCARF...
PRACTICAL GIFTS CAN BE VERY... INTIMATE.
YEAH, YEAH.
LADY MAYU, THE BREADTH OF YOUR TALENT IS SUCH THAT NO GIFT IS BEYOND YOUR MAKING!
YOU WANT A VALENTINE THAT BADLY?
OH, WELL... I...!!
HMM...

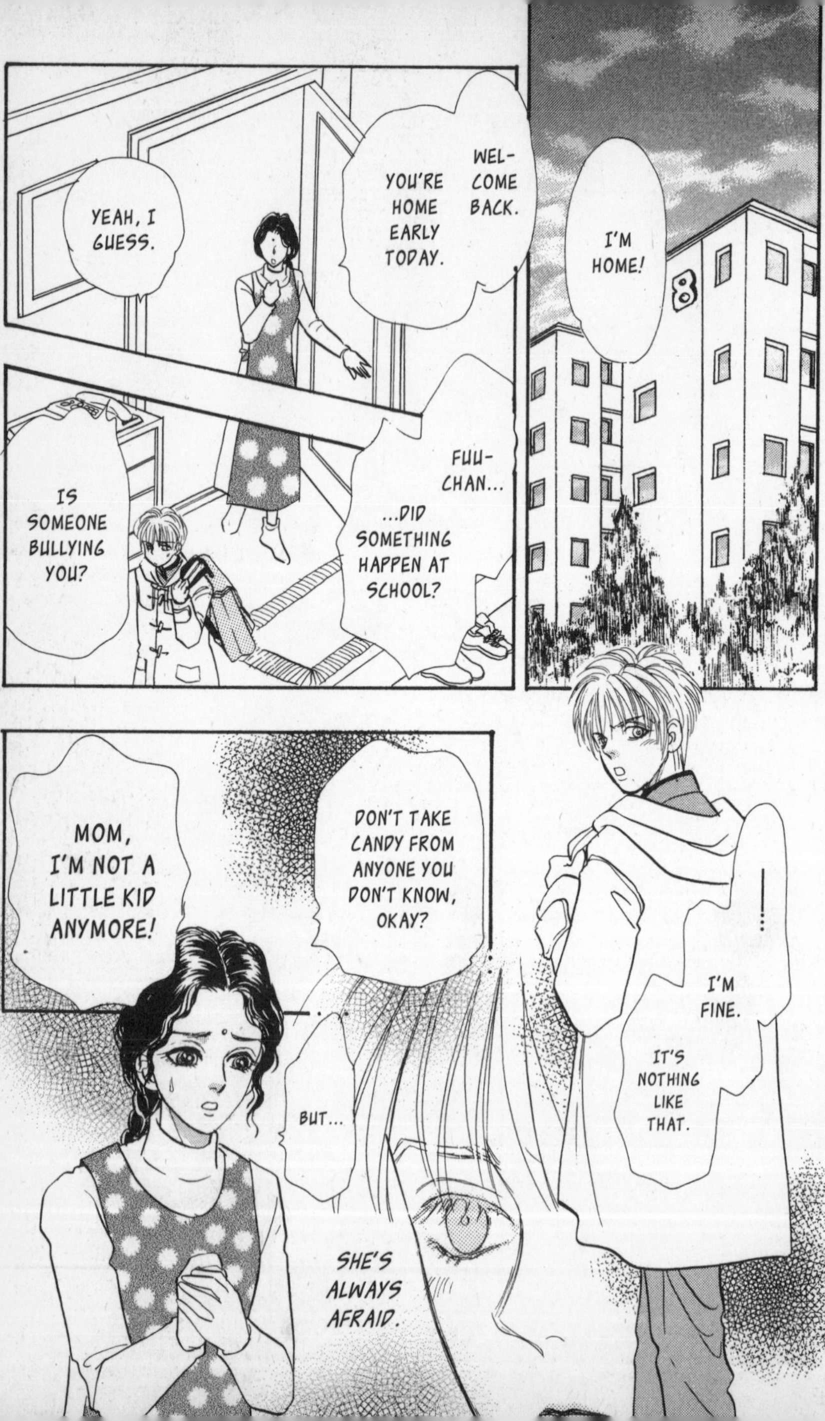
I'M HOME!
WEL-COME BACK.
YOU'RE HOME EARLY TODAY.
YEAH, I GUESS.
FUU-CHAN...
...DID SOMETHING HAPPEN AT SCHOOL?
IS SOMEONE BULLYING YOU?
I'M FINE.
IT'S NOTHING LIKE THAT.
DON'T TAKE CANDY FROM ANYONE YOU DON'T KNOW, OKAY?
MOM, I'M NOT A LITTLE KID ANYMORE!
BUT...
SHE'S ALWAYS AFRAID.

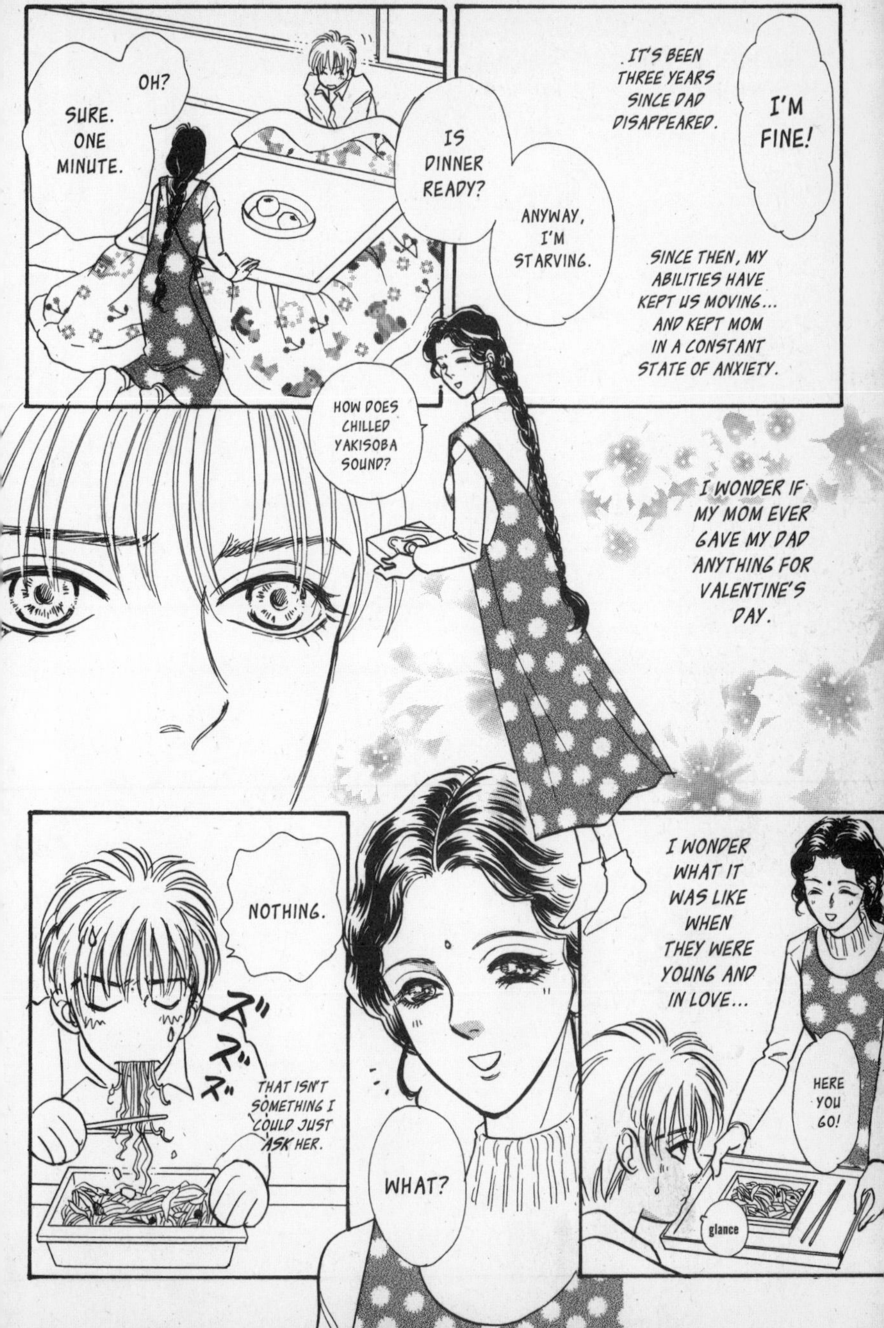
I'M FINE!
IT'S BEEN THREE YEARS SINCE DAD DISAPPEARED.
SINCE THEN, MY ABILITIES HAVE KEPT US MOVING... AND KEPT MOM IN A CONSTANT STATE OF ANXIETY.
ANYWAY, I'M STARVING.
IS DINNER READY?
OH?
SURE. ONE MINUTE.
HOW DOES CHILLED YAKISOBA SOUND?
I WONDER IF MY MOM EVER GAVE MY DAD ANYTHING FOR VALENTINE'S DAY.
I WONDER WHAT IT WAS LIKE WHEN THEY WERE YOUNG AND IN LOVE...
HERE YOU GO!
glance
WHAT?
NOTHING.
THAT ISN'T SOMETHING I COULD JUST ASK HER.

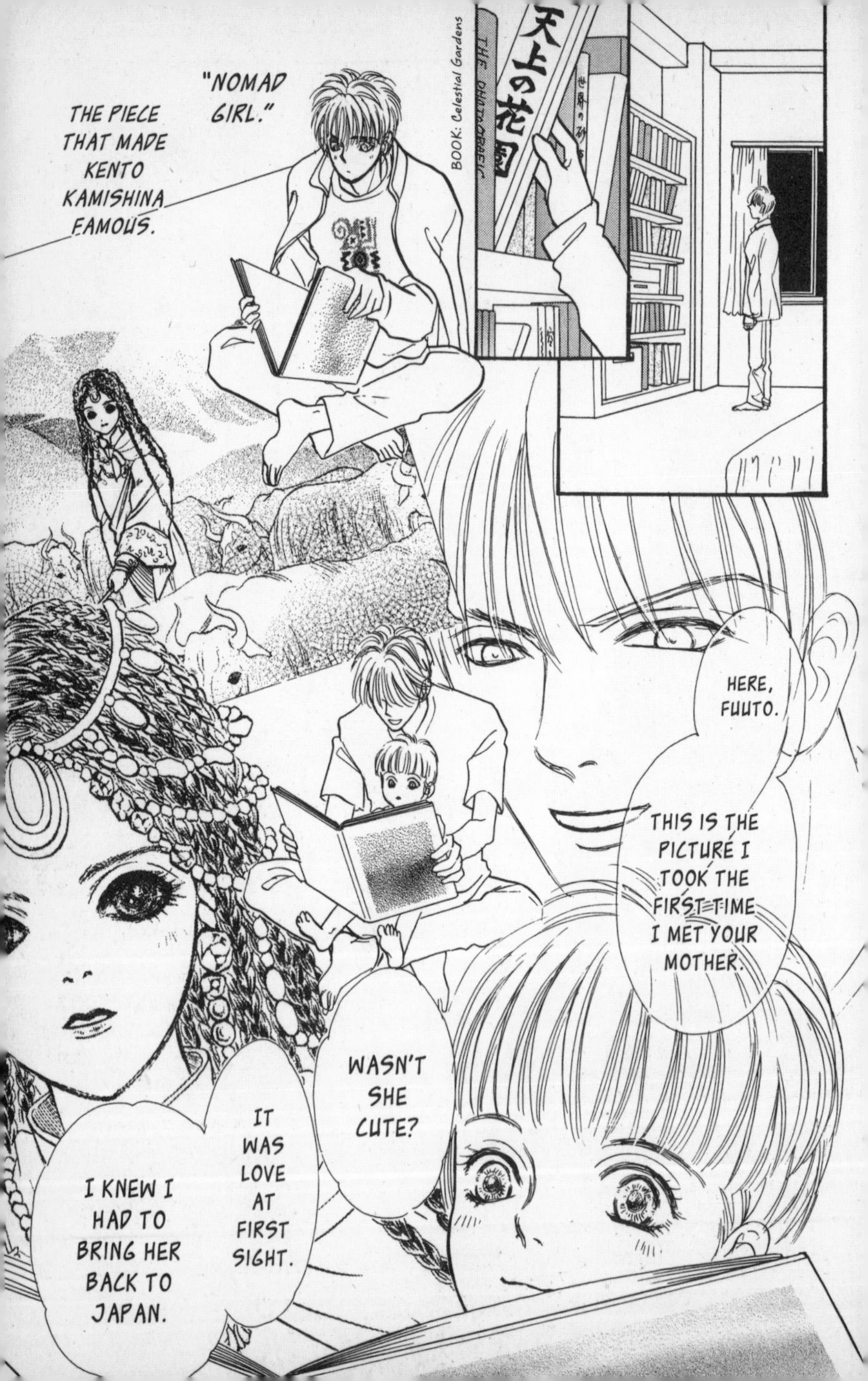
天上の花園
BOOK: Celestial Gardens
"NOMAD GIRL."
THE PIECE THAT MADE KENTO KAMISHINA FAMOUS.
HERE, FUUTO.
THIS IS THE PICTURE I TOOK THE FIRST TIME I MET YOUR MOTHER.
WASN'T SHE CUTE?
IT WAS LOVE AT FIRST SIGHT.
I KNEW I HAD TO BRING HER BACK TO JAPAN.

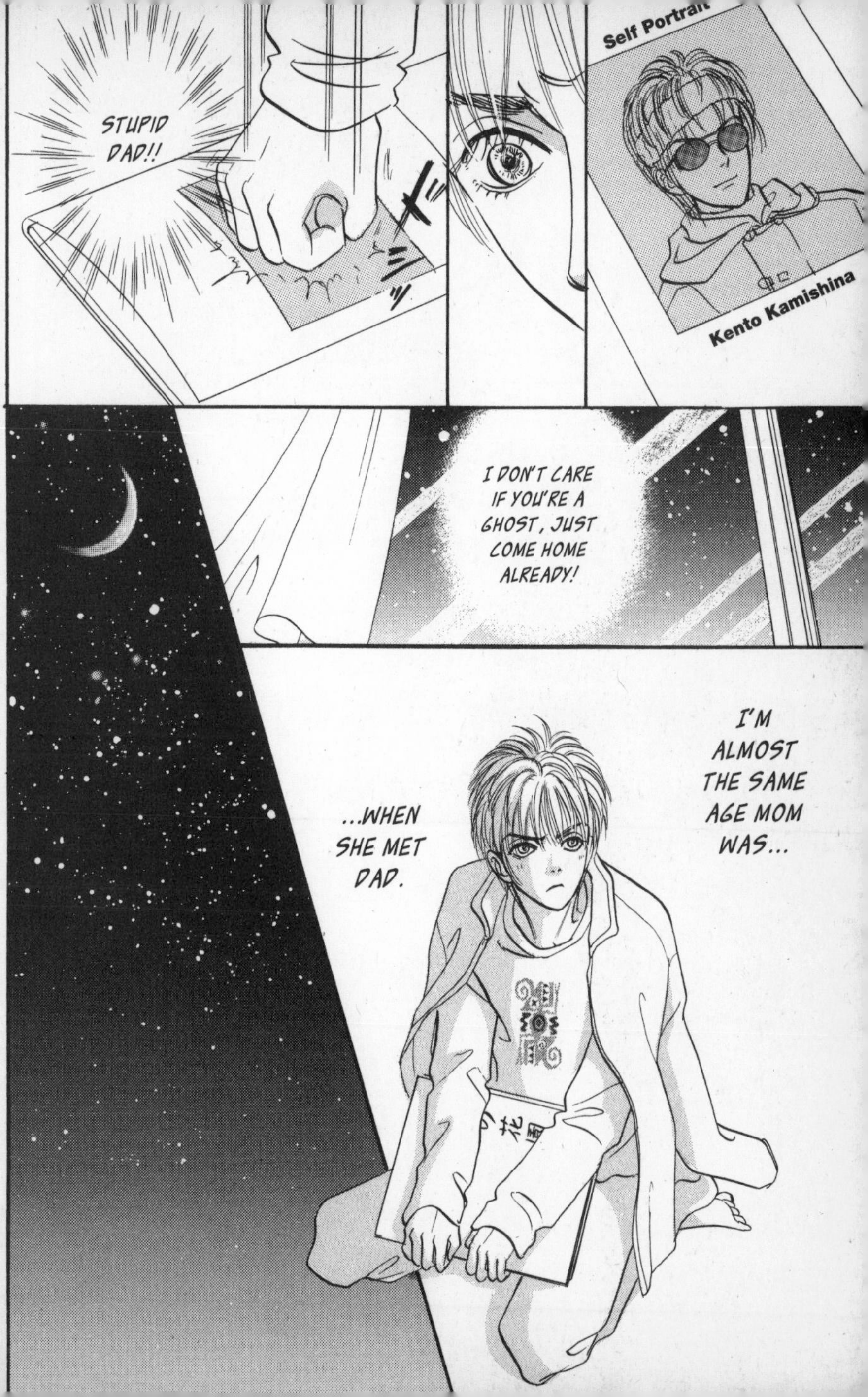
Self Portrait
Kento Kamishina
STUPID DAD!!
I DON'T CARE IF YOU'RE A GHOST, JUST COME HOME ALREADY!
I'M ALMOST THE SAME AGE MOM WAS...
...WHEN SHE MET DAD.

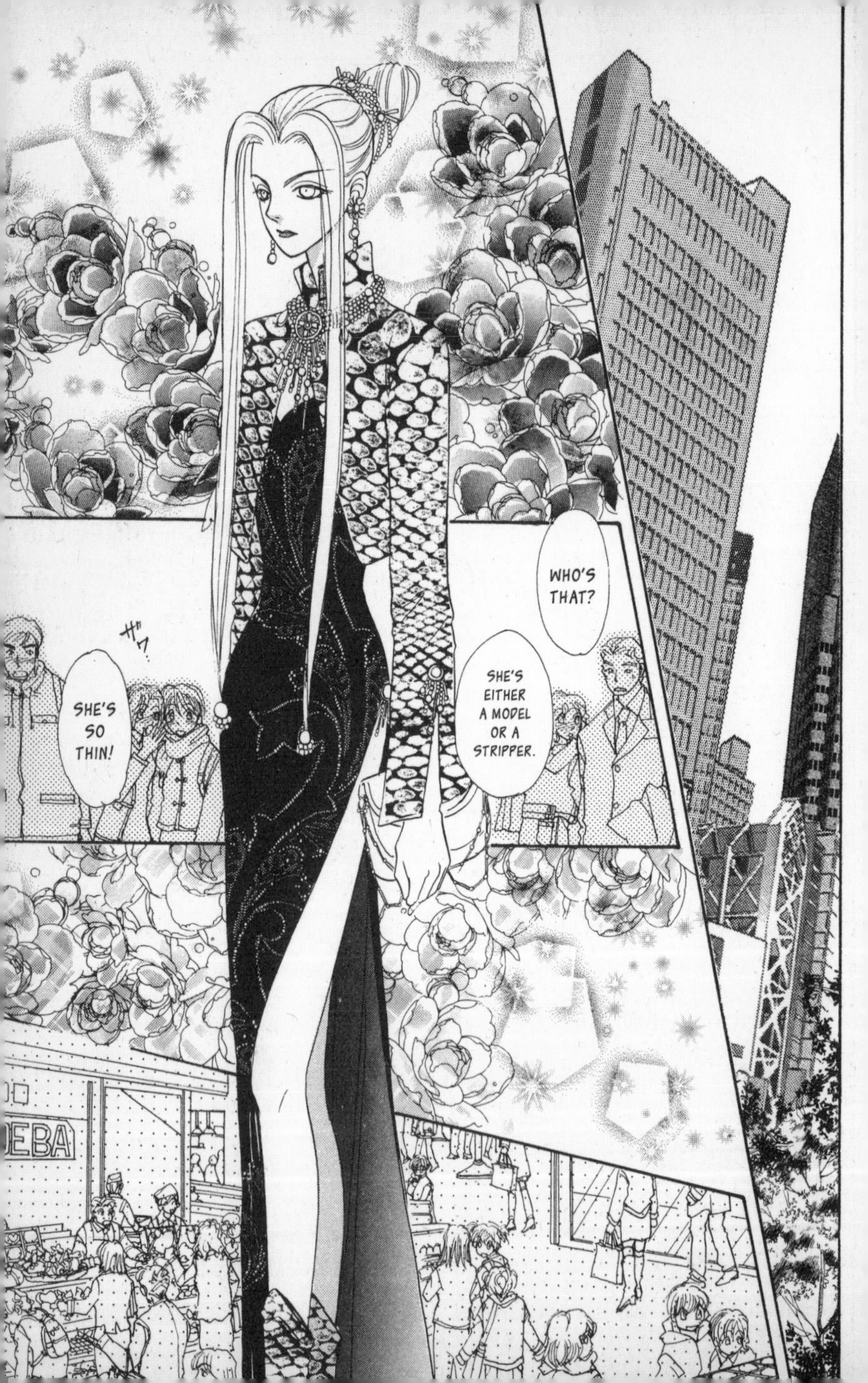
WHO'S THAT?
SHE'S EITHER A MODEL OR A STRIPPER.
SHE'S SO THIN!

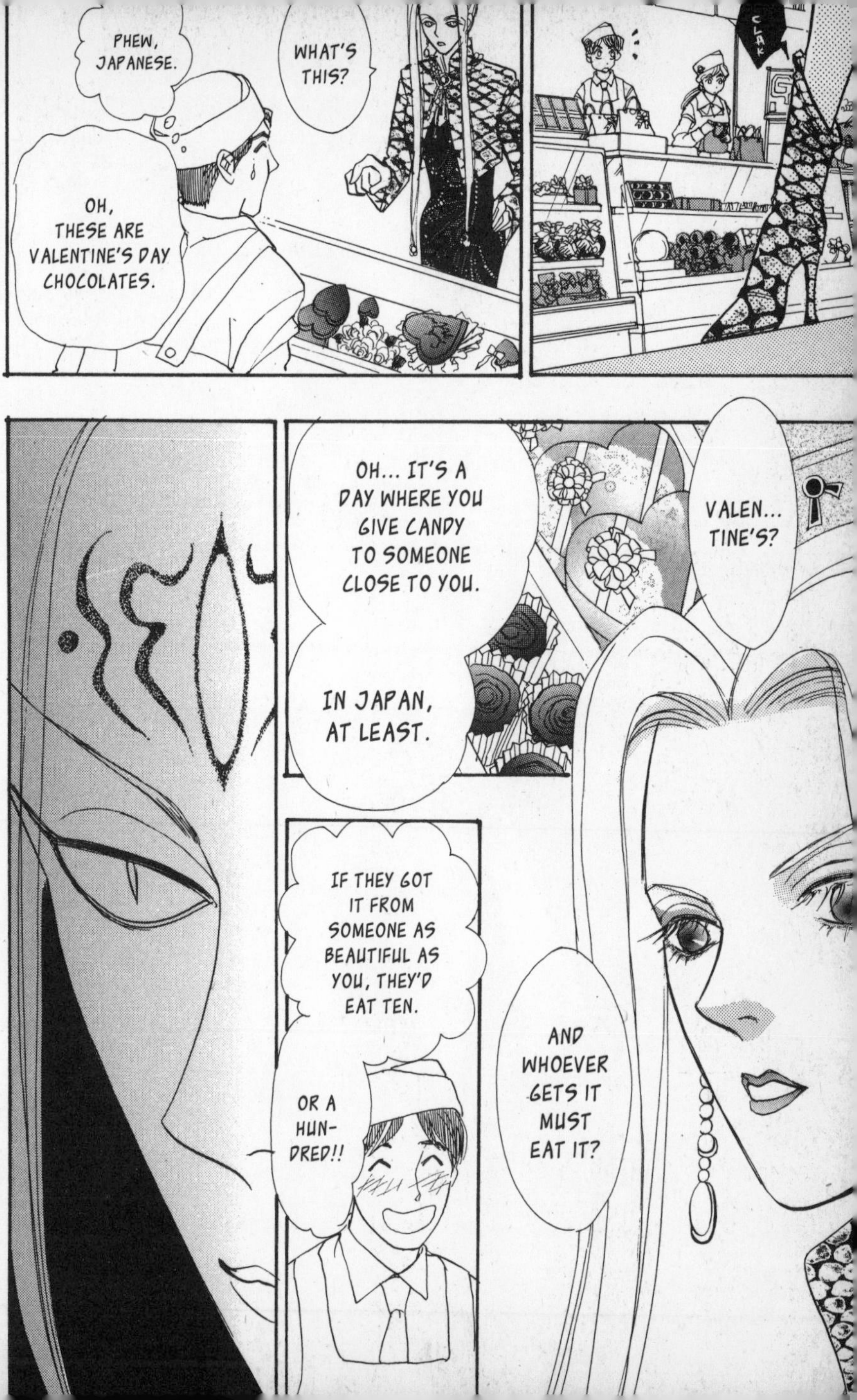
CLAK
WHAT'S THIS?
PHEW, JAPANESE.
OH, THESE ARE VALENTINE'S DAY CHOCOLATES.
VALEN... TINE'S?
OH... IT'S A DAY WHERE YOU GIVE CANDY TO SOMEONE CLOSE TO YOU.
IN JAPAN, AT LEAST.
AND WHOEVER GETS IT MUST EAT IT?
IF THEY GOT IT FROM SOMEONE AS BEAUTIFUL AS YOU, THEY'D EAT TEN.
OR A HUN-DRED!!

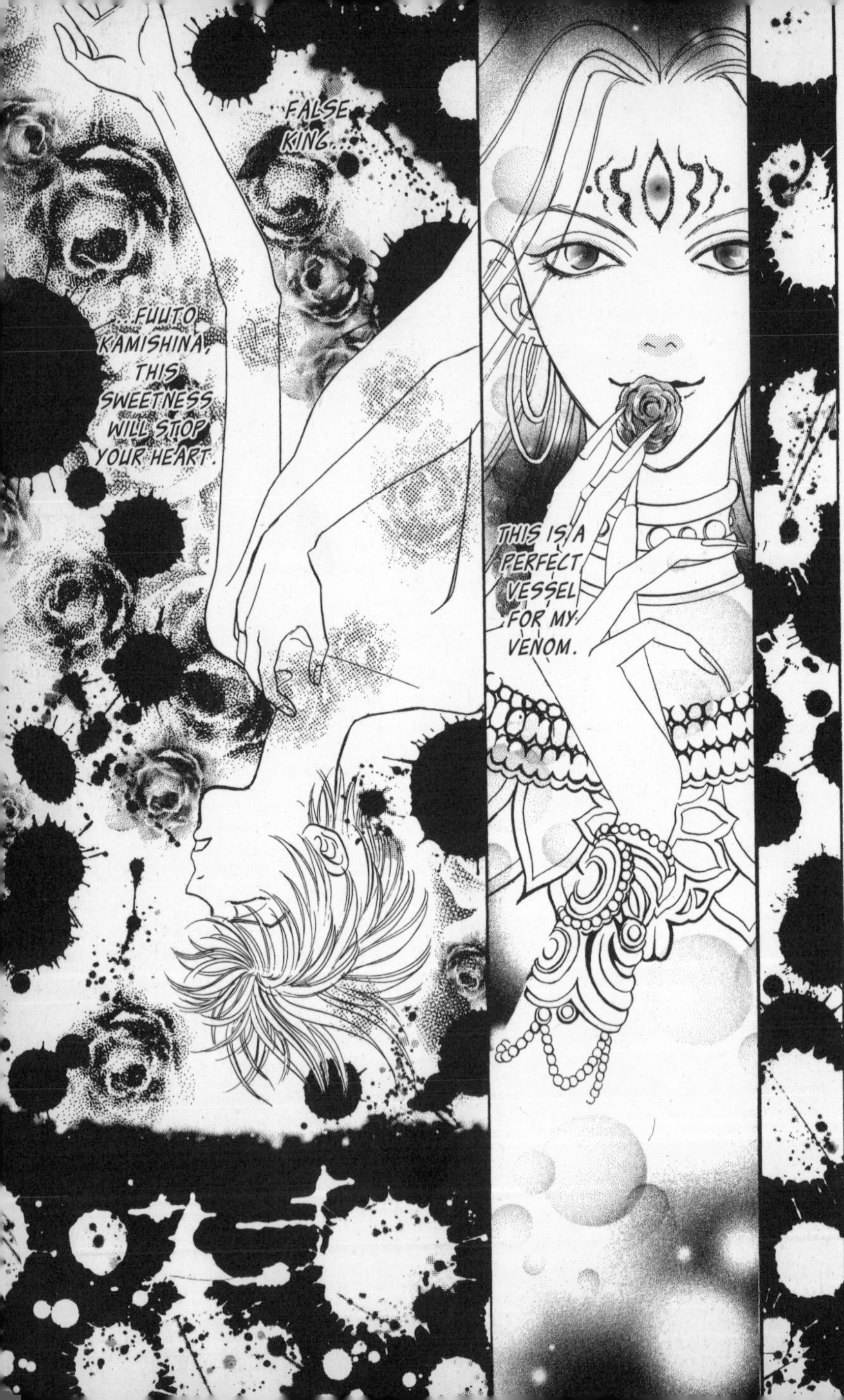
FALSE KING.
...FUUTO KAMISHINA, THIS SWEETNESS WILL STOP YOUR HEART.
THIS IS A PERFECT VESSEL FOR MY VENOM.

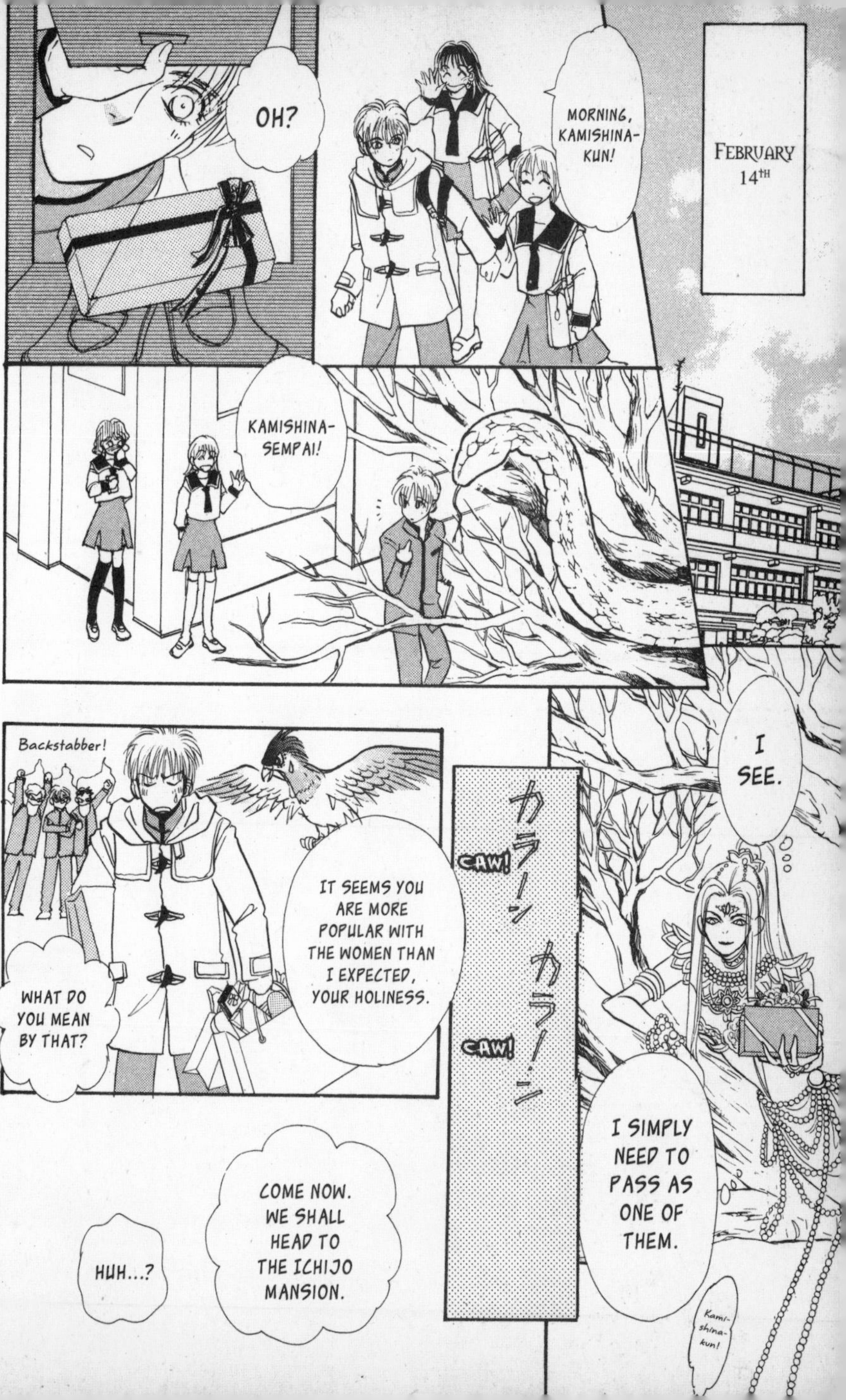

February 14th
Morning, Kamishina-kun!
Oh?
Kamishina-sempai!
I see.
I simply need to pass as one of them.
Kami-shina-kun!
CAW!
CAW!
It seems you are more popular with the women than I expected, your holiness.
What do you mean by that?
Backstabber!
Come now. We shall head to the Ichijo mansion.
Huh...?

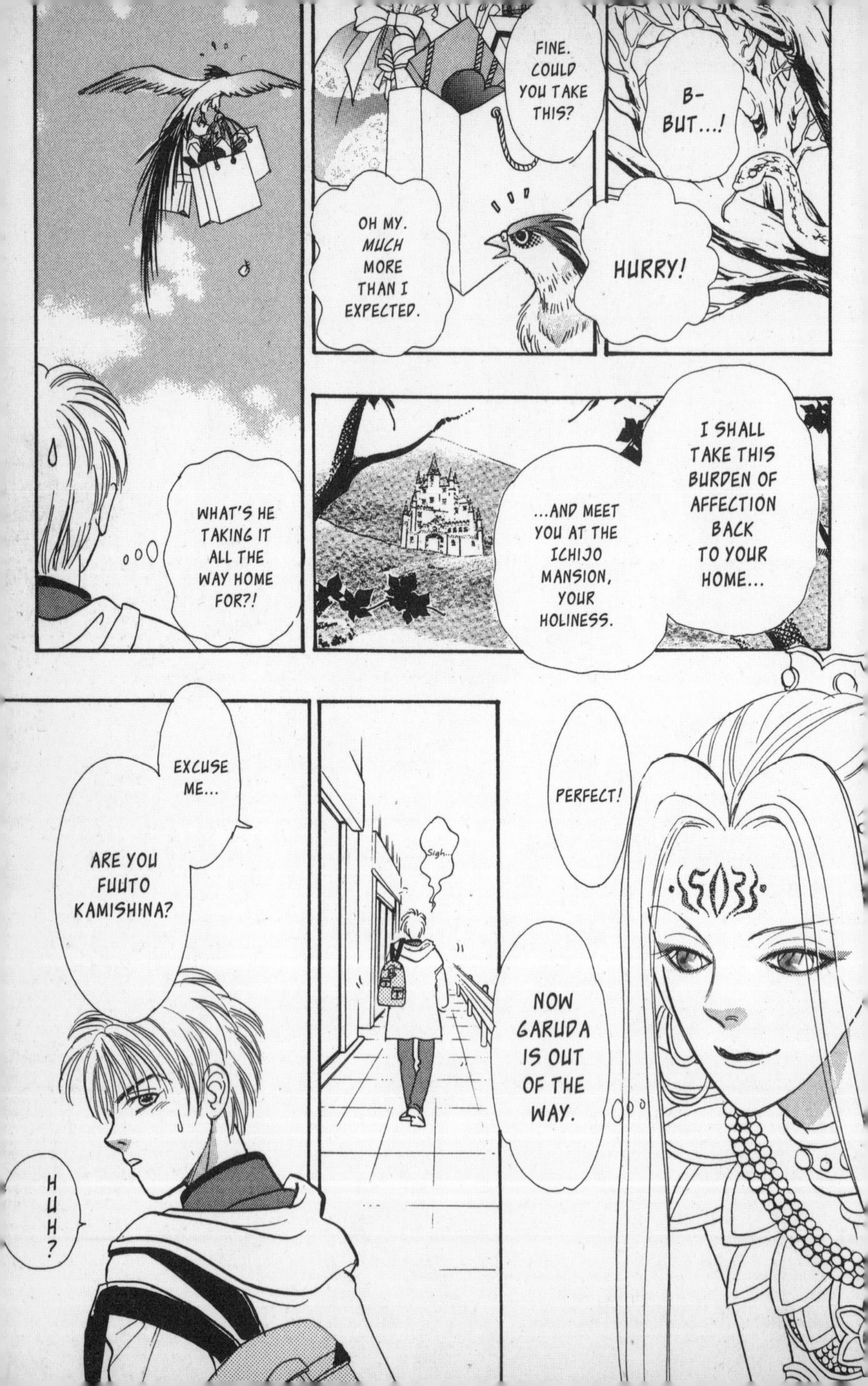
FINE. COULD YOU TAKE THIS?
OH MY. *MUCH* MORE THAN I EXPECTED.
B-BUT...!
HURRY!
WHAT'S HE TAKING IT ALL THE WAY HOME FOR?!
I SHALL TAKE THIS BURDEN OF AFFECTION BACK TO YOUR HOME...
...AND MEET YOU AT THE ICHIJO MANSION, YOUR HOLINESS.
EXCUSE ME...
ARE YOU FUUTO KAMISHINA?
HUH?
Sigh...
PERFECT!
NOW GARUDA IS OUT OF THE WAY.

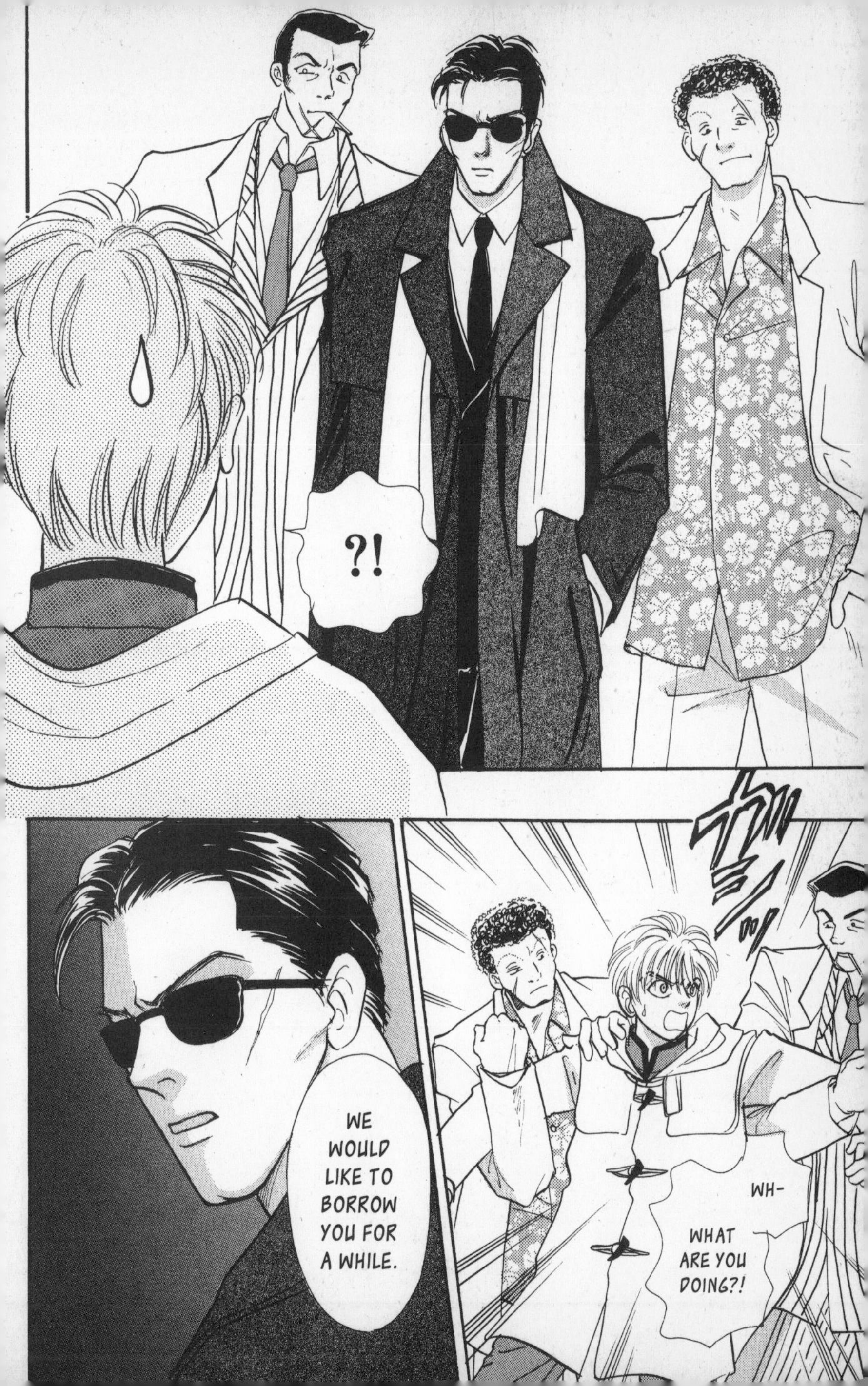
?!
WE WOULD LIKE TO BORROW YOU FOR A WHILE.
WH-
WHAT ARE YOU DOING?!

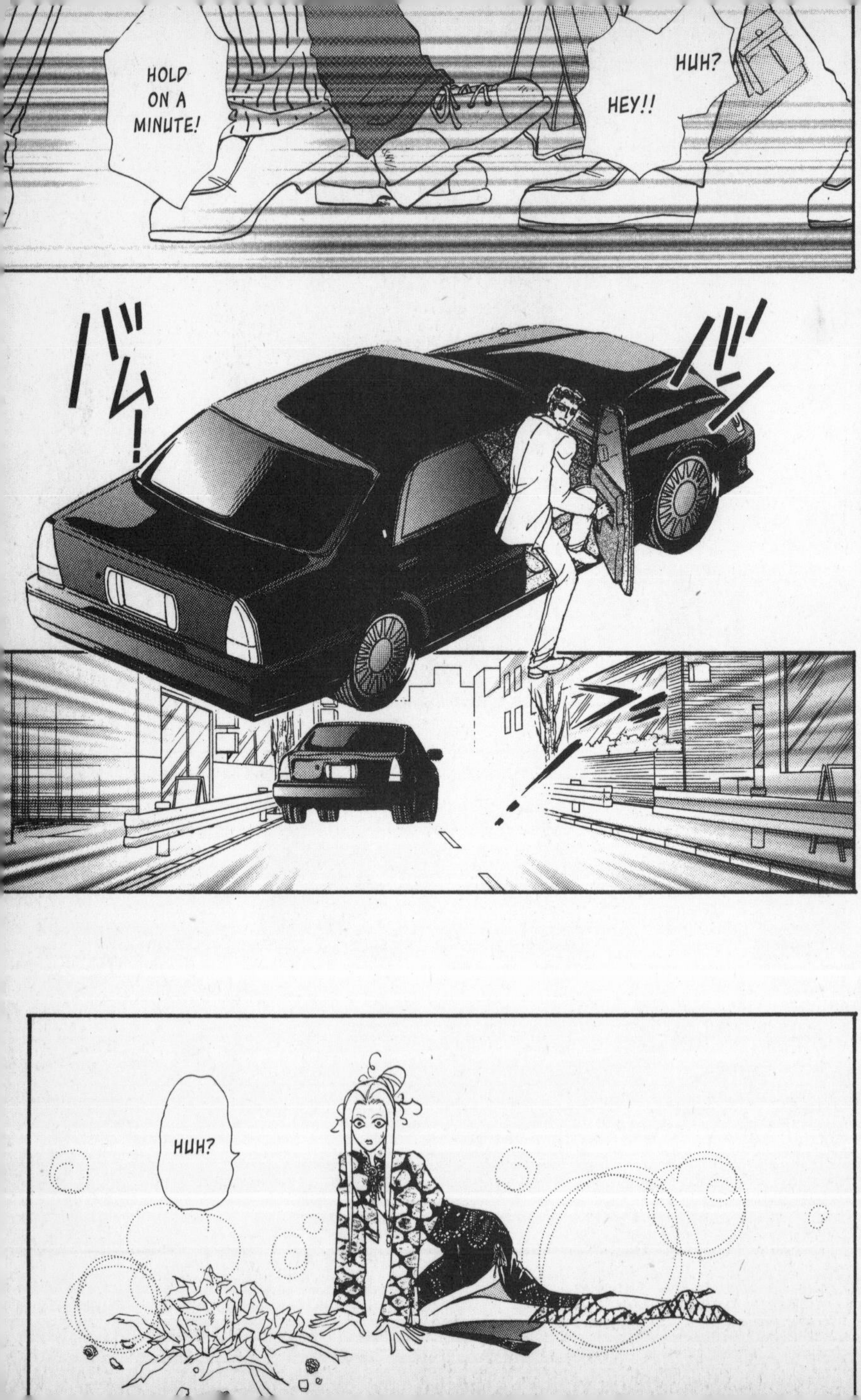
HUH?
HEY!!
HOLD ON A MINUTE!
バムー!
HUH?

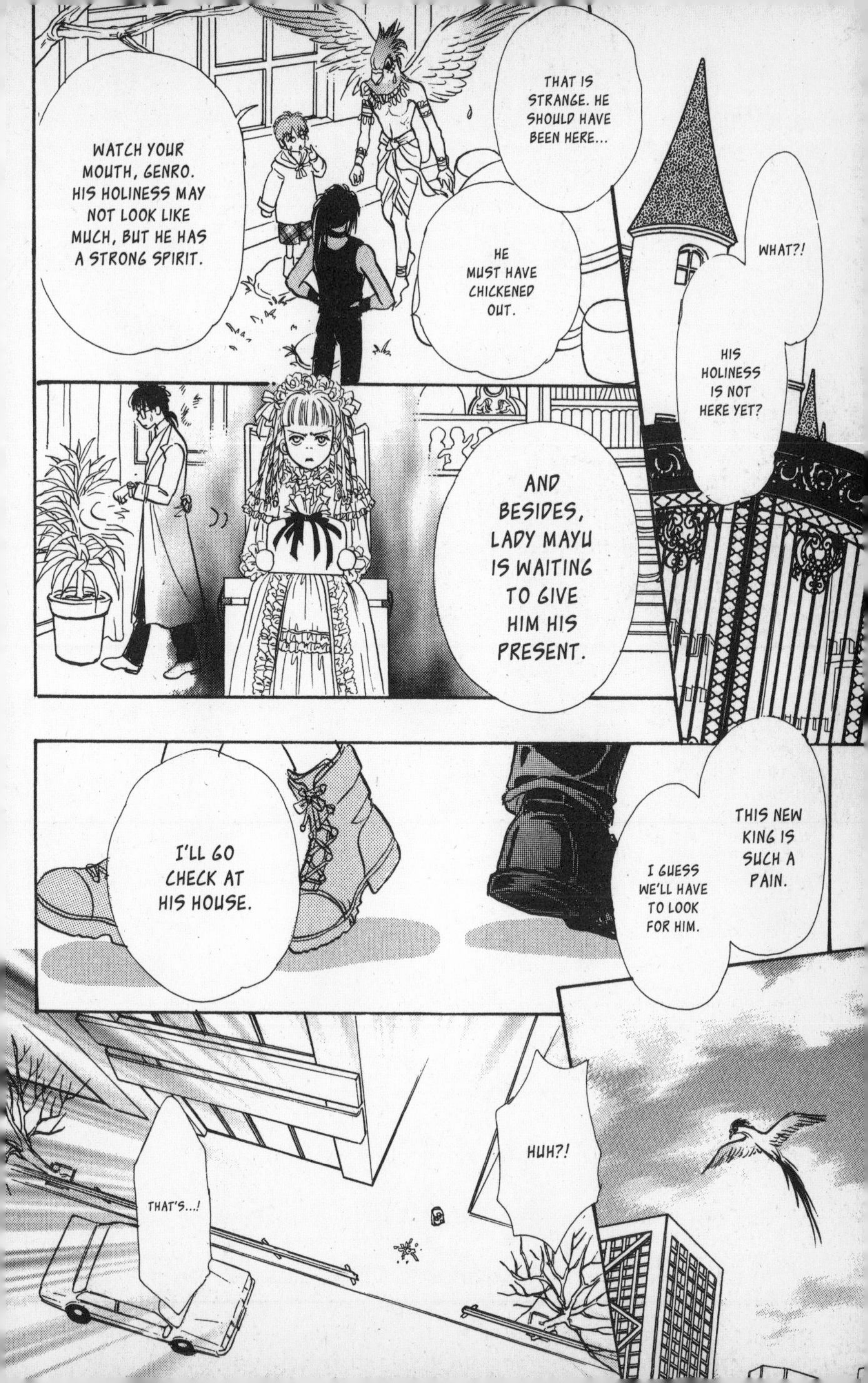

WHAT?!
HIS HOLINESS IS NOT HERE YET?
THAT IS STRANGE. HE SHOULD HAVE BEEN HERE...
HE MUST HAVE CHICKENED OUT.
WATCH YOUR MOUTH, GENRO. HIS HOLINESS MAY NOT LOOK LIKE MUCH, BUT HE HAS A STRONG SPIRIT.
AND BESIDES, LADY MAYU IS WAITING TO GIVE HIM HIS PRESENT.
THIS NEW KING IS SUCH A PAIN.
I GUESS WE'LL HAVE TO LOOK FOR HIM.
I'LL GO CHECK AT HIS HOUSE.
HUH?!
THAT'S...!

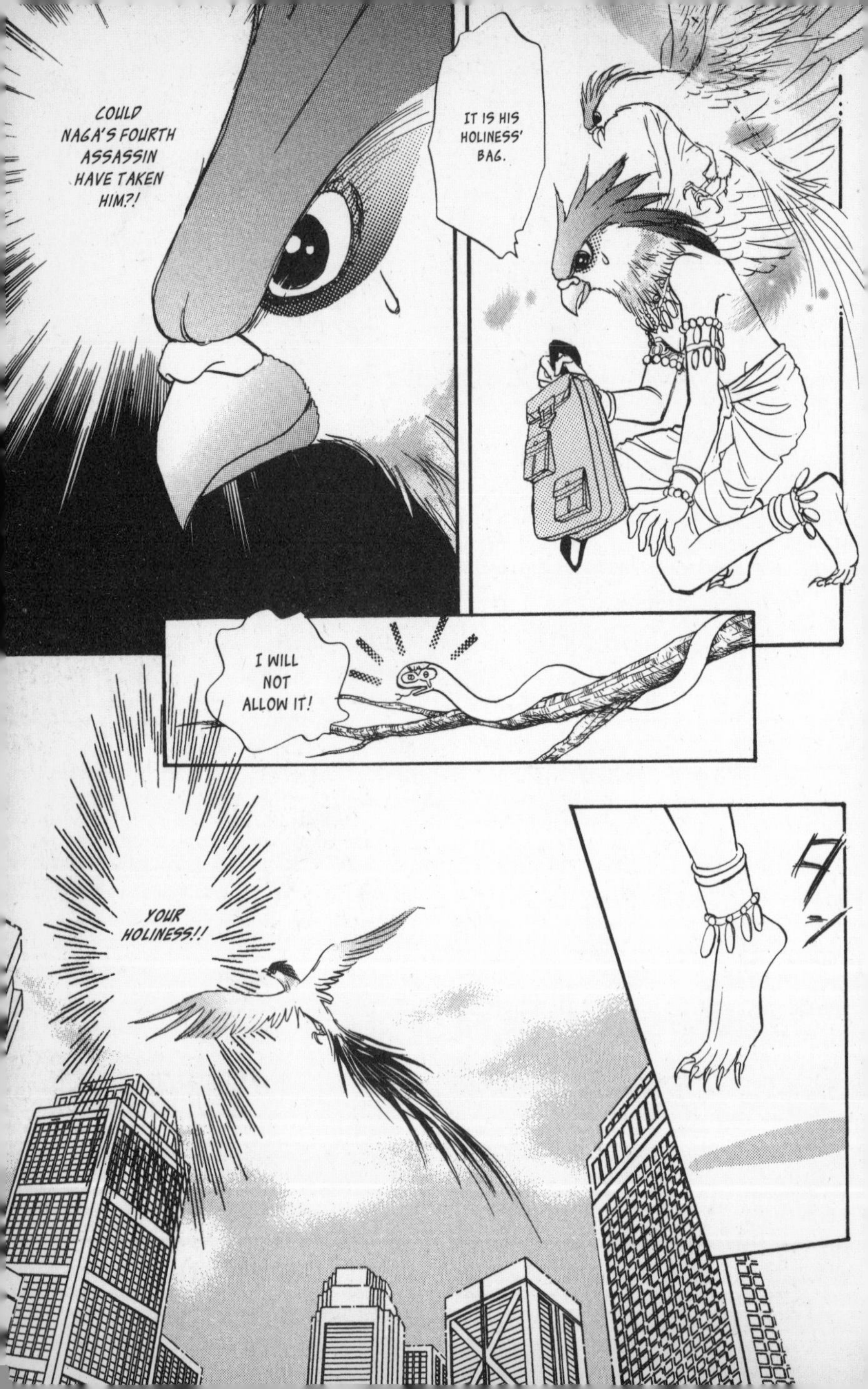
It is his Holiness' bag.
Could Naga's fourth assassin have taken him?!
I will not allow it!
Your Holiness!!

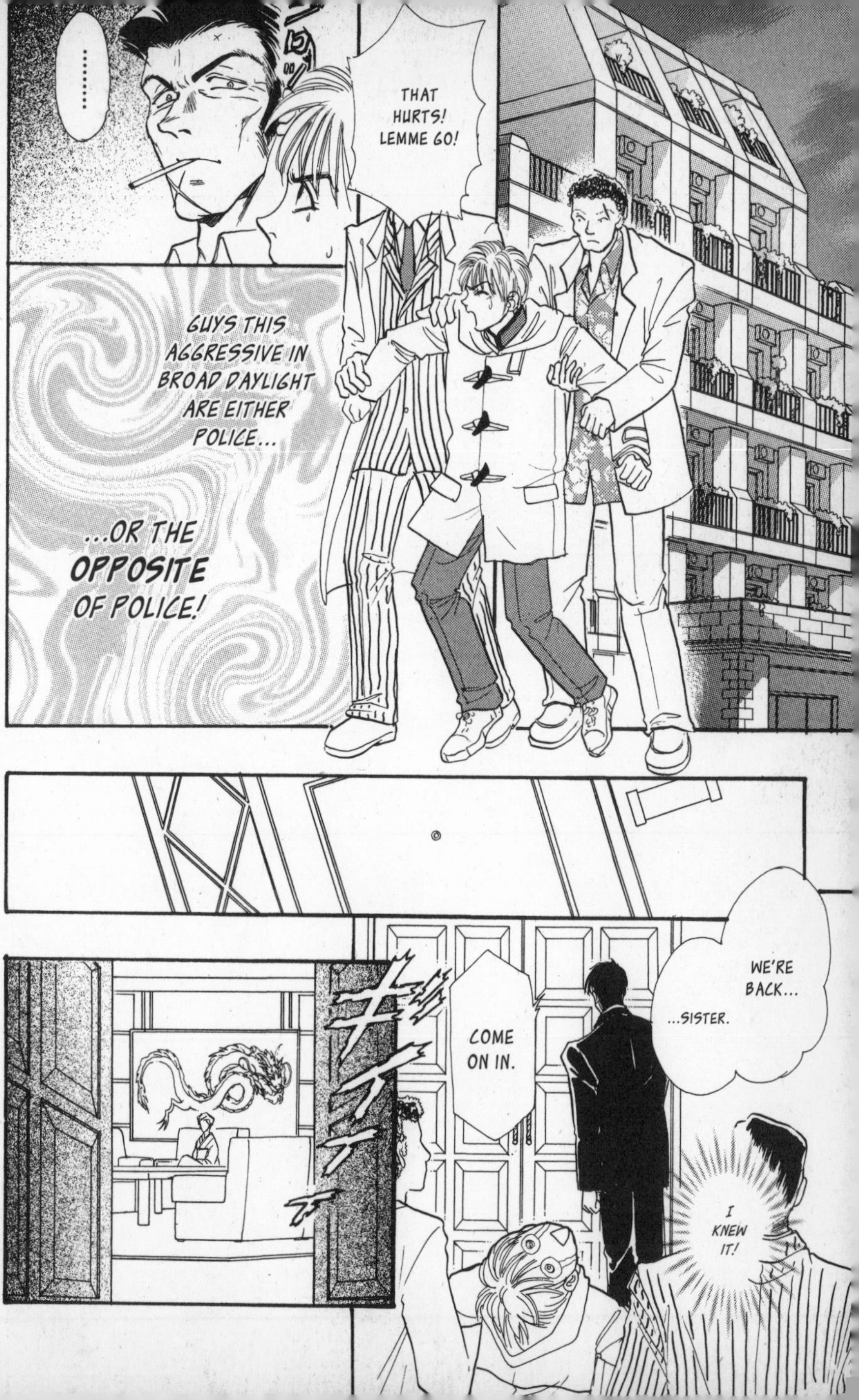

......
THAT HURTS! LEMME GO!
GUYS THIS AGGRESSIVE IN BROAD DAYLIGHT ARE EITHER POLICE...
...OR THE OPPOSITE OF POLICE!
WE'RE BACK...
...SISTER.
COME ON IN.
I KNEW IT!

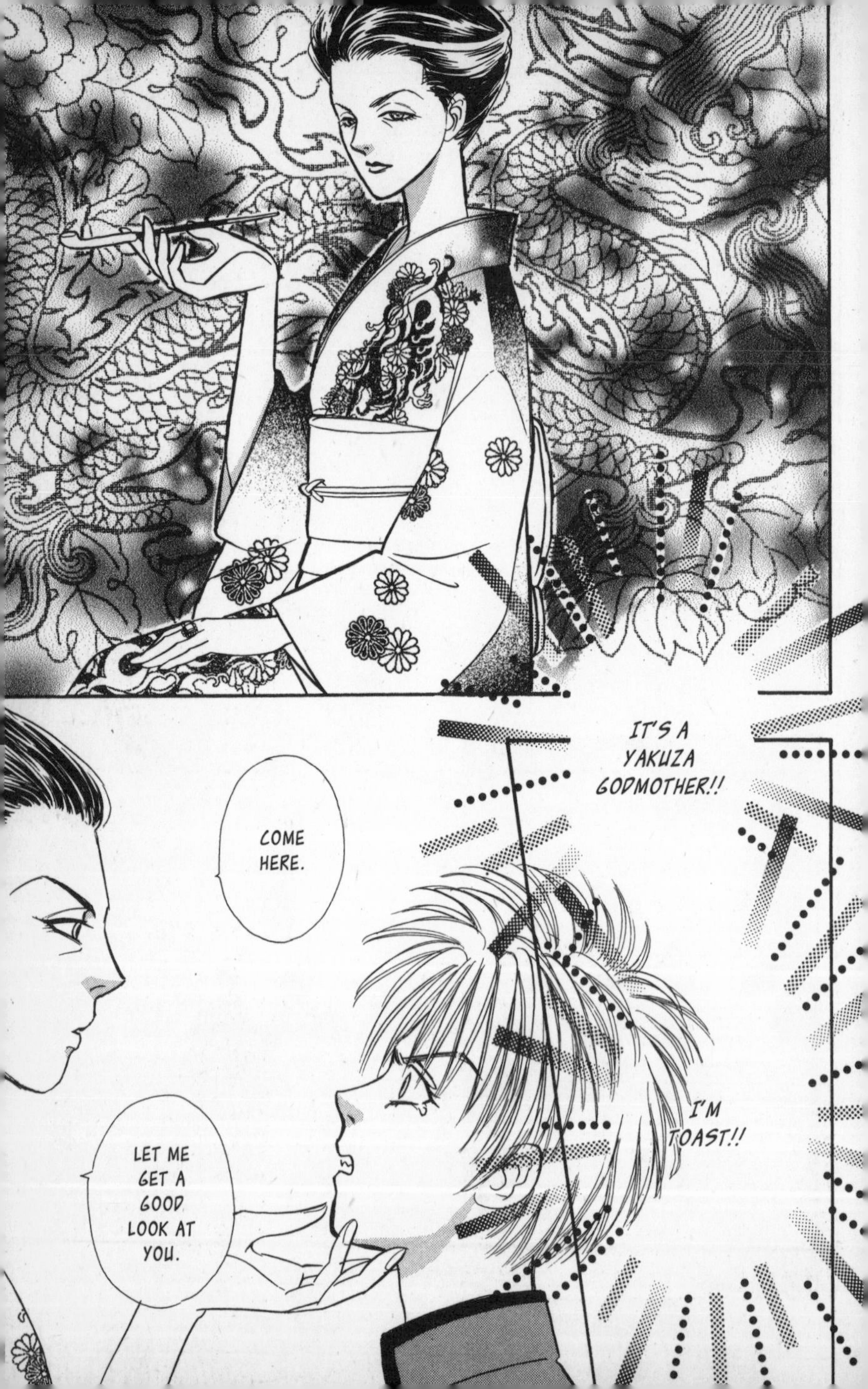
IT'S A YAKUZA GODMOTHER!!
COME HERE.
I'M TOAST!!
LET ME GET A GOOD LOOK AT YOU.

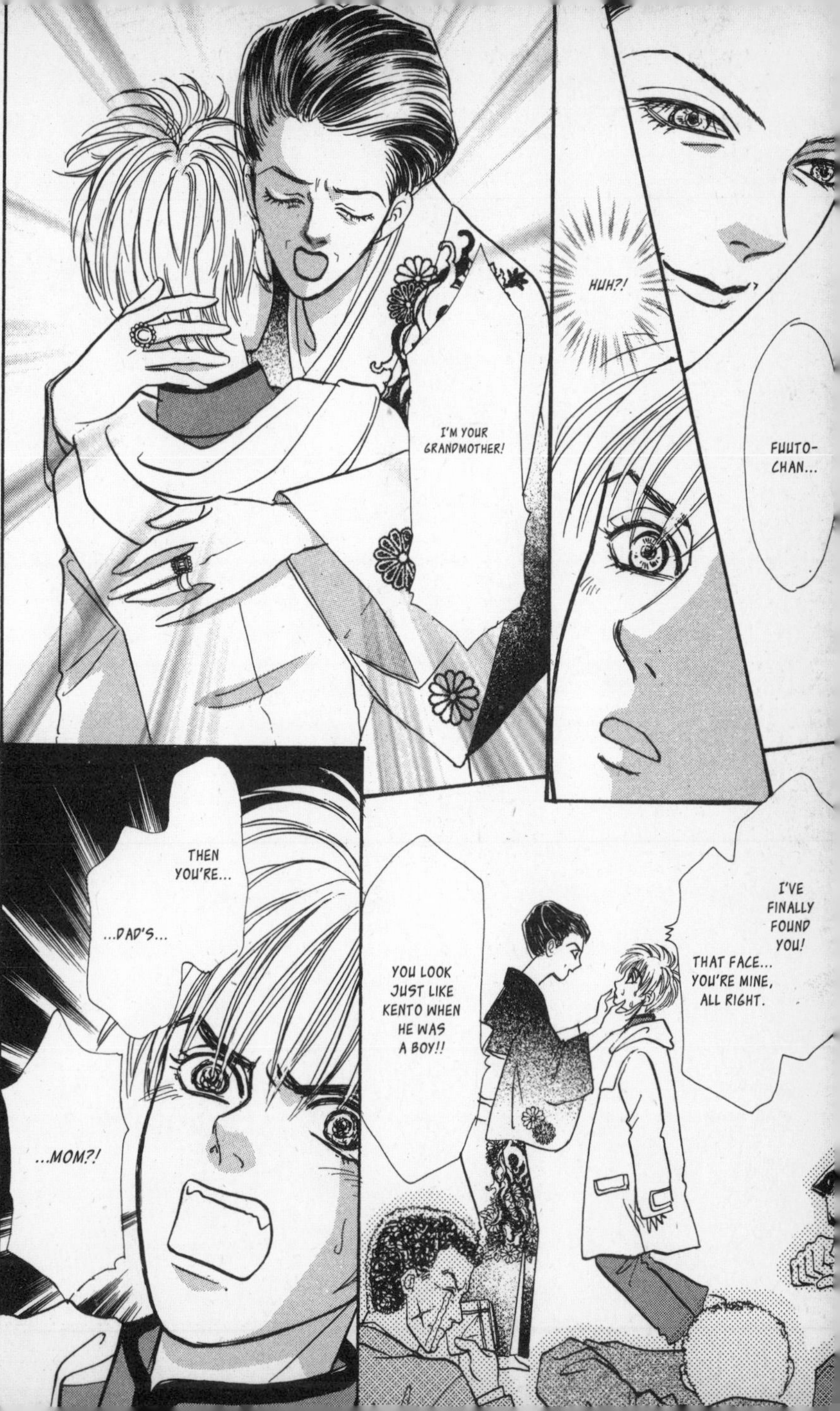
FUUTO-CHAN...
HUH?!
I'M YOUR GRANDMOTHER!
I'VE FINALLY FOUND YOU!
THAT FACE... YOU'RE MINE, ALL RIGHT.
YOU LOOK JUST LIKE KENTO WHEN HE WAS A BOY!!
THEN YOU'RE...
...DAD'S...
...MOM?!

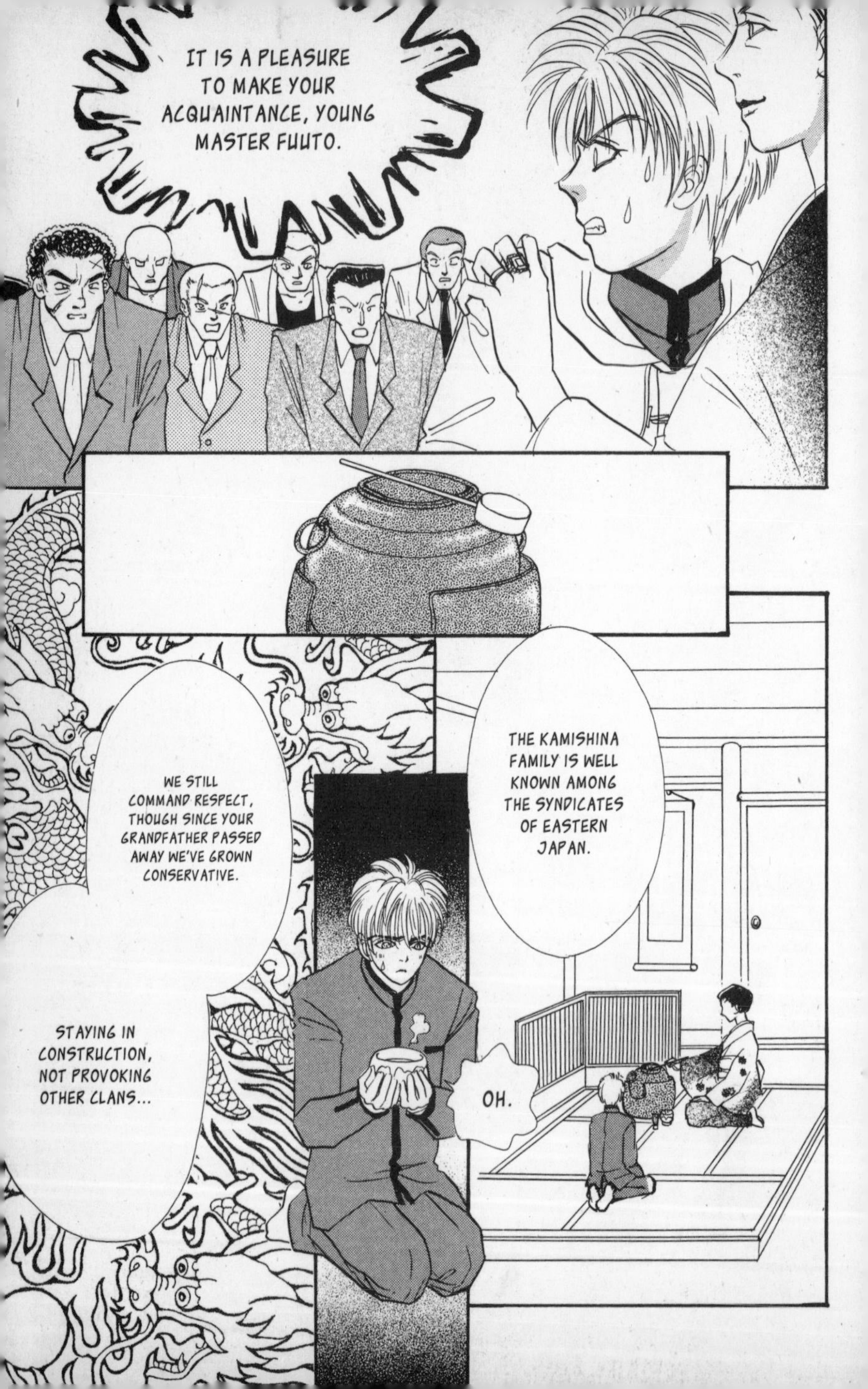
IT IS A PLEASURE TO MAKE YOUR ACQUAINTANCE, YOUNG MASTER FUUTO.
THE KAMISHINA FAMILY IS WELL KNOWN AMONG THE SYNDICATES OF EASTERN JAPAN.
WE STILL COMMAND RESPECT, THOUGH SINCE YOUR GRANDFATHER PASSED AWAY WE'VE GROWN CONSERVATIVE.
OH.
STAYING IN CONSTRUCTION, NOT PROVOKING OTHER CLANS...

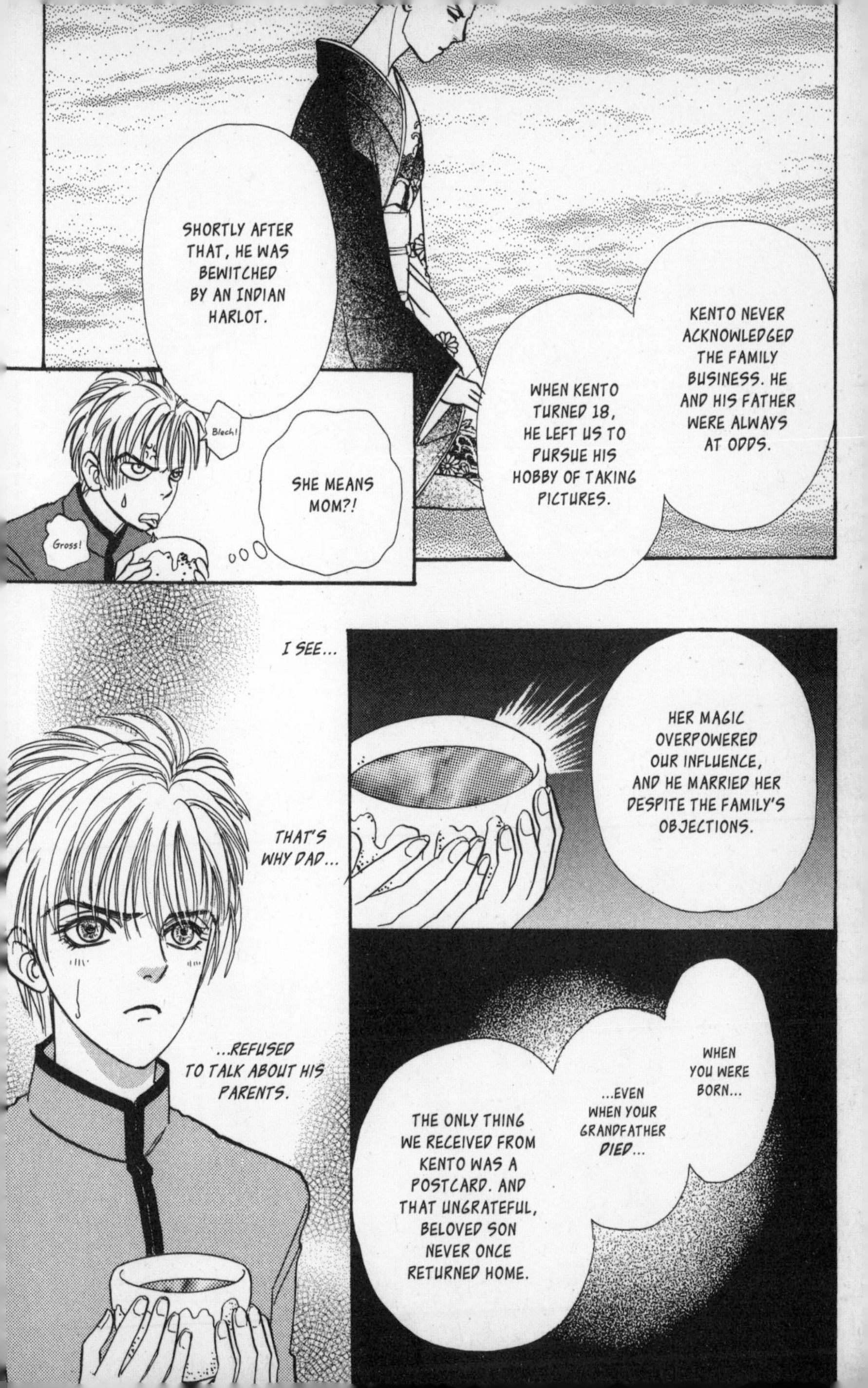

KENTO NEVER ACKNOWLEDGED THE FAMILY BUSINESS. HE AND HIS FATHER WERE ALWAYS AT ODDS.
WHEN KENTO TURNED 18, HE LEFT US TO PURSUE HIS HOBBY OF TAKING PICTURES.
SHORTLY AFTER THAT, HE WAS BEWITCHED BY AN INDIAN HARLOT.
Blech!
Gross!
SHE MEANS MOM?!
HER MAGIC OVERPOWERED OUR INFLUENCE, AND HE MARRIED HER DESPITE THE FAMILY'S OBJECTIONS.
I SEE...
THAT'S WHY DAD...
...REFUSED TO TALK ABOUT HIS PARENTS.
WHEN YOU WERE BORN...
...EVEN WHEN YOUR GRANDFATHER DIED...
THE ONLY THING WE RECEIVED FROM KENTO WAS A POSTCARD. AND THAT UNGRATEFUL, BELOVED SON NEVER ONCE RETURNED HOME.

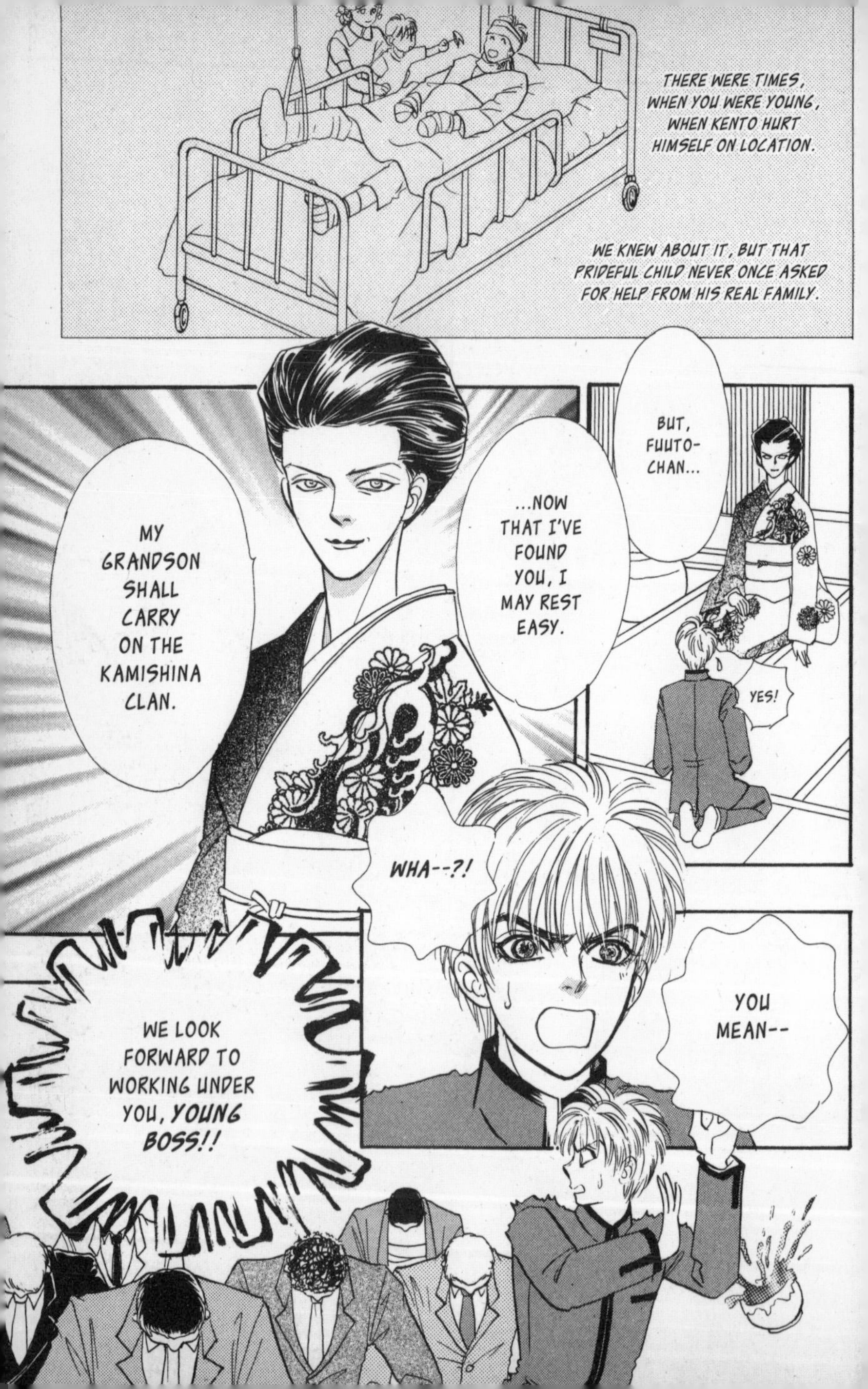
THERE WERE TIMES, WHEN YOU WERE YOUNG, WHEN KENTO HURT HIMSELF ON LOCATION.
WE KNEW ABOUT IT, BUT THAT PRIDEFUL CHILD NEVER ONCE ASKED FOR HELP FROM HIS REAL FAMILY.
BUT, FUUTO-CHAN...
YES!
...NOW THAT I'VE FOUND YOU, I MAY REST EASY.
MY GRANDSON SHALL CARRY ON THE KAMISHINA CLAN.
WHA--?!
YOU MEAN--
WE LOOK FORWARD TO WORKING UNDER YOU, *YOUNG BOSS!!*

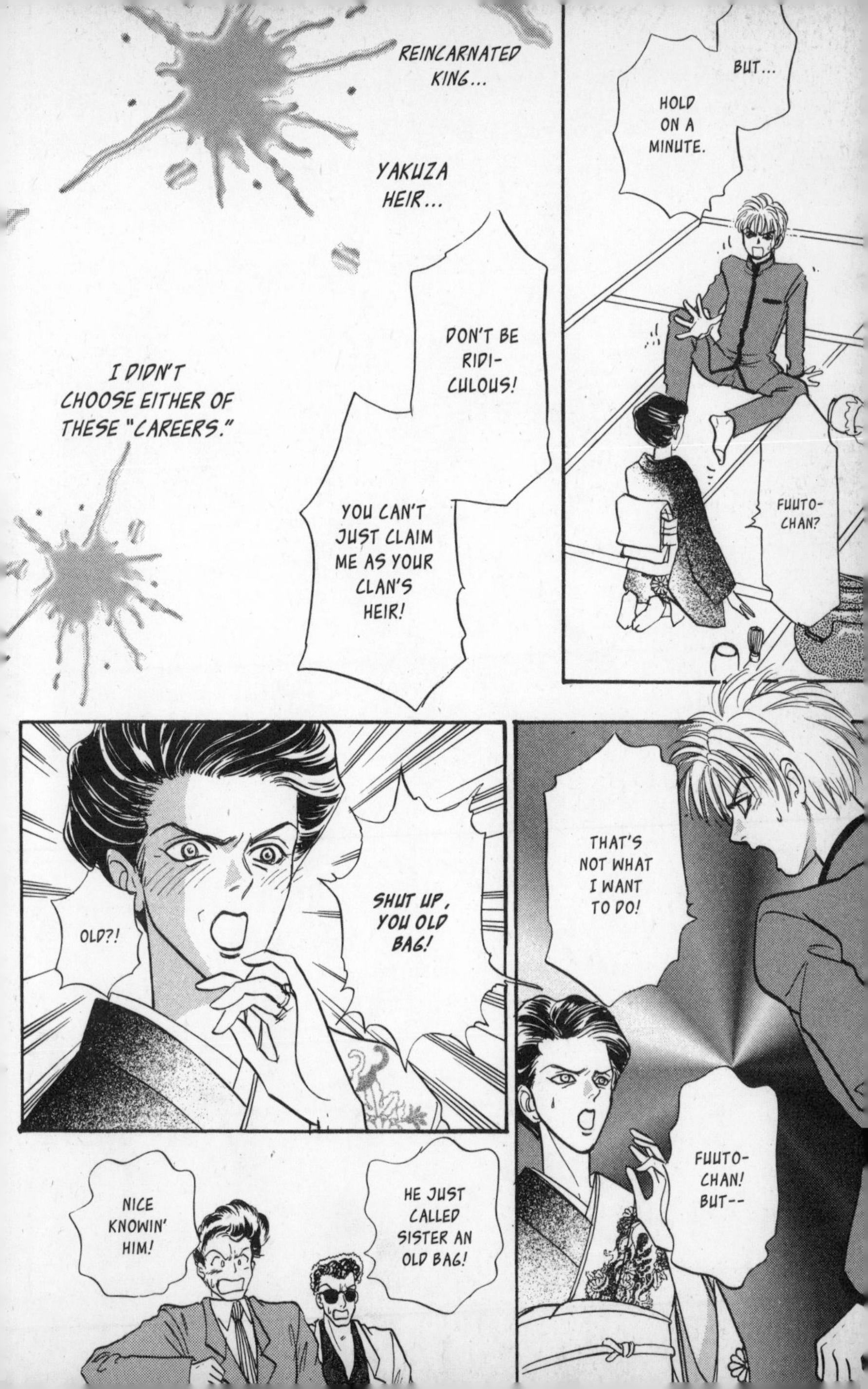

BUT...
HOLD ON A MINUTE.
FUUTO-CHAN?
REINCARNATED KING...
YAKUZA HEIR...
I DIDN'T CHOOSE EITHER OF THESE "CAREERS."
DON'T BE RIDICULOUS!
YOU CAN'T JUST CLAIM ME AS YOUR CLAN'S HEIR!
THAT'S NOT WHAT I WANT TO DO!
SHUT UP, YOU OLD BAG!
OLD?!
FUUTO-CHAN! BUT--
HE JUST CALLED SISTER AN OLD BAG!
NICE KNOWIN' HIM!

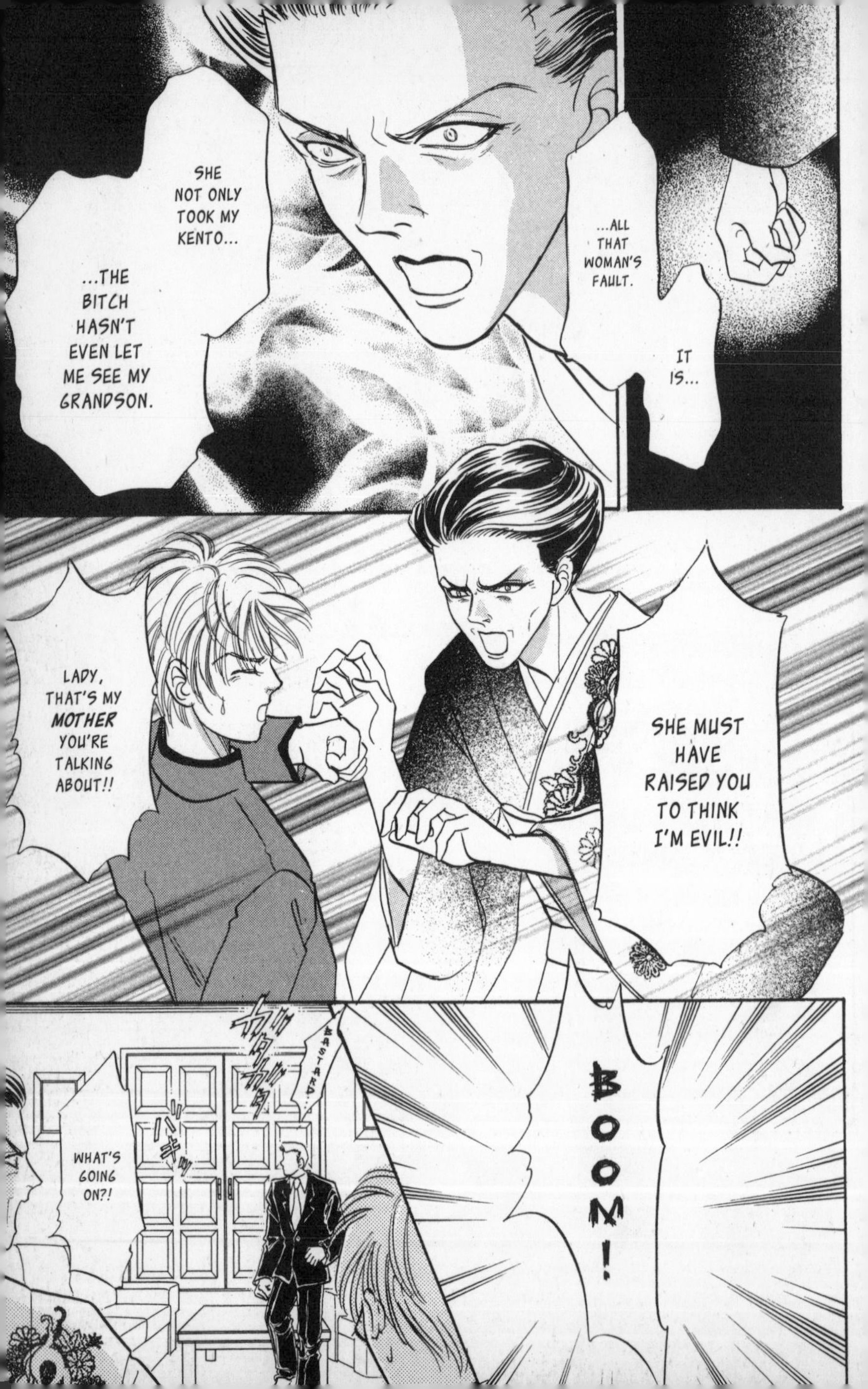
IT IS...
...ALL THAT WOMAN'S FAULT.
SHE NOT ONLY TOOK MY KENTO...
...THE BITCH HASN'T EVEN LET ME SEE MY GRANDSON.
SHE MUST HAVE RAISED YOU TO THINK I'M EVIL!!
LADY, THAT'S MY *MOTHER* YOU'RE TALKING ABOUT!!
BOOM!
BASTARD...
WHAT'S GOING ON?!

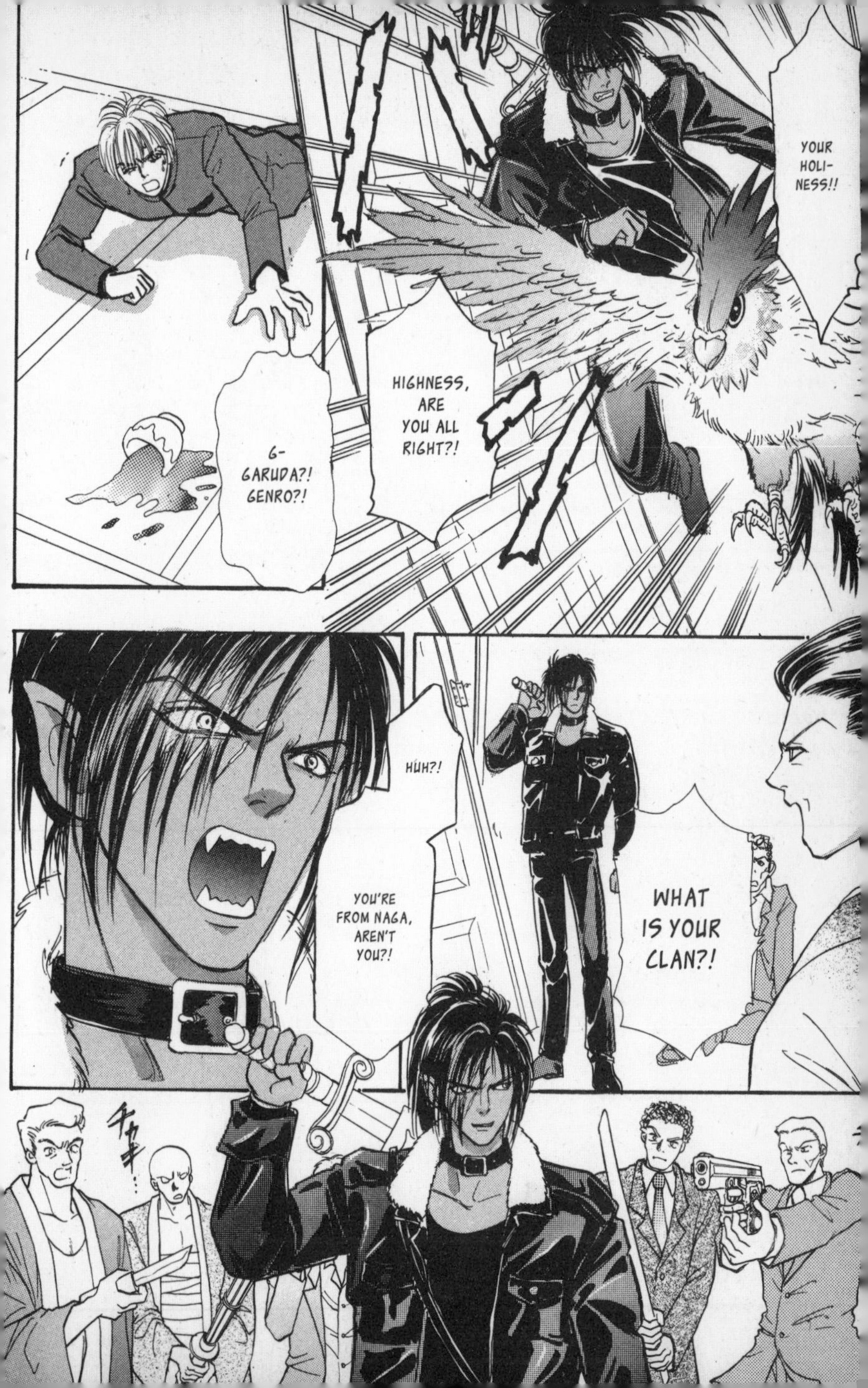
YOUR HOLINESS!!
HIGHNESS, ARE YOU ALL RIGHT?!
G-GARUDA?! GENRO?!
WHAT IS YOUR CLAN?!
HUH?!
YOU'RE FROM NAGA, AREN'T YOU?!

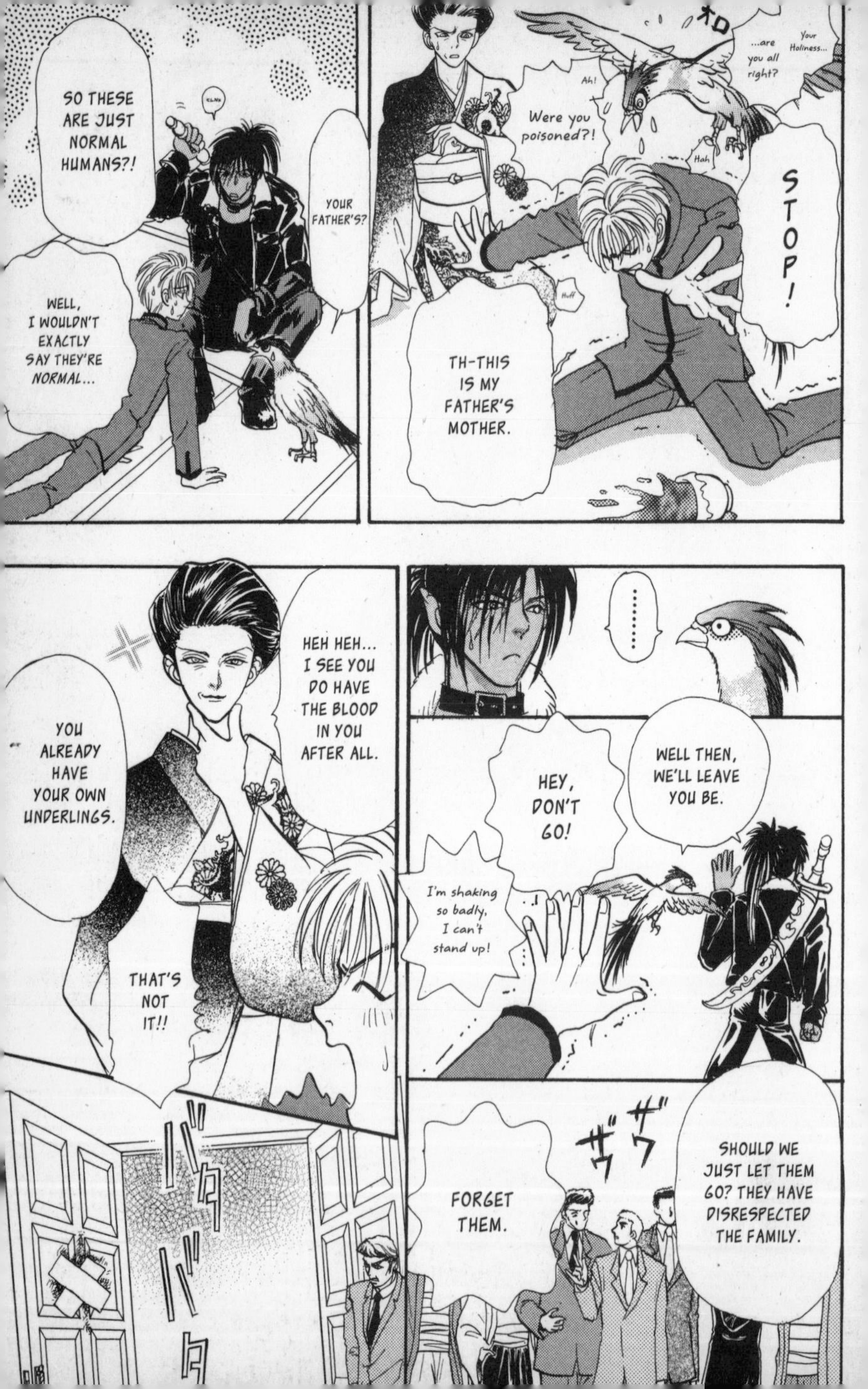

Your Holiness...
...are you all right?
オロ
Ah!
Were you poisoned?!
Hah
STOP!
Huff
TH-THIS IS MY FATHER'S MOTHER.
YOUR FATHER'S?
CLNK
SO THESE ARE JUST NORMAL HUMANS?!
WELL, I WOULDN'T EXACTLY SAY THEY'RE NORMAL...
......
WELL THEN, WE'LL LEAVE YOU BE.
HEY, DON'T GO!
I'm shaking so badly, I can't stand up!
HEH HEH... I SEE YOU DO HAVE THE BLOOD IN YOU AFTER ALL.
YOU ALREADY HAVE YOUR OWN UNDERLINGS.
THAT'S NOT IT!!
SHOULD WE JUST LET THEM GO? THEY HAVE DISRESPECTED THE FAMILY.
ザワ ザワ
FORGET THEM.
バタ バタ

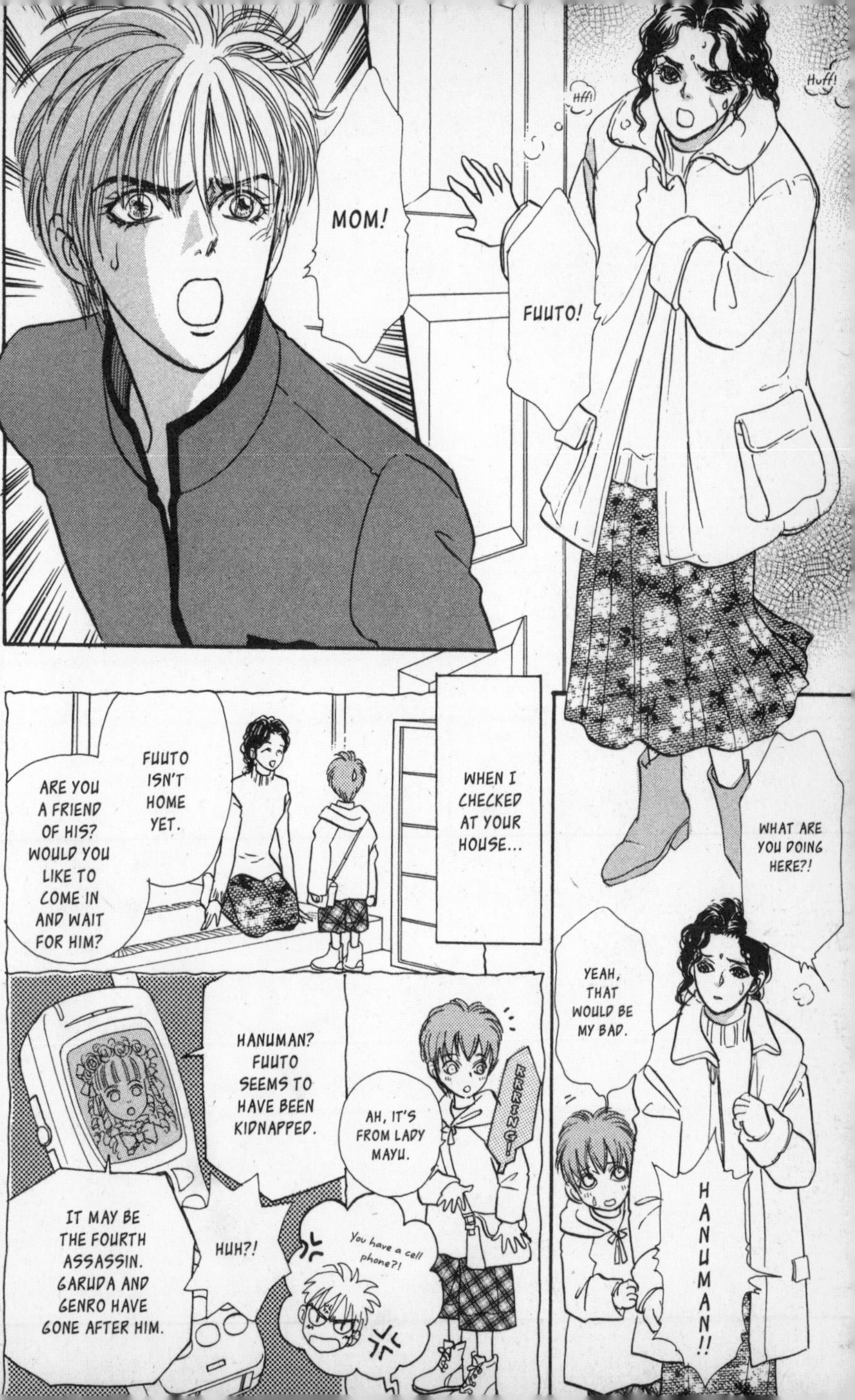
Huff!
Hff!
FUUTO!
MOM!
WHAT ARE YOU DOING HERE?!
YEAH, THAT WOULD BE MY BAD.
HANUMAN!!
WHEN I CHECKED AT YOUR HOUSE...
FUUTO ISN'T HOME YET.
ARE YOU A FRIEND OF HIS? WOULD YOU LIKE TO COME IN AND WAIT FOR HIM?
KRRRING!
AH, IT'S FROM LADY MAYU.
You have a cell phone?!
HANUMAN? FUUTO SEEMS TO HAVE BEEN KIDNAPPED.
HUH?!
IT MAY BE THE FOURTH ASSASSIN. GARUDA AND GENRO HAVE GONE AFTER HIM.

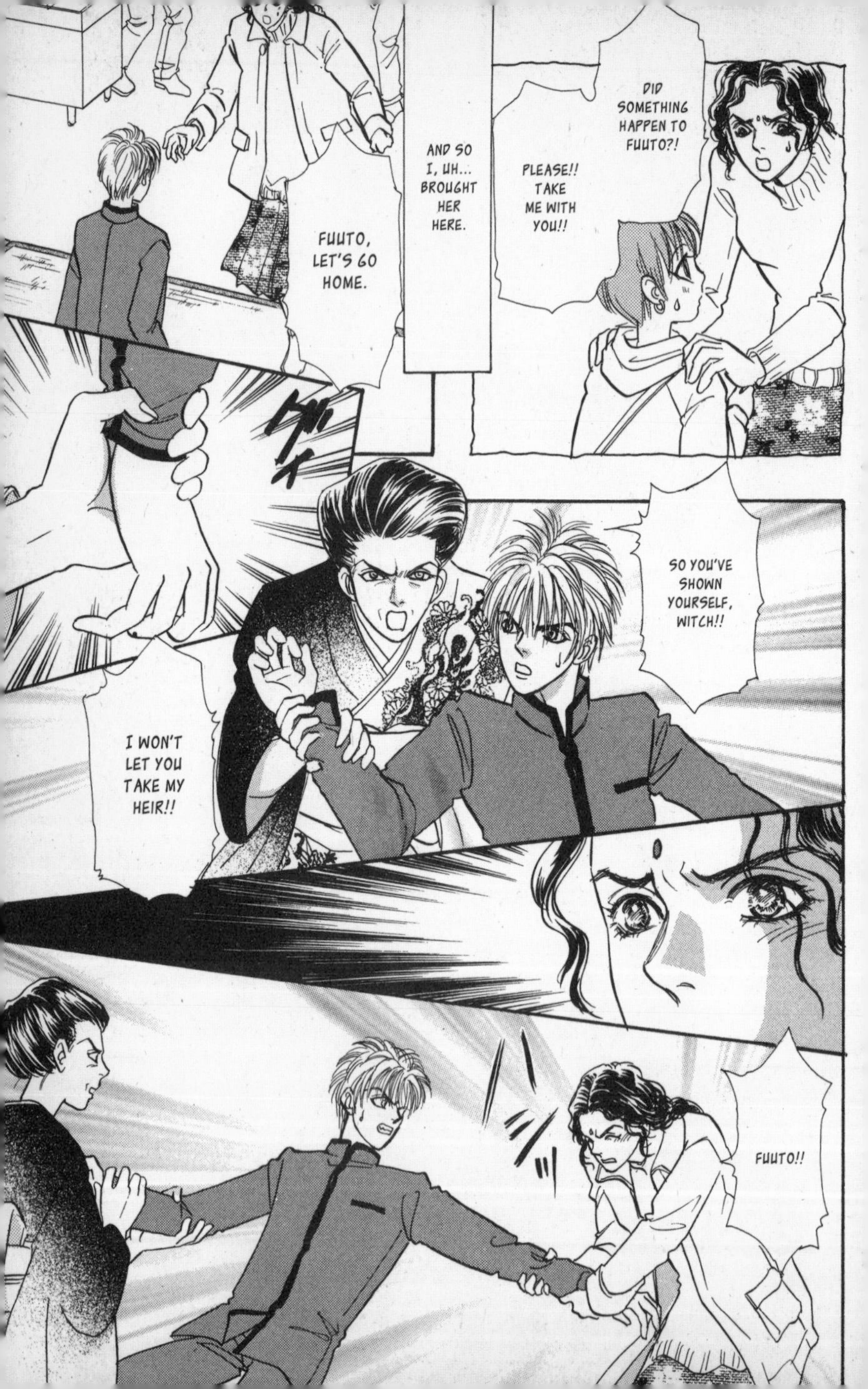
DID SOMETHING HAPPEN TO FUUTO?!
PLEASE!! TAKE ME WITH YOU!!
AND SO I, UH... BROUGHT HER HERE.
FUUTO, LET'S GO HOME.
SO YOU'VE SHOWN YOURSELF, WITCH!!
I WON'T LET YOU TAKE MY HEIR!!
FUUTO!!

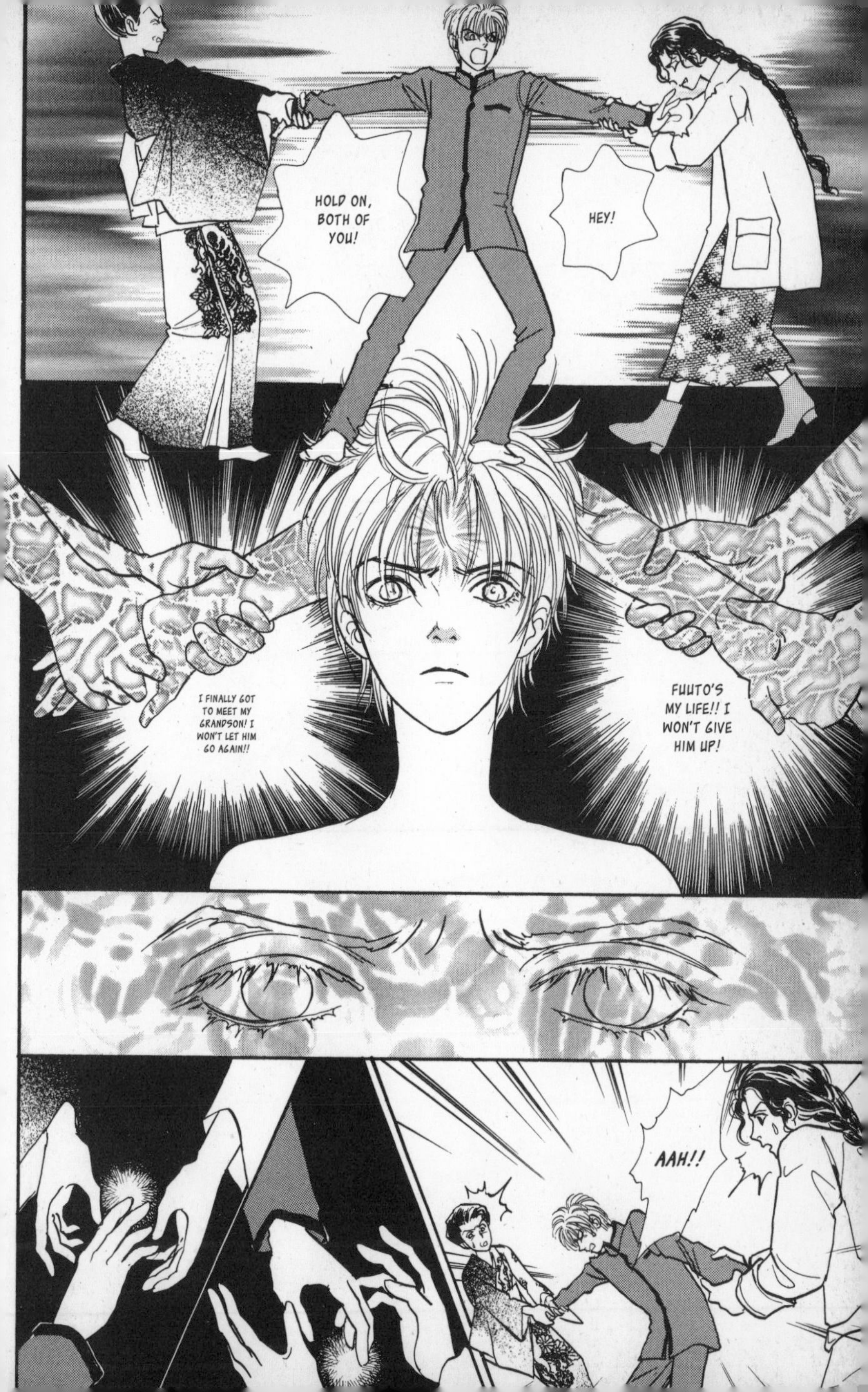
HEY!
HOLD ON, BOTH OF YOU!
FUUTO'S MY LIFE!! I WON'T GIVE HIM UP!
I FINALLY GOT TO MEET MY GRANDSON! I WON'T LET HIM GO AGAIN!!
AAH!!

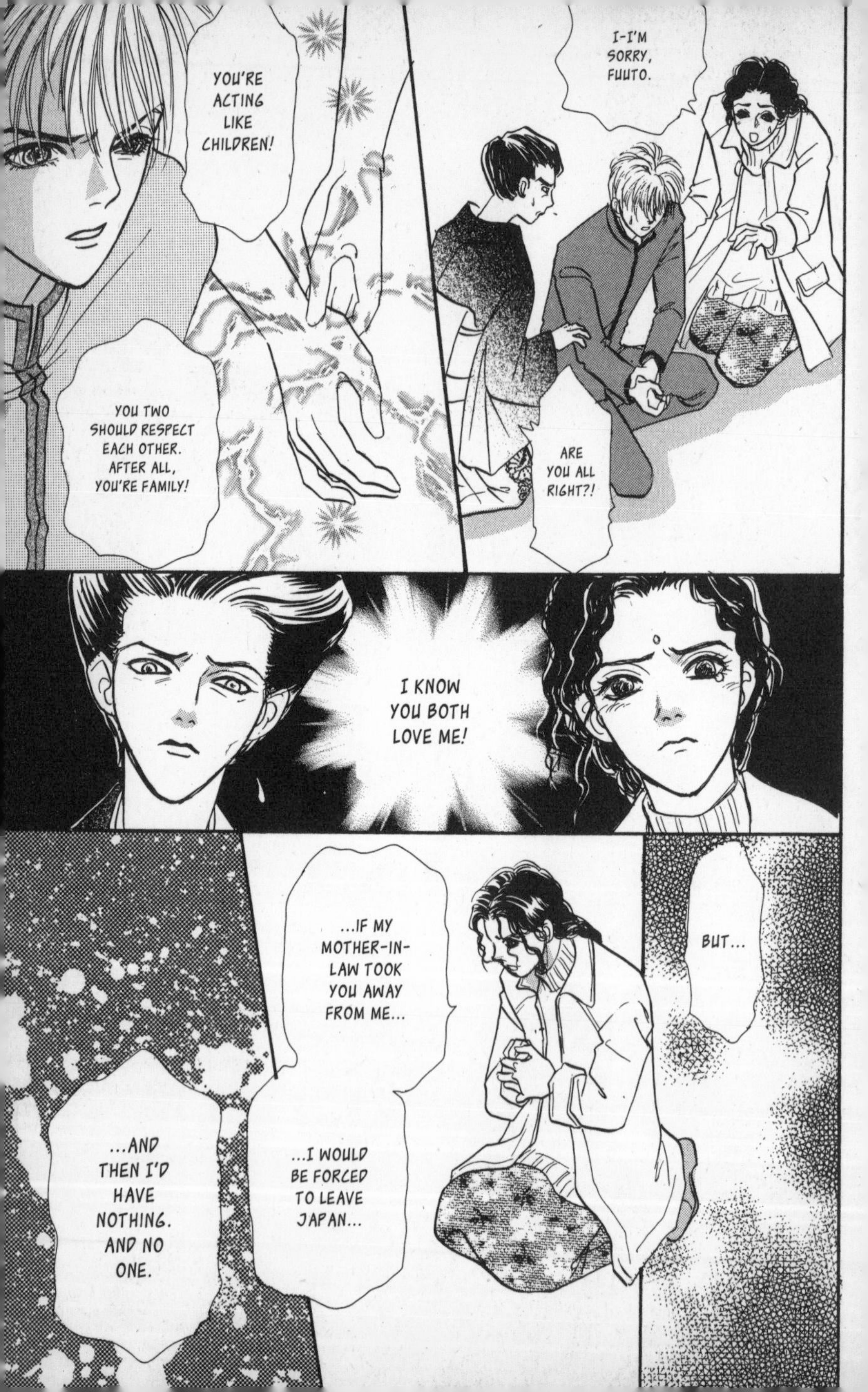
I-I'M SORRY, FUUTO.
ARE YOU ALL RIGHT?!
YOU'RE ACTING LIKE CHILDREN!
YOU TWO SHOULD RESPECT EACH OTHER. AFTER ALL, YOU'RE FAMILY!
I KNOW YOU BOTH LOVE ME!
BUT...
...IF MY MOTHER-IN-LAW TOOK YOU AWAY FROM ME...
...I WOULD BE FORCED TO LEAVE JAPAN...
...AND THEN I'D HAVE NOTHING. AND NO ONE.

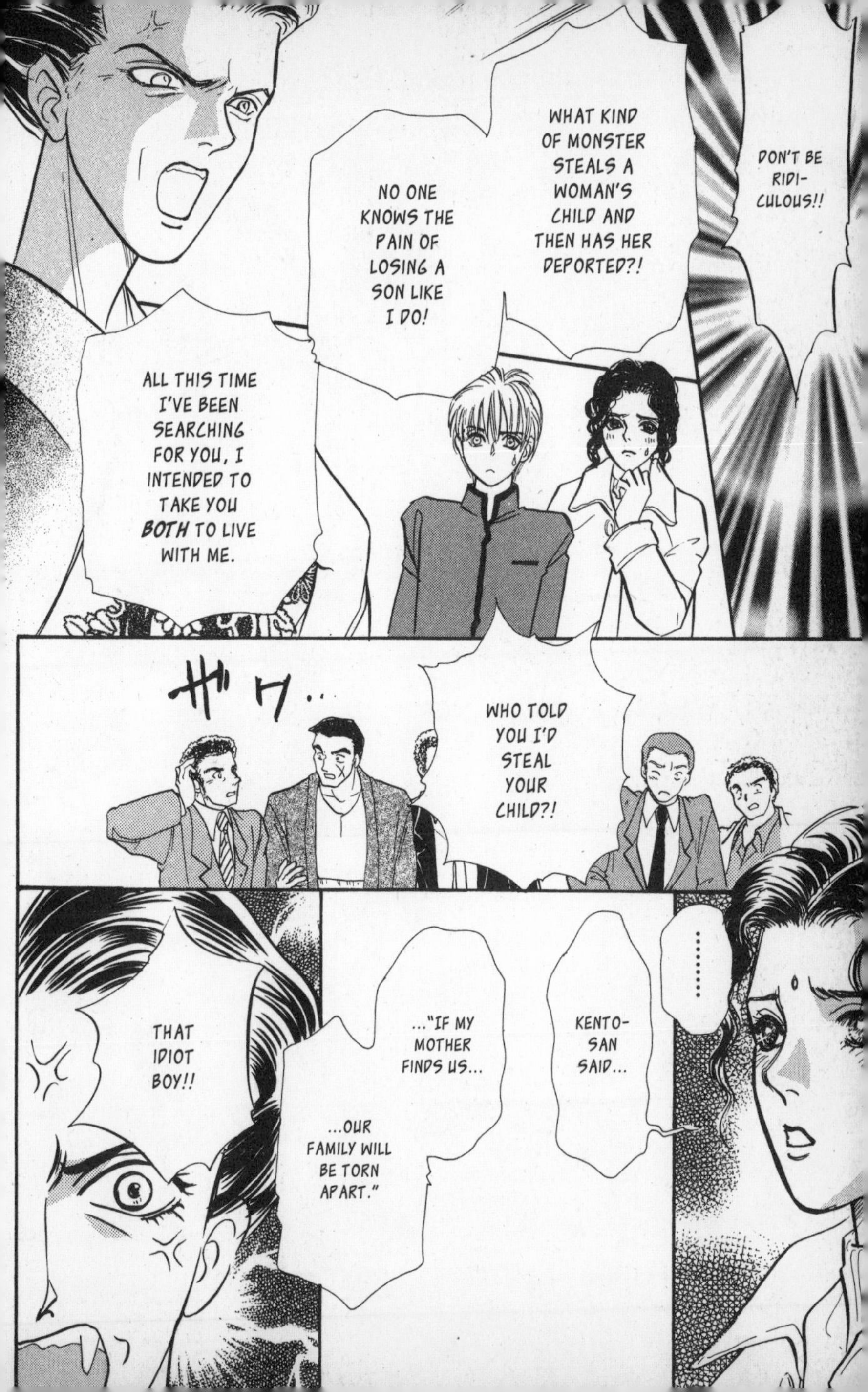
DON'T BE RIDI-CULOUS!!
WHAT KIND OF MONSTER STEALS A WOMAN'S CHILD AND THEN HAS HER DEPORTED?!
NO ONE KNOWS THE PAIN OF LOSING A SON LIKE I DO!
ALL THIS TIME I'VE BEEN SEARCHING FOR YOU, I INTENDED TO TAKE YOU *BOTH* TO LIVE WITH ME.
WHO TOLD YOU I'D STEAL YOUR CHILD?!
ザワ...
......
KENTO-SAN SAID...
..."IF MY MOTHER FINDS US...
...OUR FAMILY WILL BE TORN APART."
THAT IDIOT BOY!!

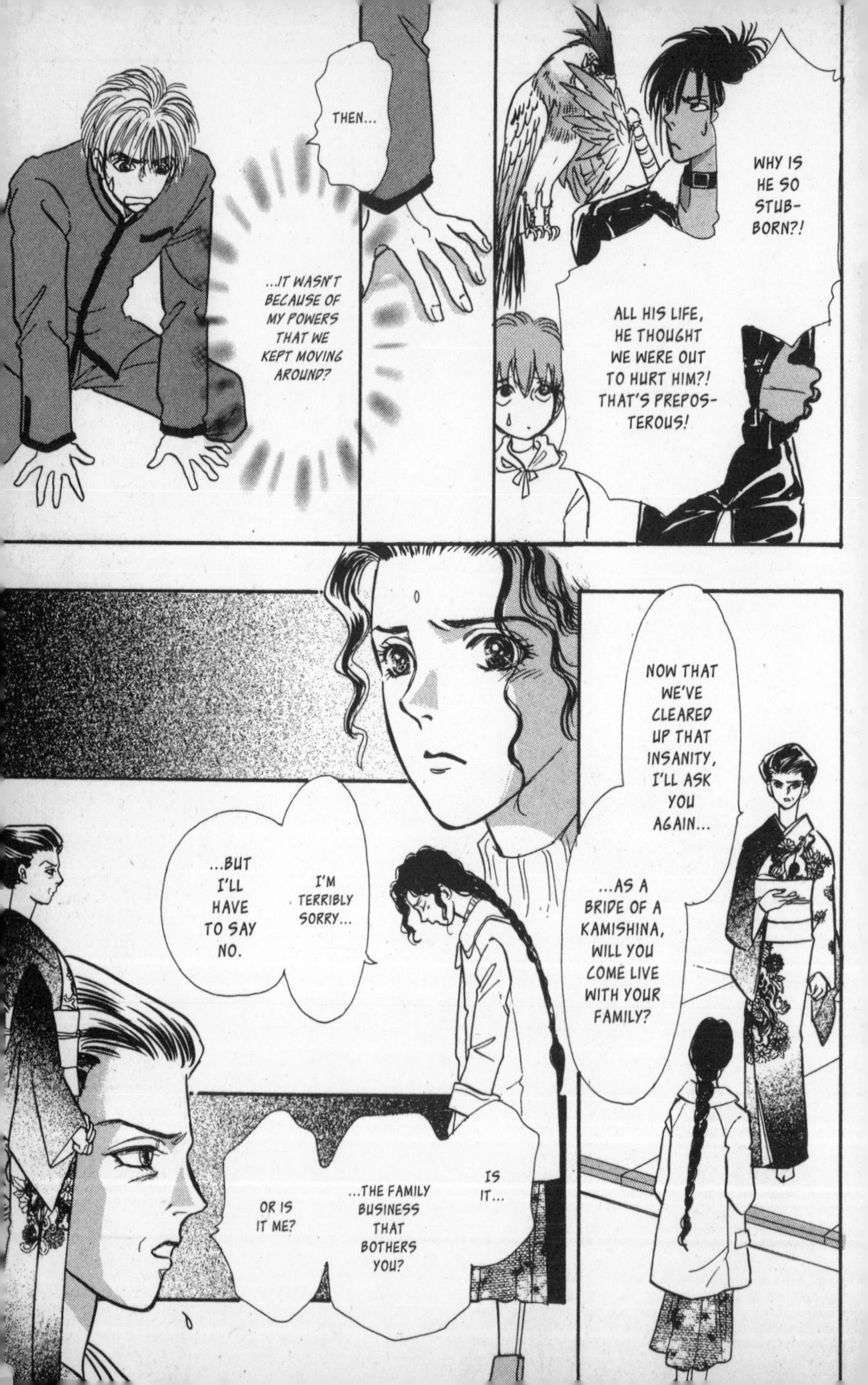
WHY IS HE SO STUB-BORN?!
ALL HIS LIFE, HE THOUGHT WE WERE OUT TO HURT HIM?! THAT'S PREPOS-TEROUS!
THEN...
...IT WASN'T BECAUSE OF MY POWERS THAT WE KEPT MOVING AROUND?
NOW THAT WE'VE CLEARED UP THAT INSANITY, I'LL ASK YOU AGAIN...
...AS A BRIDE OF A KAMISHINA, WILL YOU COME LIVE WITH YOUR FAMILY?
I'M TERRIBLY SORRY...
...BUT I'LL HAVE TO SAY NO.
IS IT...
...THE FAMILY BUSINESS THAT BOTHERS YOU?
OR IS IT ME?

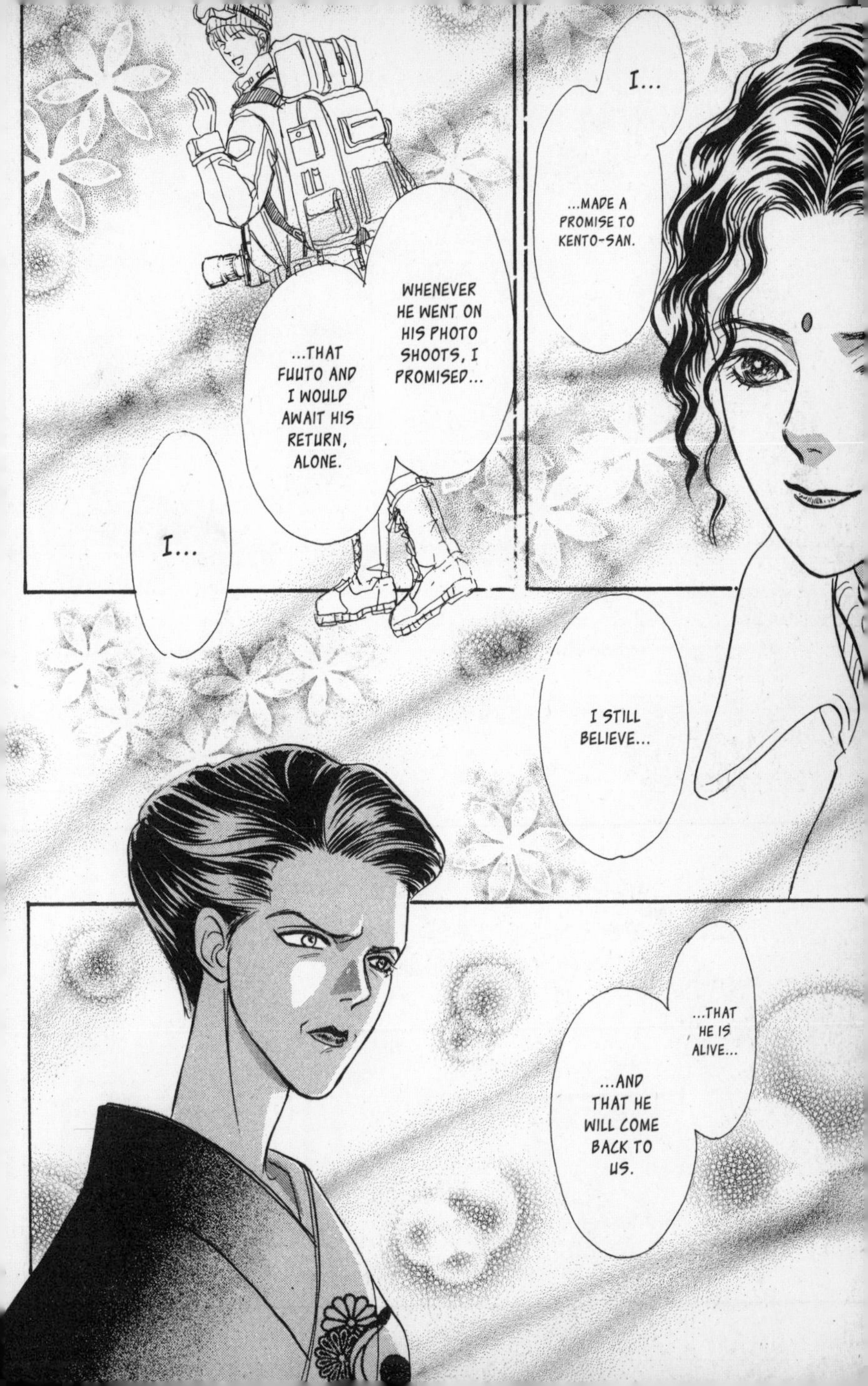
I...
...MADE A PROMISE TO KENTO-SAN.
WHENEVER HE WENT ON HIS PHOTO SHOOTS, I PROMISED...
...THAT FUUTO AND I WOULD AWAIT HIS RETURN, ALONE.
I...
I STILL BELIEVE...
...THAT HE IS ALIVE...
...AND THAT HE WILL COME BACK TO US.

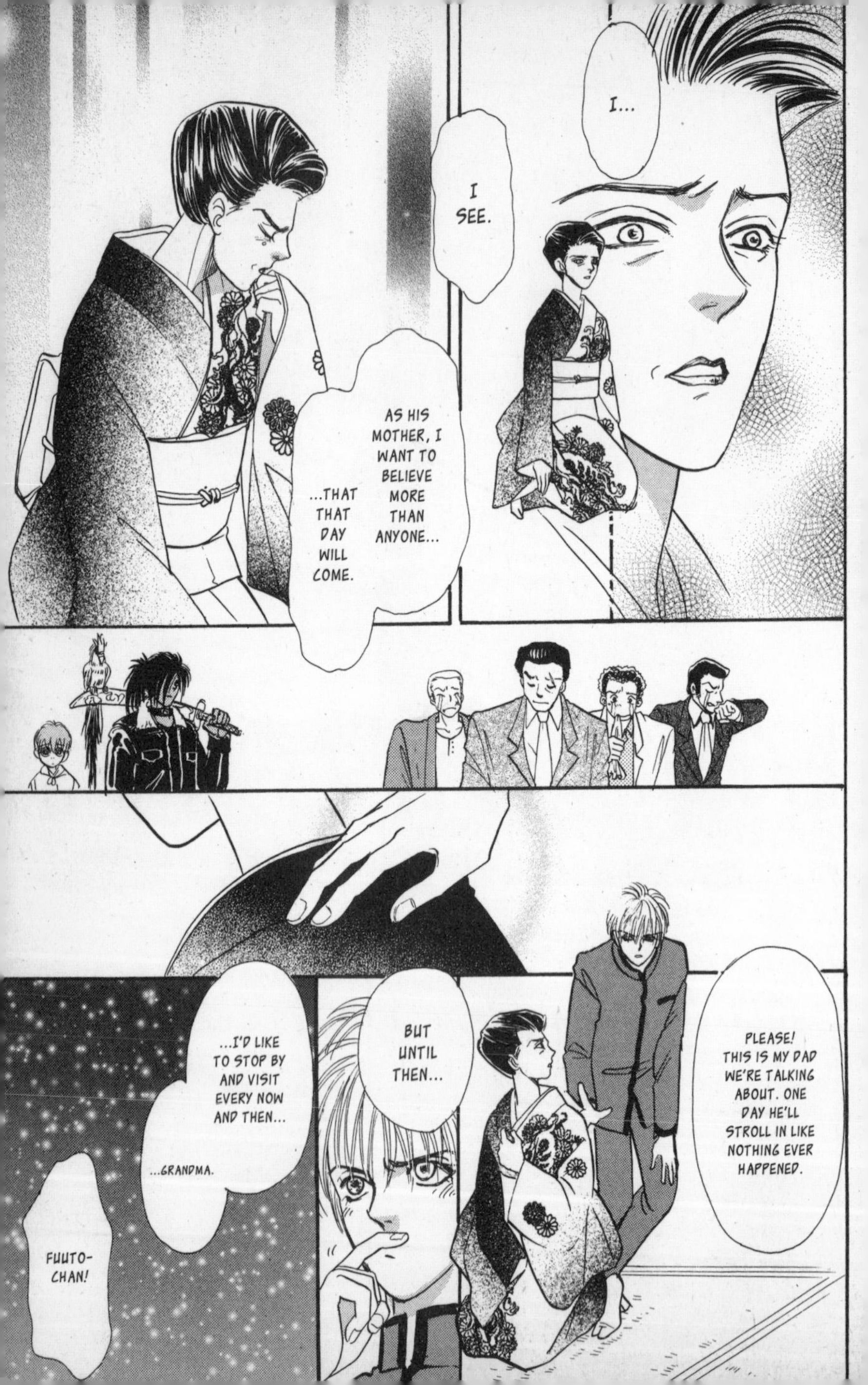
I...
I SEE.
AS HIS MOTHER, I WANT TO BELIEVE MORE THAN ANYONE...
...THAT THAT DAY WILL COME.
PLEASE! THIS IS MY DAD WE'RE TALKING ABOUT. ONE DAY HE'LL STROLL IN LIKE NOTHING EVER HAPPENED.
BUT UNTIL THEN...
...I'D LIKE TO STOP BY AND VISIT EVERY NOW AND THEN...
...GRANDMA.
FUUTO-CHAN!

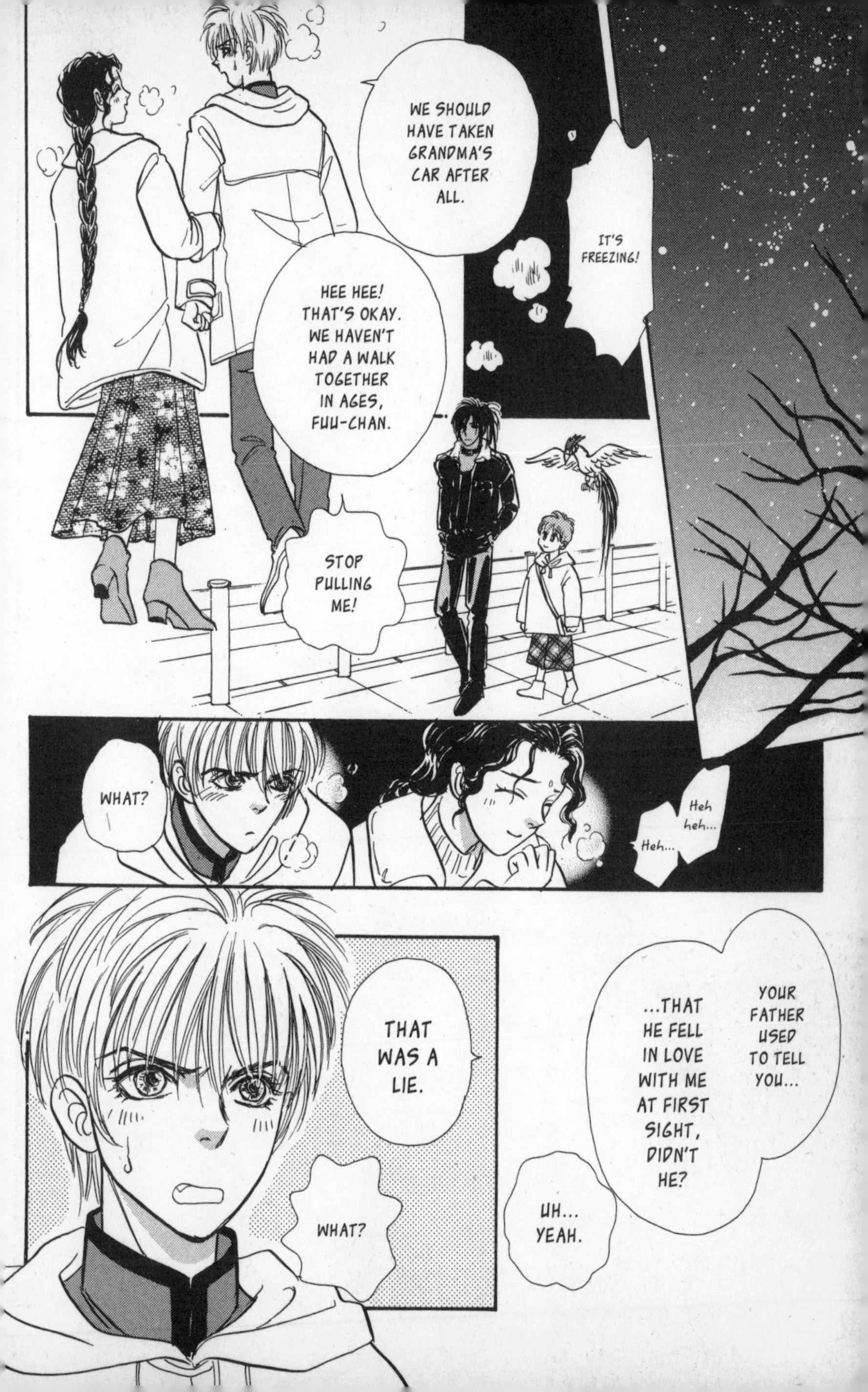
IT'S FREEZING!
WE SHOULD HAVE TAKEN GRANDMA'S CAR AFTER ALL.
HEE HEE! THAT'S OKAY. WE HAVEN'T HAD A WALK TOGETHER IN AGES, FUU-CHAN.
STOP PULLING ME!
Heh heh... Heh...
WHAT?
YOUR FATHER USED TO TELL YOU...
...THAT HE FELL IN LOVE WITH ME AT FIRST SIGHT, DIDN'T HE?
UH... YEAH.
THAT WAS A LIE.
WHAT?

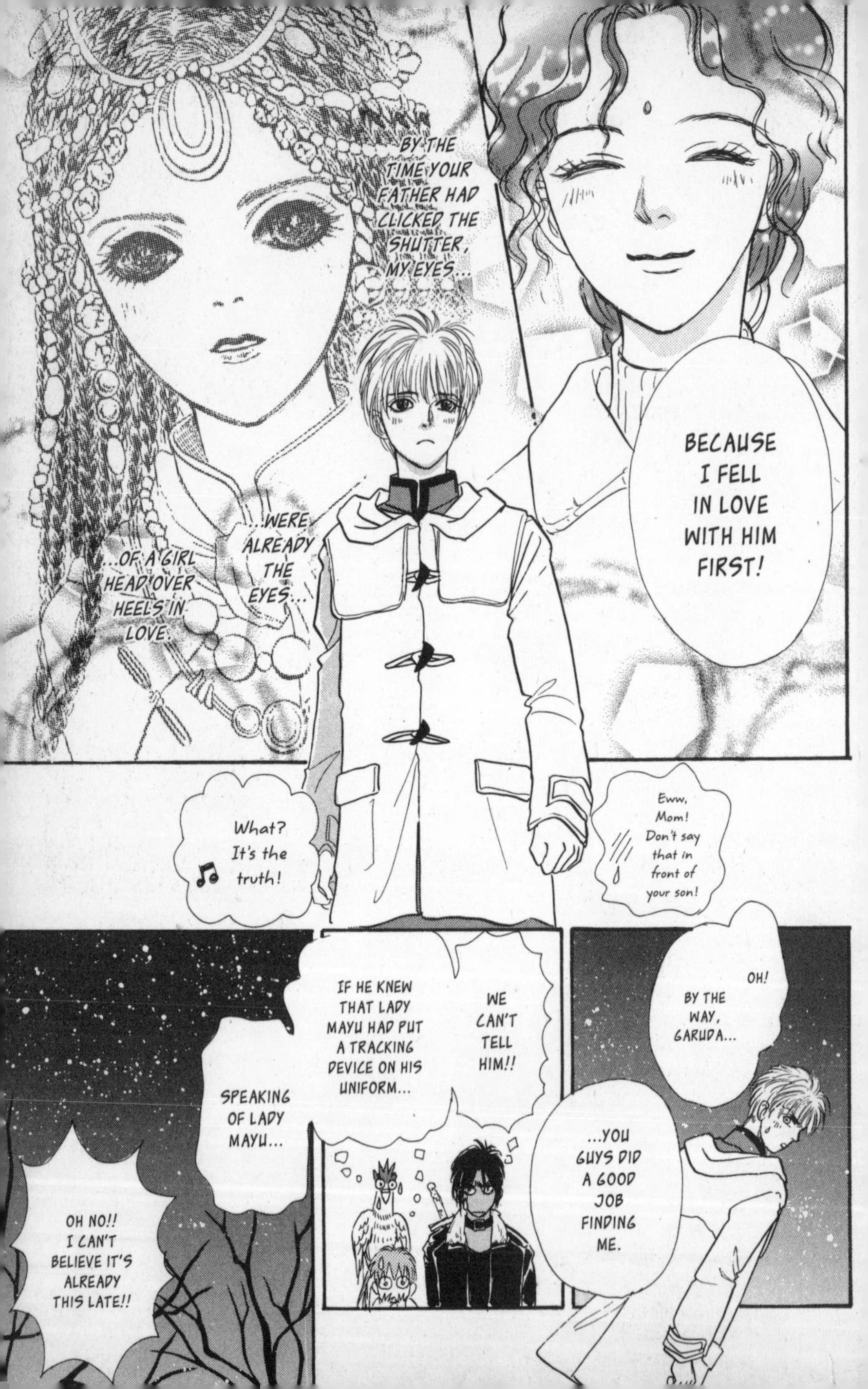
BECAUSE I FELL IN LOVE WITH HIM FIRST!
BY THE TIME YOUR FATHER HAD CLICKED THE SHUTTER, MY EYES...
...WERE ALREADY THE EYES...
...OF A GIRL HEAD OVER HEELS IN LOVE.
Eww, Mom! Don't say that in front of your son!
What? It's the truth!
OH!
BY THE WAY, GARUDA...
...YOU GUYS DID A GOOD JOB FINDING ME.
WE CAN'T TELL HIM!!
IF HE KNEW THAT LADY MAYU HAD PUT A TRACKING DEVICE ON HIS UNIFORM...
SPEAKING OF LADY MAYU...
OH NO!! I CAN'T BELIEVE IT'S ALREADY THIS LATE!!

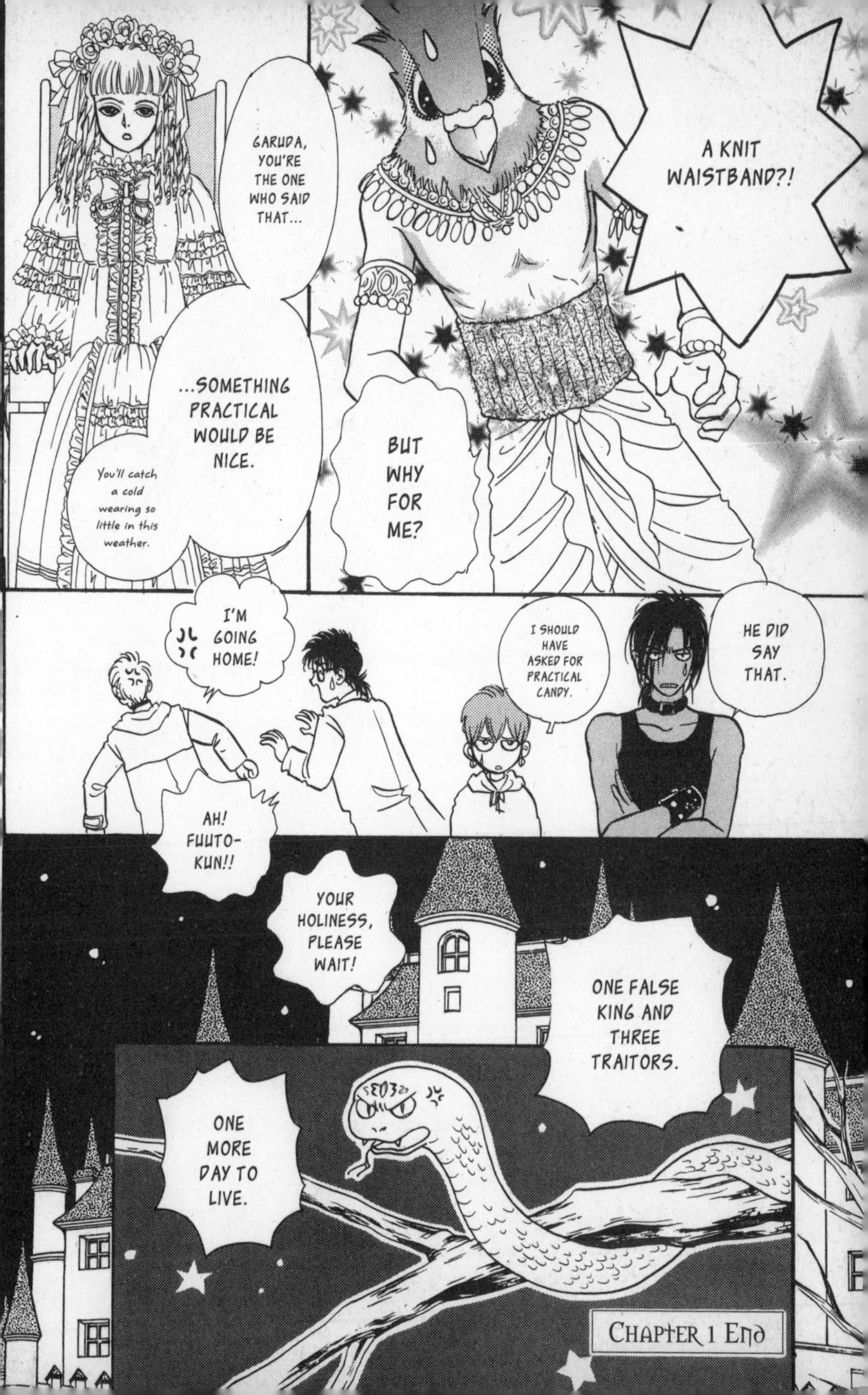
A KNIT WAISTBAND?!
GARUDA, YOU'RE THE ONE WHO SAID THAT...
BUT WHY FOR ME?
...SOMETHING PRACTICAL WOULD BE NICE.
You'll catch a cold wearing so little in this weather.
HE DID SAY THAT.
I SHOULD HAVE ASKED FOR PRACTICAL CANDY.
I'M GOING HOME!
AH! FUUTO-KUN!!
YOUR HOLINESS, PLEASE WAIT!
ONE FALSE KING AND THREE TRAITORS.
ONE MORE DAY TO LIVE.
Chapter 1 End

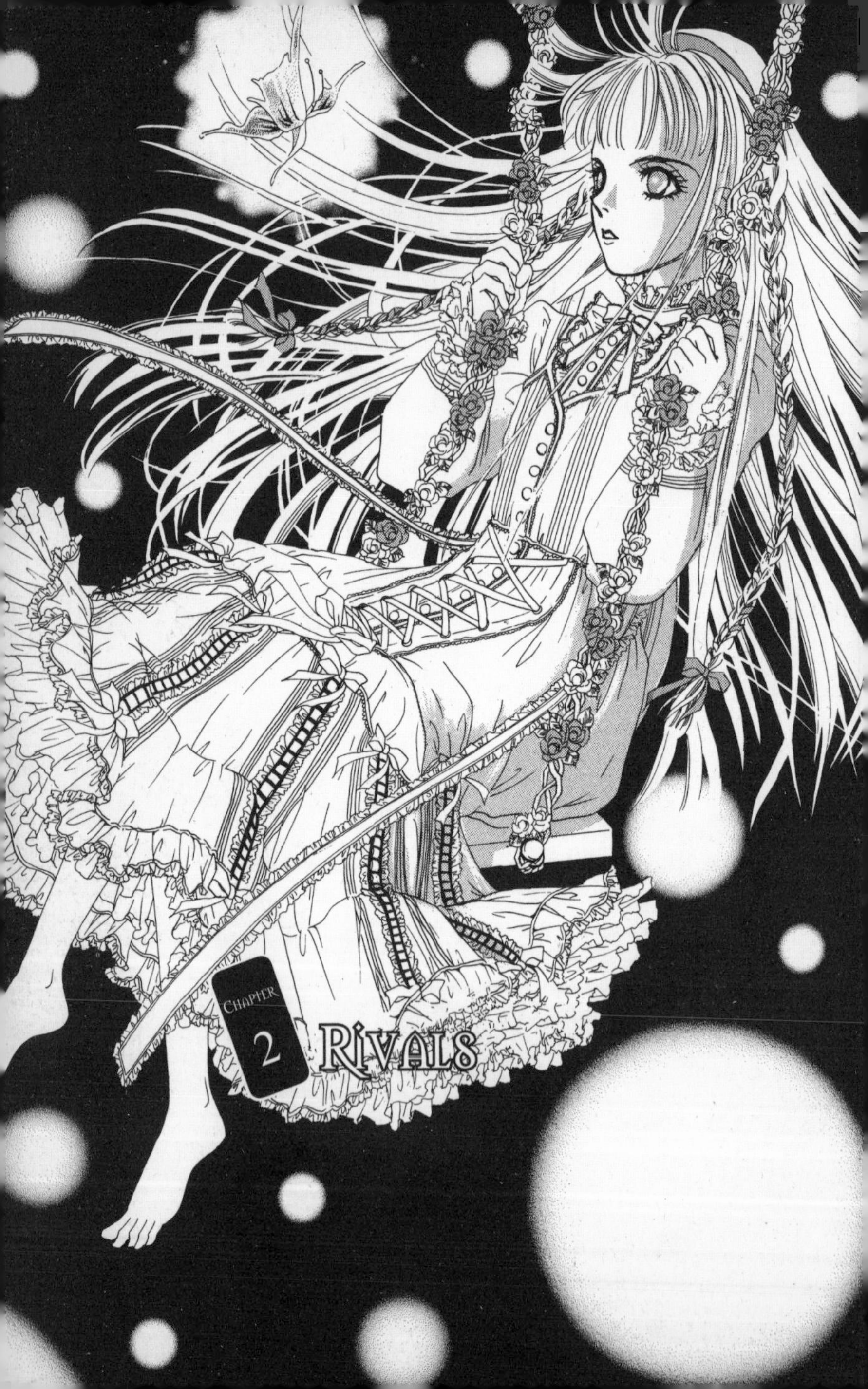

Chapter 2
Rivals

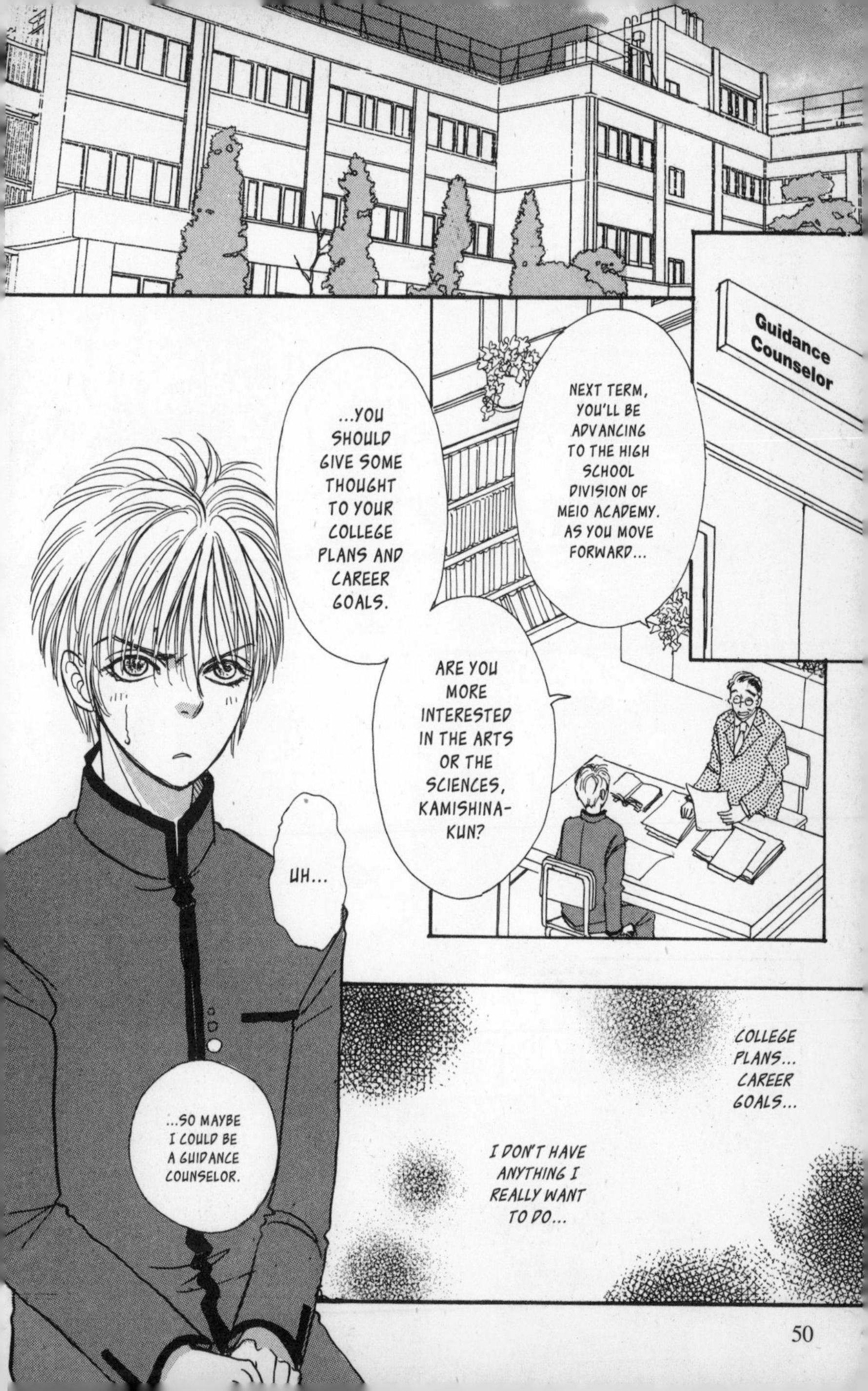
Guidance Counselor
NEXT TERM, YOU'LL BE ADVANCING TO THE HIGH SCHOOL DIVISION OF MEIO ACADEMY. AS YOU MOVE FORWARD...
...YOU SHOULD GIVE SOME THOUGHT TO YOUR COLLEGE PLANS AND CAREER GOALS.
ARE YOU MORE INTERESTED IN THE ARTS OR THE SCIENCES, KAMISHINA-KUN?
UH...
COLLEGE PLANS... CAREER GOALS...
I DON'T HAVE ANYTHING I REALLY WANT TO DO...
...SO MAYBE I COULD BE A GUIDANCE COUNSELOR.

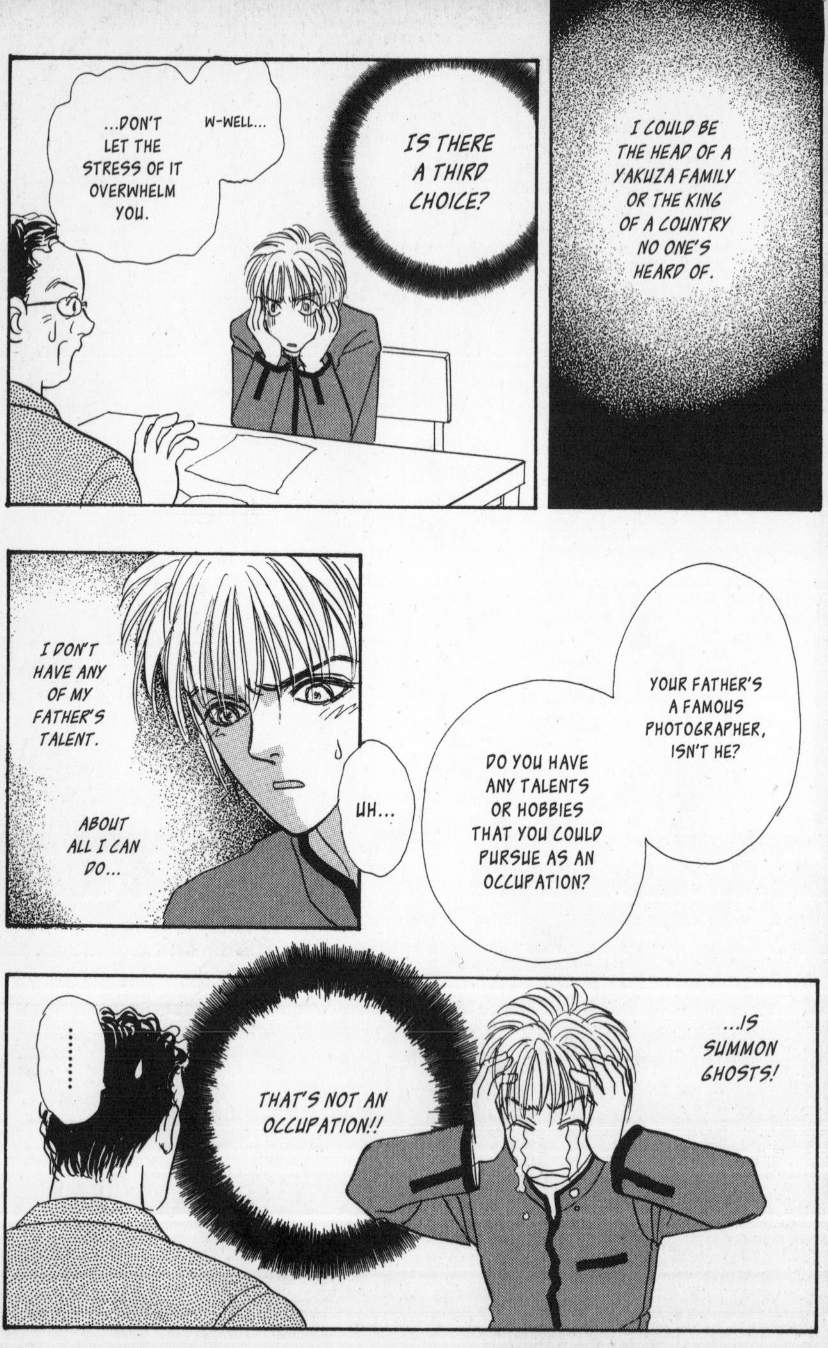
I COULD BE THE HEAD OF A YAKUZA FAMILY OR THE KING OF A COUNTRY NO ONE'S HEARD OF.
IS THERE A THIRD CHOICE?
W-WELL...
...DON'T LET THE STRESS OF IT OVERWHELM YOU.
YOUR FATHER'S A FAMOUS PHOTOGRAPHER, ISN'T HE?
DO YOU HAVE ANY TALENTS OR HOBBIES THAT YOU COULD PURSUE AS AN OCCUPATION?
UH...
I DON'T HAVE ANY OF MY FATHER'S TALENT.
ABOUT ALL I CAN DO...
...IS SUMMON GHOSTS!
THAT'S NOT AN OCCUPATION!!
....

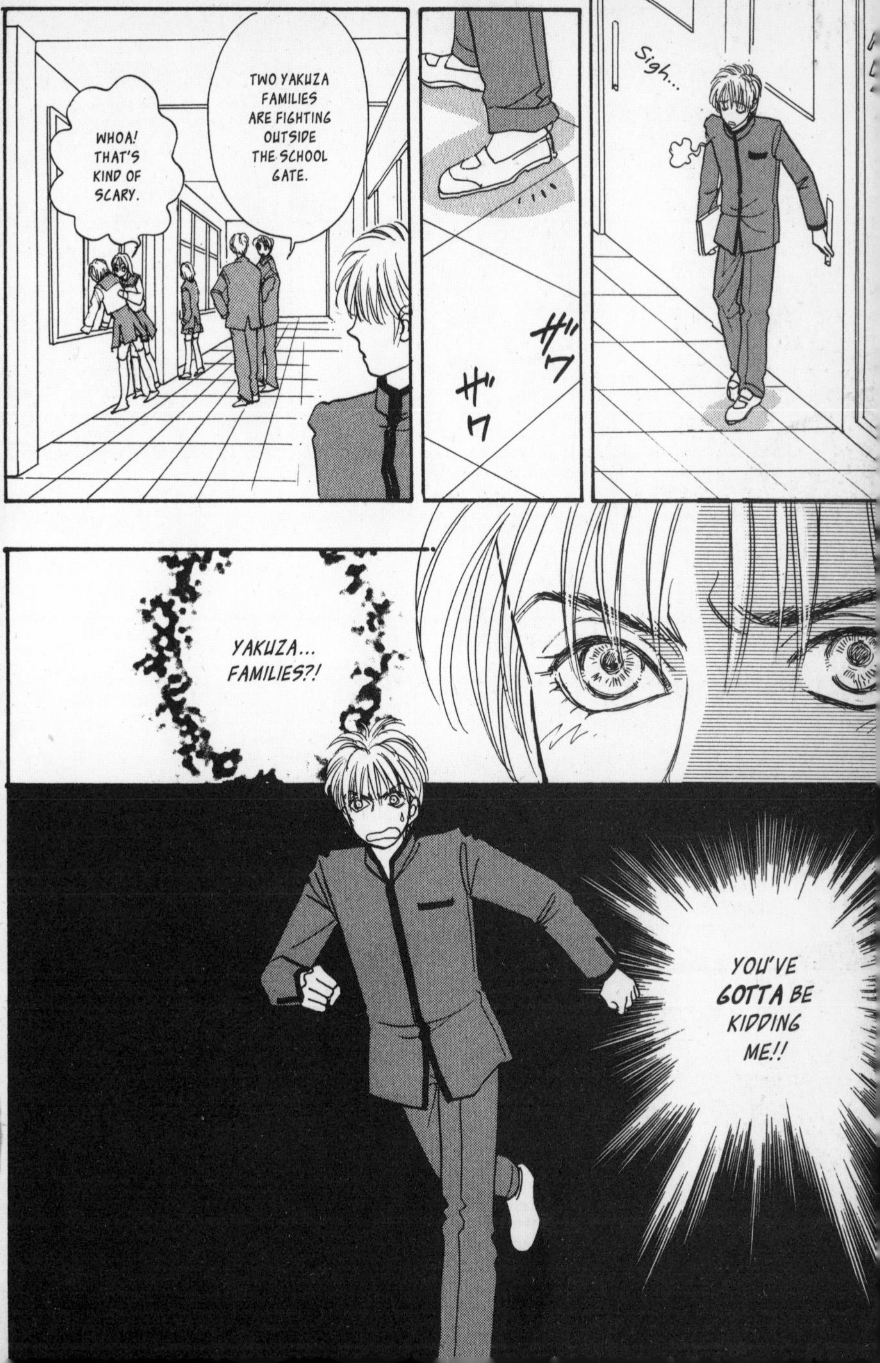
Sigh...
ザワ
ザワ
TWO YAKUZA FAMILIES ARE FIGHTING OUTSIDE THE SCHOOL GATE.
WHOA! THAT'S KIND OF SCARY.
YAKUZA... FAMILIES?!
YOU'VE GOTTA BE KIDDING ME!!

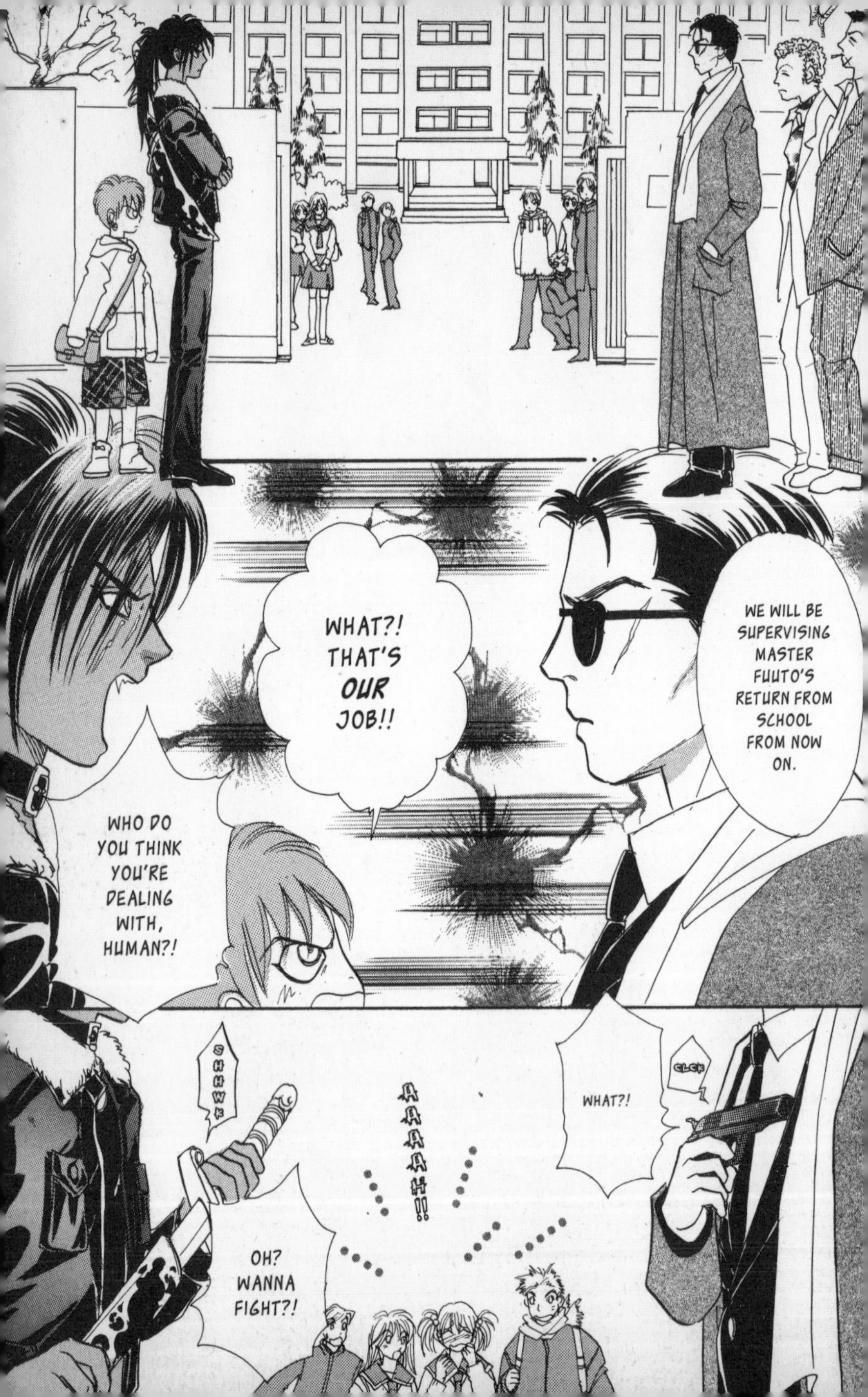
WE WILL BE SUPERVISING MASTER FUUTO'S RETURN FROM SCHOOL FROM NOW ON.
WHAT?! THAT'S OUR JOB!!
WHO DO YOU THINK YOU'RE DEALING WITH, HUMAN?!
CLCK
WHAT?!
AAAAAH!!
SHHWK
OH? WANNA FIGHT?!

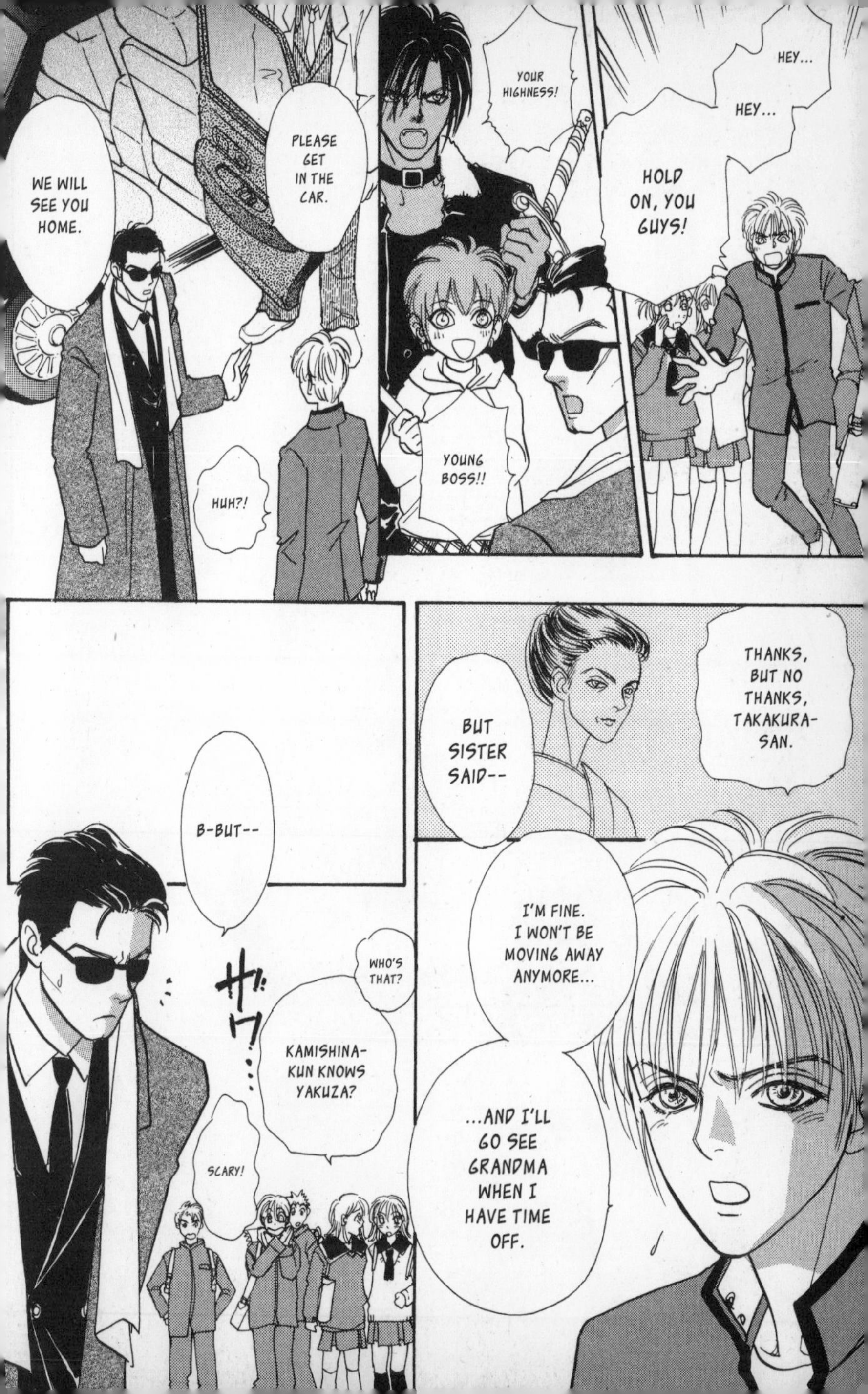

HEY...
HEY...
HOLD ON, YOU GUYS!
YOUR HIGHNESS!
YOUNG BOSS!!
PLEASE GET IN THE CAR.
WE WILL SEE YOU HOME.
HUH?!
THANKS, BUT NO THANKS, TAKAKURA-SAN.
BUT SISTER SAID--
B-BUT--
I'M FINE. I WON'T BE MOVING AWAY ANYMORE...
...AND I'LL GO SEE GRANDMA WHEN I HAVE TIME OFF.
WHO'S THAT?
KAMISHINA-KUN KNOWS YAKUZA?
ザワ...
SCARY!

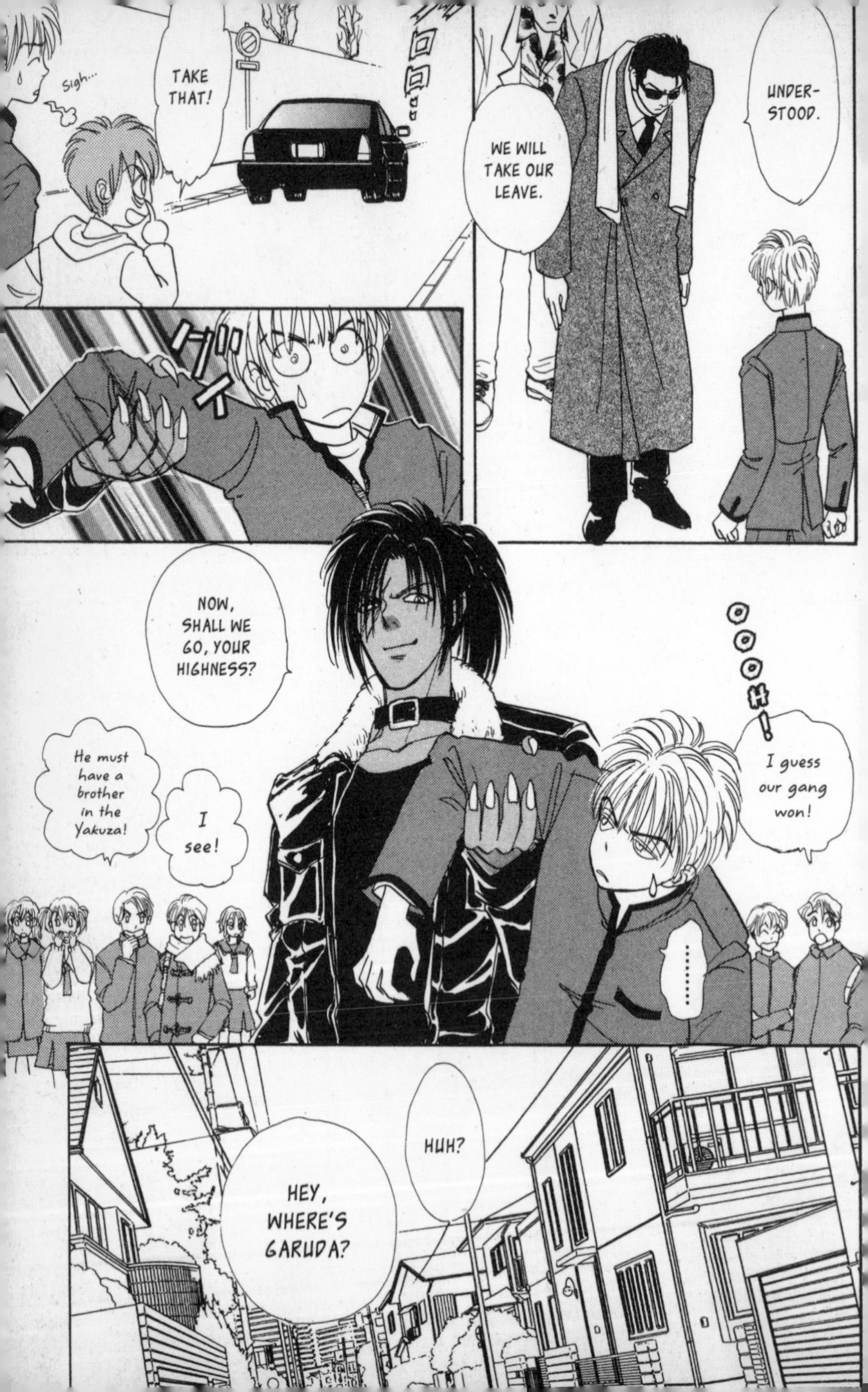
UNDER-STOOD.
WE WILL TAKE OUR LEAVE.
TAKE THAT!
Sigh...
OOOOH!
I guess our gang won!
NOW, SHALL WE GO, YOUR HIGHNESS?
He must have a brother in the Yakuza!
I see!
....
HUH?
HEY, WHERE'S GARUDA?

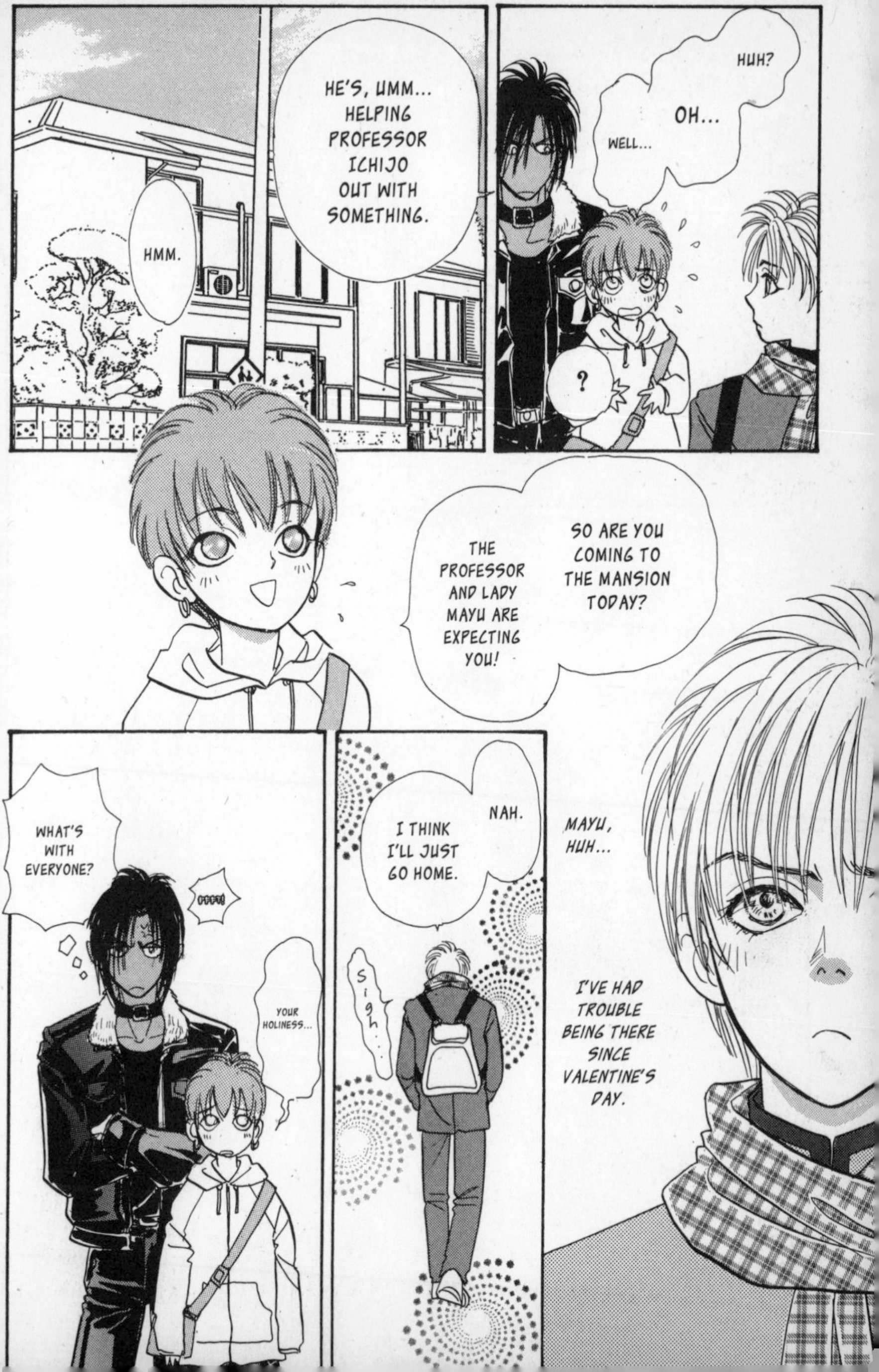
HUH?
OH...
WELL...
HE'S, UMM... HELPING PROFESSOR ICHIJO OUT WITH SOMETHING.
HMM.
?
SO ARE YOU COMING TO THE MANSION TODAY?
THE PROFESSOR AND LADY MAYU ARE EXPECTING YOU!
MAYU, HUH...
I'VE HAD TROUBLE BEING THERE SINCE VALENTINE'S DAY.
NAH.
I THINK I'LL JUST GO HOME.
sigh...
WHAT'S WITH EVERYONE?
YOUR HOLINESS...

BECAUSE I RAISED THE ISSUE ON VALENTINE'S DAY...

...HIS HOLINESS FEELS HURT.

I CANNOT YET SHOW MY FACE AROUND HIM.

S i g h . . .

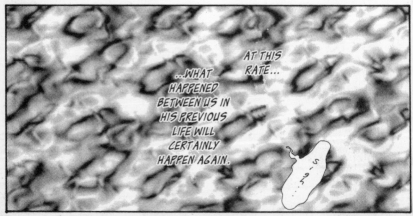

AT THIS RATE...

...WHAT HAPPENED BETWEEN US IN HIS PREVIOUS LIFE WILL CERTAINLY HAPPEN AGAIN.

S - i - g - h . . .

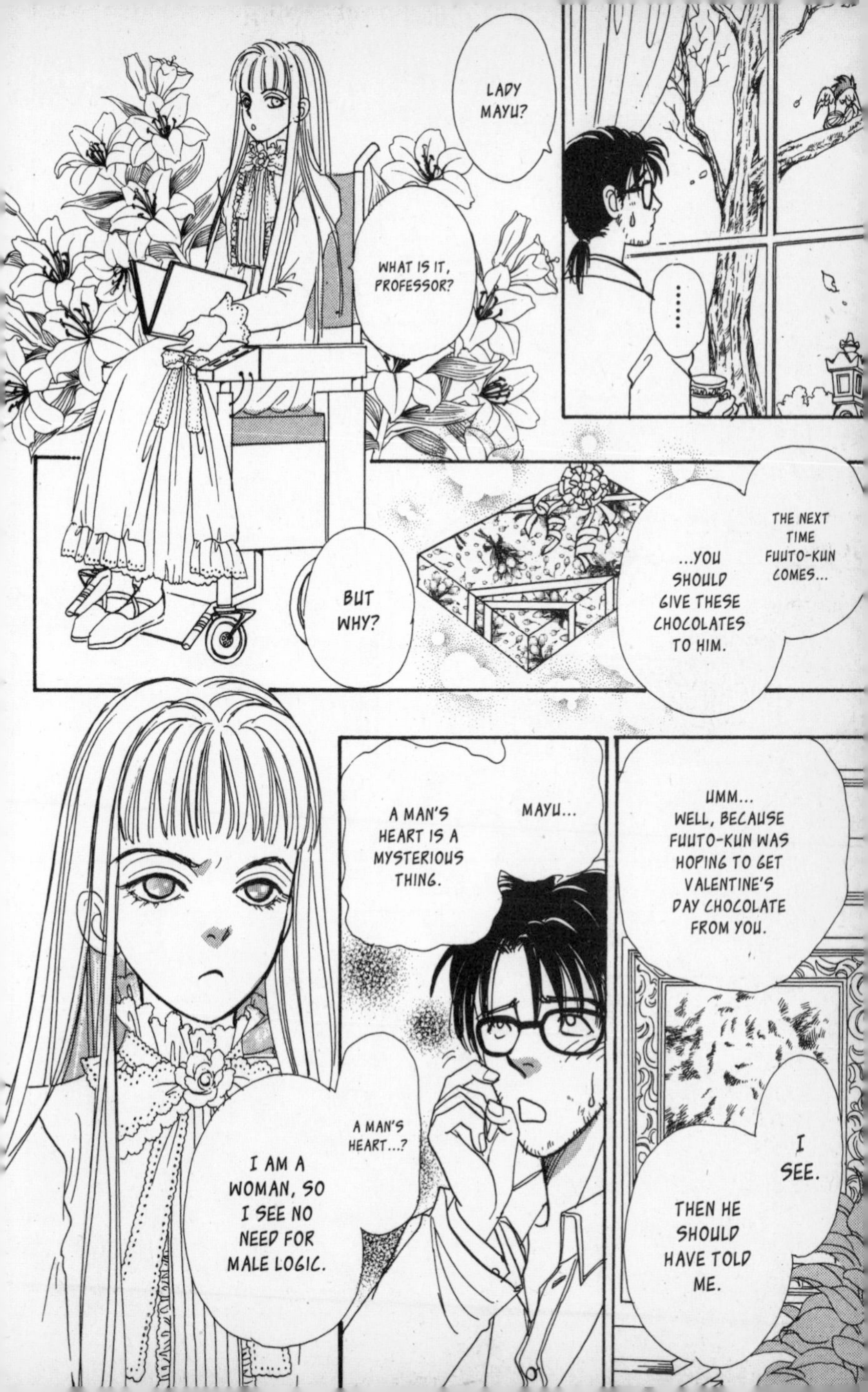
LADY MAYU?
......
WHAT IS IT, PROFESSOR?
THE NEXT TIME FUUTO-KUN COMES...
...YOU SHOULD GIVE THESE CHOCOLATES TO HIM.
BUT WHY?
UMM... WELL, BECAUSE FUUTO-KUN WAS HOPING TO GET VALENTINE'S DAY CHOCOLATE FROM YOU.
MAYU...
A MAN'S HEART IS A MYSTERIOUS THING.
I SEE.
THEN HE SHOULD HAVE TOLD ME.
A MAN'S HEART...?
I AM A WOMAN, SO I SEE NO NEED FOR MALE LOGIC.

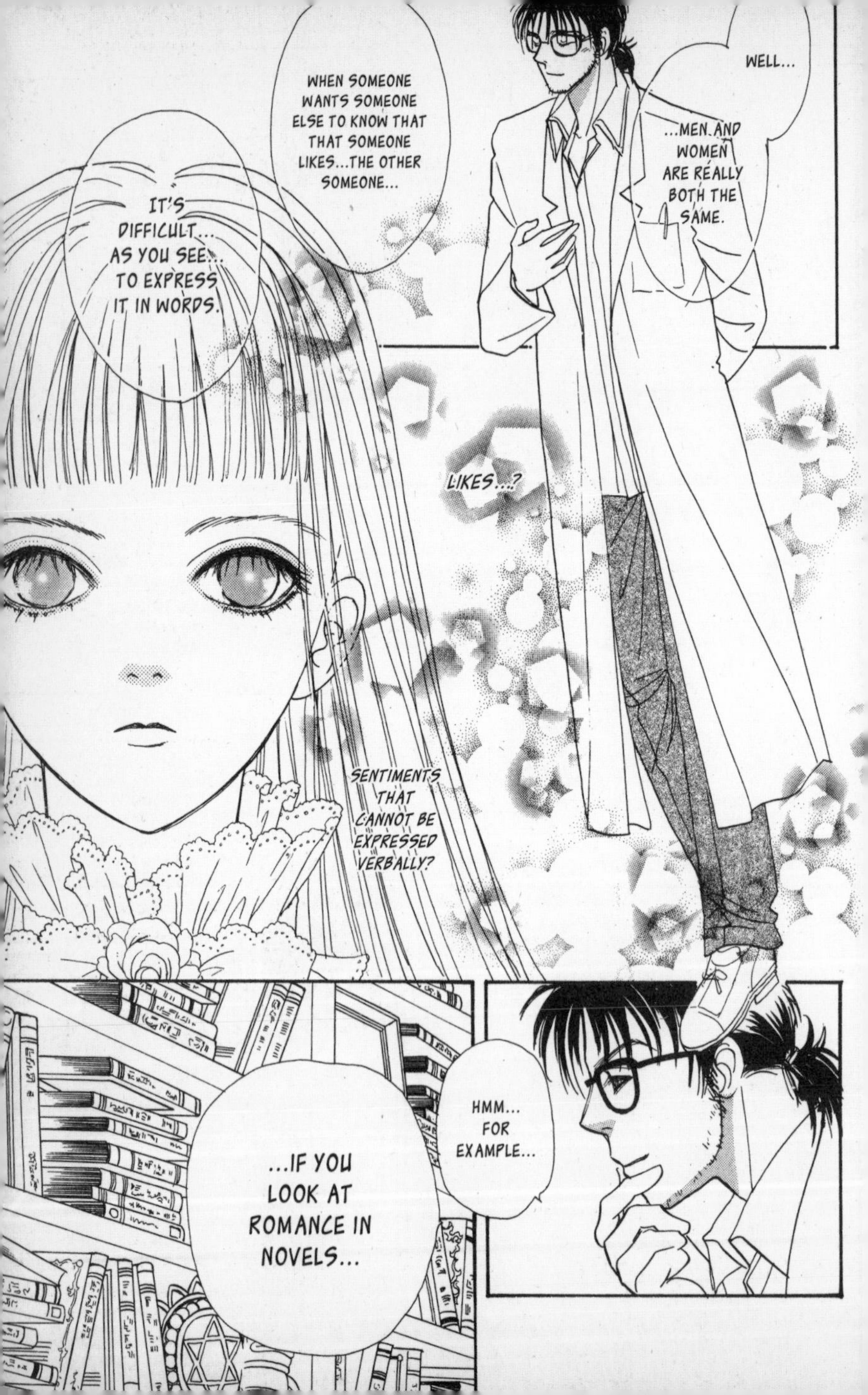
WELL...
...MEN AND WOMEN ARE REALLY BOTH THE SAME.
WHEN SOMEONE WANTS SOMEONE ELSE TO KNOW THAT THAT SOMEONE LIKES...THE OTHER SOMEONE...
IT'S DIFFICULT... AS YOU SEE... TO EXPRESS IT IN WORDS.
LIKES...?
SENTIMENTS THAT CANNOT BE EXPRESSED VERBALLY?
HMM... FOR EXAMPLE...
...IF YOU LOOK AT ROMANCE IN NOVELS...

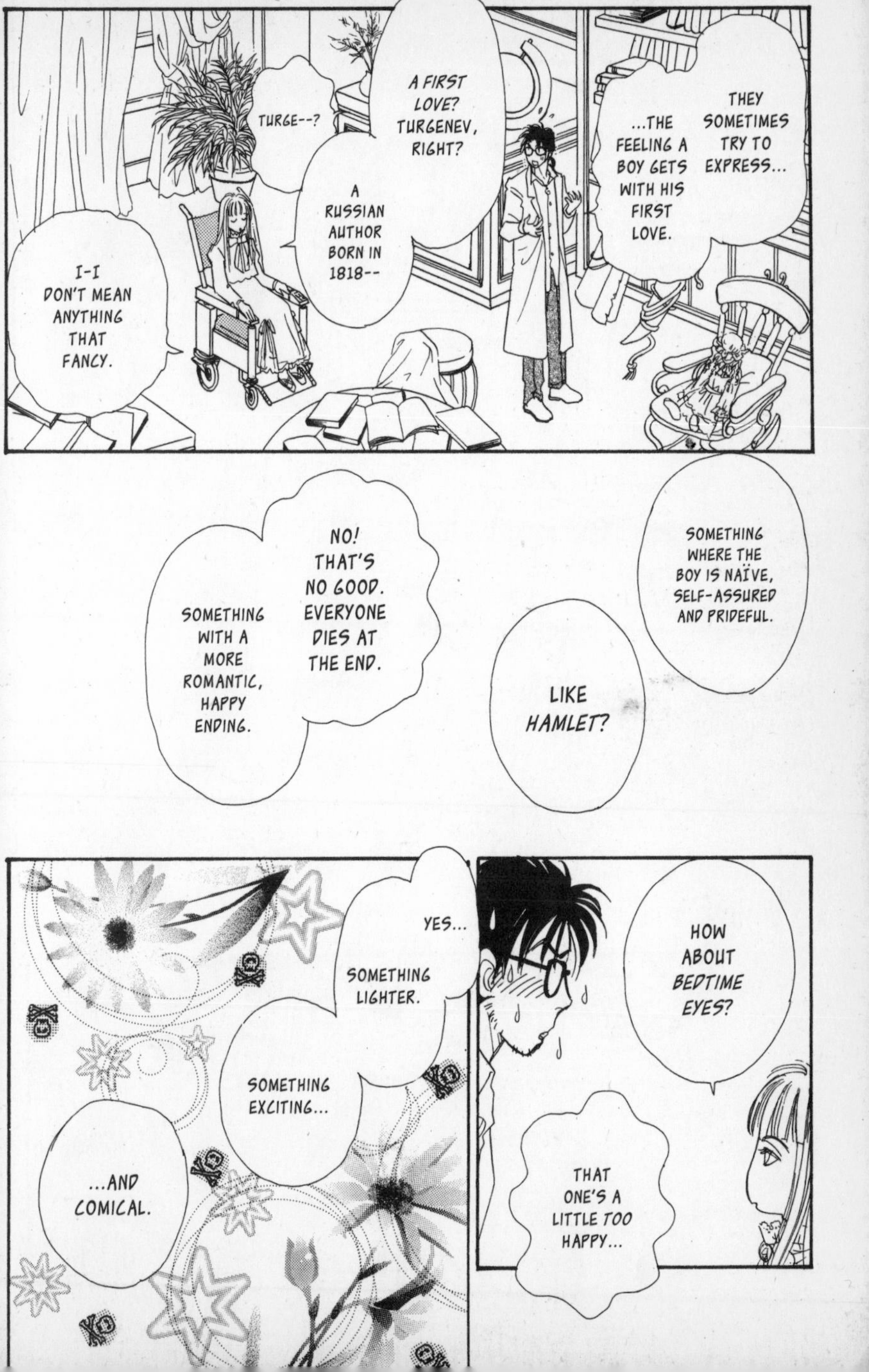
THEY SOMETIMES TRY TO EXPRESS...
...THE FEELING A BOY GETS WITH HIS FIRST LOVE.
A FIRST LOVE? TURGENEV, RIGHT?
TURGE--?
A RUSSIAN AUTHOR BORN IN 1818--
I-I DON'T MEAN ANYTHING THAT FANCY.
SOMETHING WHERE THE BOY IS NAÏVE, SELF-ASSURED AND PRIDEFUL.
LIKE *HAMLET*?
NO! THAT'S NO GOOD. EVERYONE DIES AT THE END.
SOMETHING WITH A MORE ROMANTIC, HAPPY ENDING.
HOW ABOUT *BEDTIME EYES*?
THAT ONE'S A LITTLE *TOO* HAPPY...
YES...
SOMETHING LIGHTER.
SOMETHING EXCITING...
...AND COMICAL.

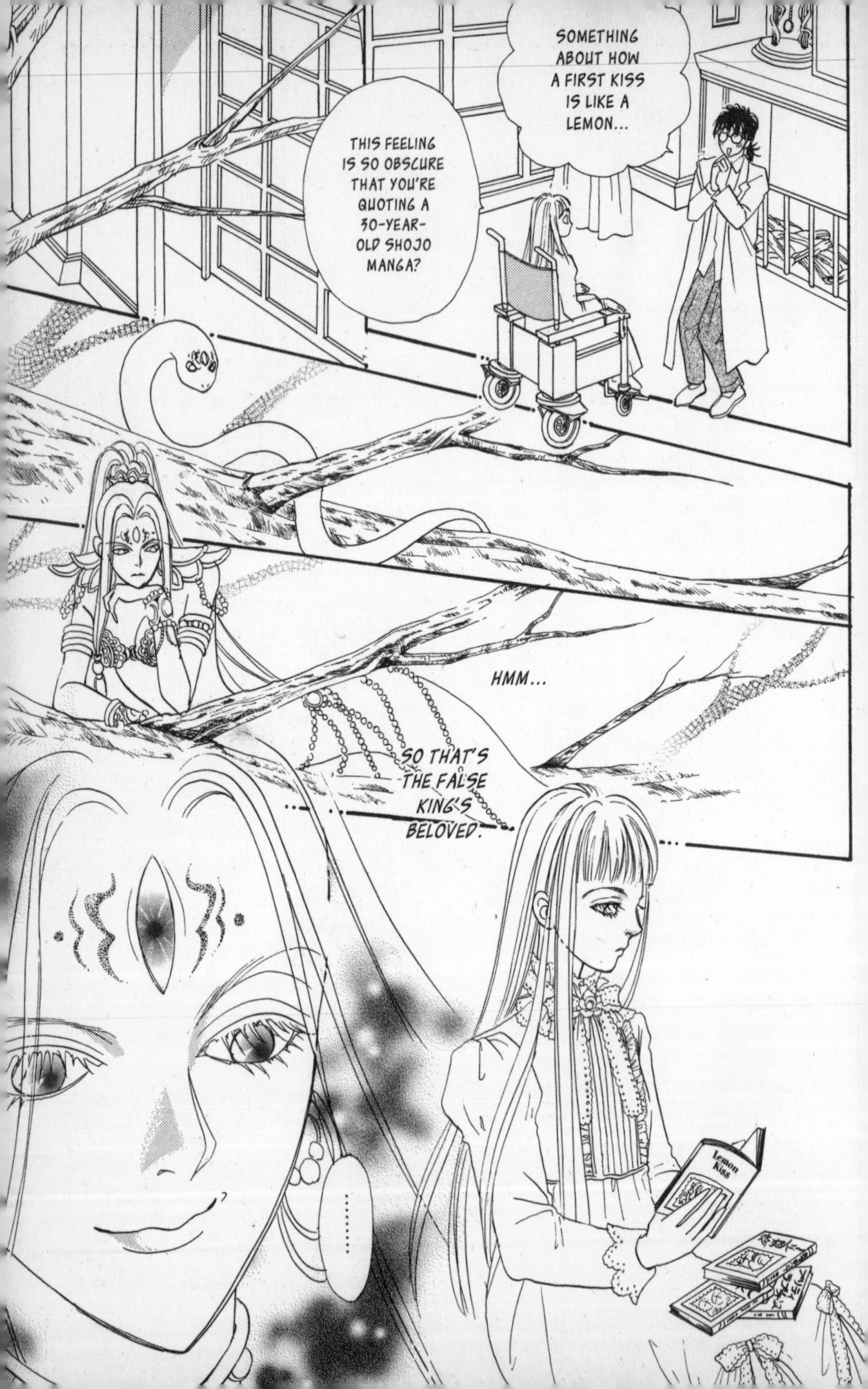
SOMETHING ABOUT HOW A FIRST KISS IS LIKE A LEMON...
THIS FEELING IS SO OBSCURE THAT YOU'RE QUOTING A 30-YEAR-OLD SHOJO MANGA?
HMM...
SO THAT'S THE FALSE KING'S BELOVED.
......
Lemon Kiss

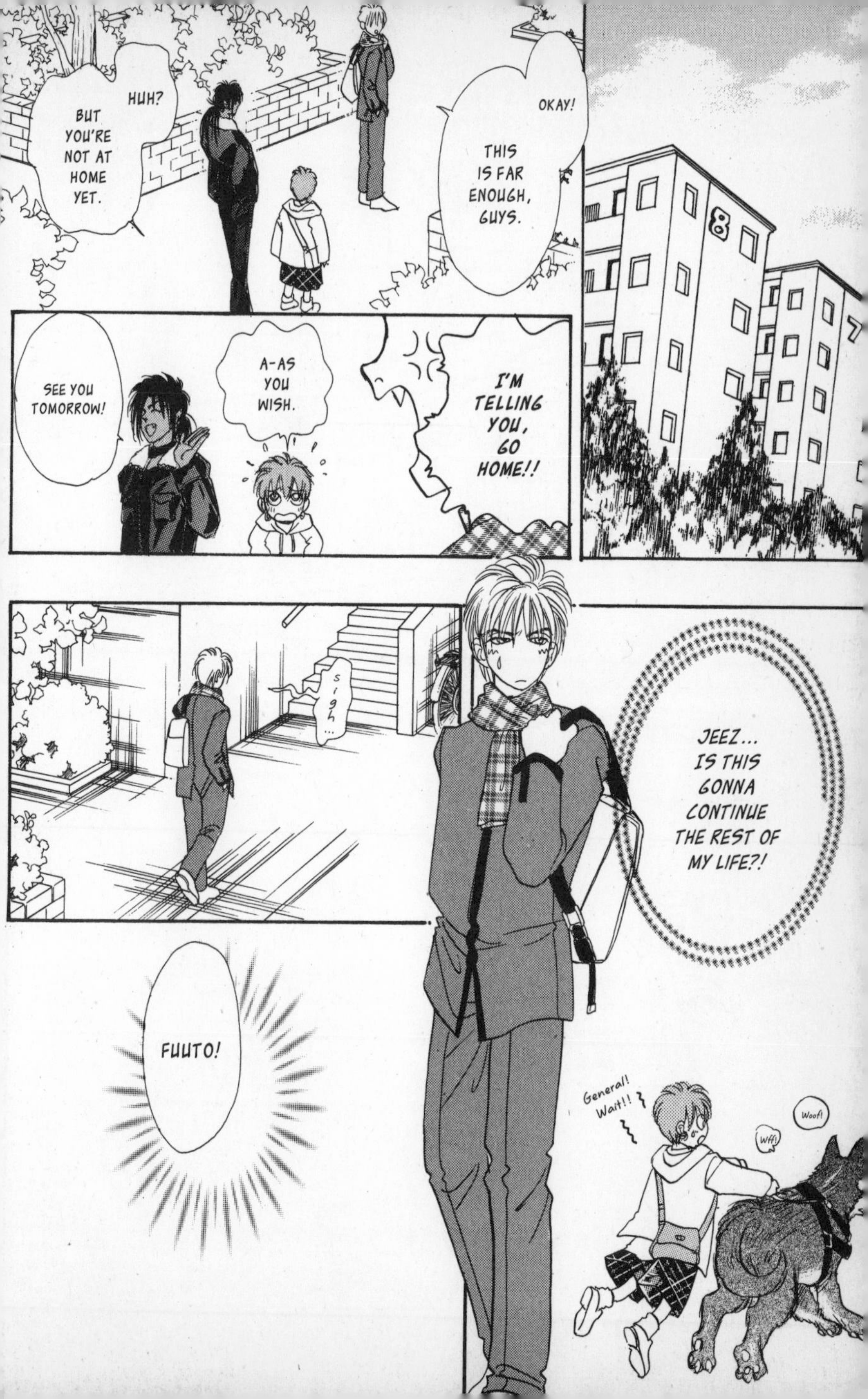
OKAY!
THIS IS FAR ENOUGH, GUYS.
HUH?
BUT YOU'RE NOT AT HOME YET.
I'M TELLING YOU, GO HOME!!
A-AS YOU WISH.
SEE YOU TOMORROW!
JEEZ... IS THIS GONNA CONTINUE THE REST OF MY LIFE?!
sigh...
FUUTO!
Woof!
Wf!
General! Wait!!

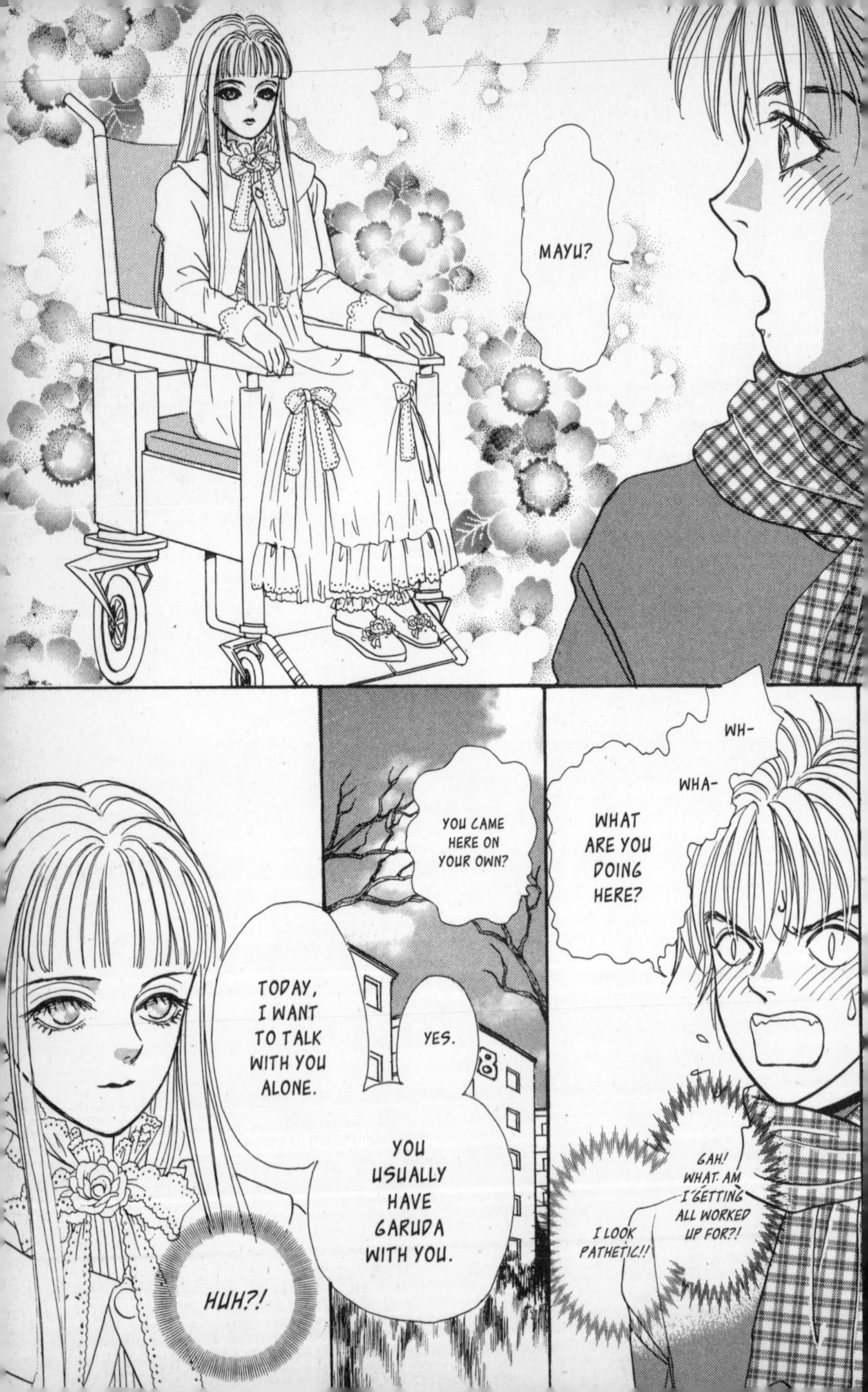
MAYU?
WH-
WHA-
WHAT ARE YOU DOING HERE?
GAH! WHAT AM I GETTING ALL WORKED UP FOR?!
I LOOK PATHETIC!!
YOU CAME HERE ON YOUR OWN?
YES.
YOU USUALLY HAVE GARUDA WITH YOU.
TODAY, I WANT TO TALK WITH YOU ALONE.
HUH?!

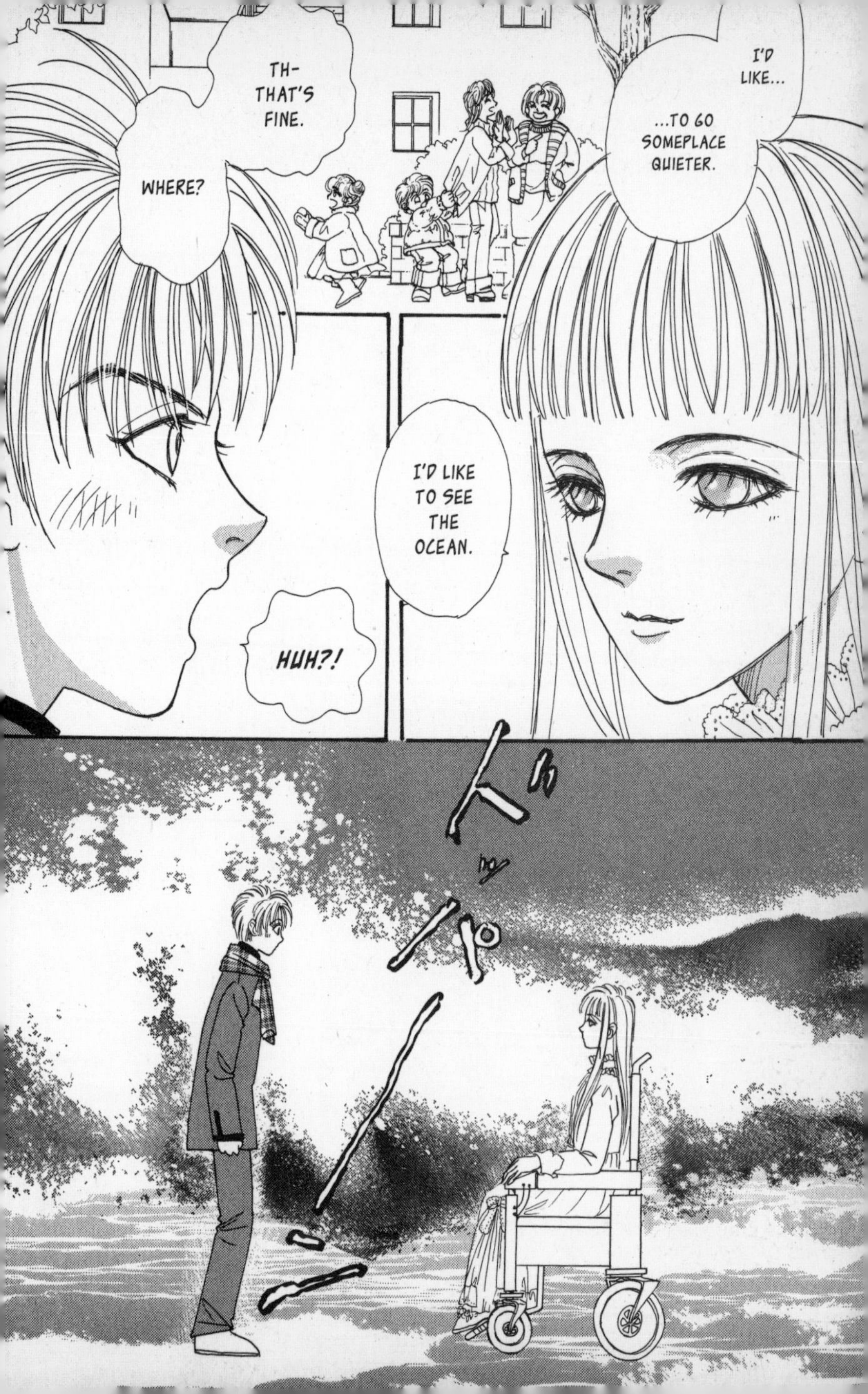
I'D LIKE...
...TO GO SOMEPLACE QUIETER.
TH- THAT'S FINE.
WHERE?
I'D LIKE TO SEE THE OCEAN.
HUH?!

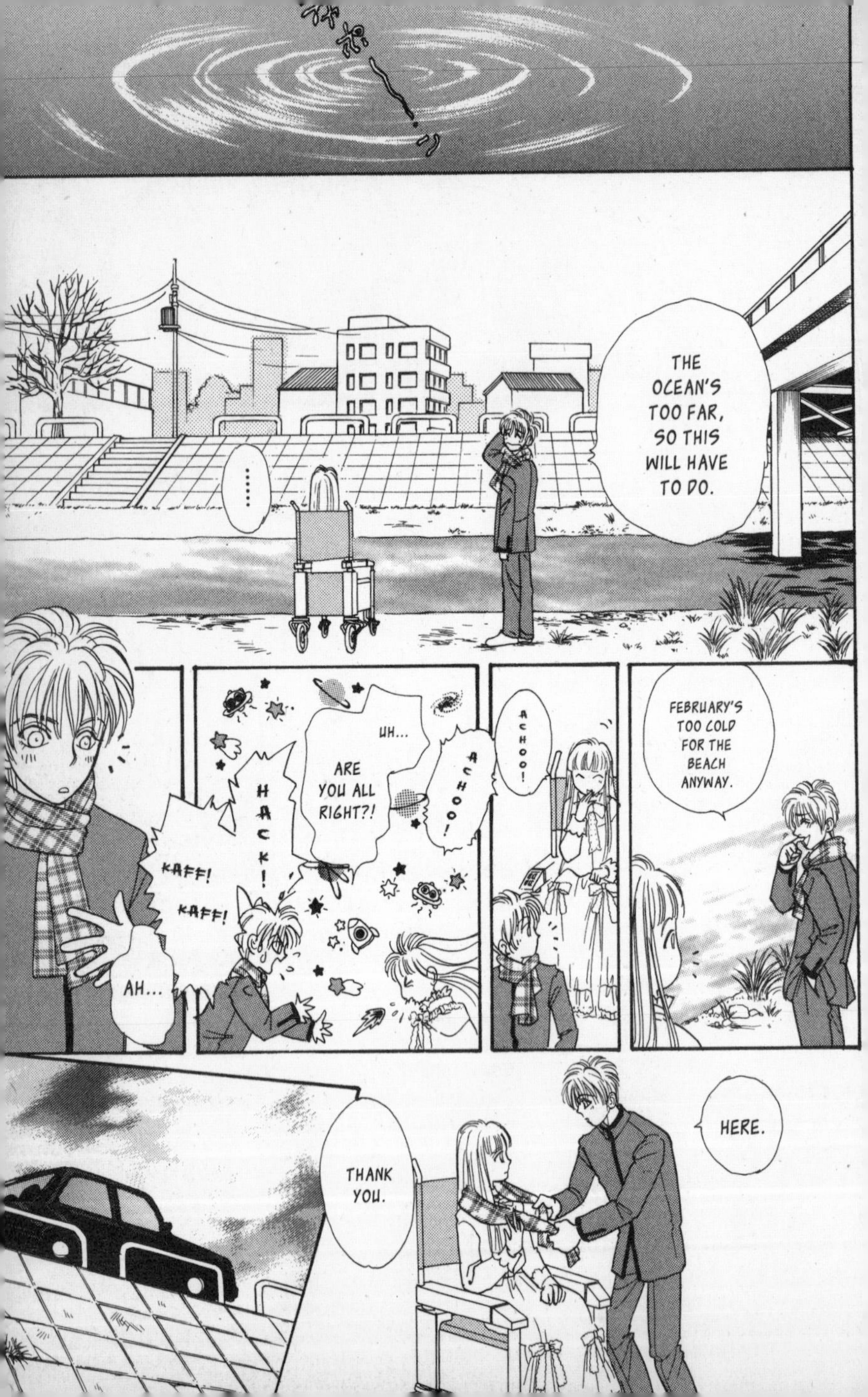
THE OCEAN'S TOO FAR, SO THIS WILL HAVE TO DO.
......
FEBRUARY'S TOO COLD FOR THE BEACH ANYWAY.
ACHOO!
ACHOO!
UH...
ARE YOU ALL RIGHT?!
HACK!
KAFF!
KAFF!
AH...
HERE.
THANK YOU.

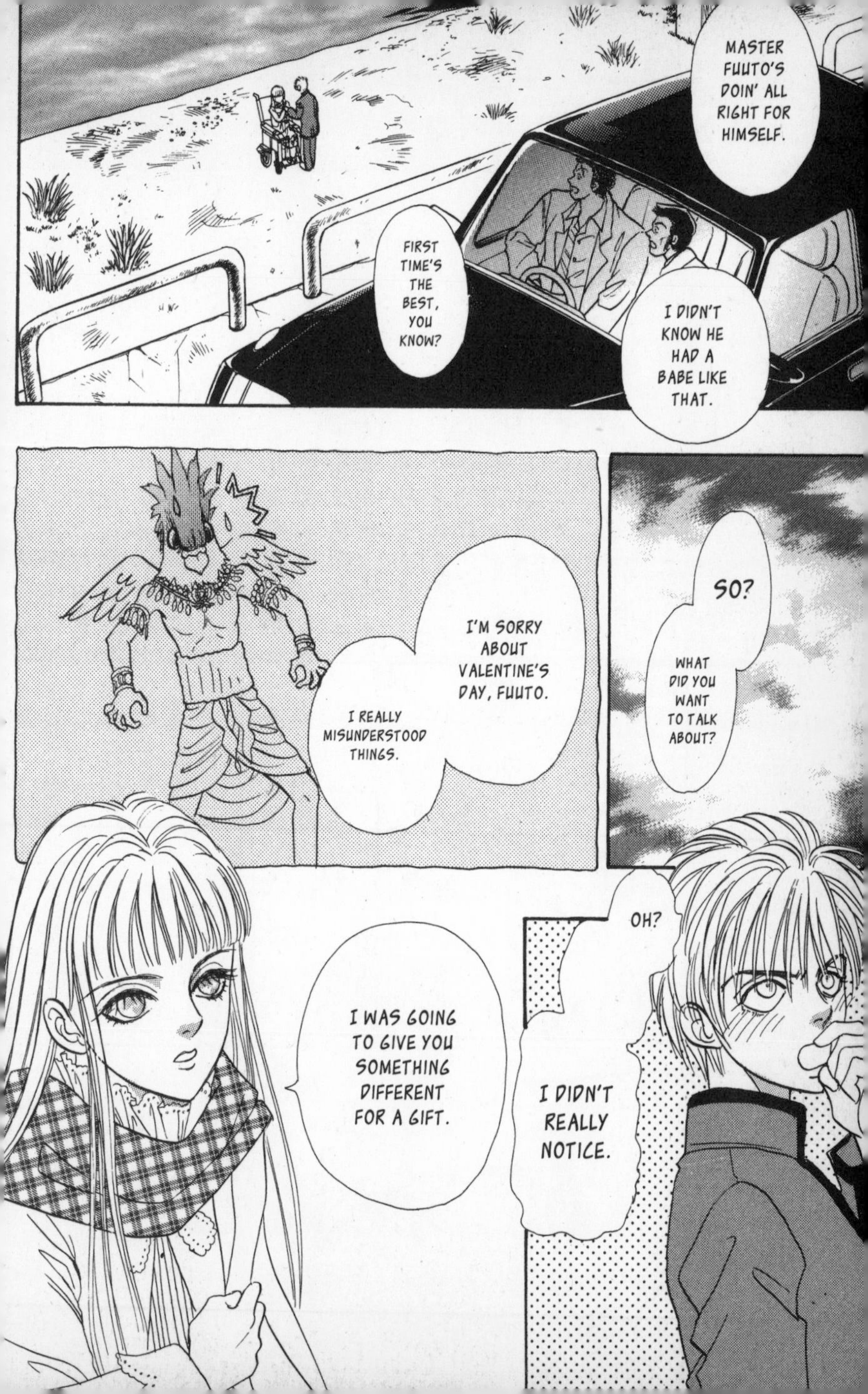
MASTER FUUTO'S DOIN' ALL RIGHT FOR HIMSELF.
I DIDN'T KNOW HE HAD A BABE LIKE THAT.
FIRST TIME'S THE BEST, YOU KNOW?
SO?
WHAT DID YOU WANT TO TALK ABOUT?
I'M SORRY ABOUT VALENTINE'S DAY, FUUTO.
I REALLY MISUNDERSTOOD THINGS.
OH?
I DIDN'T REALLY NOTICE.
I WAS GOING TO GIVE YOU SOMETHING DIFFERENT FOR A GIFT.

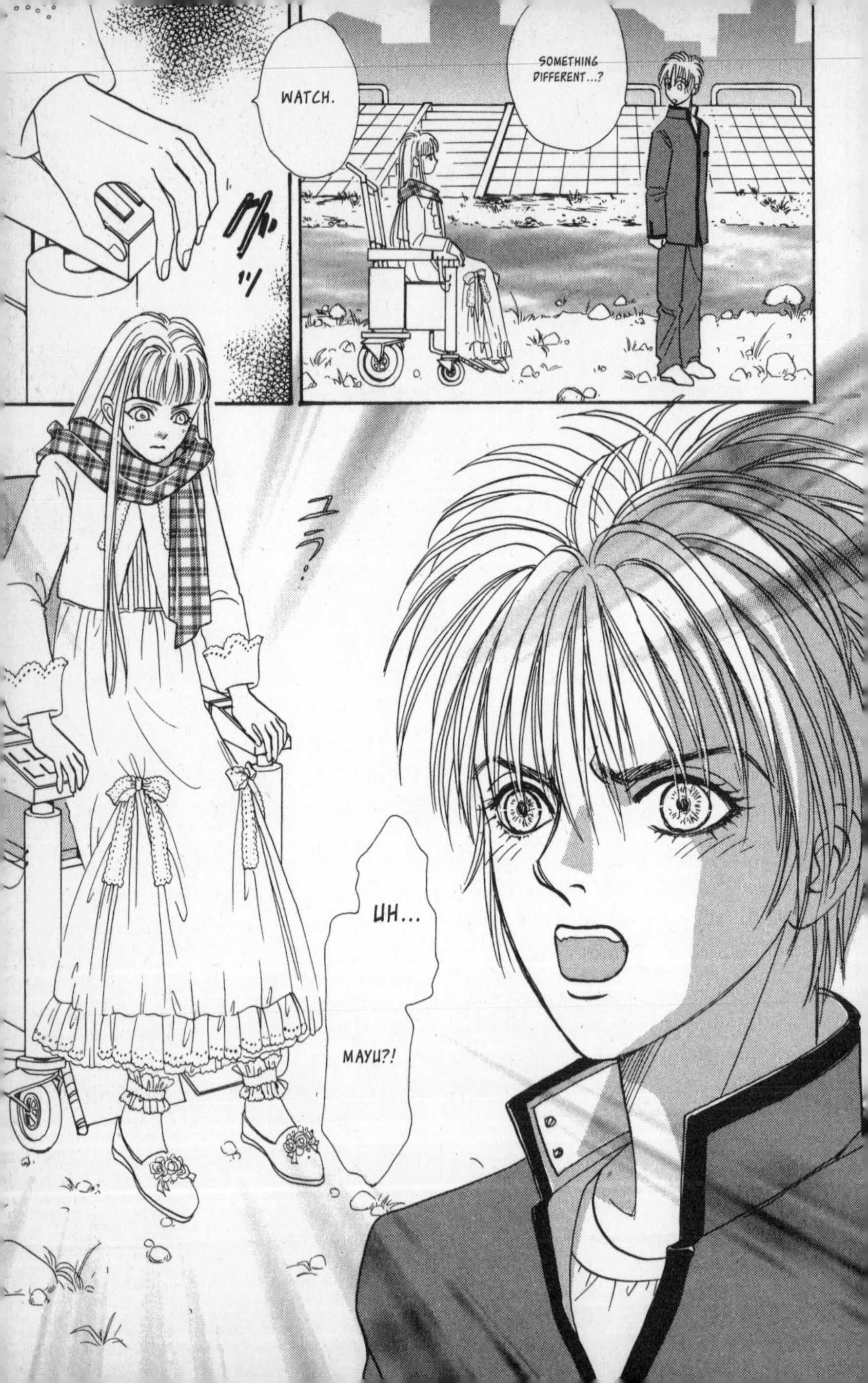
SOMETHING DIFFERENT...?
WATCH.
UH...
MAYU?!

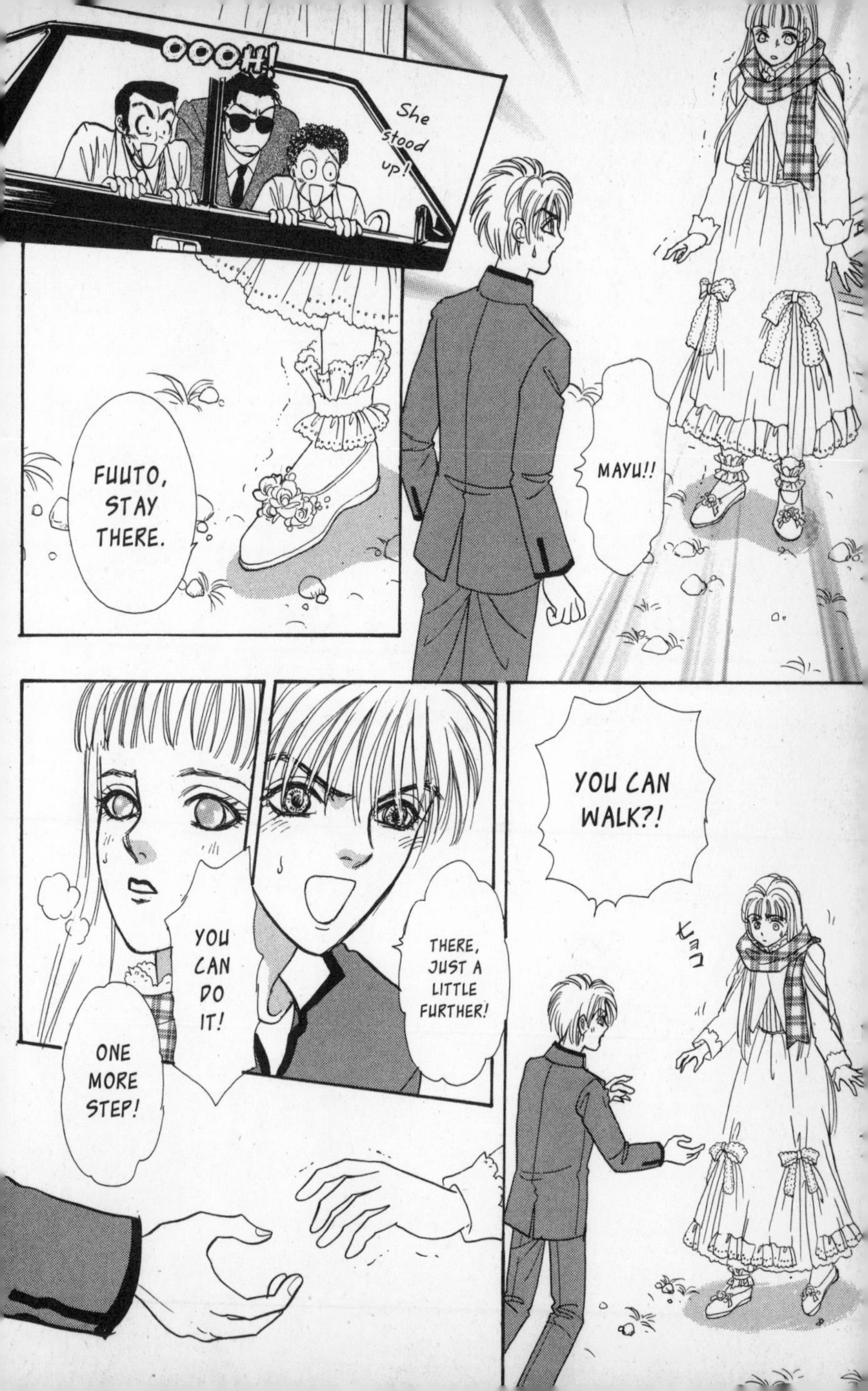
OOOH!
She stood up!
MAYU!!
FUUTO, STAY THERE.
YOU CAN WALK?!
ヒョコ
THERE, JUST A LITTLE FURTHER!
YOU CAN DO IT!
ONE MORE STEP!

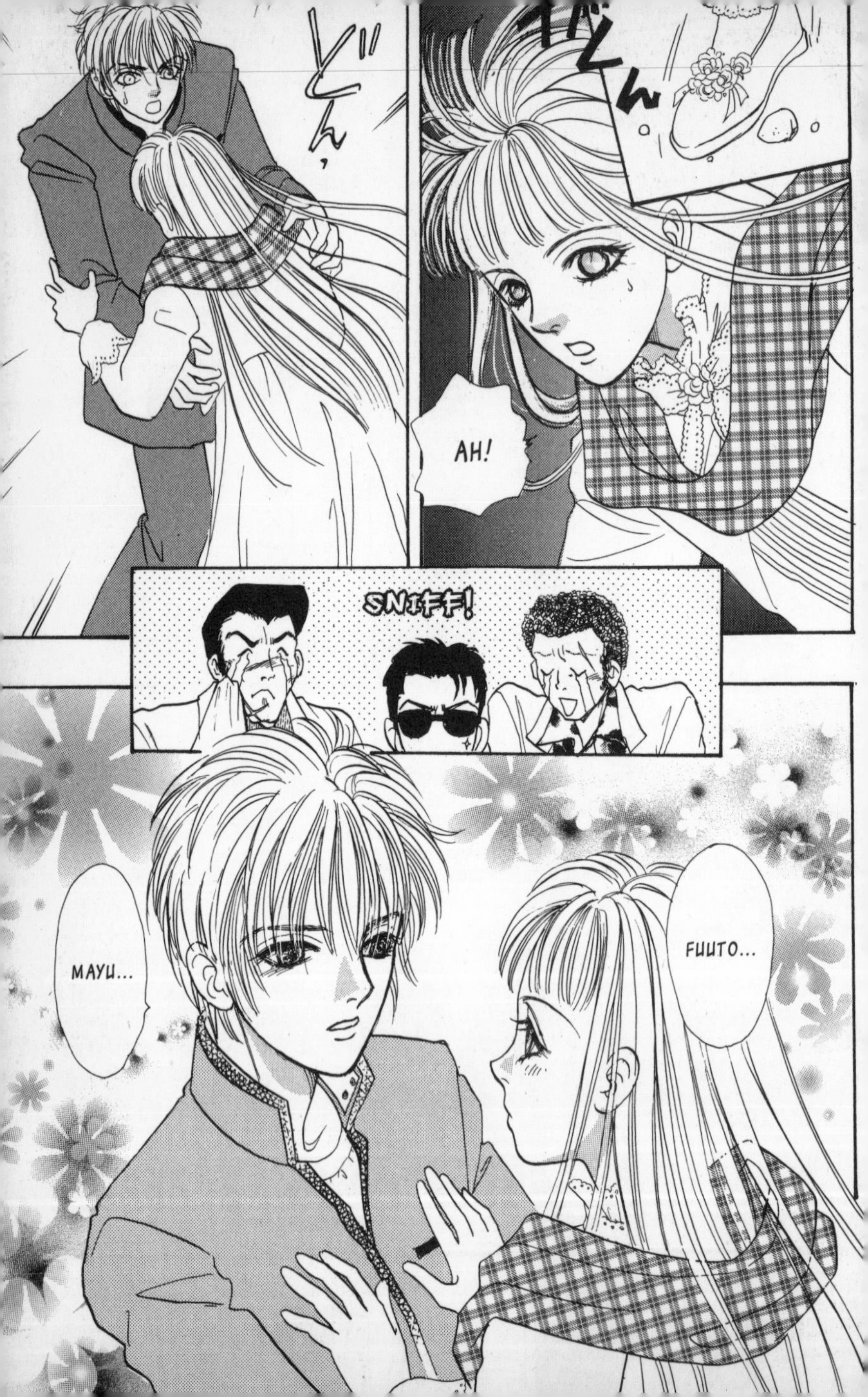
AH!
SNIFF!
FUUTO...
MAYU...

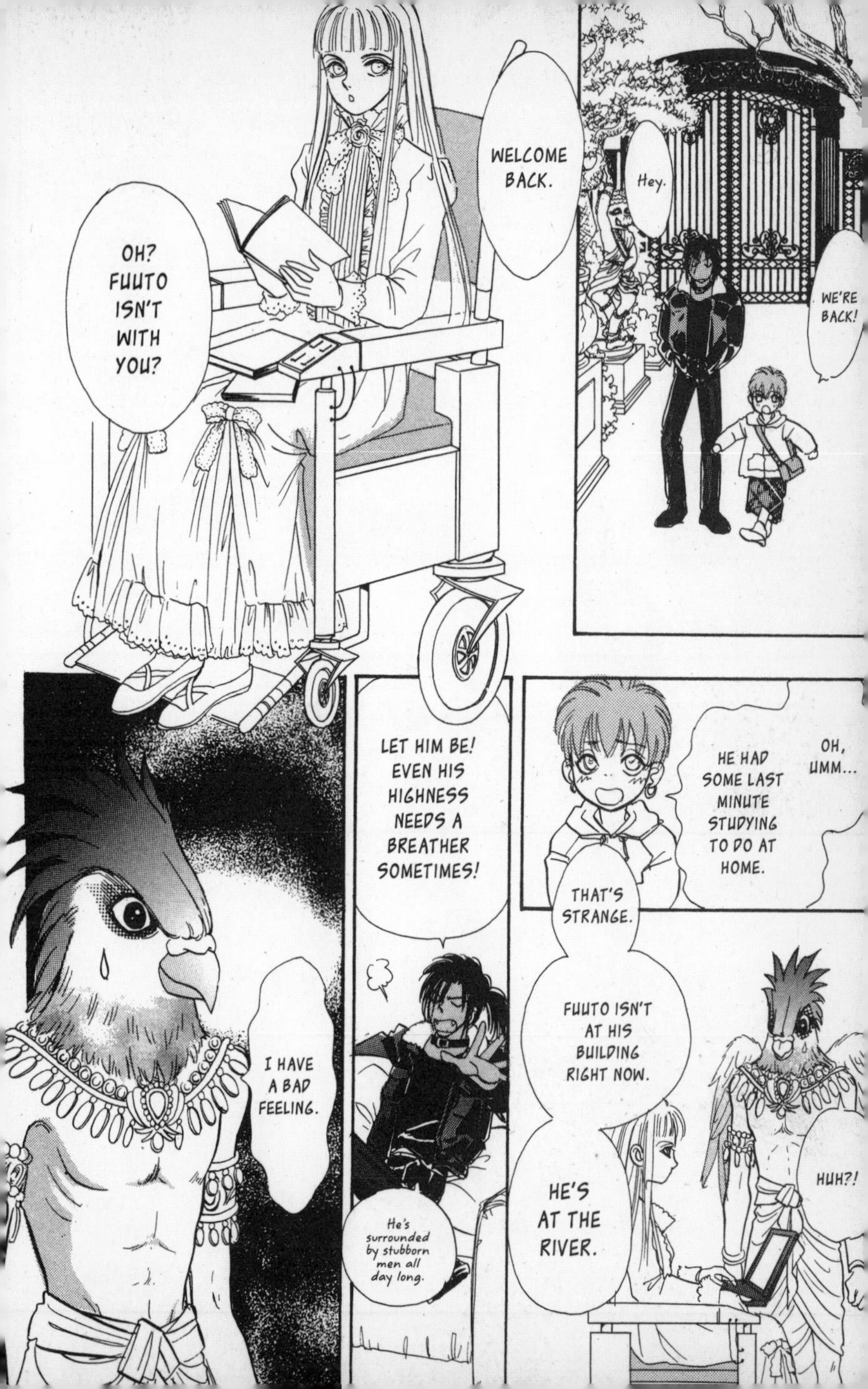

Hey.
WE'RE BACK!
WELCOME BACK.
OH? FUUTO ISN'T WITH YOU?
OH, UMM...
HE HAD SOME LAST MINUTE STUDYING TO DO AT HOME.
LET HIM BE! EVEN HIS HIGHNESS NEEDS A BREATHER SOMETIMES!
He's surrounded by stubborn men all day long.
THAT'S STRANGE.
FUUTO ISN'T AT HIS BUILDING RIGHT NOW.
HE'S AT THE RIVER.
HUH?!
I HAVE A BAD FEELING.

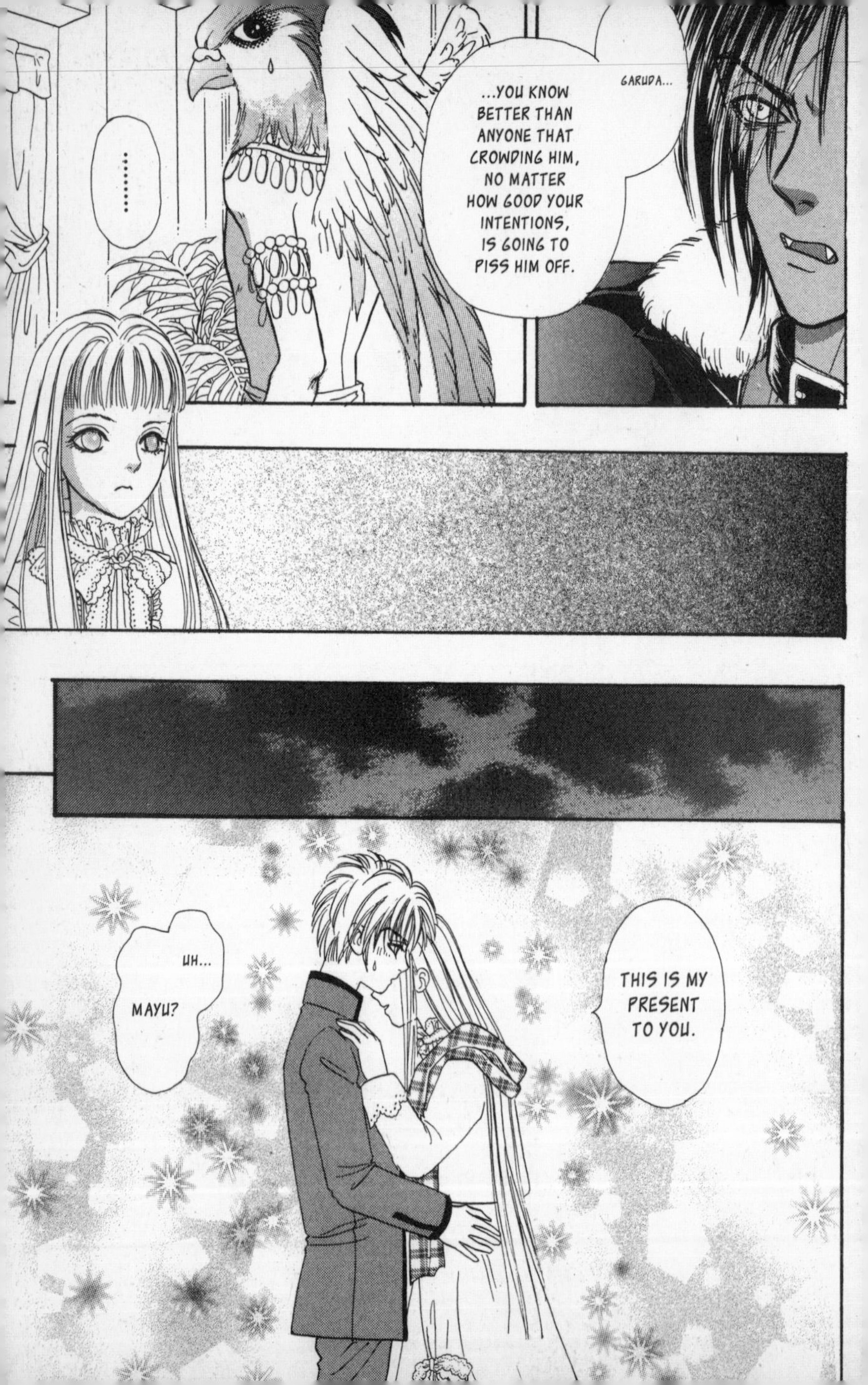
GARUDA...
...YOU KNOW BETTER THAN ANYONE THAT CROWDING HIM, NO MATTER HOW GOOD YOUR INTENTIONS, IS GOING TO PISS HIM OFF.
....
THIS IS MY PRESENT TO YOU.
UH... MAYU?

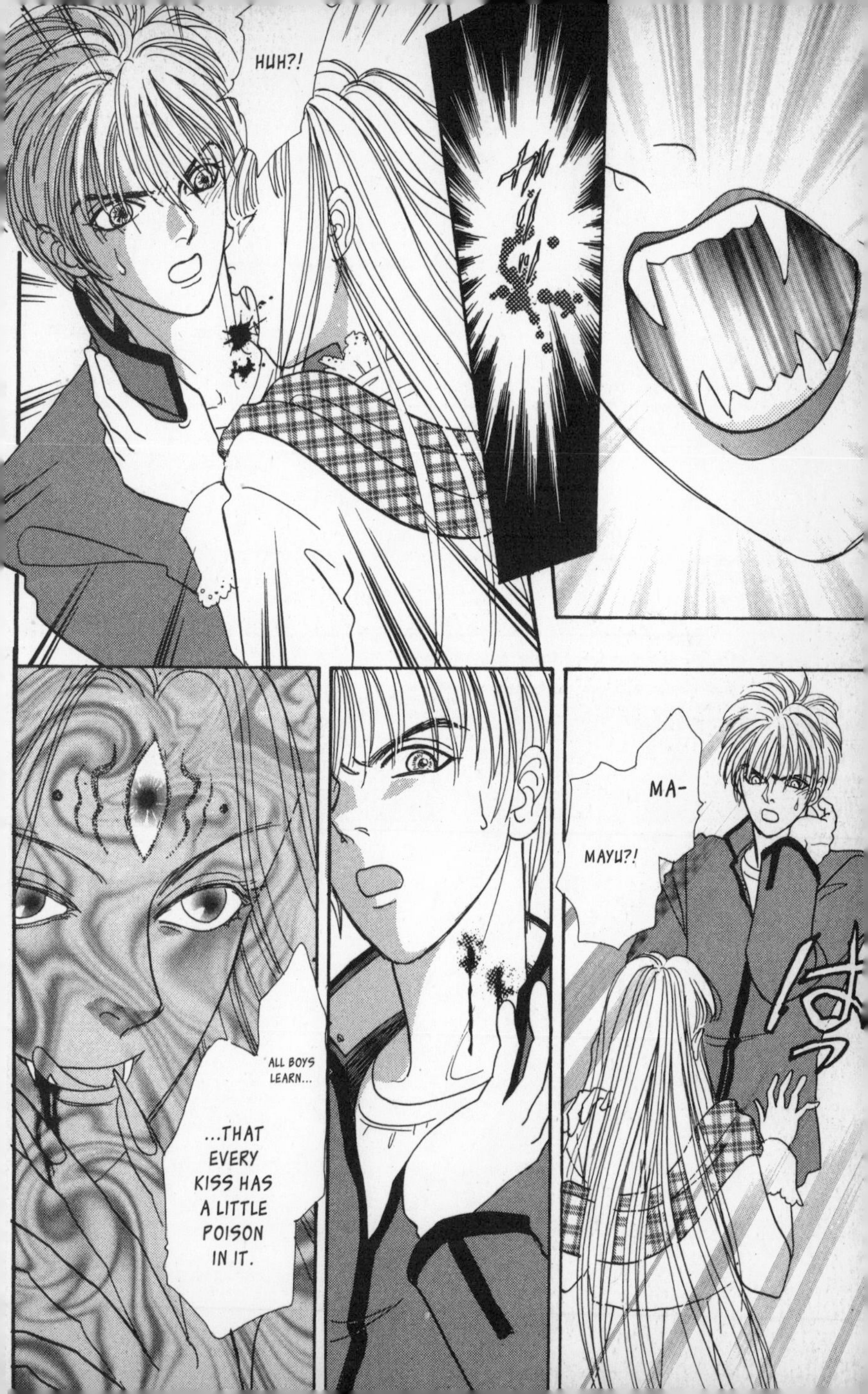
HUH?!
MA-
MAYU?!
はっ
ALL BOYS LEARN...
...THAT EVERY KISS HAS A LITTLE POISON IN IT.

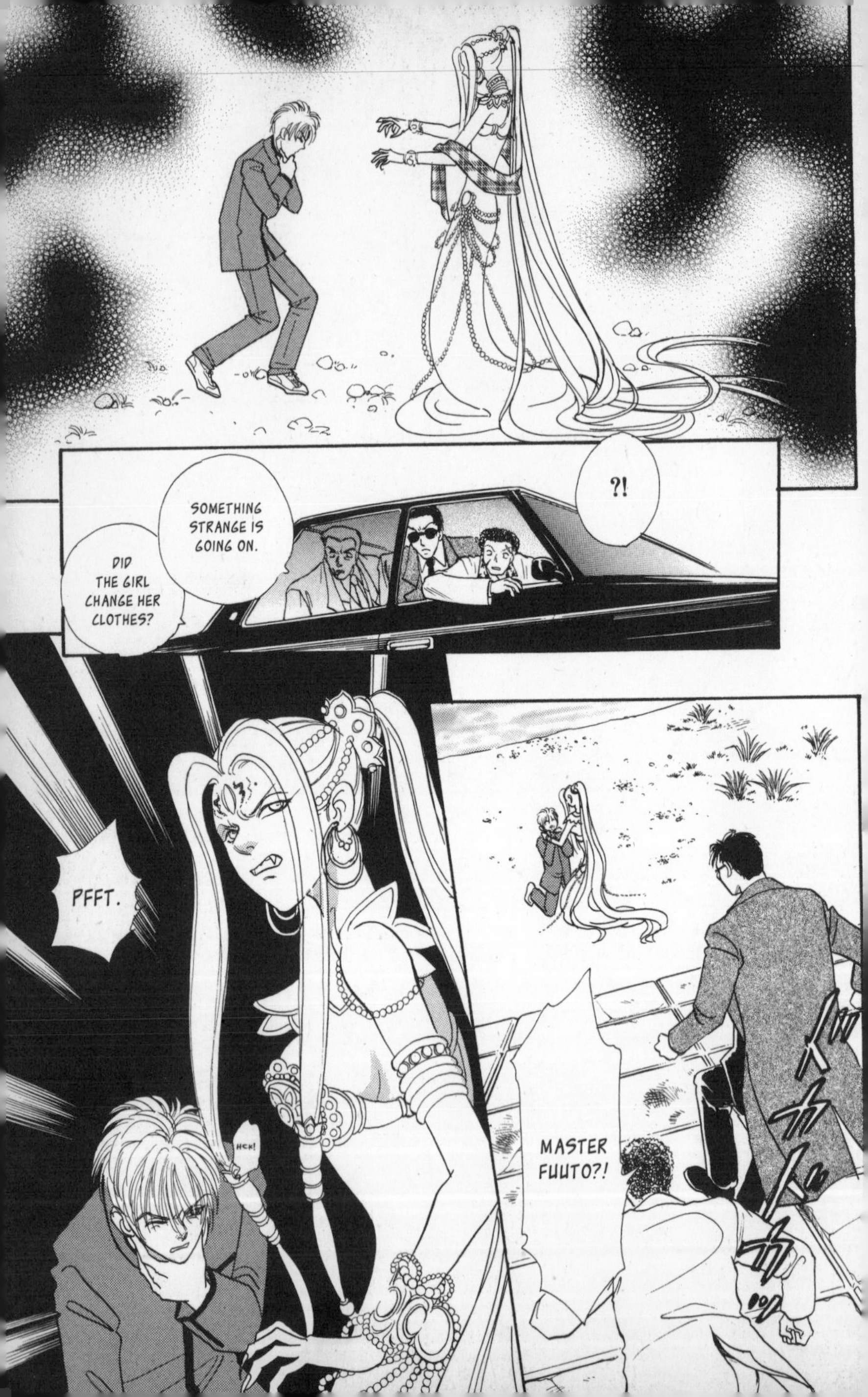
?!
SOMETHING STRANGE IS GOING ON.
DID THE GIRL CHANGE HER CLOTHES?
MASTER FUUTO?!
PFFT.
HCK!

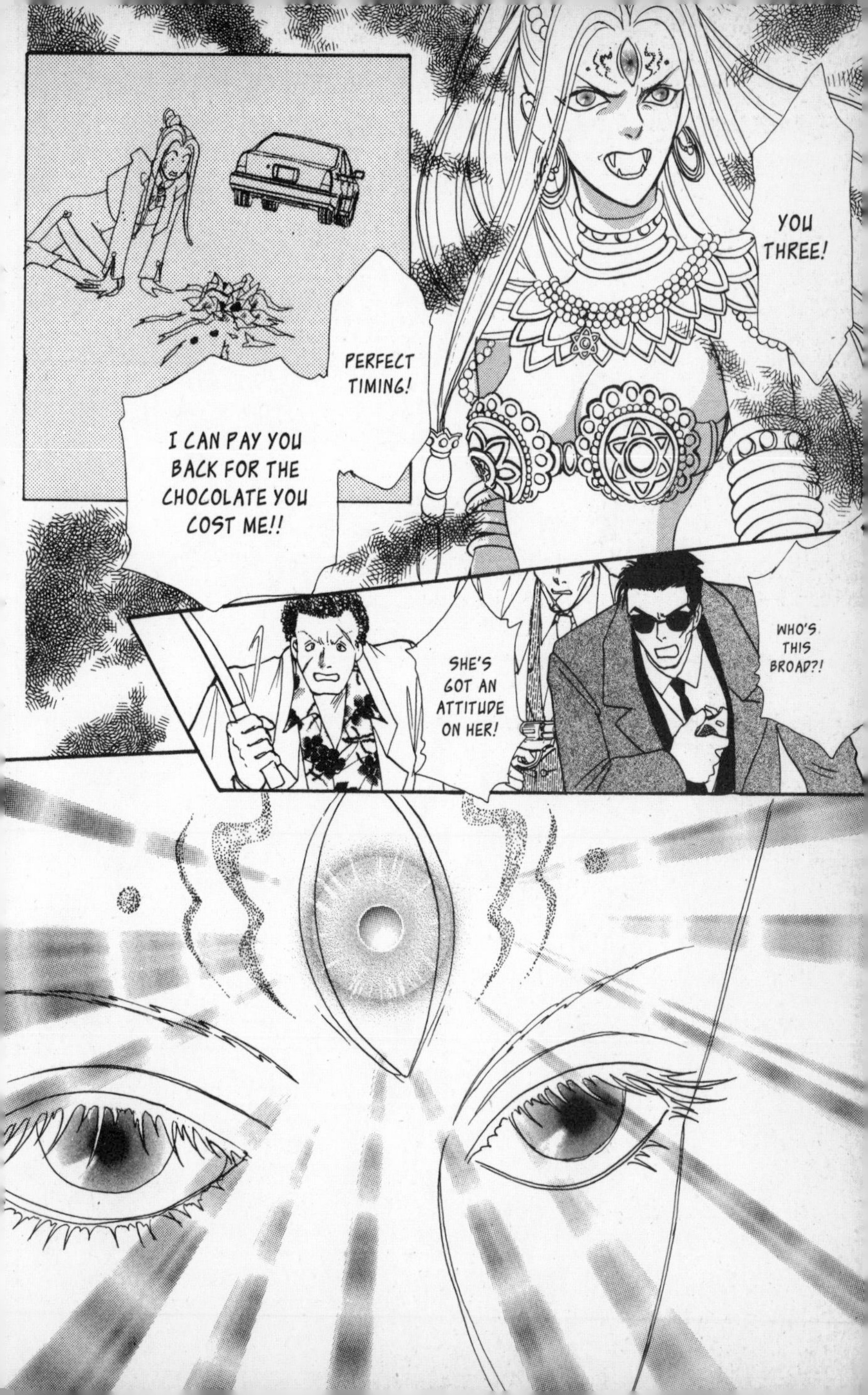

YOU THREE!
PERFECT TIMING!
I CAN PAY YOU BACK FOR THE CHOCOLATE YOU COST ME!!
WHO'S THIS BROAD?!
SHE'S GOT AN ATTITUDE ON HER!

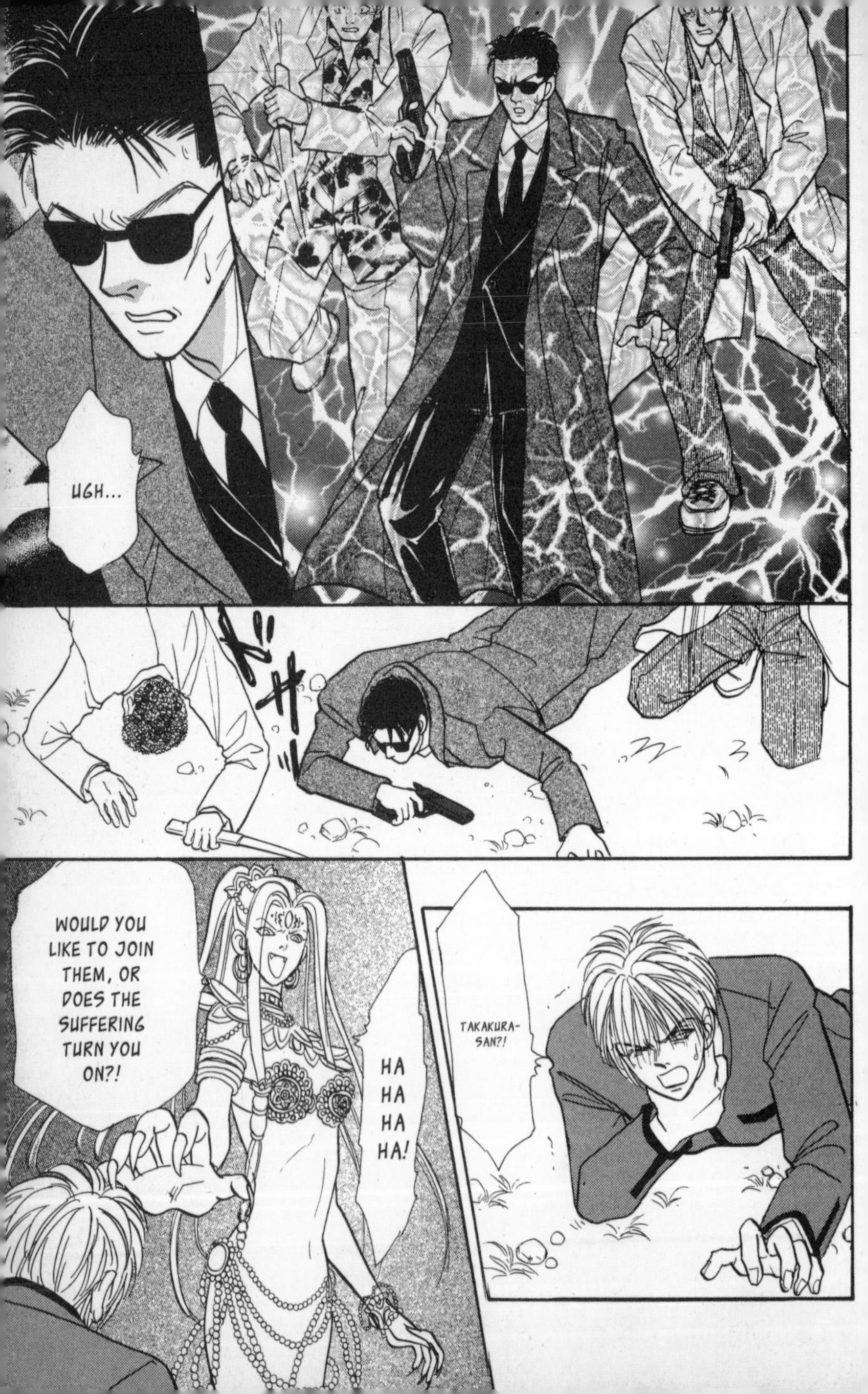
UGH...
WOULD YOU LIKE TO JOIN THEM, OR DOES THE SUFFERING TURN YOU ON?!
HA HA HA HA!
TAKAKURA-SAN?!

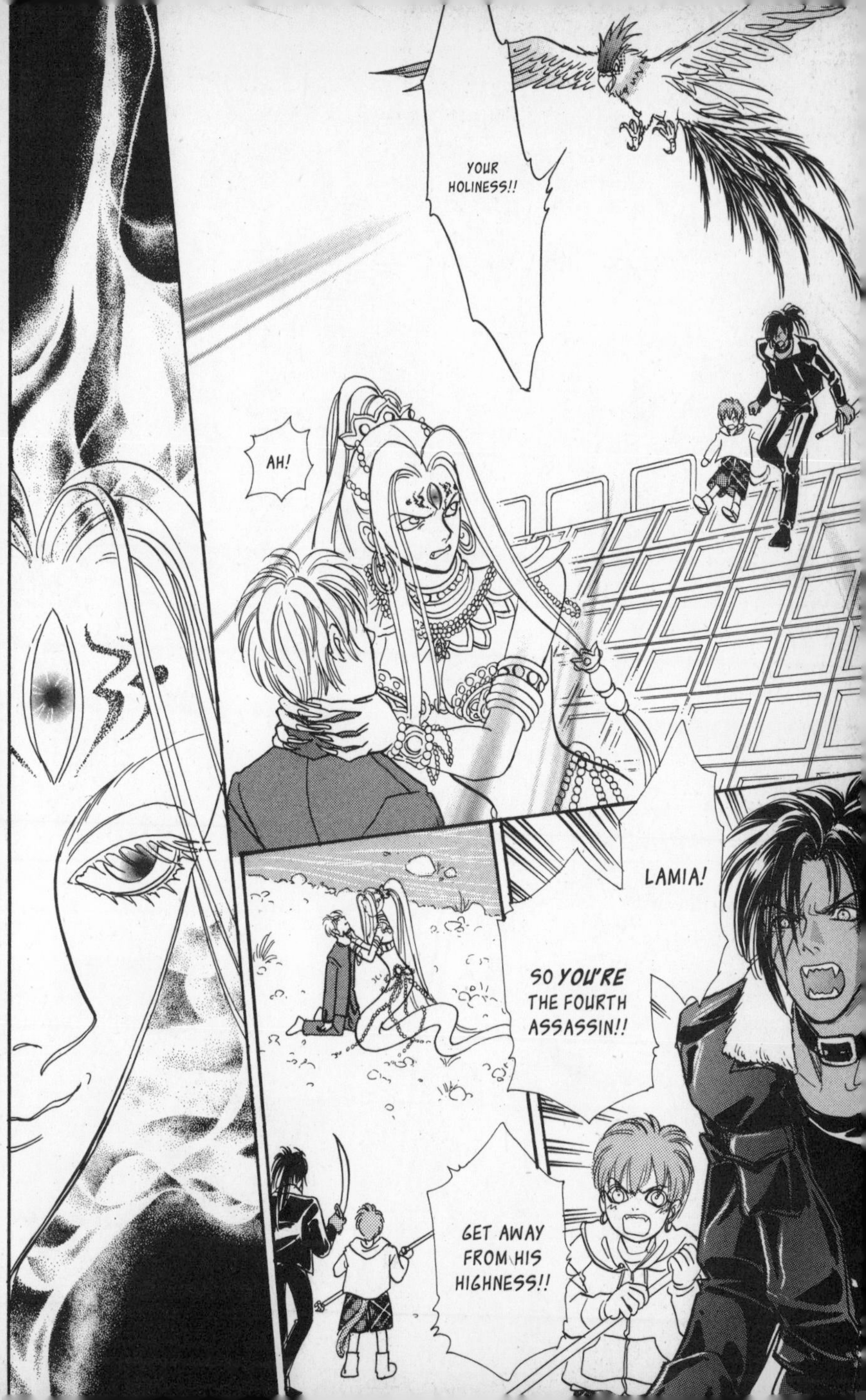
YOUR HOLINESS!!
AH!
LAMIA!
SO YOU'RE THE FOURTH ASSASSIN!!
GET AWAY FROM HIS HIGHNESS!!

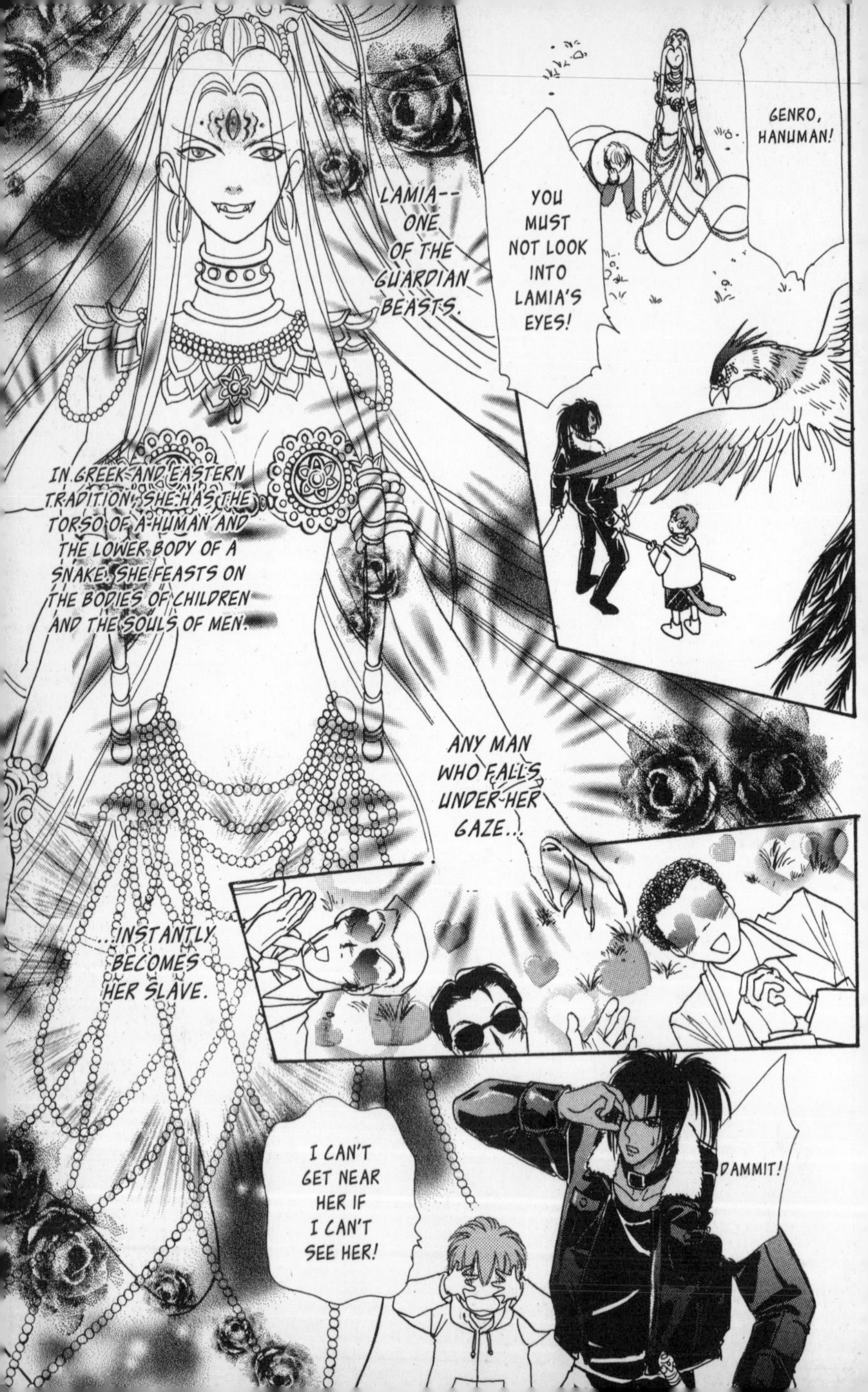
GENRO, HANUMAN!
YOU MUST NOT LOOK INTO LAMIA'S EYES!
LAMIA-- ONE OF THE GUARDIAN BEASTS.
IN GREEK AND EASTERN TRADITION, SHE HAS THE TORSO OF A HUMAN AND THE LOWER BODY OF A SNAKE. SHE FEASTS ON THE BODIES OF CHILDREN AND THE SOULS OF MEN.
ANY MAN WHO FALLS UNDER HER GAZE...
...INSTANTLY BECOMES HER SLAVE.
DAMMIT!
I CAN'T GET NEAR HER IF I CAN'T SEE HER!

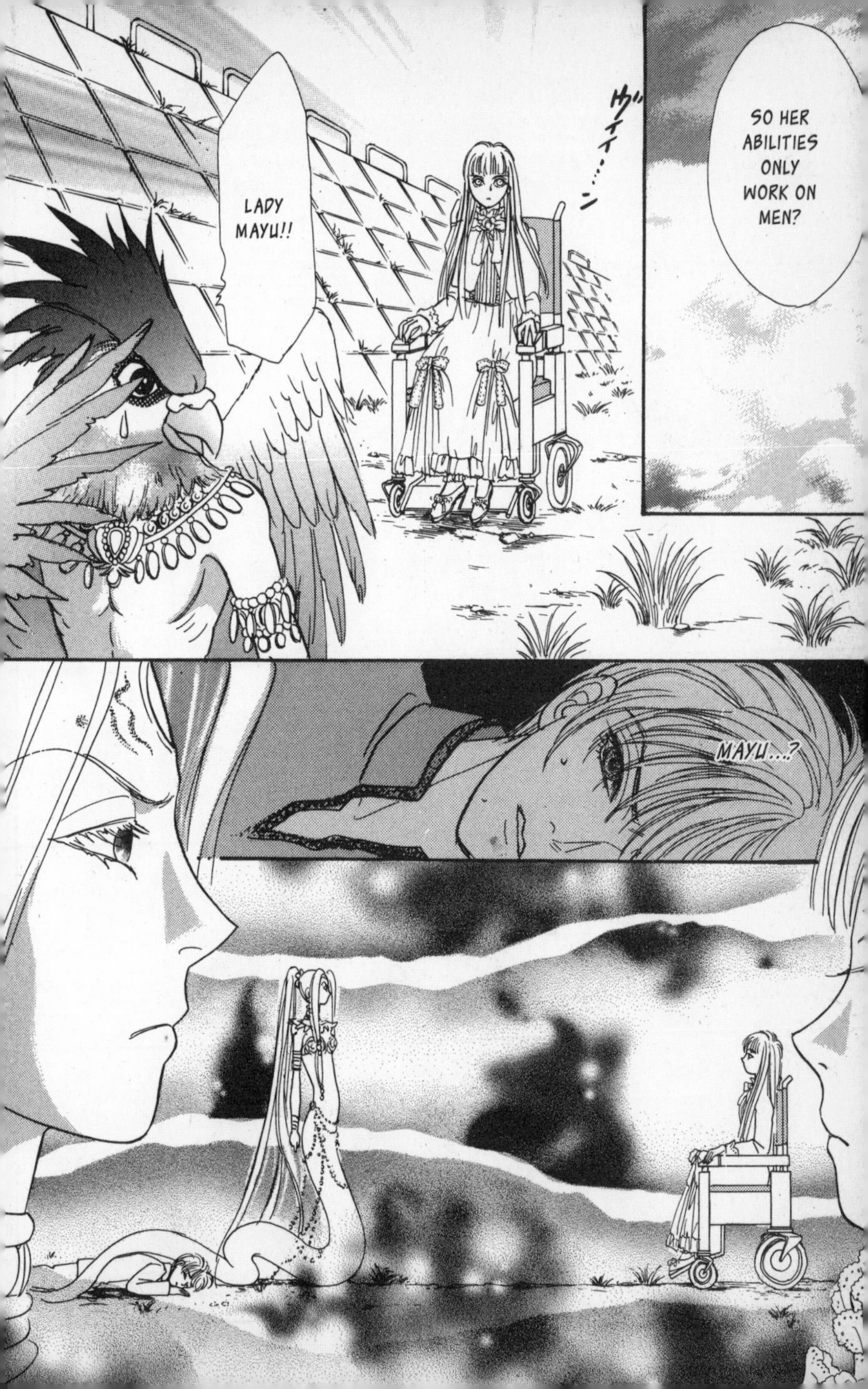
SO HER ABILITIES ONLY WORK ON MEN?
ヴィイ…ン
LADY MAYU!!
MAYU...?

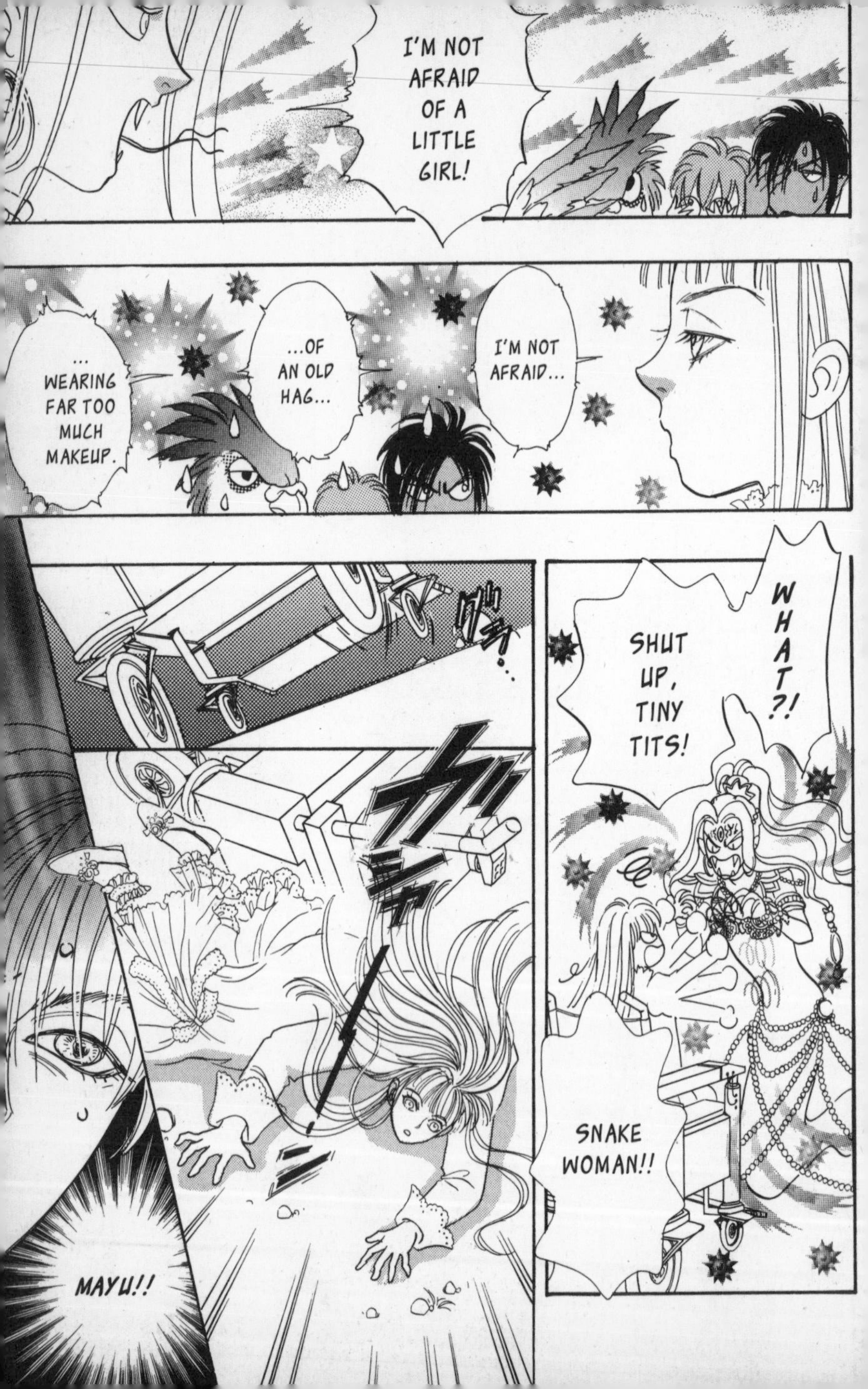
I'M NOT AFRAID OF A LITTLE GIRL!
I'M NOT AFRAID...
...OF AN OLD HAG...
...WEARING FAR TOO MUCH MAKEUP.
WHAT?!
SHUT UP, TINY TITS!
SNAKE WOMAN!!
MAYU!!

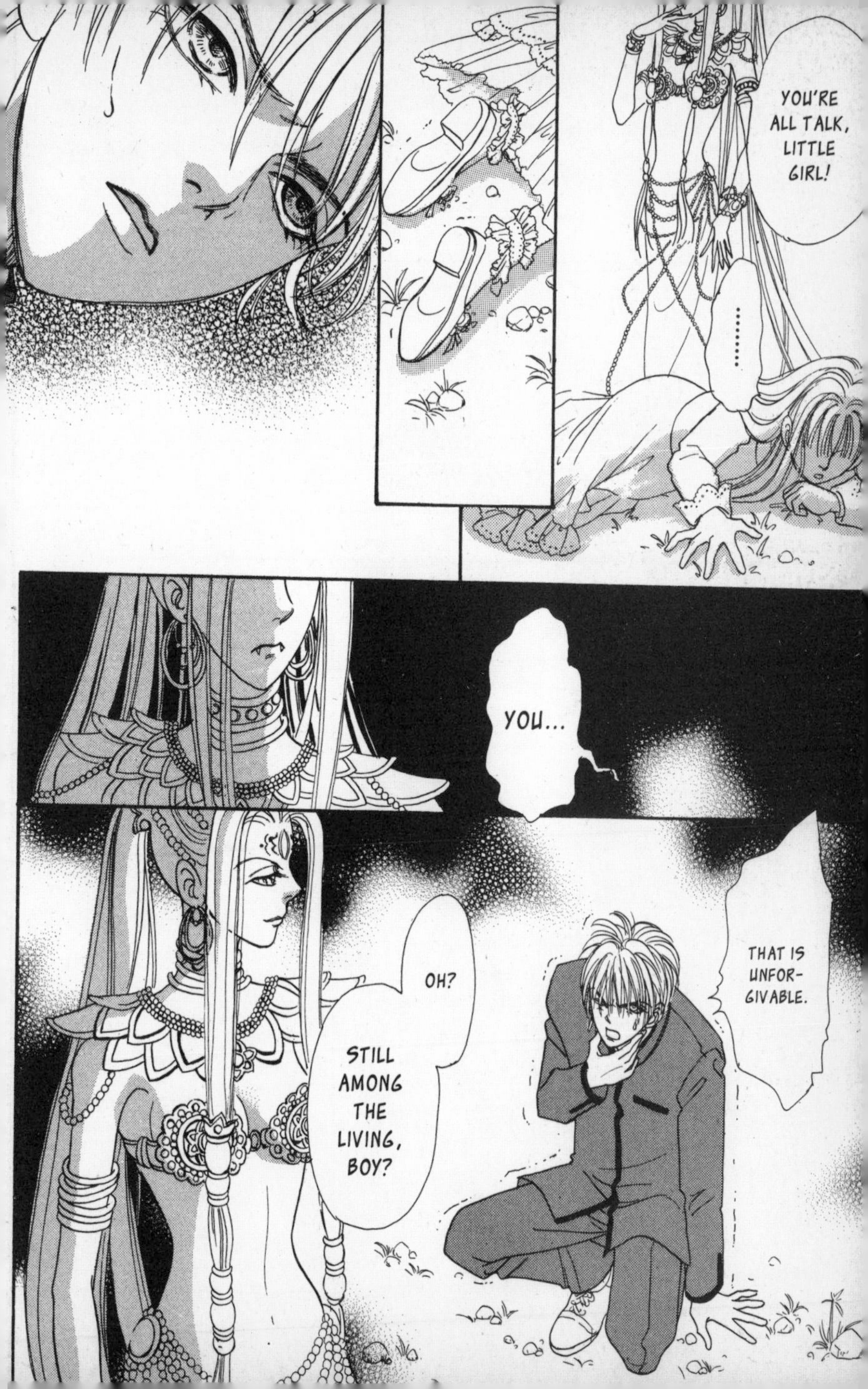
YOU'RE ALL TALK, LITTLE GIRL!
......
YOU...
THAT IS UNFOR-GIVABLE.
OH?
STILL AMONG THE LIVING, BOY?

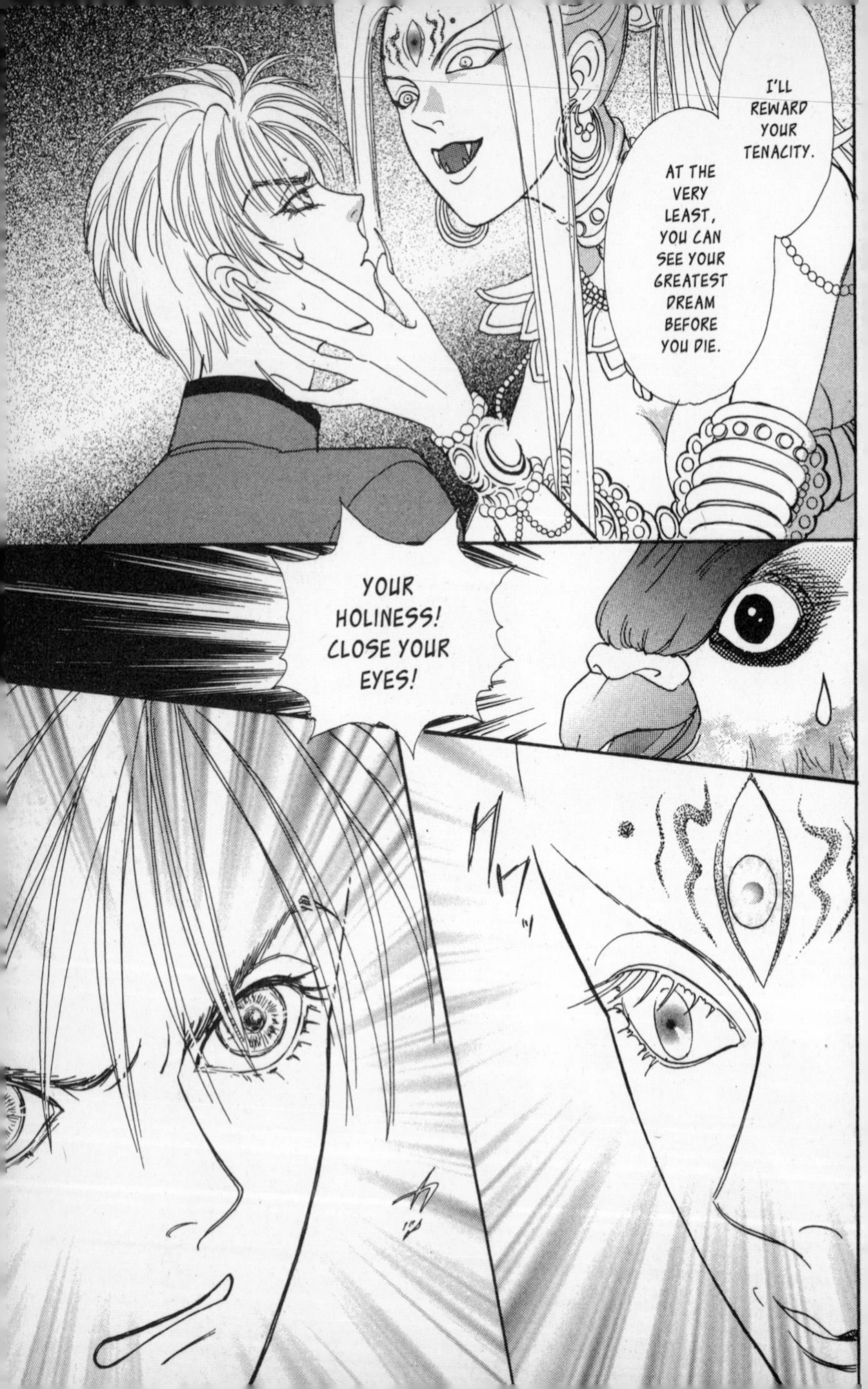
I'LL REWARD YOUR TENACITY.
AT THE VERY LEAST, YOU CAN SEE YOUR GREATEST DREAM BEFORE YOU DIE.
YOUR HOLINESS! CLOSE YOUR EYES!

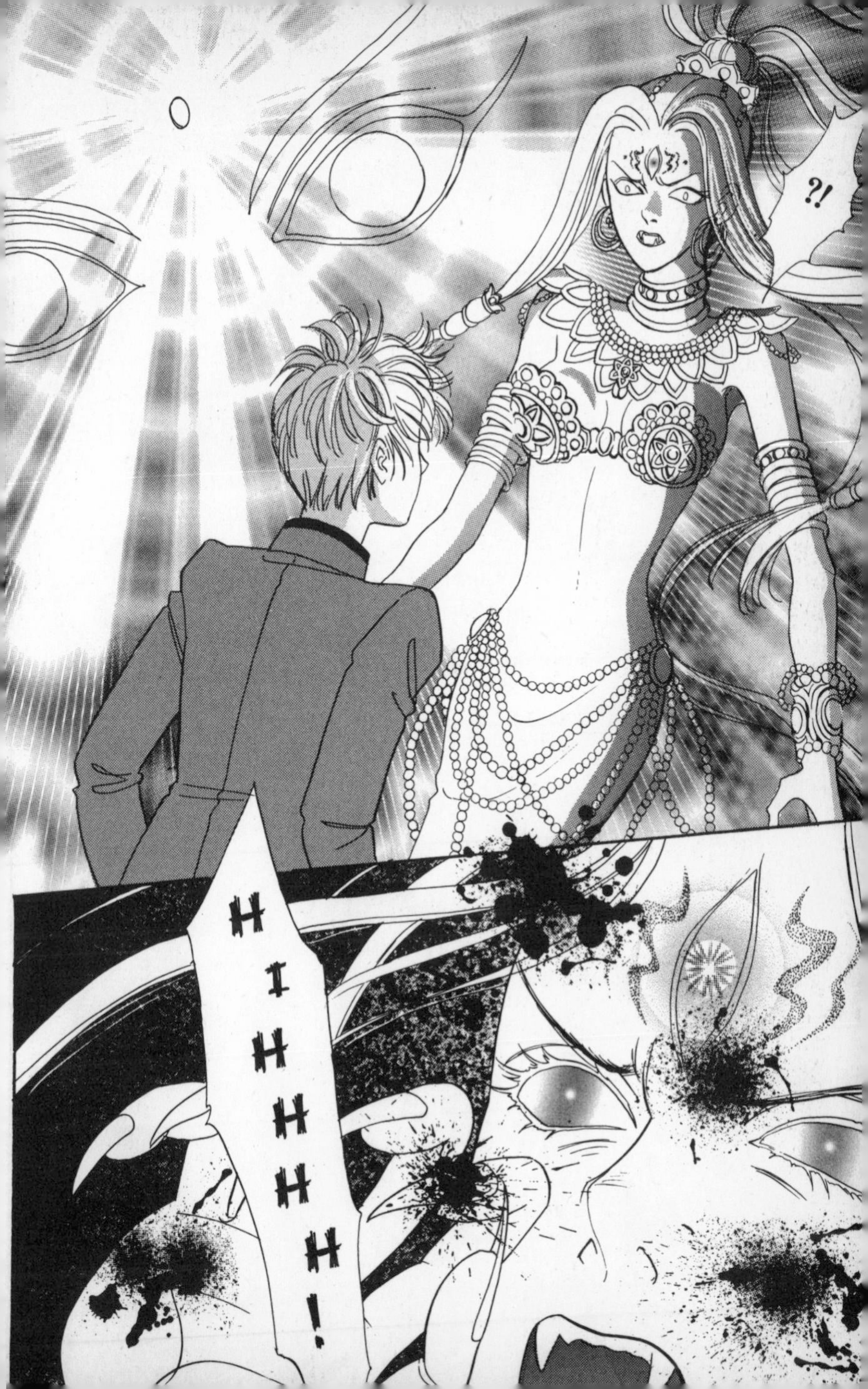
?!
HIHHHHH!

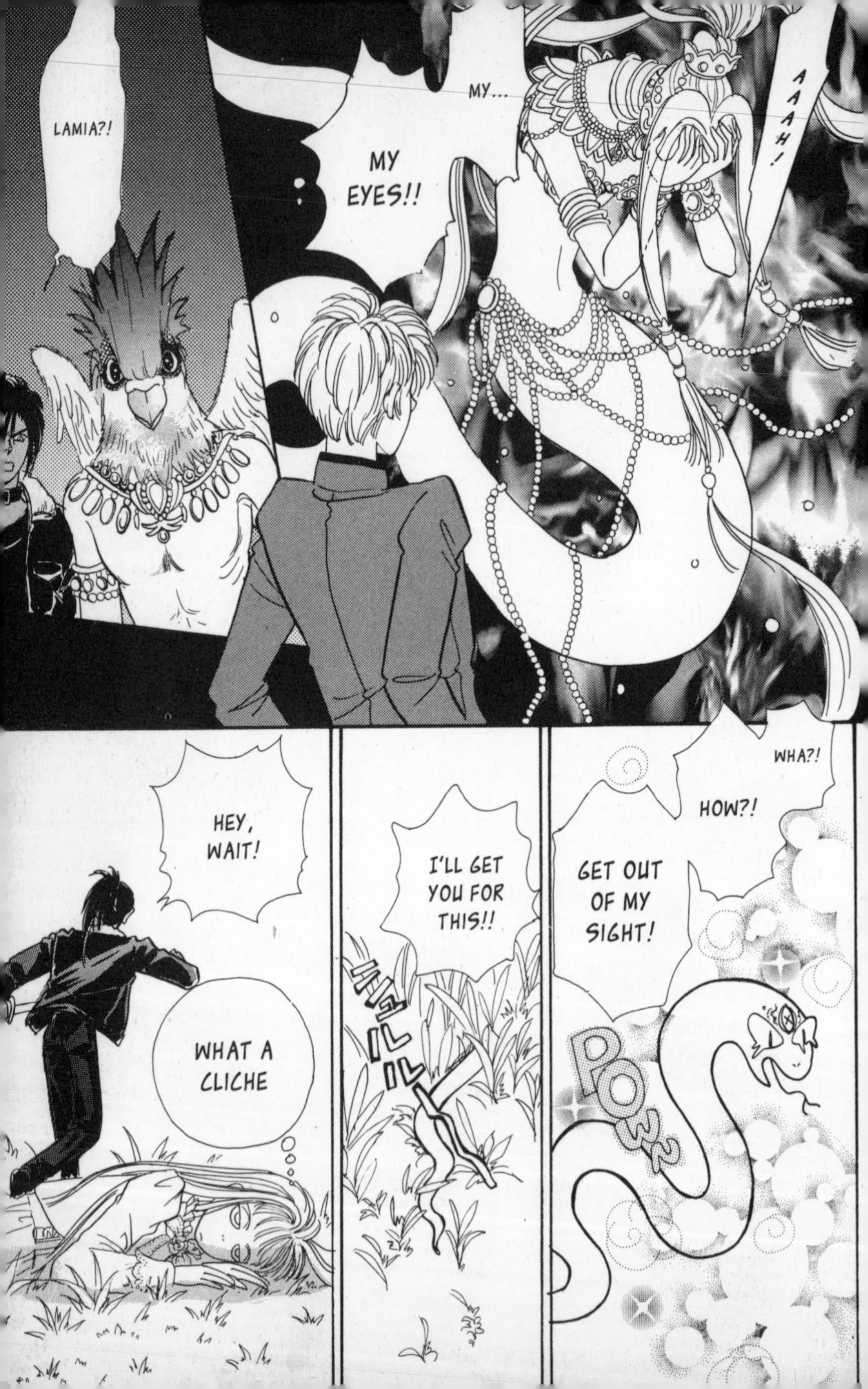
AAAH!
MY...
MY EYES!!
LAMIA?!
WHA?!
HOW?!
GET OUT OF MY SIGHT!
POW
I'LL GET YOU FOR THIS!!
HEY, WAIT!
WHAT A CLICHE

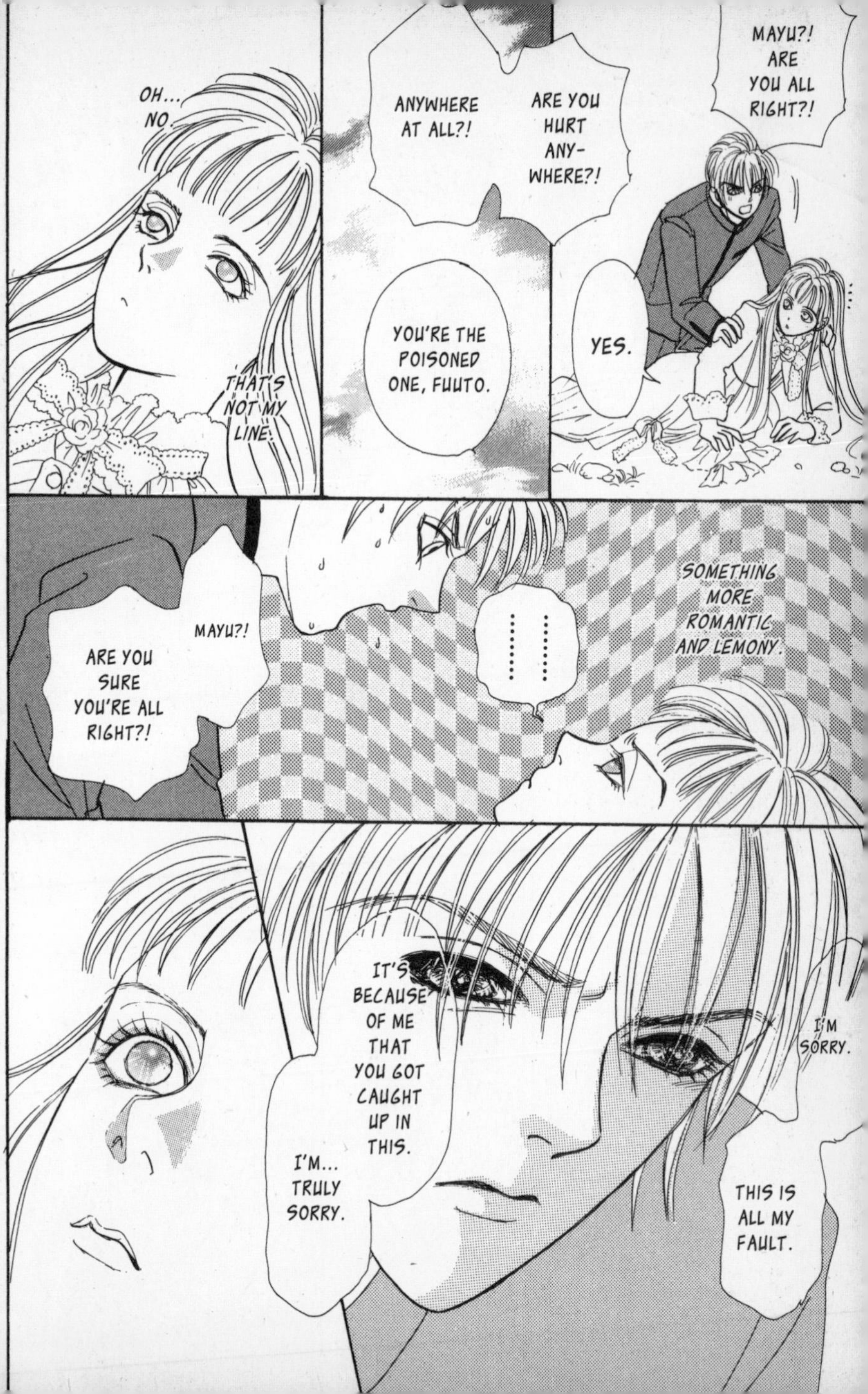
MAYU?! ARE YOU ALL RIGHT?!
YES.
ARE YOU HURT ANY-WHERE?!
ANYWHERE AT ALL?!
YOU'RE THE POISONED ONE, FUUTO.
OH... NO.
THAT'S NOT MY LINE.
SOMETHING MORE ROMANTIC AND LEMONY.
......
MAYU?!
ARE YOU SURE YOU'RE ALL RIGHT?!
I'M SORRY.
THIS IS ALL MY FAULT.
IT'S BECAUSE OF ME THAT YOU GOT CAUGHT UP IN THIS.
I'M... TRULY SORRY.

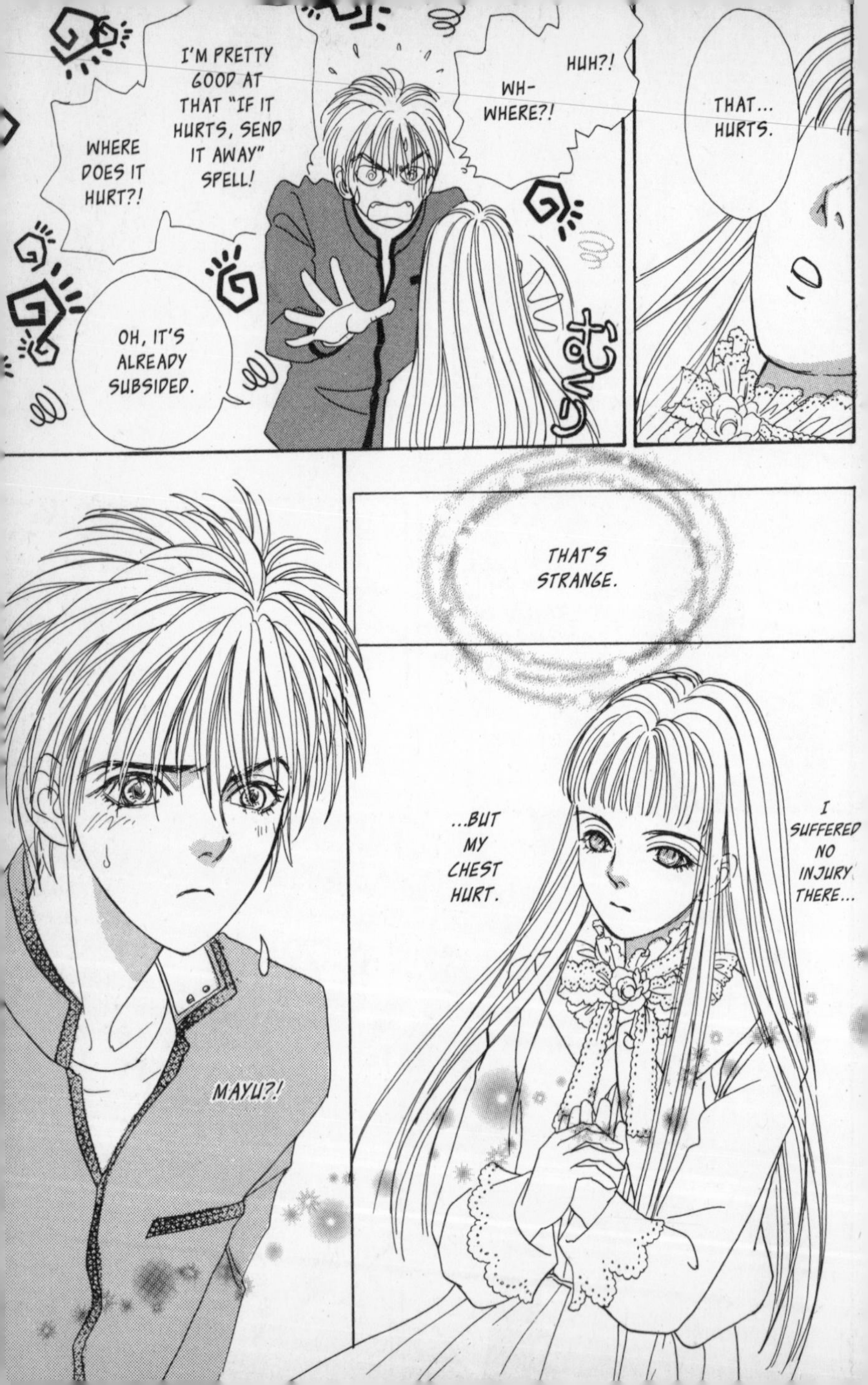

THAT... HURTS.
HUH?!
WH- WHERE?!
I'M PRETTY GOOD AT THAT "IF IT HURTS, SEND IT AWAY" SPELL!
WHERE DOES IT HURT?!
OH, IT'S ALREADY SUBSIDED.
THAT'S STRANGE.
I SUFFERED NO INJURY THERE...
...BUT MY CHEST HURT.
MAYU?!

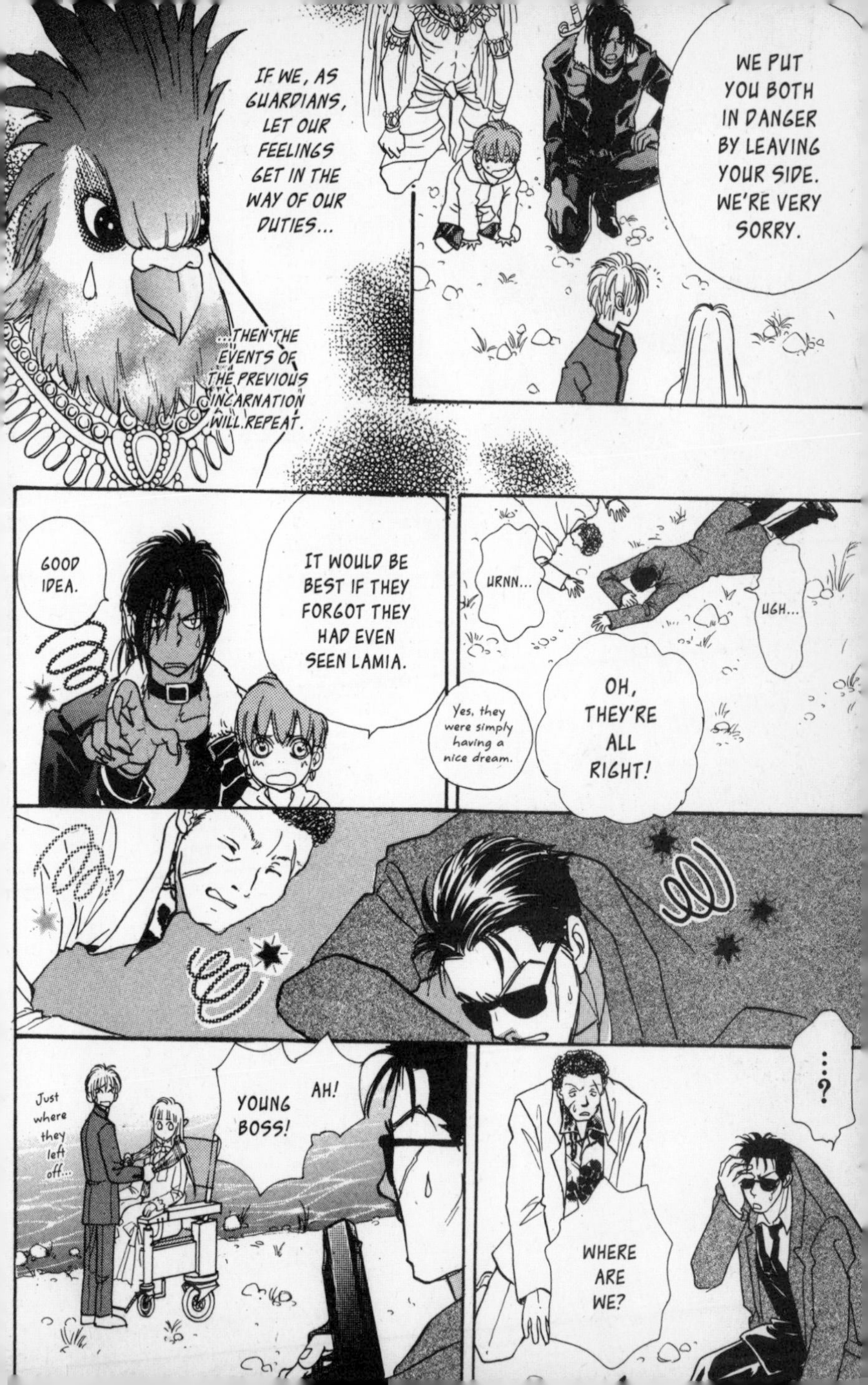
WE PUT YOU BOTH IN DANGER BY LEAVING YOUR SIDE. WE'RE VERY SORRY.
IF WE, AS GUARDIANS, LET OUR FEELINGS GET IN THE WAY OF OUR DUTIES...
...THEN THE EVENTS OF THE PREVIOUS INCARNATION WILL REPEAT.
UGH...
URNN...
OH, THEY'RE ALL RIGHT!
Yes, they were simply having a nice dream.
IT WOULD BE BEST IF THEY FORGOT THEY HAD EVEN SEEN LAMIA.
GOOD IDEA.
...?
WHERE ARE WE?
AH!
YOUNG BOSS!
Just where they left off...

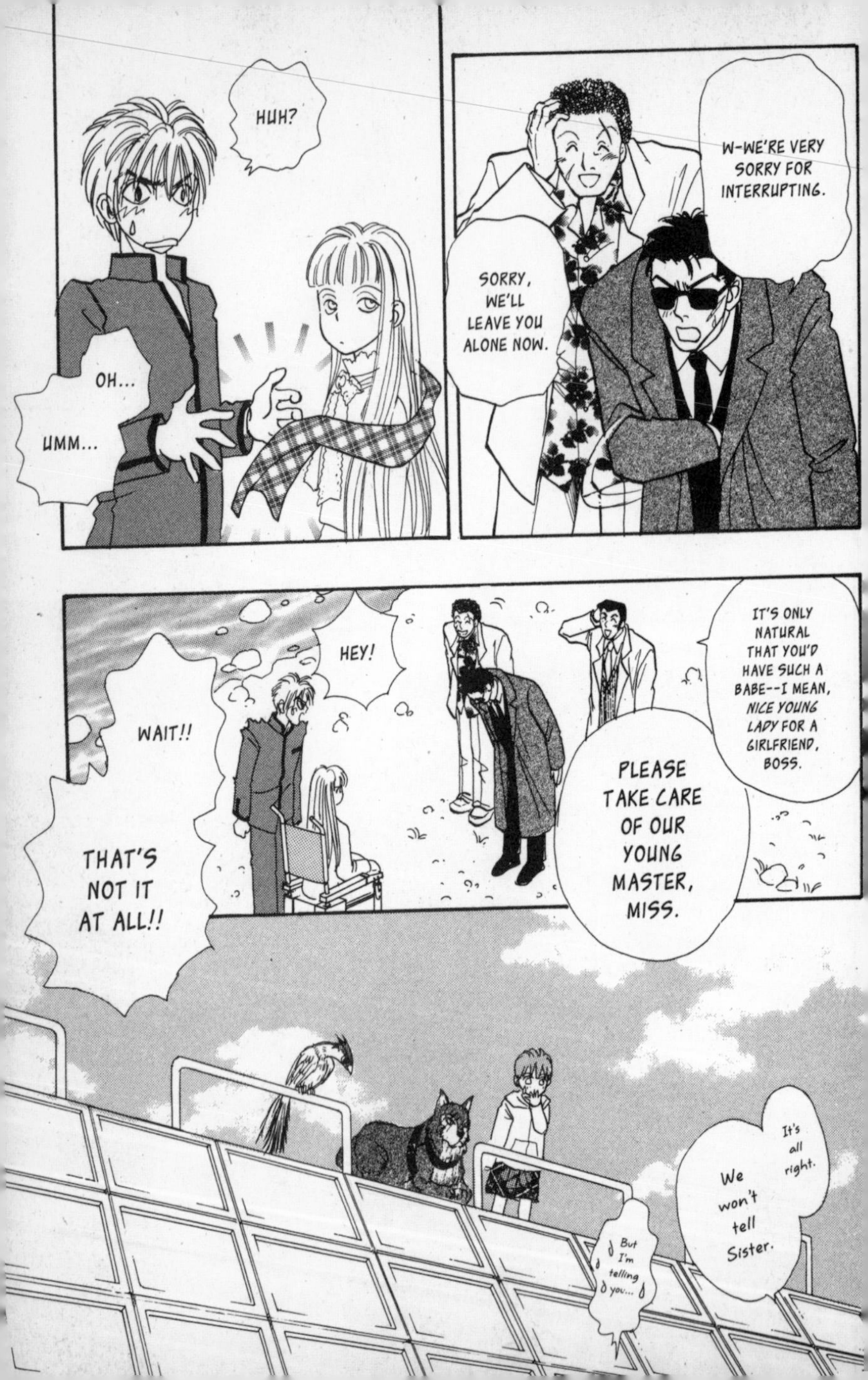
W-WE'RE VERY SORRY FOR INTERRUPTING.
SORRY, WE'LL LEAVE YOU ALONE NOW.
HUH?
OH... UMM...
IT'S ONLY NATURAL THAT YOU'D HAVE SUCH A BABE--I MEAN, *NICE YOUNG LADY* FOR A GIRLFRIEND, BOSS.
PLEASE TAKE CARE OF OUR YOUNG MASTER, MISS.
HEY!
WAIT!!
THAT'S NOT IT AT ALL!!
It's all right.
We won't tell Sister.
But I'm telling you...

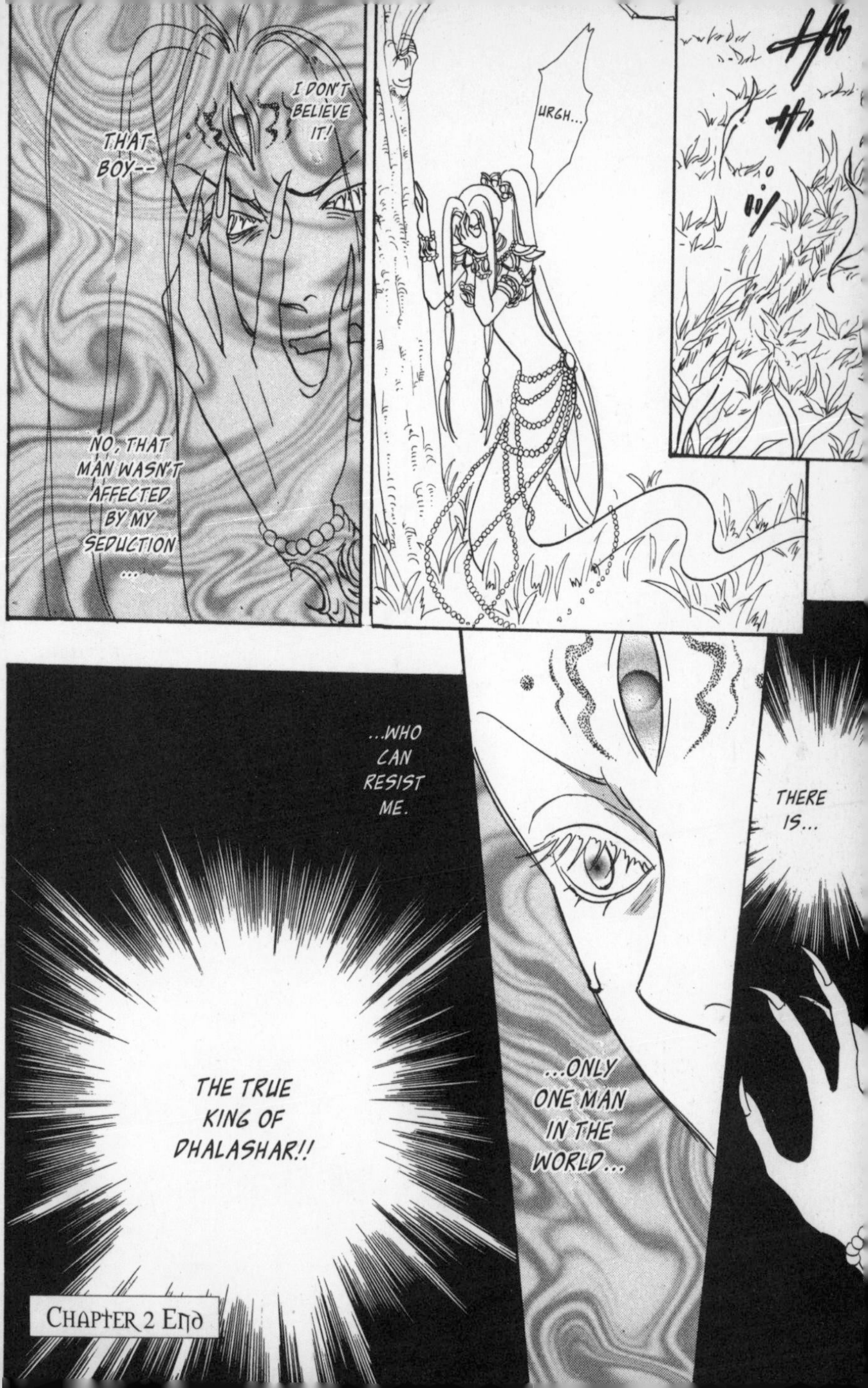
URGH...
I DON'T BELIEVE IT!
THAT BOY--
NO, THAT MAN WASN'T AFFECTED BY MY SEDUCTION ...
THERE IS...
...ONLY ONE MAN IN THE WORLD...
...WHO CAN RESIST ME.
THE TRUE KING OF DHALASHAR!!
CHAPTER 2 END

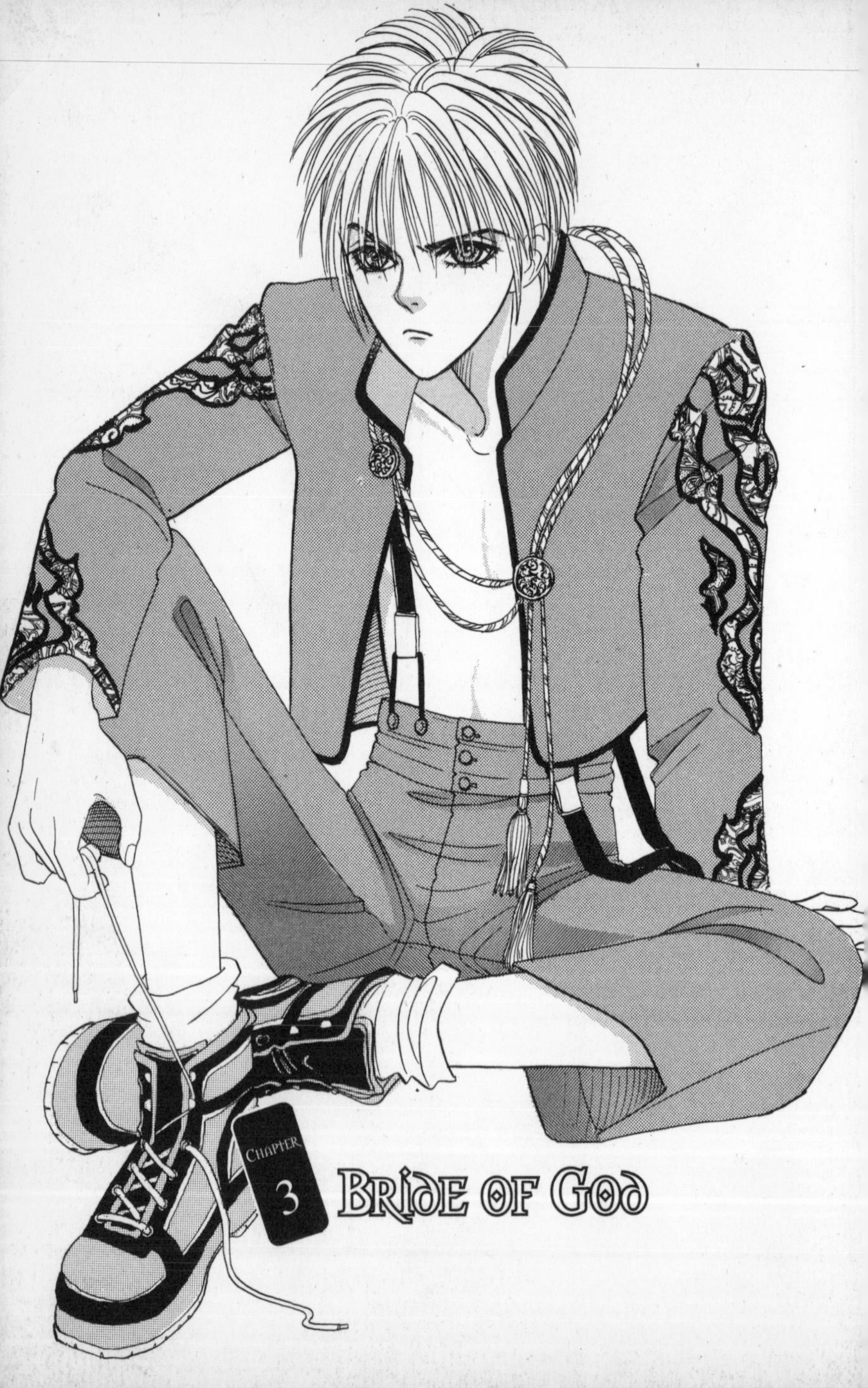
CHAPTER
3
BRIDE OF GOD

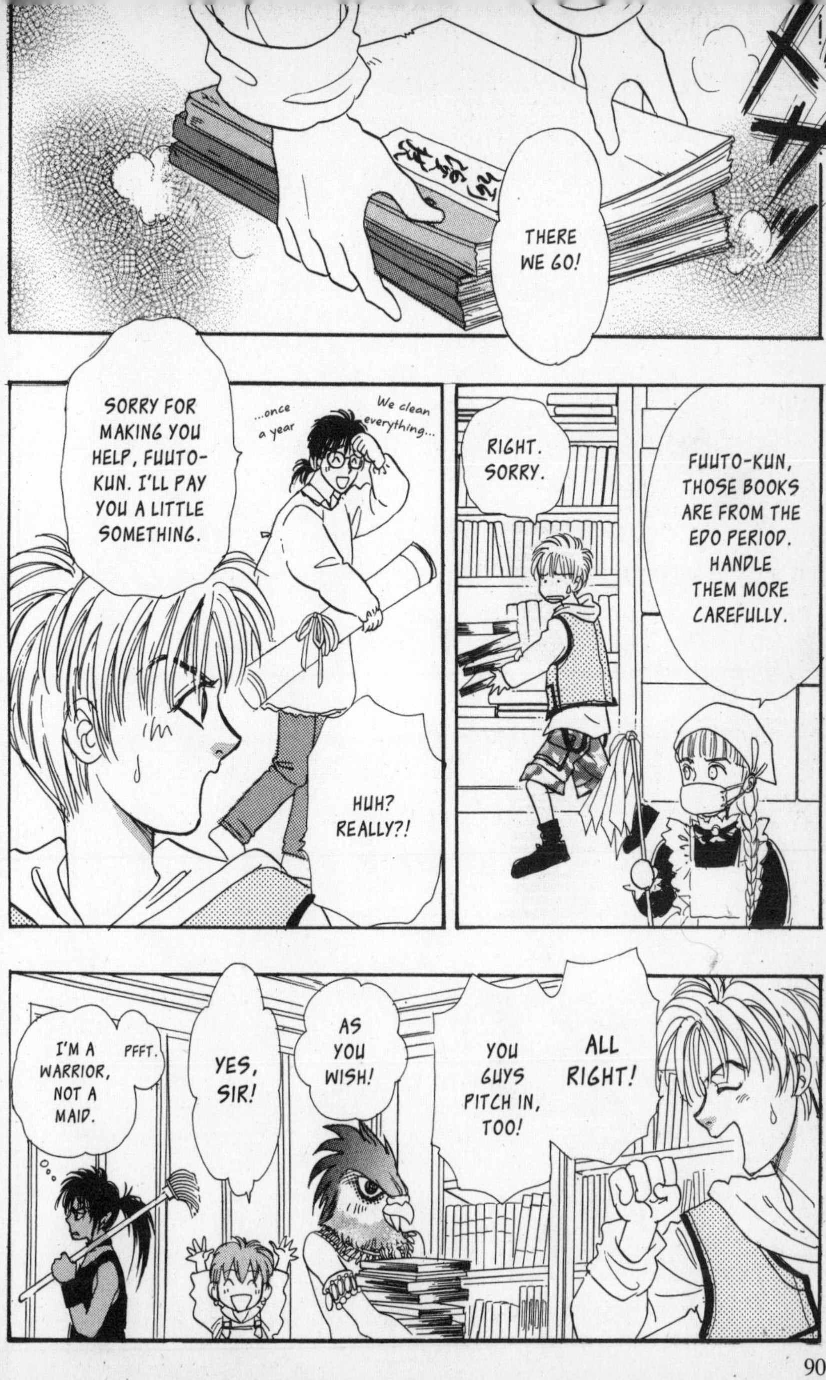
THERE WE GO!
FUUTO-KUN, THOSE BOOKS ARE FROM THE EDO PERIOD. HANDLE THEM MORE CAREFULLY.
RIGHT. SORRY.
We clean everything...
...once a year
SORRY FOR MAKING YOU HELP, FUUTO-KUN. I'LL PAY YOU A LITTLE SOMETHING.
HUH? REALLY?!
ALL RIGHT!
YOU GUYS PITCH IN, TOO!
AS YOU WISH!
YES, SIR!
PFFT.
I'M A WARRIOR, NOT A MAID.

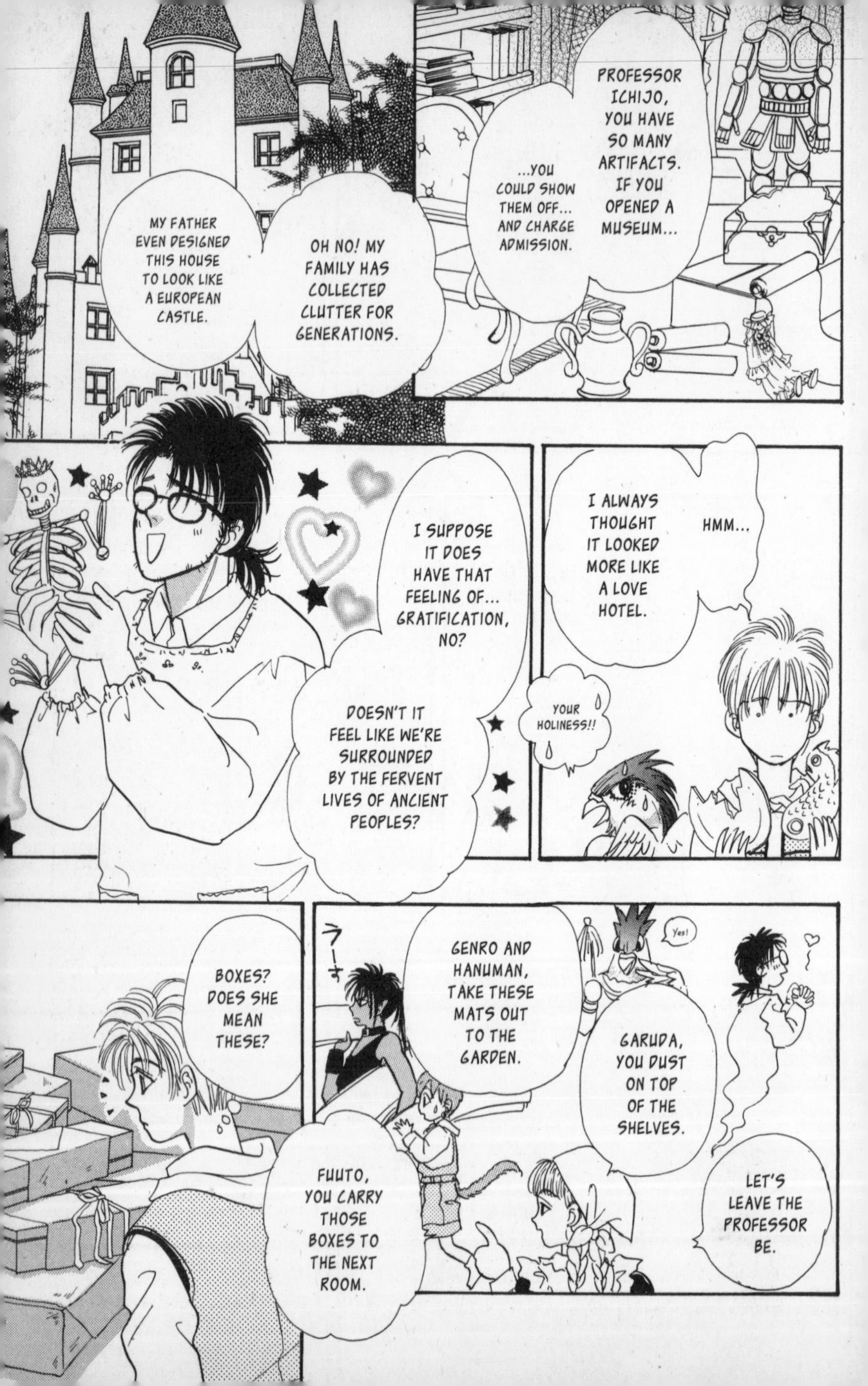
PROFESSOR ICHIJO, YOU HAVE SO MANY ARTIFACTS. IF YOU OPENED A MUSEUM...
...YOU COULD SHOW THEM OFF... AND CHARGE ADMISSION.
OH NO! MY FAMILY HAS COLLECTED CLUTTER FOR GENERATIONS.
MY FATHER EVEN DESIGNED THIS HOUSE TO LOOK LIKE A EUROPEAN CASTLE.
HMM...
I ALWAYS THOUGHT IT LOOKED MORE LIKE A LOVE HOTEL.
YOUR HOLINESS!!
I SUPPOSE IT DOES HAVE THAT FEELING OF... GRATIFICATION, NO?
DOESN'T IT FEEL LIKE WE'RE SURROUNDED BY THE FERVENT LIVES OF ANCIENT PEOPLES?
LET'S LEAVE THE PROFESSOR BE.
Yes!
GARUDA, YOU DUST ON TOP OF THE SHELVES.
GENRO AND HANUMAN, TAKE THESE MATS OUT TO THE GARDEN.
FUUTO, YOU CARRY THOSE BOXES TO THE NEXT ROOM.
BOXES? DOES SHE MEAN THESE?

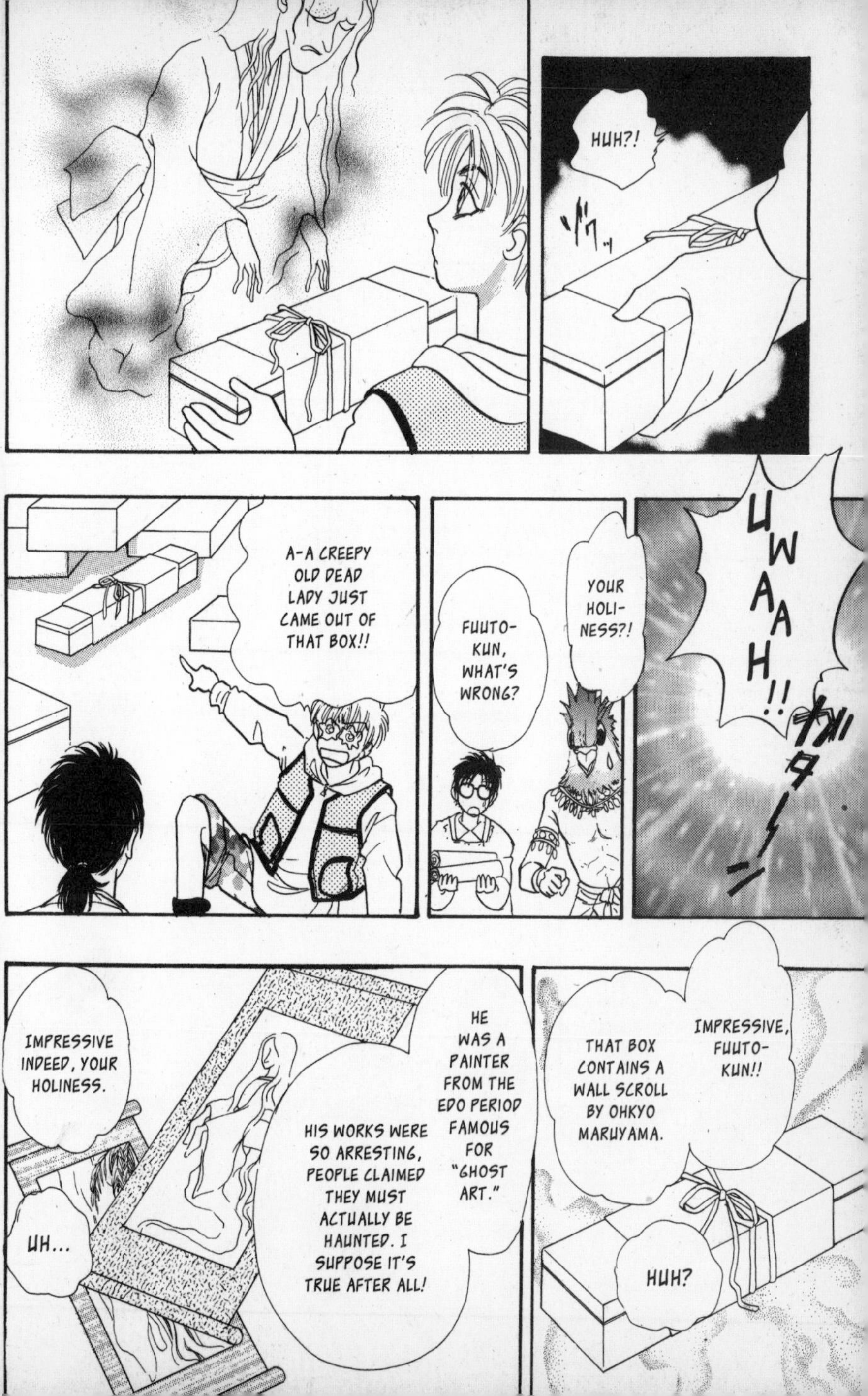
HUH?!
UWAAH!!
YOUR HOLINESS?!
FUUTO-KUN, WHAT'S WRONG?
A-A CREEPY OLD DEAD LADY JUST CAME OUT OF THAT BOX!!
IMPRESSIVE, FUUTO-KUN!!
THAT BOX CONTAINS A WALL SCROLL BY OHKYO MARUYAMA.
HUH?
HE WAS A PAINTER FROM THE EDO PERIOD FAMOUS FOR "GHOST ART."
HIS WORKS WERE SO ARRESTING, PEOPLE CLAIMED THEY MUST ACTUALLY BE HAUNTED. I SUPPOSE IT'S TRUE AFTER ALL!
IMPRESSIVE INDEED, YOUR HOLINESS.
UH...

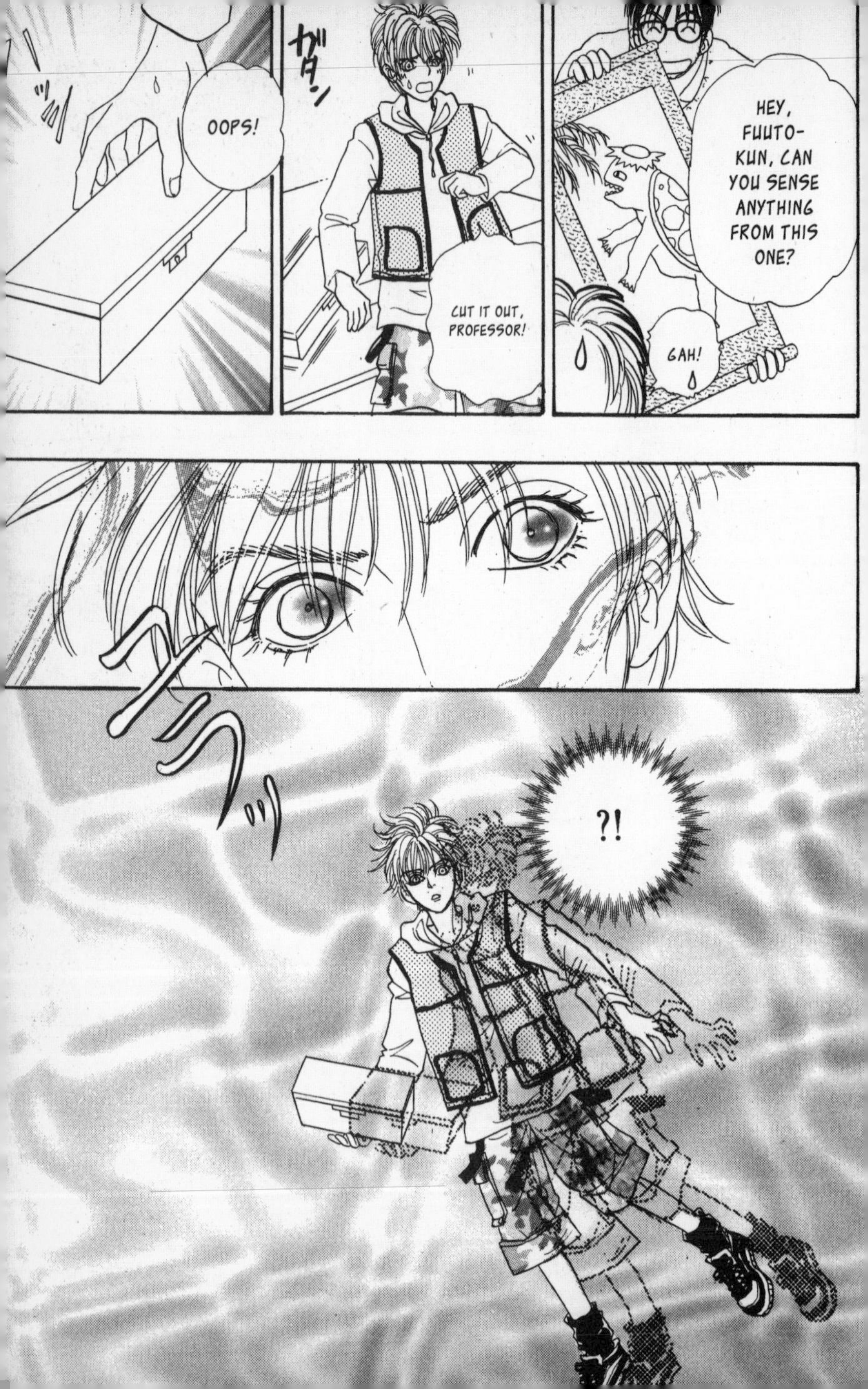
HEY, FUUTO-KUN, CAN YOU SENSE ANYTHING FROM THIS ONE?
GAH!
CUT IT OUT, PROFESSOR!
OOPS!
?!

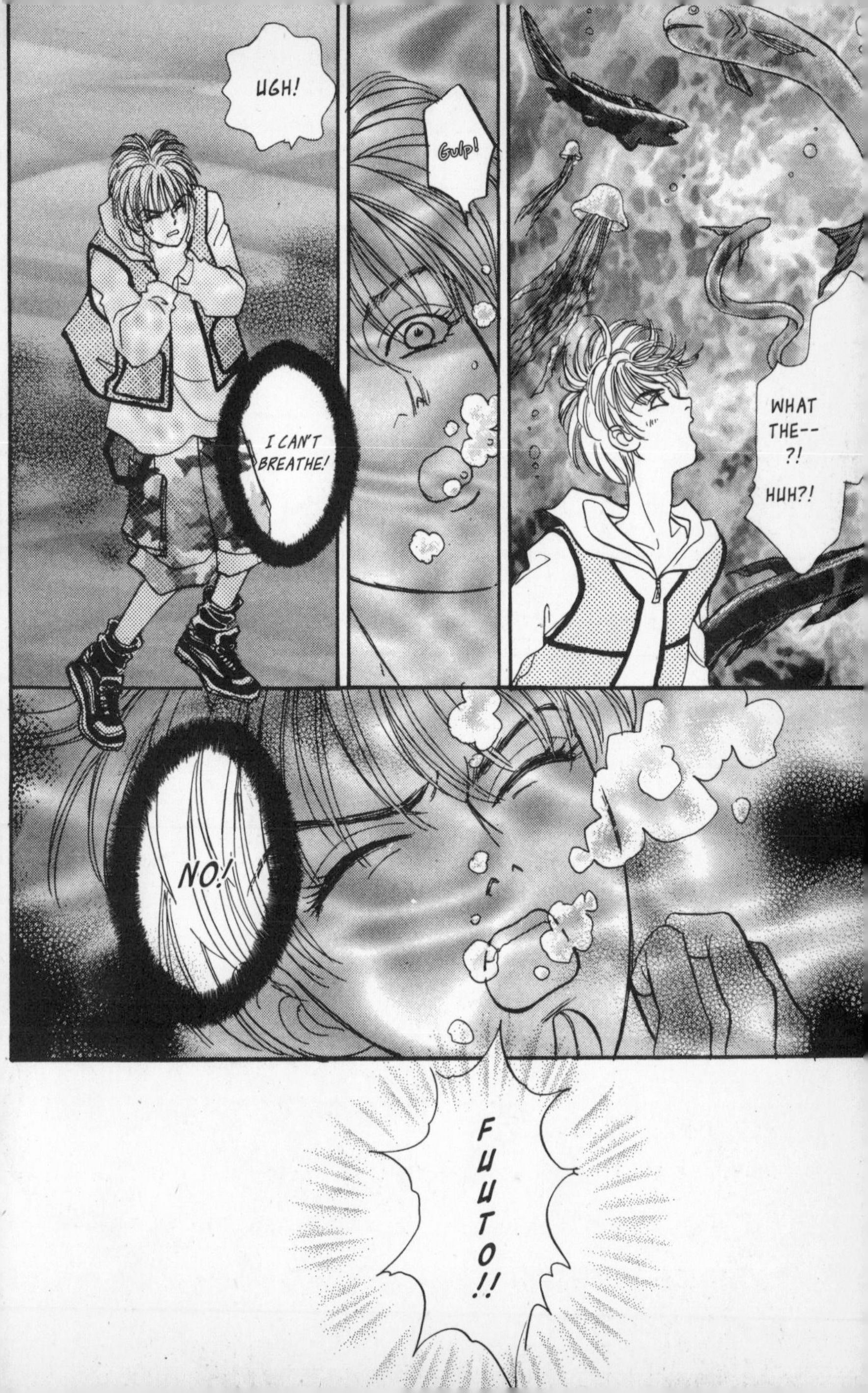
WHAT THE-- ?! HUH?!
Gulp!
UGH!
I CAN'T BREATHE!
NO!
FUUTO!!

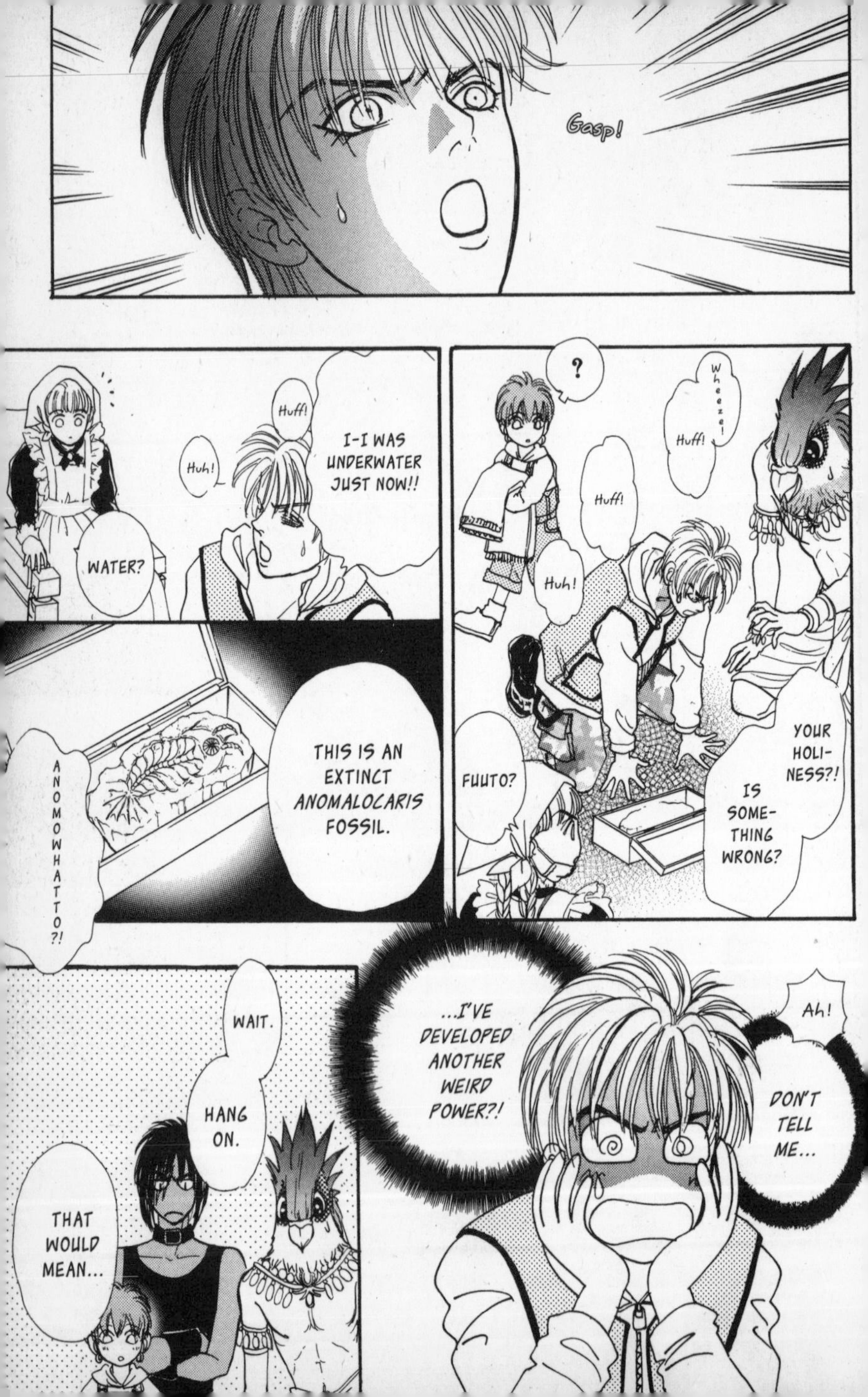
Gasp!
?
Wheeze!
Huff!
Huff!
Huh!
FUUTO?
YOUR HOLINESS?!
IS SOMETHING WRONG?
Huff!
Huh!
I-I WAS UNDERWATER JUST NOW!!
WATER?
THIS IS AN EXTINCT ANOMALOCARIS FOSSIL.
ANOMOWHATTO?!
Ah!
DON'T TELL ME...
...I'VE DEVELOPED ANOTHER WEIRD POWER?!
WAIT.
HANG ON.
THAT WOULD MEAN...

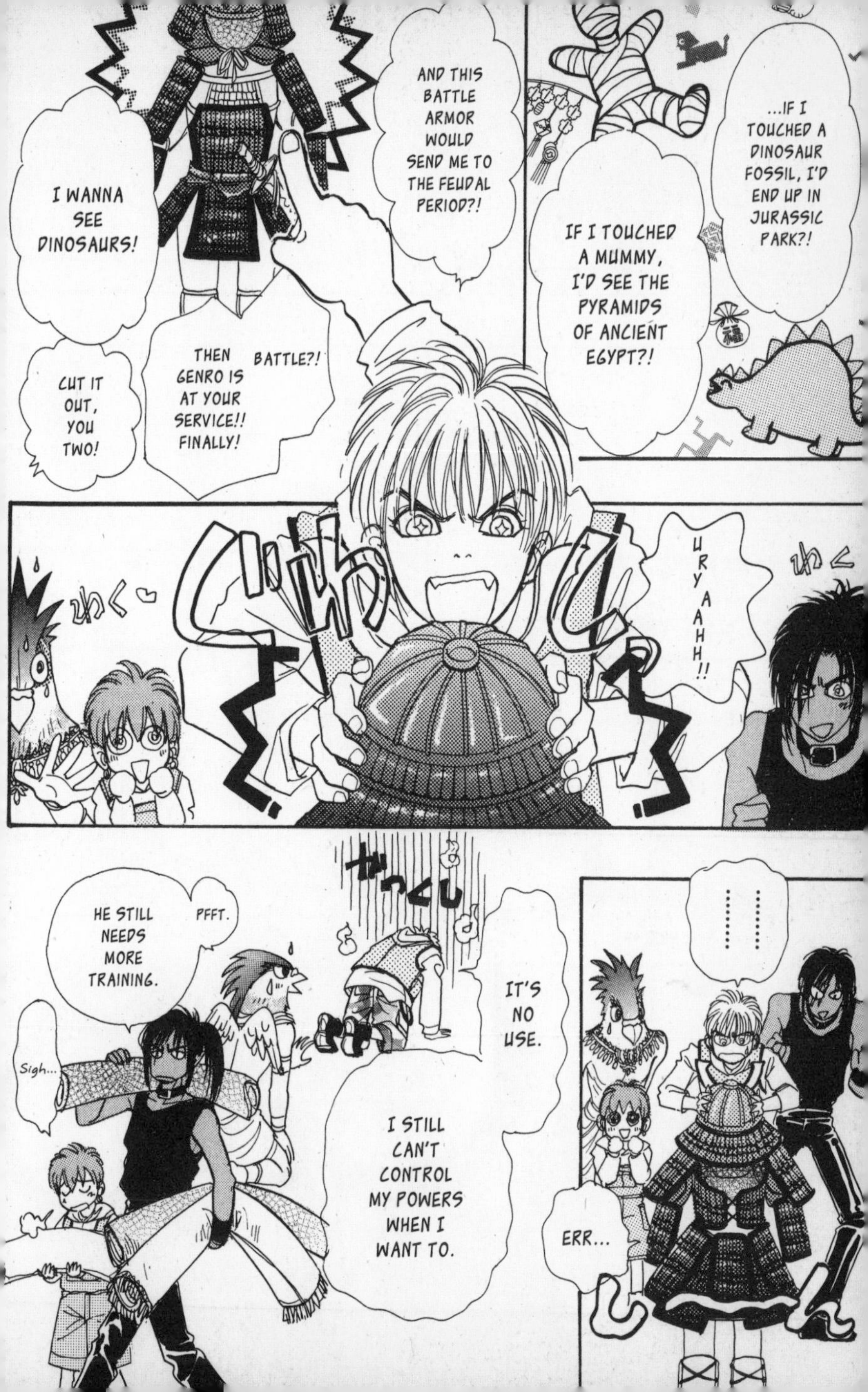
...IF I TOUCHED A DINOSAUR FOSSIL, I'D END UP IN JURASSIC PARK?!
IF I TOUCHED A MUMMY, I'D SEE THE PYRAMIDS OF ANCIENT EGYPT?!
AND THIS BATTLE ARMOR WOULD SEND ME TO THE FEUDAL PERIOD?!
I WANNA SEE DINOSAURS!
BATTLE?! FINALLY!
THEN GENRO IS AT YOUR SERVICE!!
CUT IT OUT, YOU TWO!
URYAAHH!!
......
ERR...
IT'S NO USE.
I STILL CAN'T CONTROL MY POWERS WHEN I WANT TO.
PFFT.
HE STILL NEEDS MORE TRAINING.
Sigh...

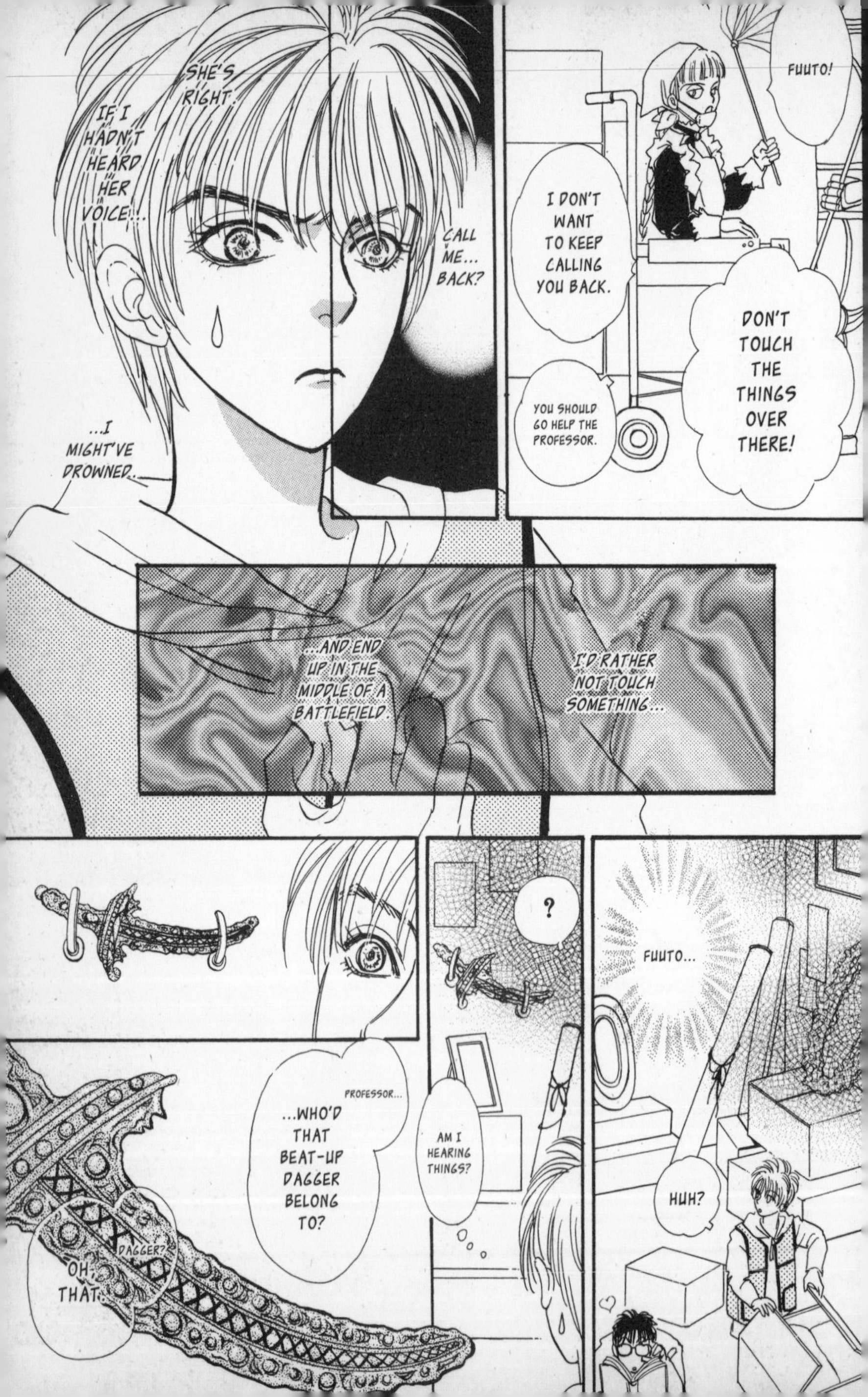
FUUTO!
DON'T TOUCH THE THINGS OVER THERE!
I DON'T WANT TO KEEP CALLING YOU BACK.
YOU SHOULD GO HELP THE PROFESSOR.
CALL ME... BACK?
SHE'S RIGHT.
IF I HADN'T HEARD HER VOICE...
...I MIGHT'VE DROWNED...
I'D RATHER NOT TOUCH SOMETHING...
...AND END UP IN THE MIDDLE OF A BATTLEFIELD.
FUUTO...
HUH?
?
AM I HEARING THINGS?
PROFESSOR...
...WHO'D THAT BEAT-UP DAGGER BELONG TO?
DAGGER?
OH, THAT.

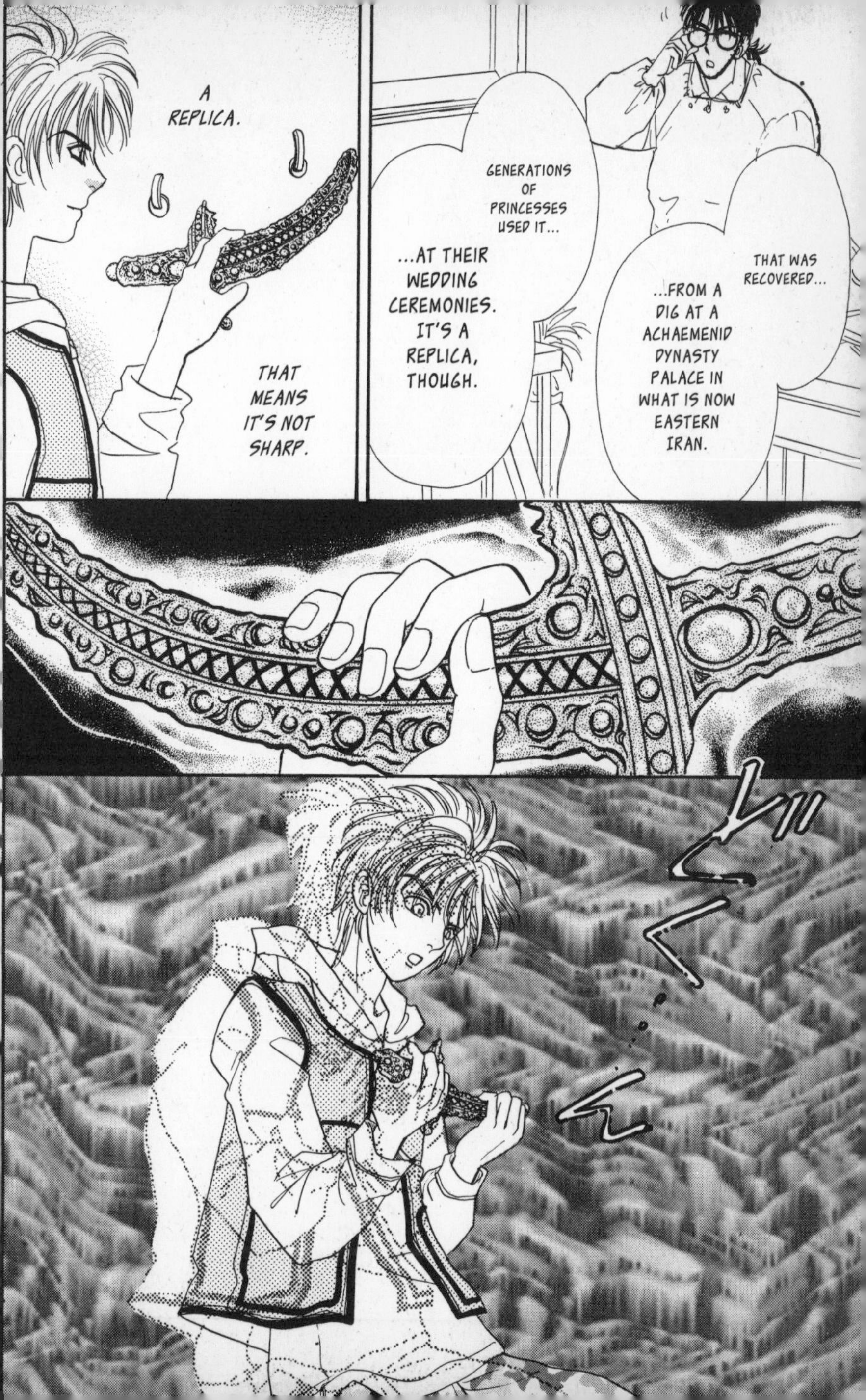
THAT WAS RECOVERED...
...FROM A DIG AT A ACHAEMENID DYNASTY PALACE IN WHAT IS NOW EASTERN IRAN.
GENERATIONS OF PRINCESSES USED IT...
...AT THEIR WEDDING CEREMONIES. IT'S A REPLICA, THOUGH.
A REPLICA.
THAT MEANS IT'S NOT SHARP.

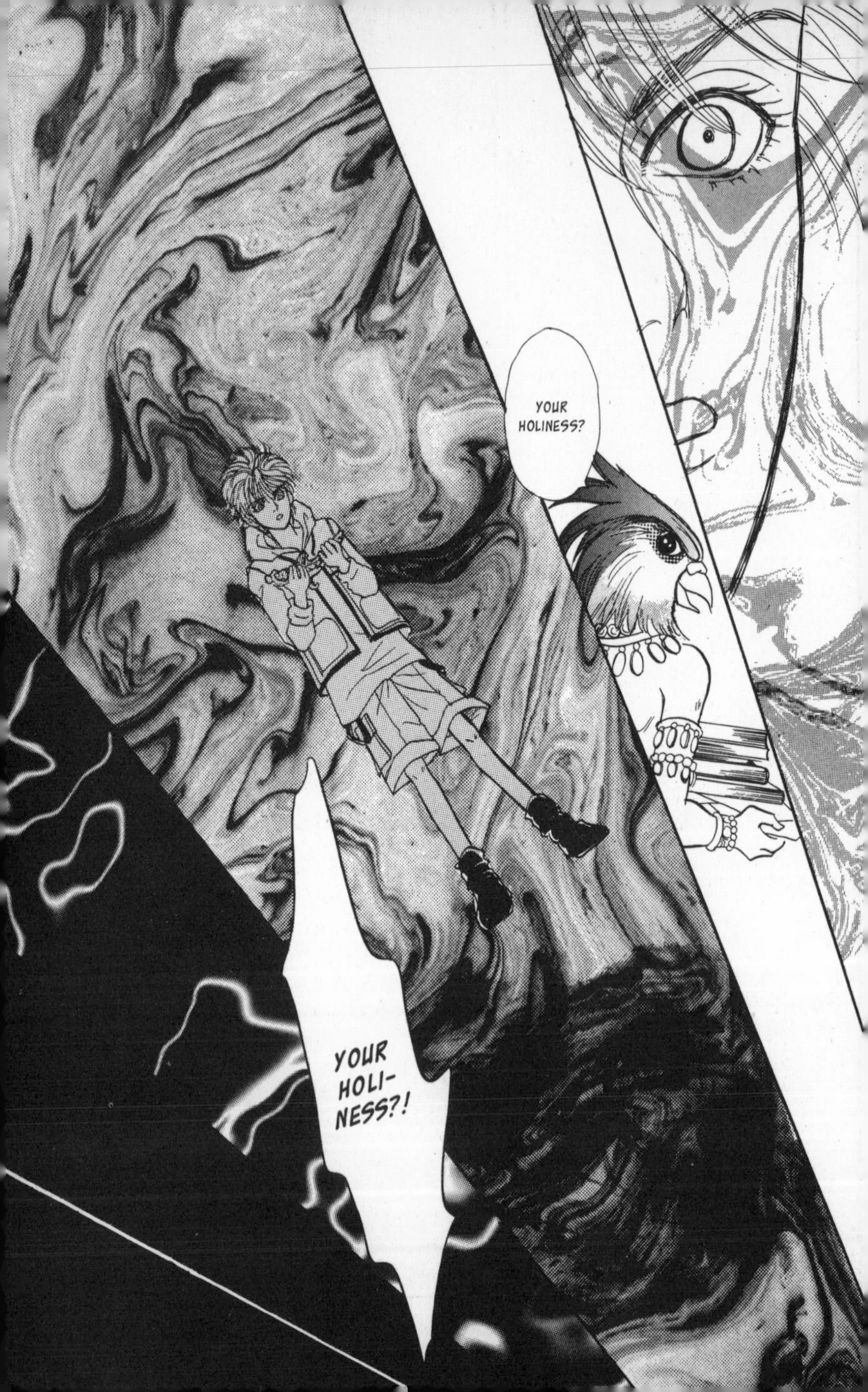
YOUR HOLINESS?
YOUR HOLI- NESS?!

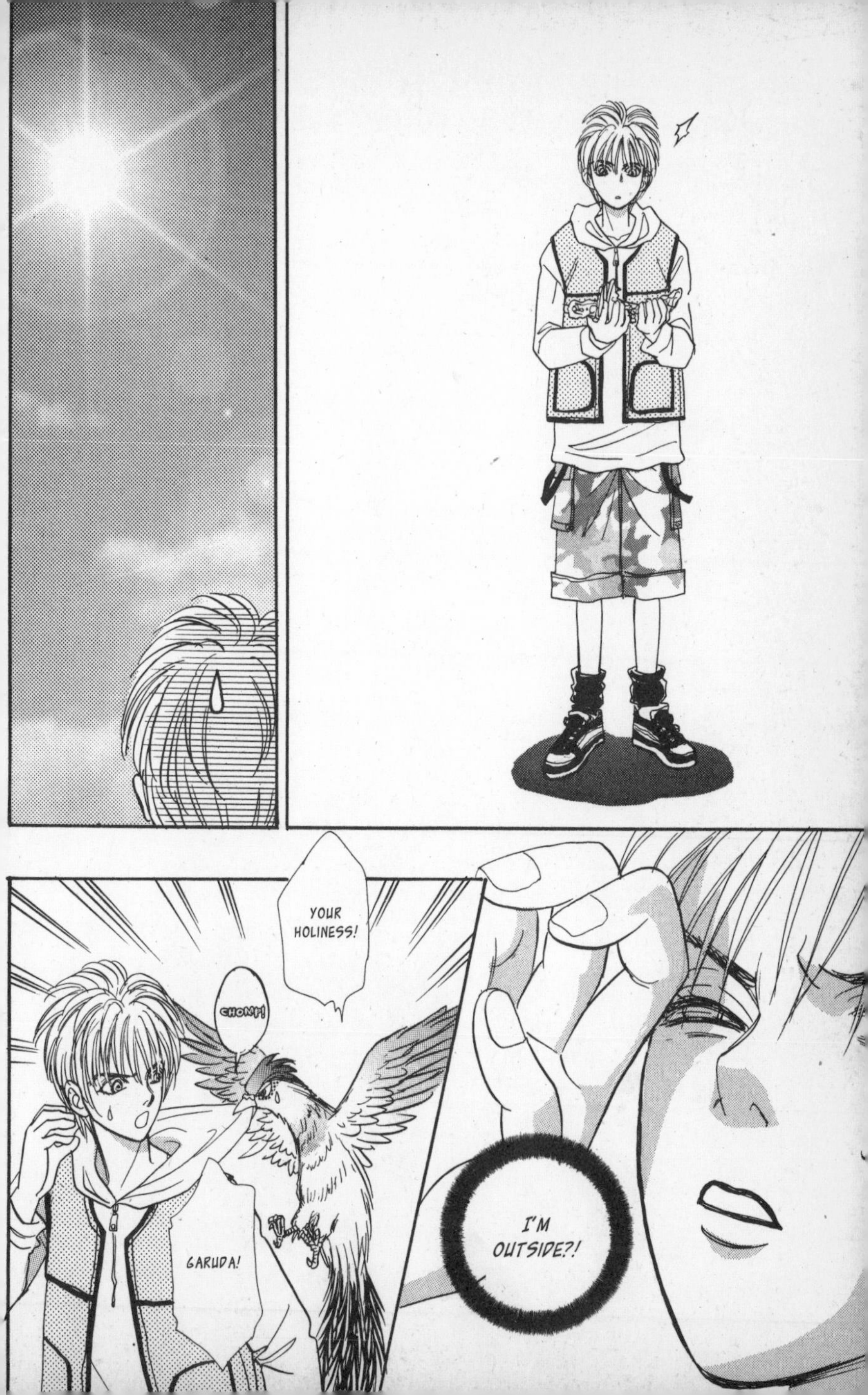
I'M OUTSIDE?!
YOUR HOLINESS!
CHOMP!
GARUDA!

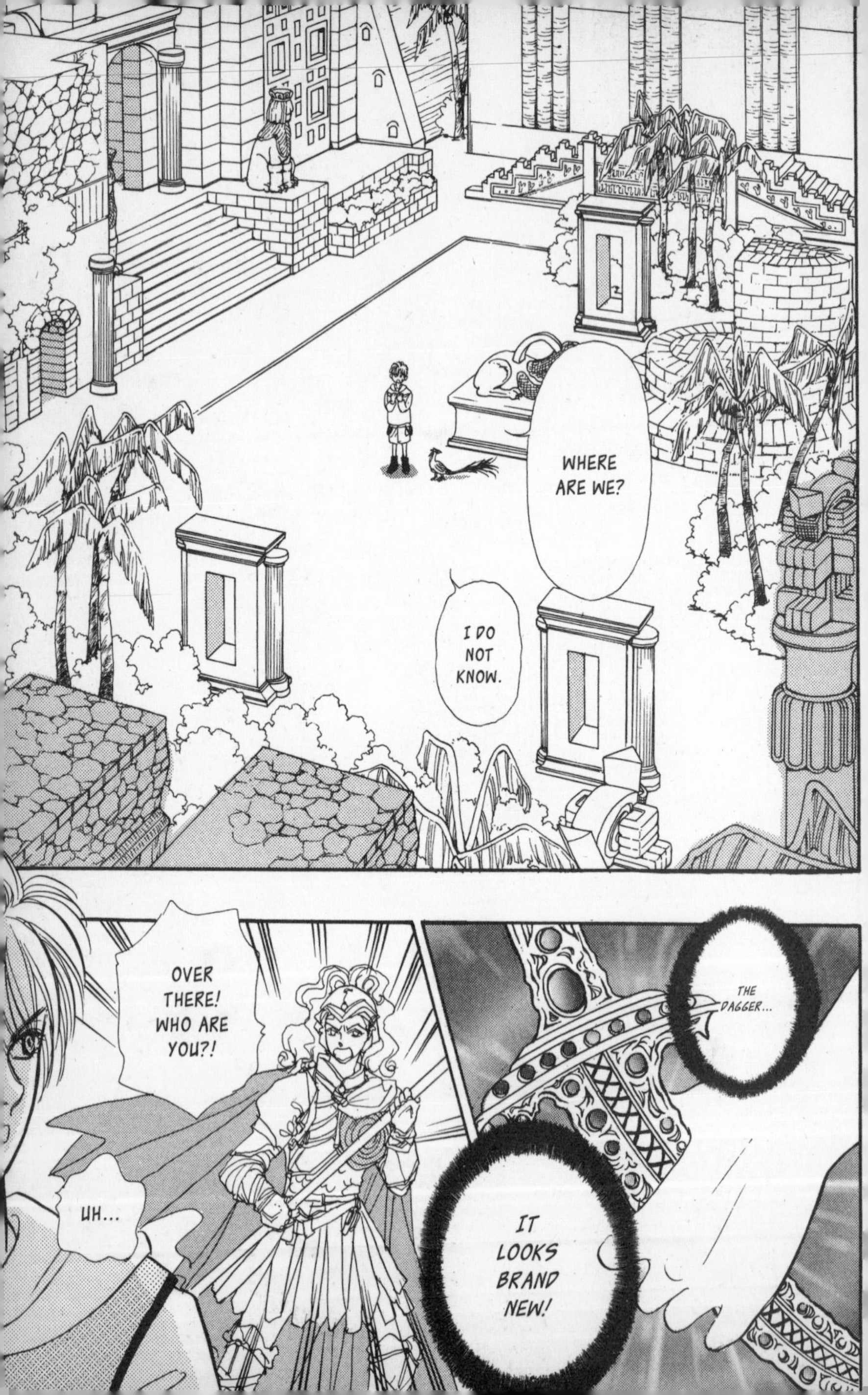
WHERE ARE WE?
I DO NOT KNOW.
OVER THERE! WHO ARE YOU?!
UH...
THE DAGGER...
IT LOOKS BRAND NEW!

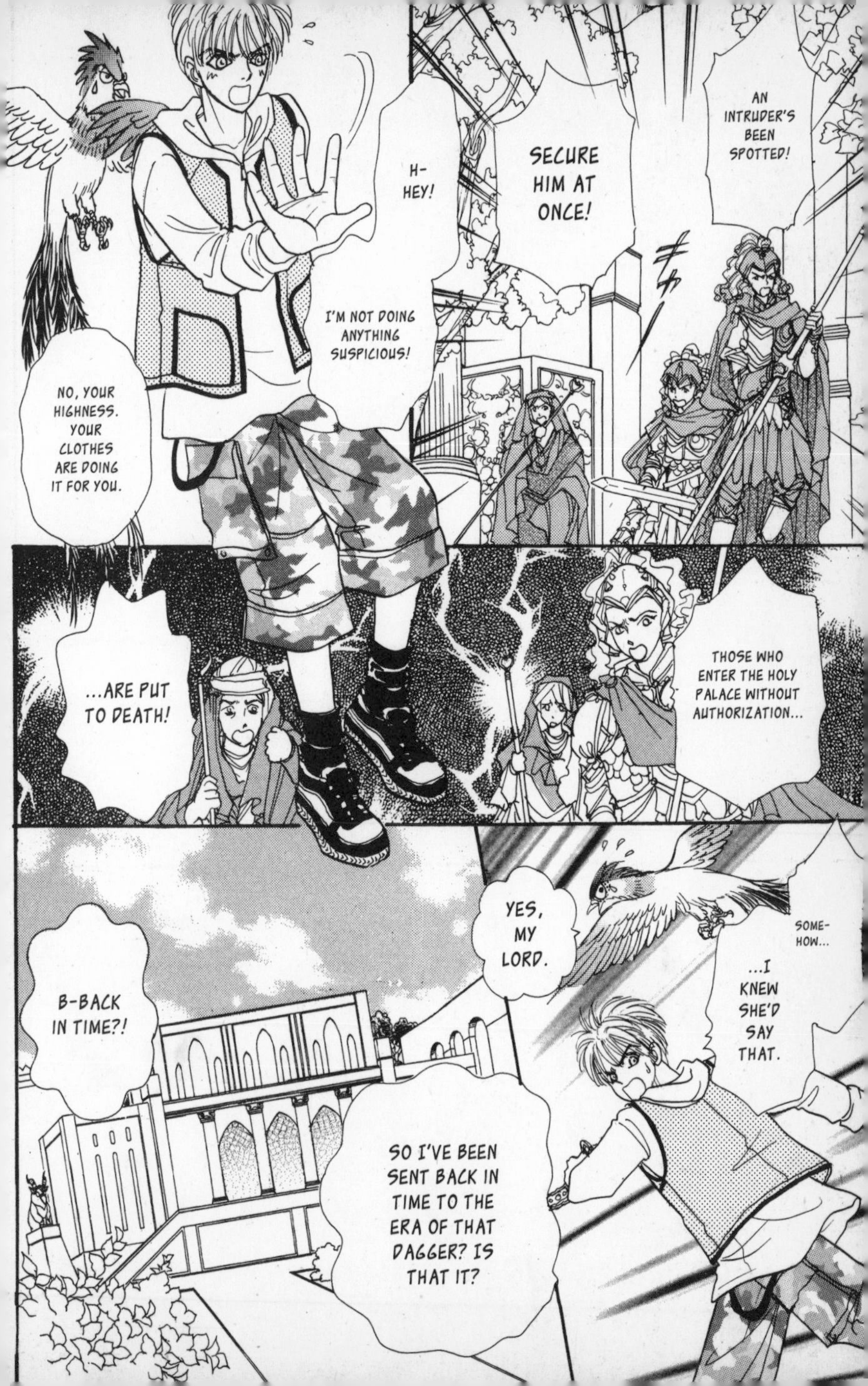
AN INTRUDER'S BEEN SPOTTED!
SECURE HIM AT ONCE!
H- HEY!
I'M NOT DOING ANYTHING SUSPICIOUS!
NO, YOUR HIGHNESS. YOUR CLOTHES ARE DOING IT FOR YOU.
THOSE WHO ENTER THE HOLY PALACE WITHOUT AUTHORIZATION...
...ARE PUT TO DEATH!
SO I'VE BEEN SENT BACK IN TIME TO THE ERA OF THAT DAGGER? IS THAT IT?
YES, MY LORD.
SOME-HOW...
...I KNEW SHE'D SAY THAT.
B-BACK IN TIME?!

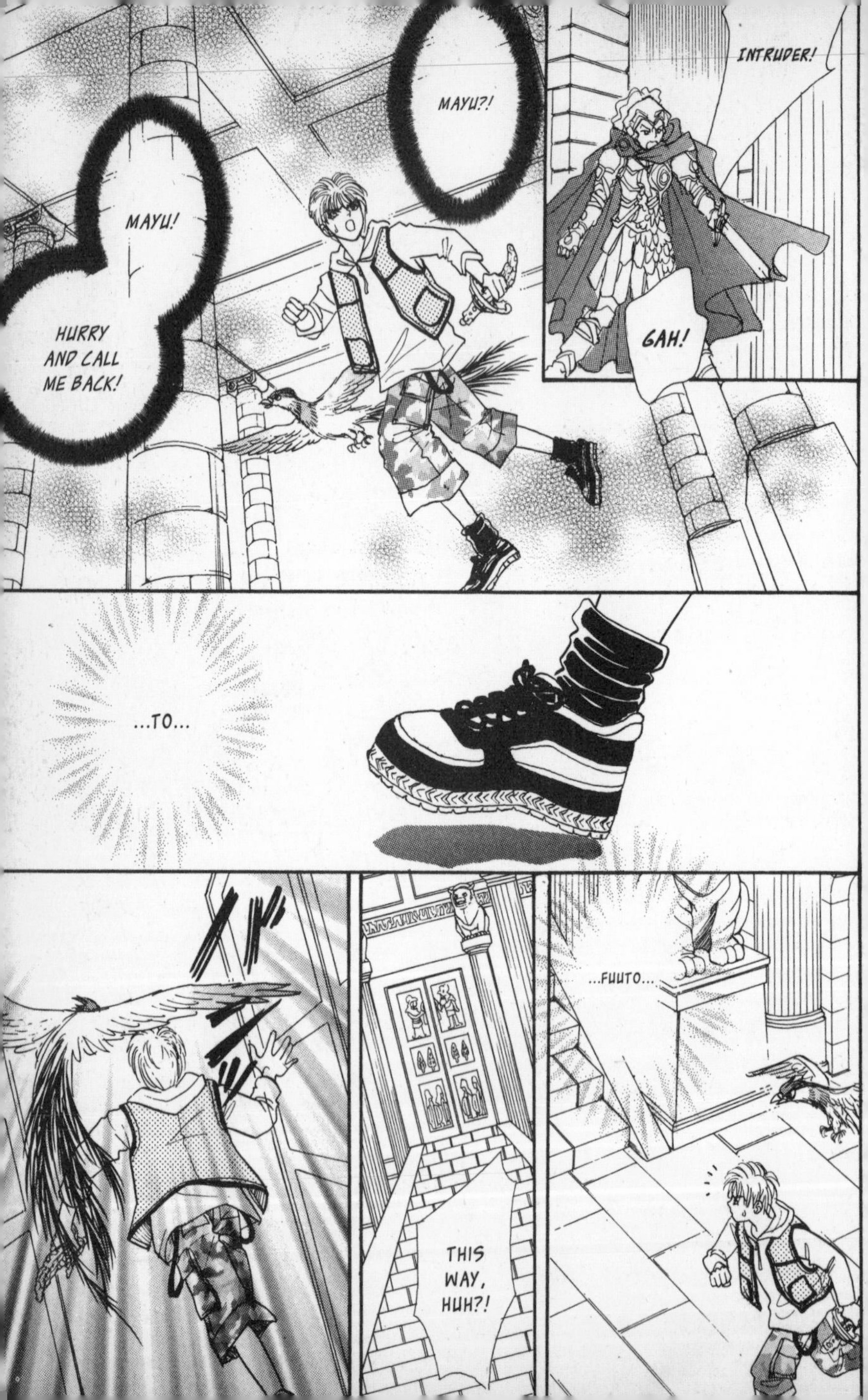
INTRUDER!
GAH!
MAYU?!
MAYU!
HURRY AND CALL ME BACK!
...TO...
...FUUTO...
THIS WAY, HUH?!

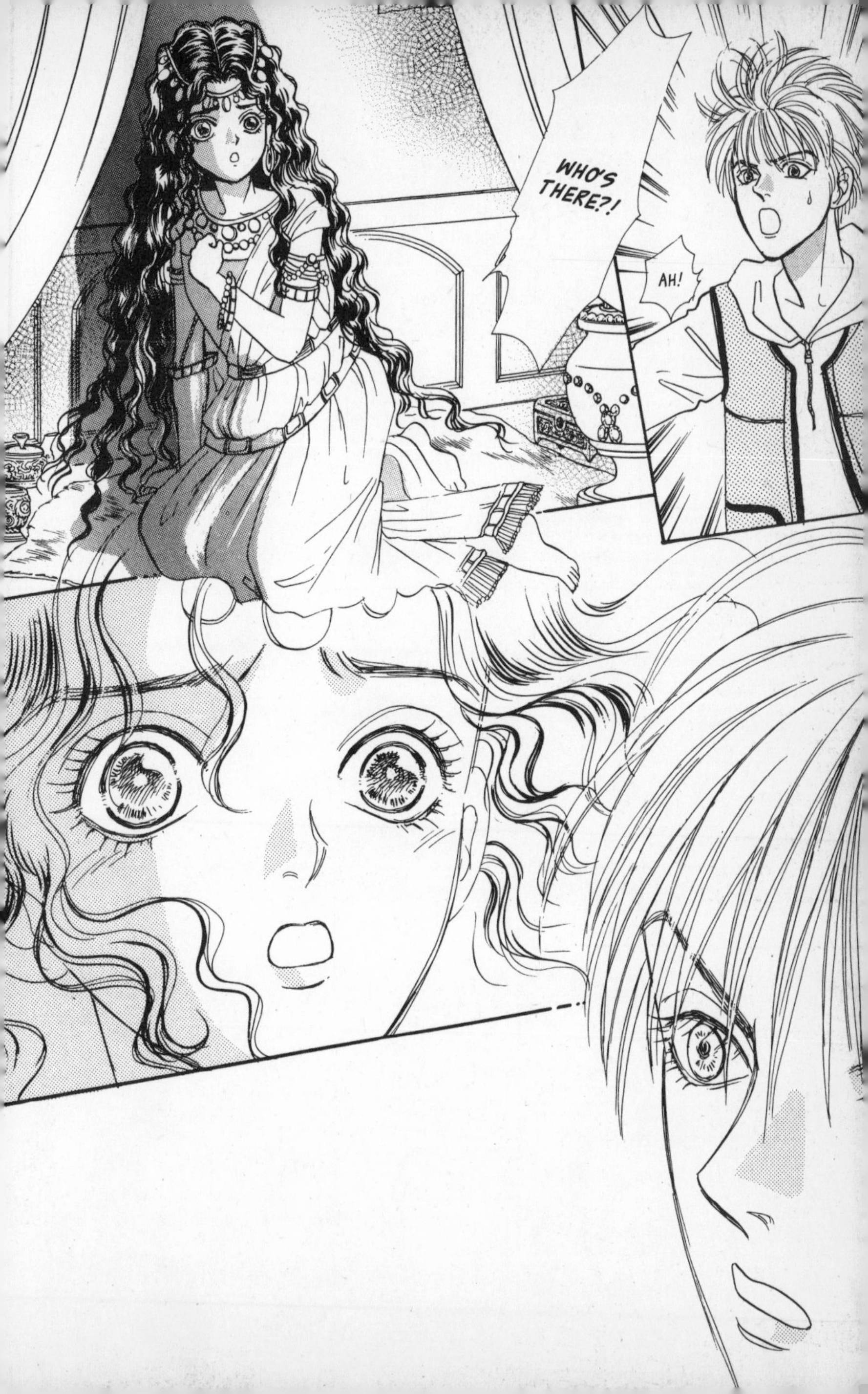
WHO'S THERE?!
AH!

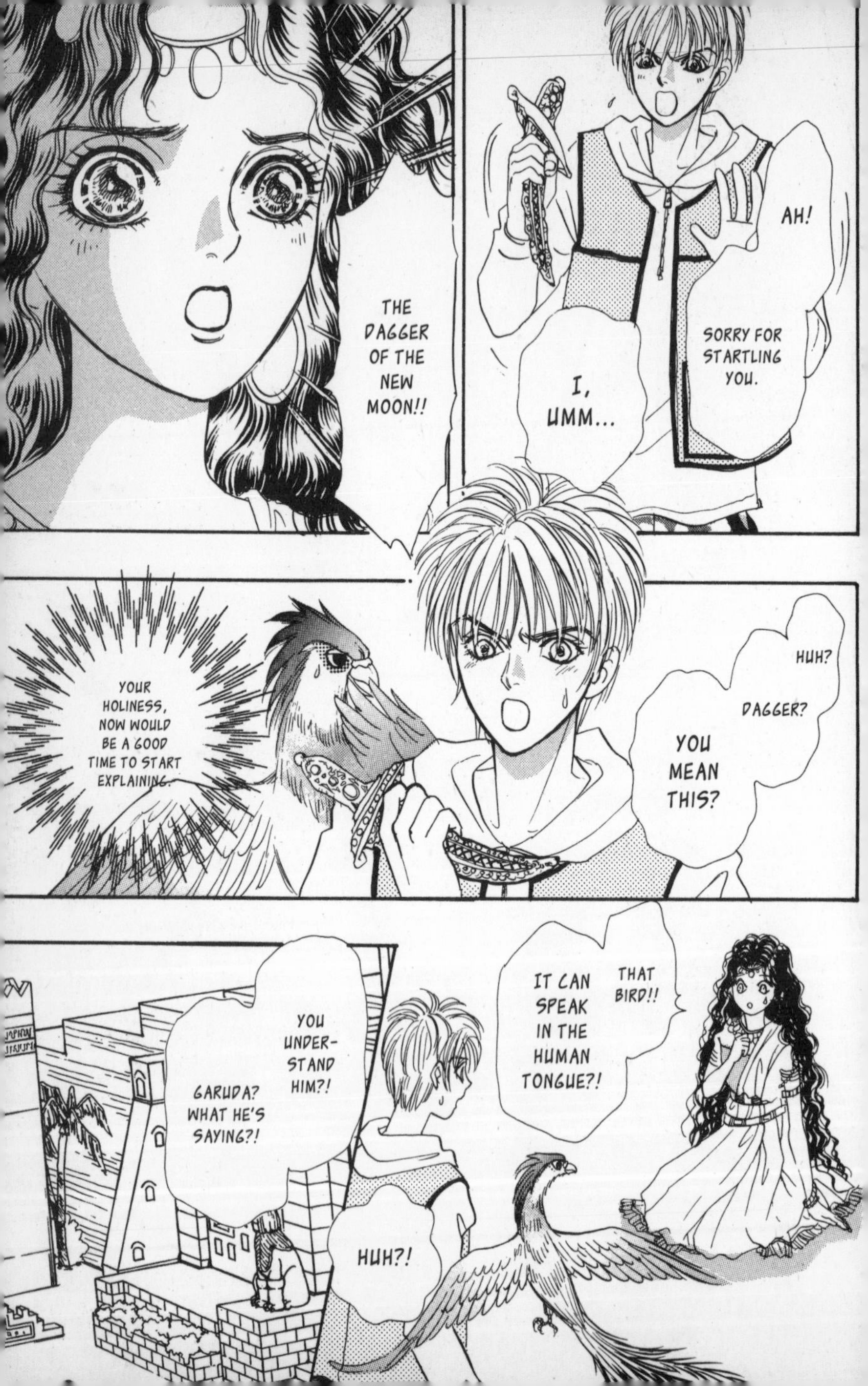
AH!
SORRY FOR STARTLING YOU.
I, UMM...
THE DAGGER OF THE NEW MOON!!
HUH?
DAGGER?
YOU MEAN THIS?
YOUR HOLINESS, NOW WOULD BE A GOOD TIME TO START EXPLAINING.
THAT BIRD!!
IT CAN SPEAK IN THE HUMAN TONGUE?!
YOU UNDER-STAND HIM?!
GARUDA? WHAT HE'S SAYING?!
HUH?!

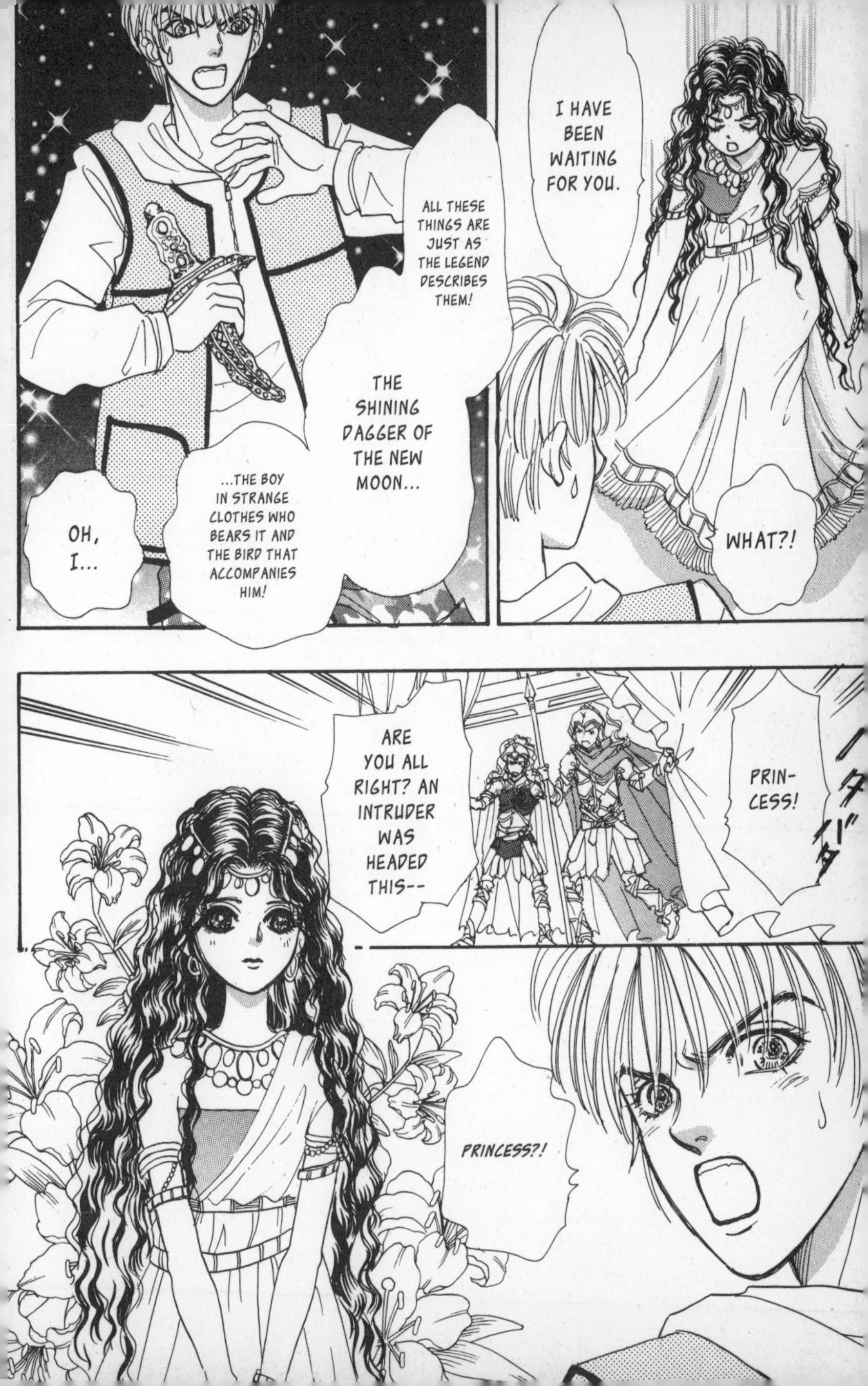
I HAVE BEEN WAITING FOR YOU.
WHAT?!
ALL THESE THINGS ARE JUST AS THE LEGEND DESCRIBES THEM!
THE SHINING DAGGER OF THE NEW MOON...
...THE BOY IN STRANGE CLOTHES WHO BEARS IT AND THE BIRD THAT ACCOMPANIES HIM!
OH, I...
PRIN-CESS!
ARE YOU ALL RIGHT? AN INTRUDER WAS HEADED THIS--
PRINCESS?!

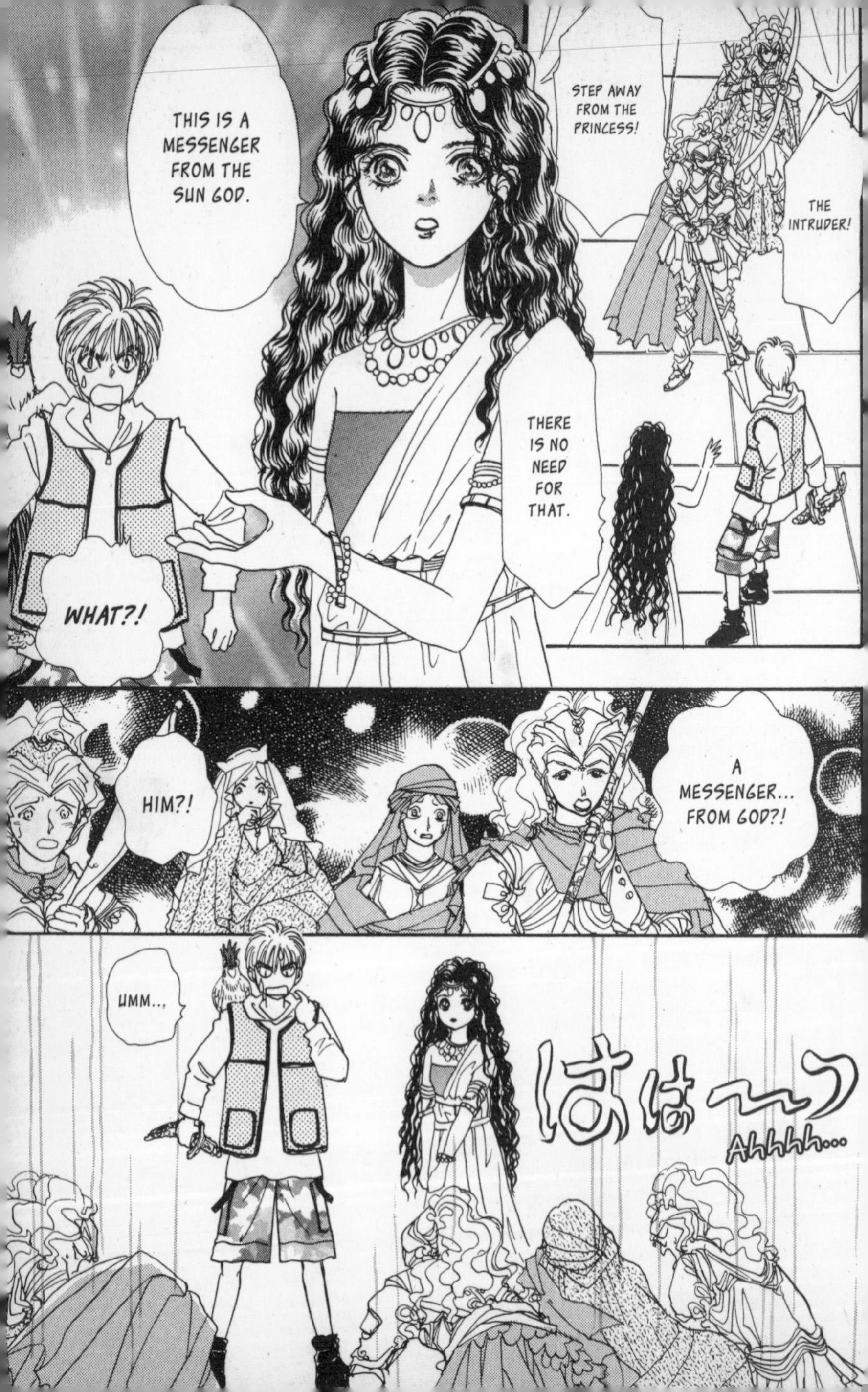
STEP AWAY FROM THE PRINCESS!
THE INTRUDER!
THERE IS NO NEED FOR THAT.
THIS IS A MESSENGER FROM THE SUN GOD.
WHAT?!
A MESSENGER... FROM GOD?!
HIM?!
はは〜っ
Ahhhh...
UMM...,

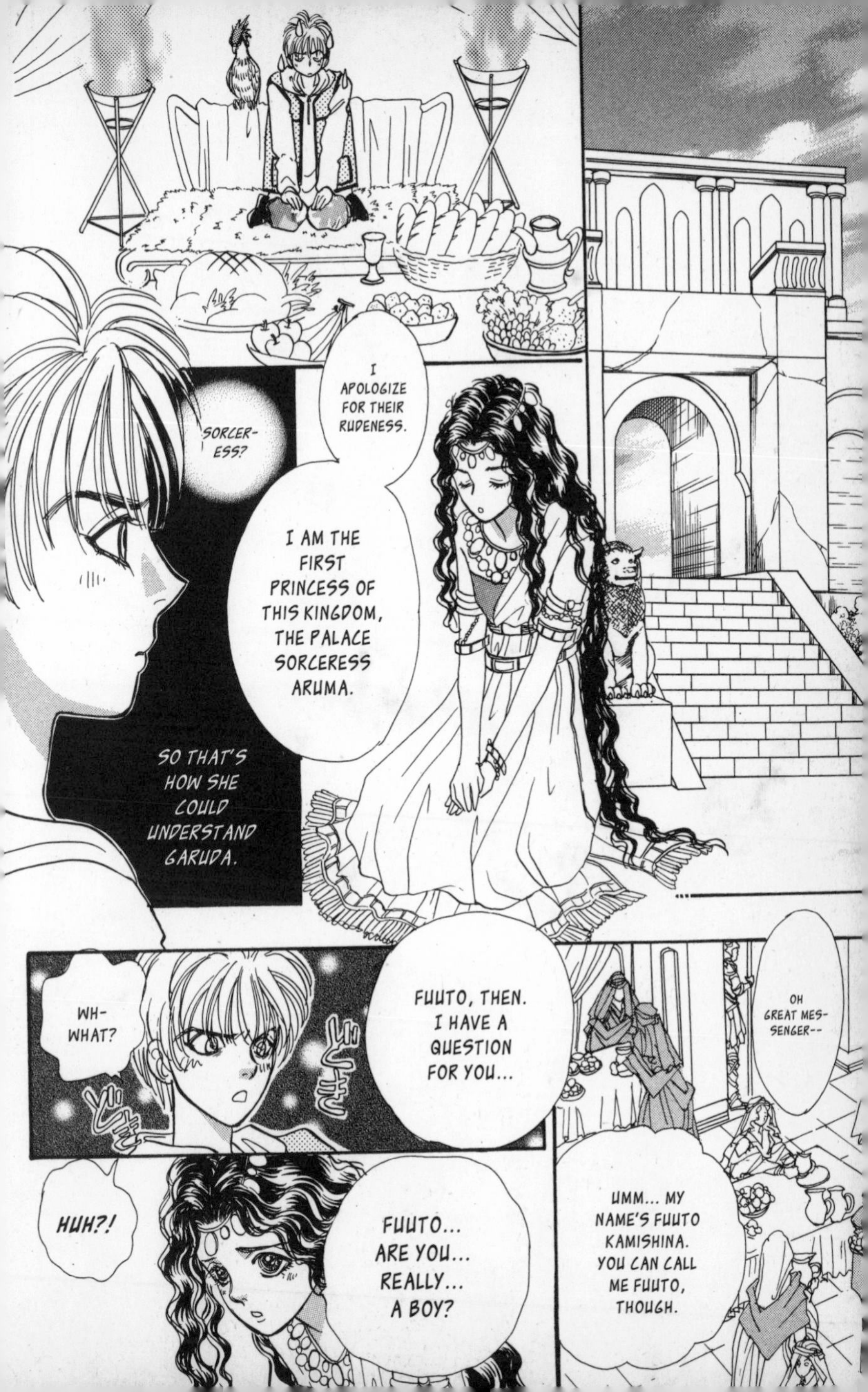
I APOLOGIZE FOR THEIR RUDENESS.
I AM THE FIRST PRINCESS OF THIS KINGDOM, THE PALACE SORCERESS ARUMA.
SORCER-ESS?
SO THAT'S HOW SHE COULD UNDERSTAND GARUDA.
OH GREAT MES-SENGER--
UMM... MY NAME'S FUUTO KAMISHINA. YOU CAN CALL ME FUUTO, THOUGH.
FUUTO, THEN. I HAVE A QUESTION FOR YOU...
WH-WHAT?
FUUTO... ARE YOU... REALLY... A BOY?
HUH?!

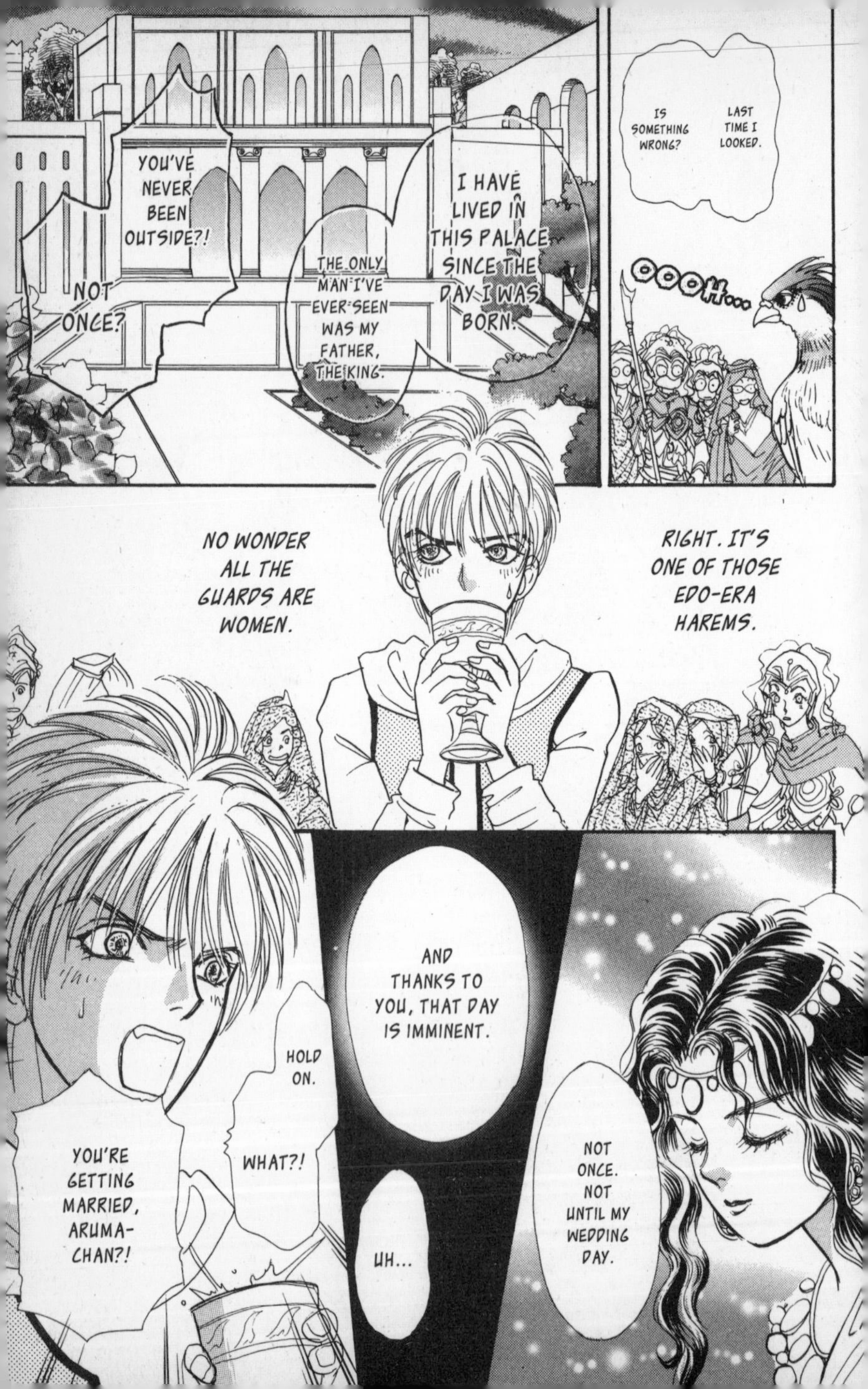
LAST TIME I LOOKED.
IS SOMETHING WRONG?
OOOH...
I HAVE LIVED IN THIS PALACE SINCE THE DAY I WAS BORN.
THE ONLY MAN I'VE EVER SEEN WAS MY FATHER, THE KING.
YOU'VE NEVER BEEN OUTSIDE?!
NOT ONCE?
RIGHT. IT'S ONE OF THOSE EDO-ERA HAREMS.
NO WONDER ALL THE GUARDS ARE WOMEN.
NOT ONCE. NOT UNTIL MY WEDDING DAY.
AND THANKS TO YOU, THAT DAY IS IMMINENT.
UH...
WHAT?!
HOLD ON.
YOU'RE GETTING MARRIED, ARUMA-CHAN?!

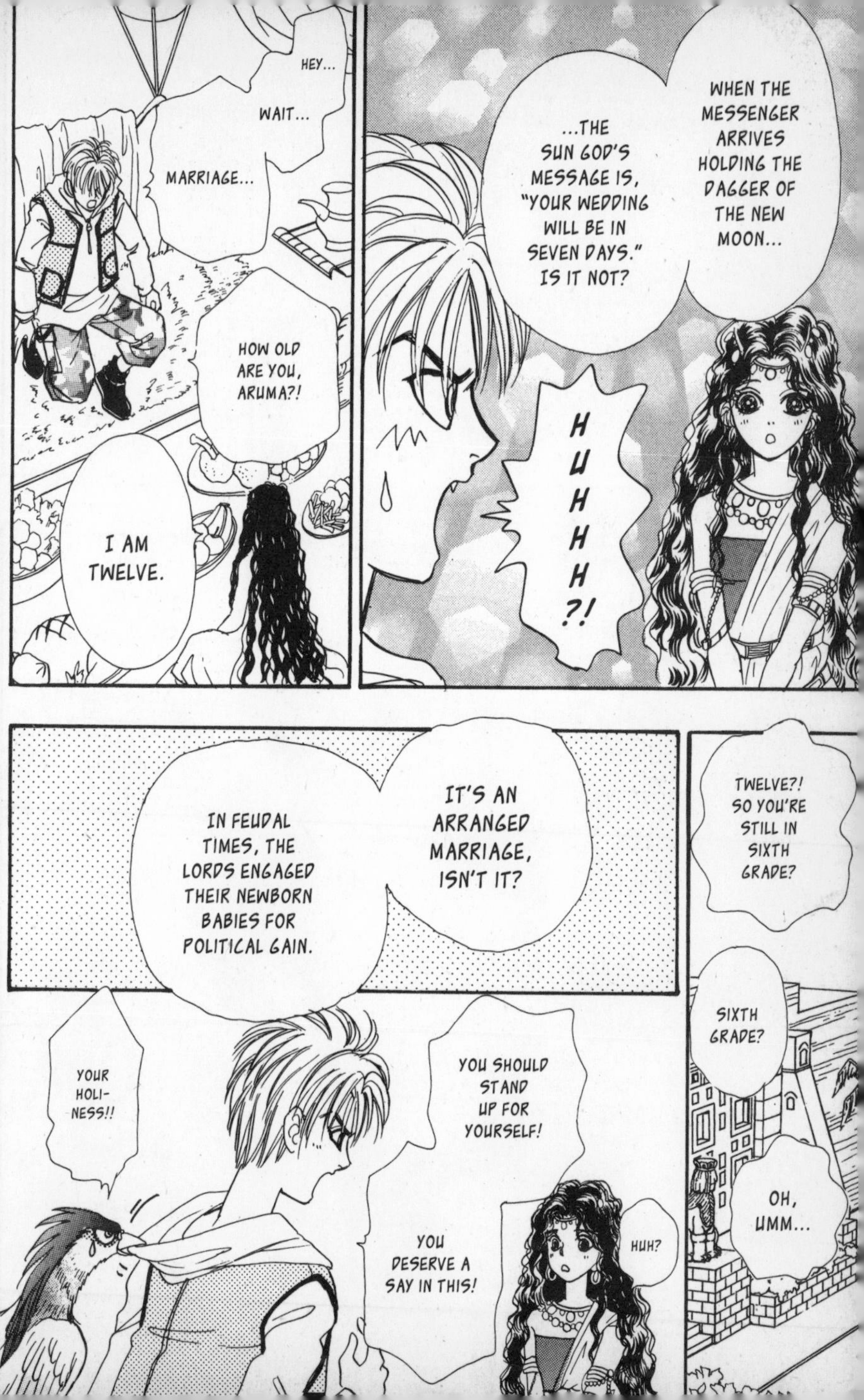
WHEN THE MESSENGER ARRIVES HOLDING THE DAGGER OF THE NEW MOON...
...THE SUN GOD'S MESSAGE IS, "YOUR WEDDING WILL BE IN SEVEN DAYS." IS IT NOT?
HUHHHH?!
HEY...
WAIT...
MARRIAGE...
HOW OLD ARE YOU, ARUMA?!
I AM TWELVE.
TWELVE?! SO YOU'RE STILL IN SIXTH GRADE?
IT'S AN ARRANGED MARRIAGE, ISN'T IT?
IN FEUDAL TIMES, THE LORDS ENGAGED THEIR NEWBORN BABIES FOR POLITICAL GAIN.
SIXTH GRADE?
OH, UMM...
YOU SHOULD STAND UP FOR YOURSELF!
HUH?
YOU DESERVE A SAY IN THIS!
YOUR HOLI-NESS!!

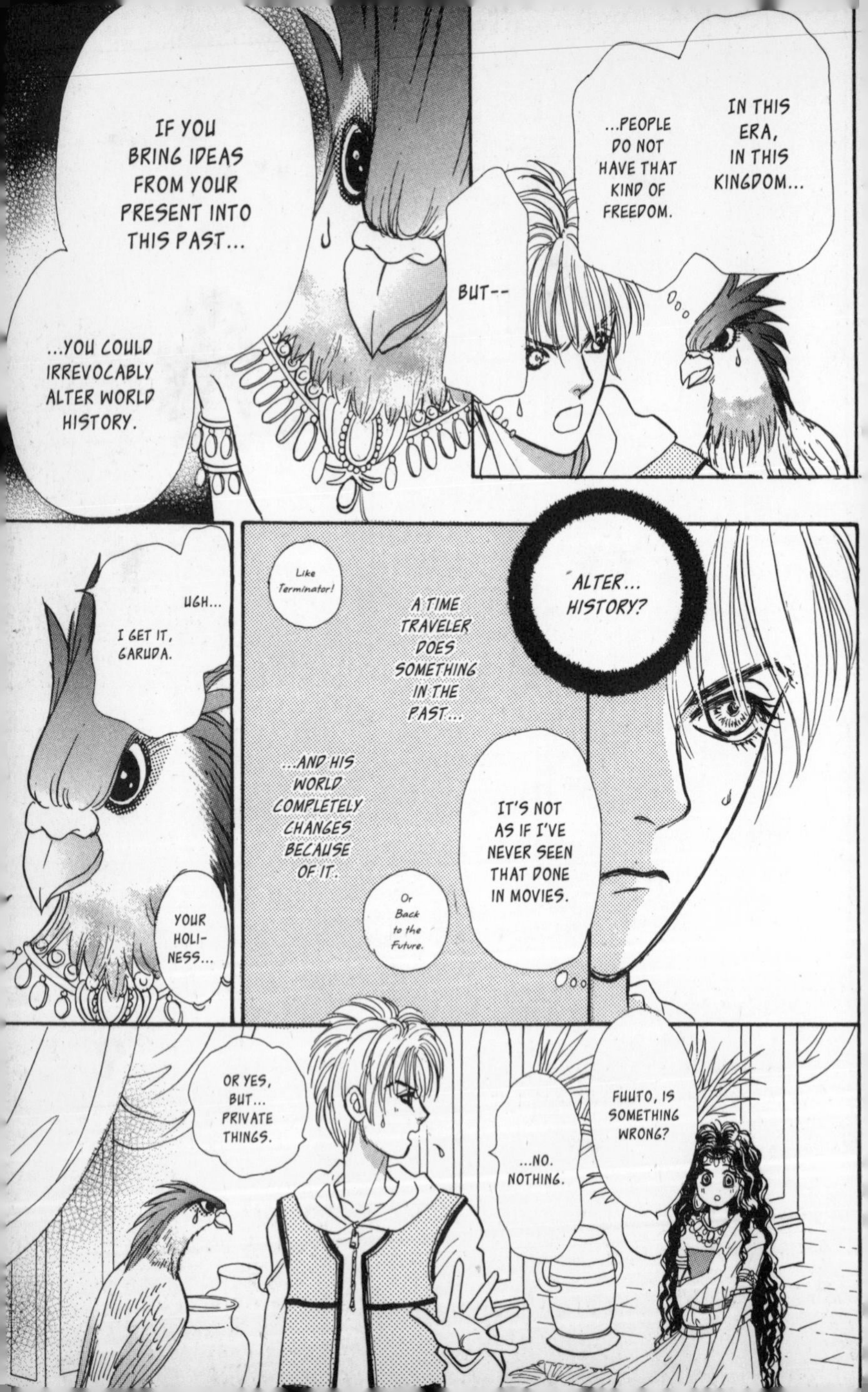
IF YOU BRING IDEAS FROM YOUR PRESENT INTO THIS PAST...
...YOU COULD IRREVOCABLY ALTER WORLD HISTORY.
BUT--
...PEOPLE DO NOT HAVE THAT KIND OF FREEDOM.
IN THIS ERA, IN THIS KINGDOM...
UGH...
I GET IT, GARUDA.
YOUR HOLI-NESS...
Like Terminator!
A TIME TRAVELER DOES SOMETHING IN THE PAST...
...AND HIS WORLD COMPLETELY CHANGES BECAUSE OF IT.
Or Back to the Future.
"ALTER... HISTORY?
IT'S NOT AS IF I'VE NEVER SEEN THAT DONE IN MOVIES.
OR YES, BUT... PRIVATE THINGS.
...NO. NOTHING.
FUUTO, IS SOMETHING WRONG?

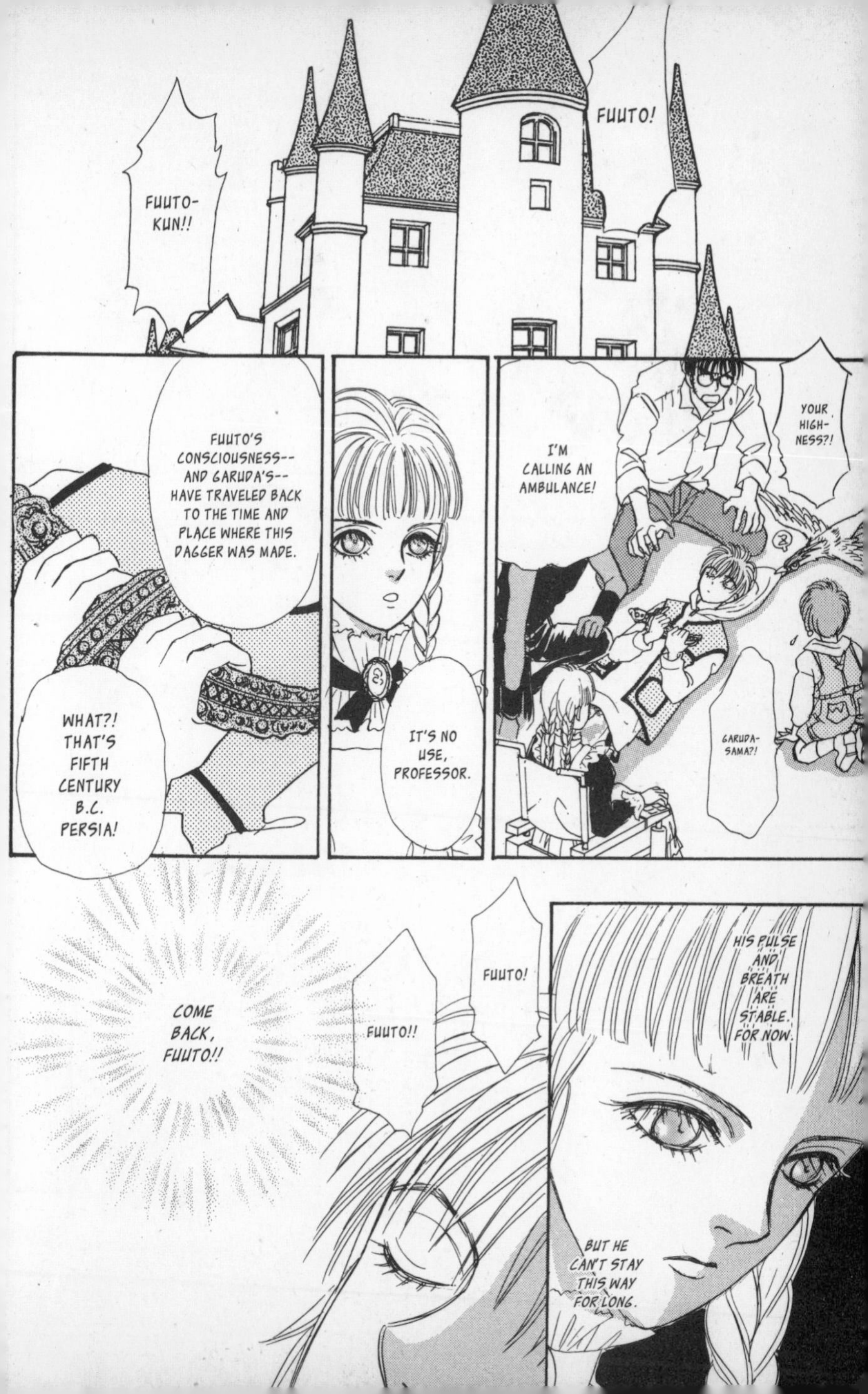
FUUTO!
FUUTO-KUN!!
YOUR HIGHNESS?!
I'M CALLING AN AMBULANCE!
GARUDA-SAMA?!
IT'S NO USE, PROFESSOR.
FUUTO'S CONSCIOUSNESS-- AND GARUDA'S-- HAVE TRAVELED BACK TO THE TIME AND PLACE WHERE THIS DAGGER WAS MADE.
WHAT?! THAT'S FIFTH CENTURY B.C. PERSIA!
HIS PULSE AND BREATH ARE STABLE. FOR NOW.
BUT HE CAN'T STAY THIS WAY FOR LONG.
FUUTO!
FUUTO!!
COME BACK, FUUTO!!

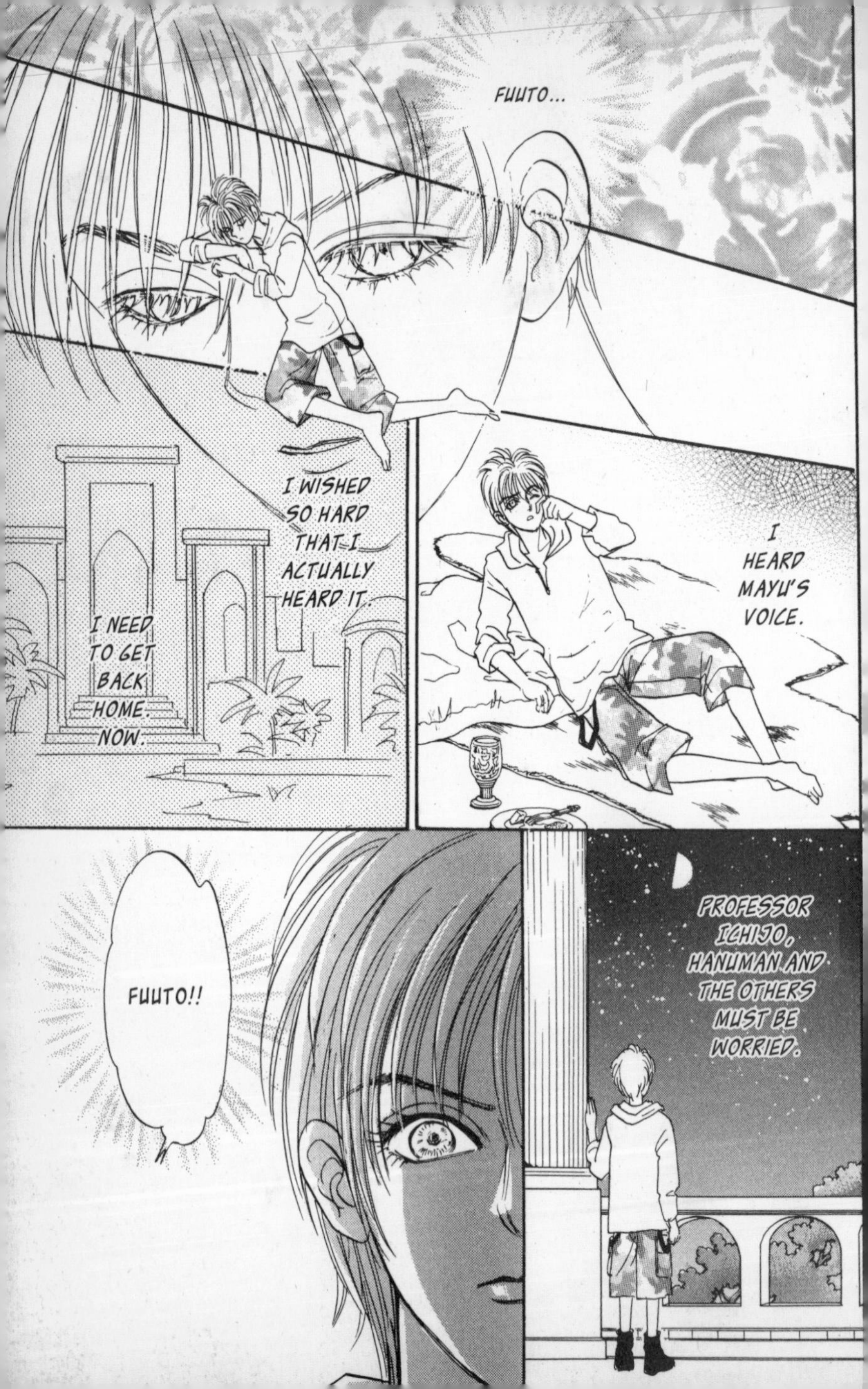
FUUTO...
I HEARD MAYU'S VOICE.
I WISHED SO HARD THAT I ACTUALLY HEARD IT.
I NEED TO GET BACK HOME. NOW.
PROFESSOR ICHIJO, HANUMAN AND THE OTHERS MUST BE WORRIED.
FUUTO!!

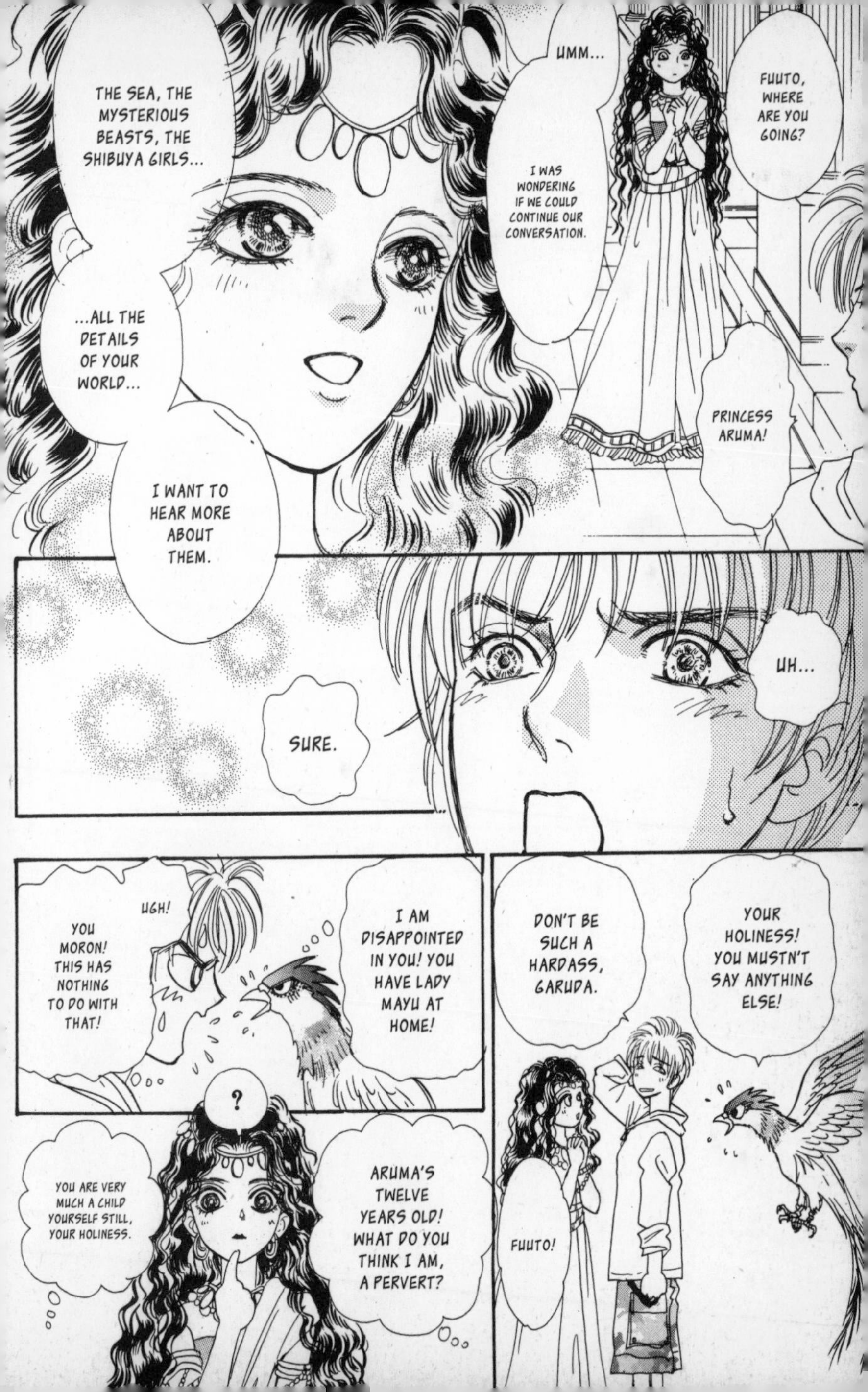
FUUTO, WHERE ARE YOU GOING?
PRINCESS ARUMA!
UMM...
I WAS WONDERING IF WE COULD CONTINUE OUR CONVERSATION.
THE SEA, THE MYSTERIOUS BEASTS, THE SHIBUYA GIRLS...
...ALL THE DETAILS OF YOUR WORLD...
I WANT TO HEAR MORE ABOUT THEM.
UH...
SURE.
YOUR HOLINESS! YOU MUSTN'T SAY ANYTHING ELSE!
DON'T BE SUCH A HARDASS, GARUDA.
FUUTO!
I AM DISAPPOINTED IN YOU! YOU HAVE LADY MAYU AT HOME!
UGH!
YOU MORON! THIS HAS NOTHING TO DO WITH THAT!
?
ARUMA'S TWELVE YEARS OLD! WHAT DO YOU THINK I AM, A PERVERT?
YOU ARE VERY MUCH A CHILD YOURSELF STILL, YOUR HOLINESS.

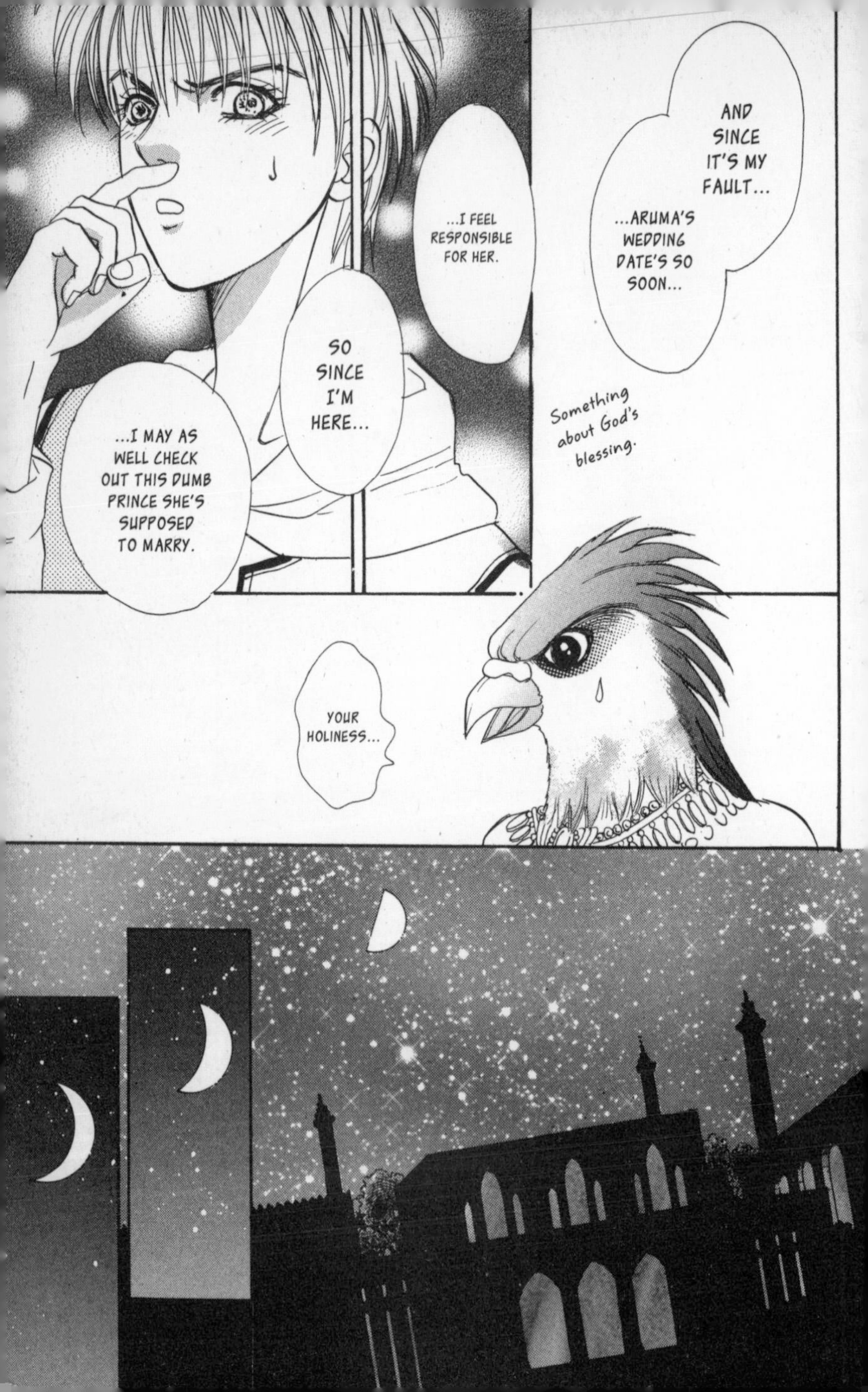
AND SINCE IT'S MY FAULT...
...ARUMA'S WEDDING DATE'S SO SOON...
Something about God's blessing.
...I FEEL RESPONSIBLE FOR HER.
SO SINCE I'M HERE...
...I MAY AS WELL CHECK OUT THIS DUMB PRINCE SHE'S SUPPOSED TO MARRY.
YOUR HOLINESS...

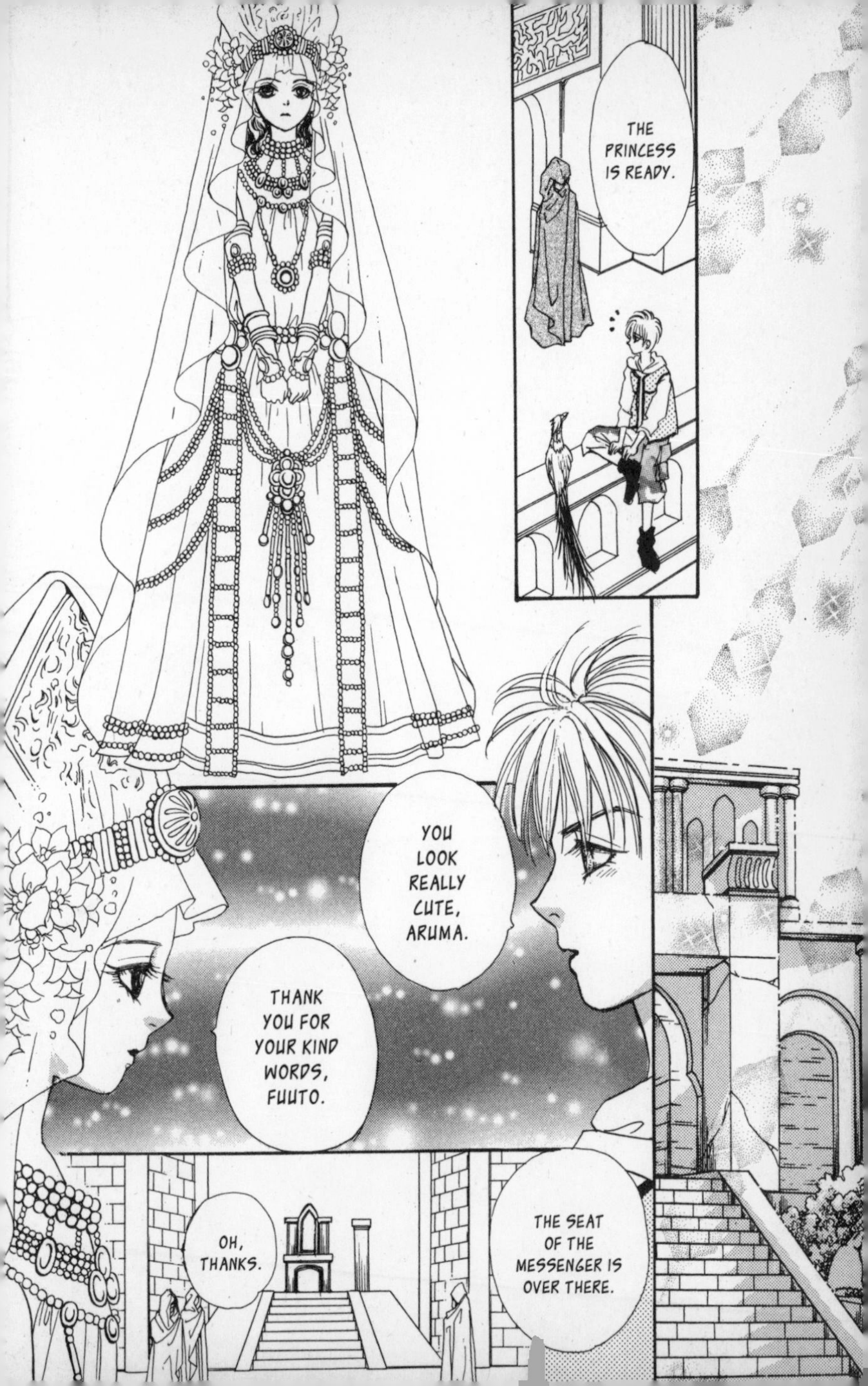
THE PRINCESS IS READY.
YOU LOOK REALLY CUTE, ARUMA.
THANK YOU FOR YOUR KIND WORDS, FUUTO.
THE SEAT OF THE MESSENGER IS OVER THERE.
OH, THANKS.

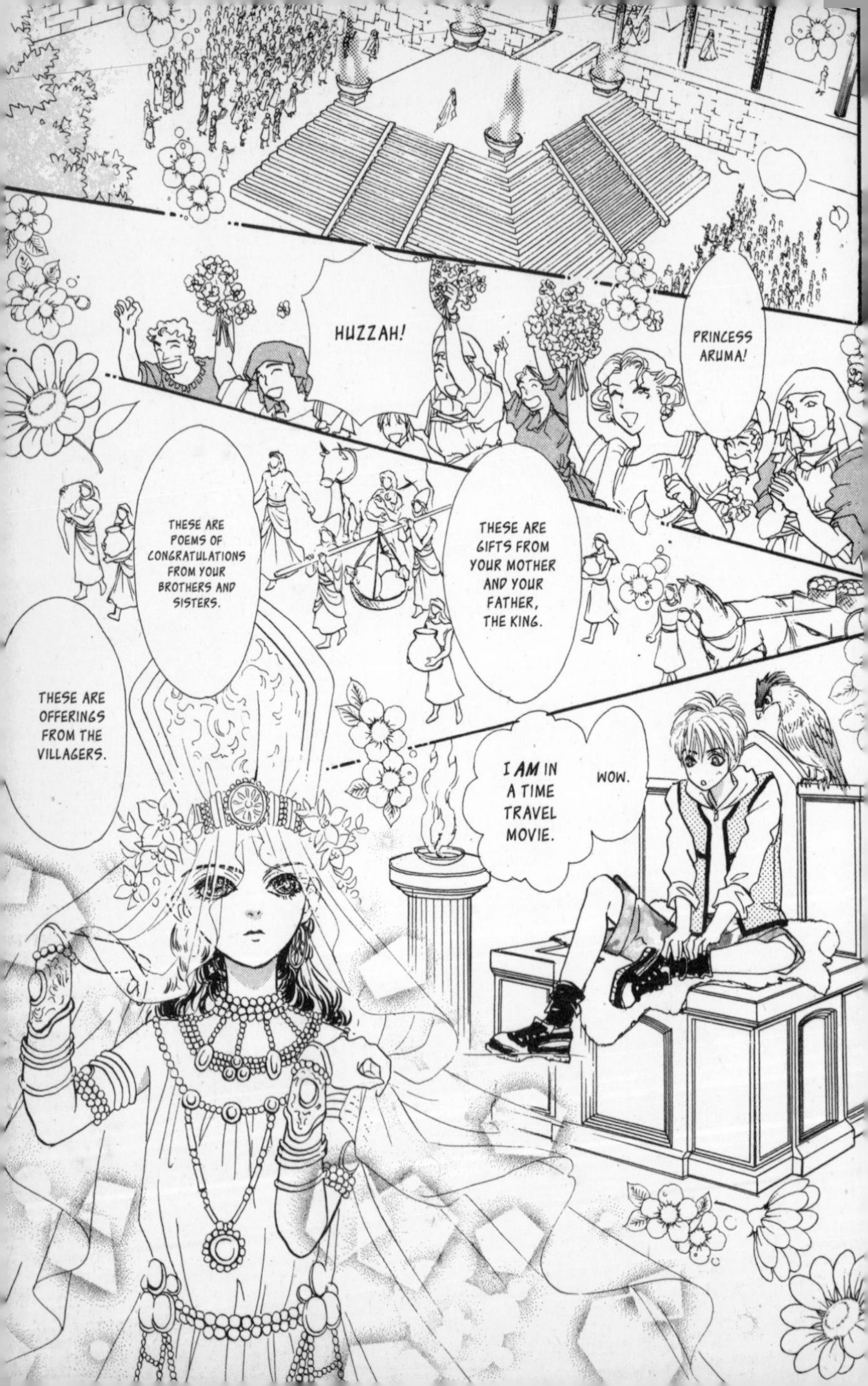
HUZZAH!
PRINCESS ARUMA!
THESE ARE POEMS OF CONGRATULATIONS FROM YOUR BROTHERS AND SISTERS.
THESE ARE GIFTS FROM YOUR MOTHER AND YOUR FATHER, THE KING.
THESE ARE OFFERINGS FROM THE VILLAGERS.
WOW.
I AM IN A TIME TRAVEL MOVIE.

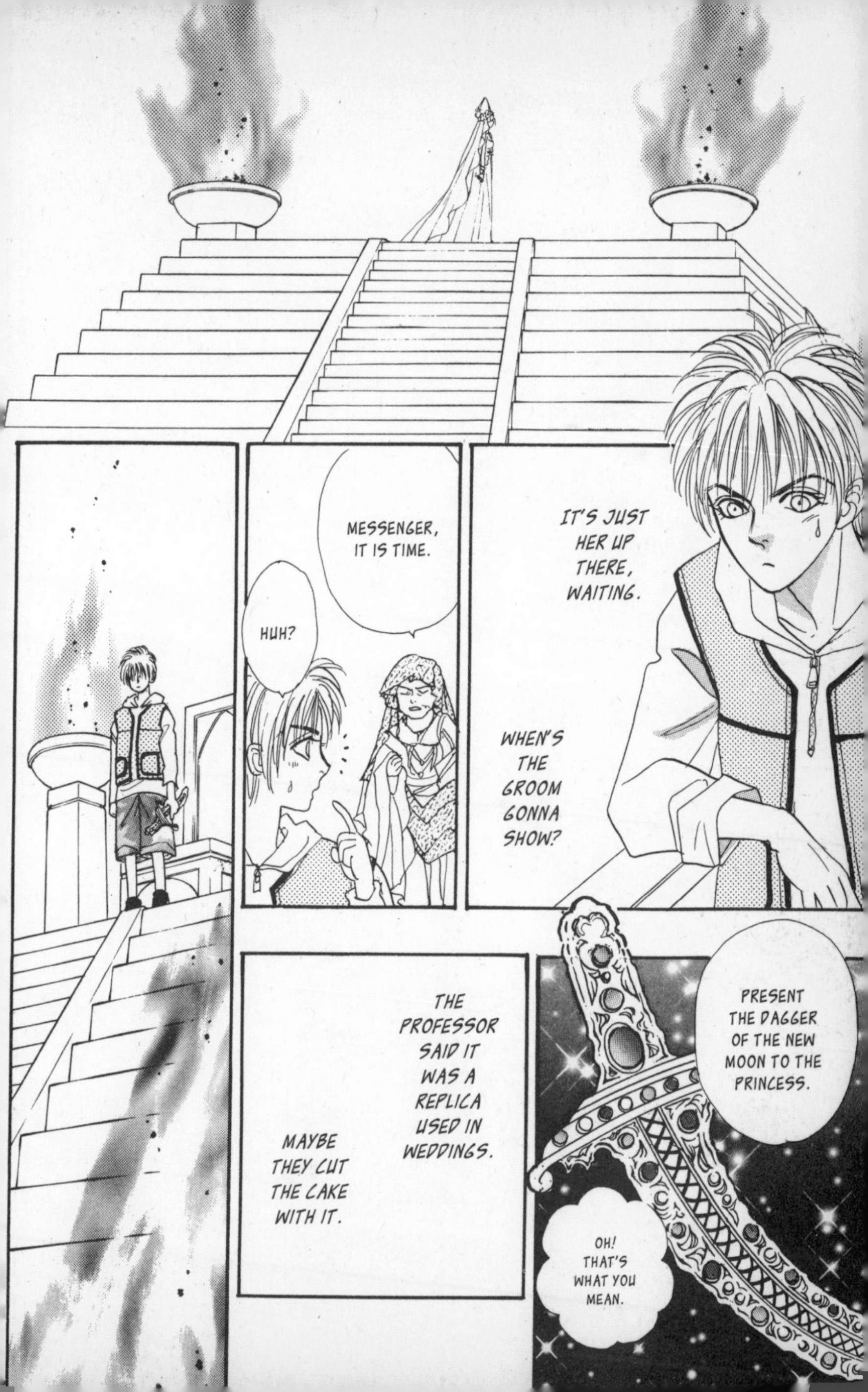
IT'S JUST HER UP THERE, WAITING.
WHEN'S THE GROOM GONNA SHOW?
MESSENGER, IT IS TIME.
HUH?
PRESENT THE DAGGER OF THE NEW MOON TO THE PRINCESS.
OH! THAT'S WHAT YOU MEAN.
THE PROFESSOR SAID IT WAS A REPLICA USED IN WEDDINGS.
MAYBE THEY CUT THE CAKE WITH IT.

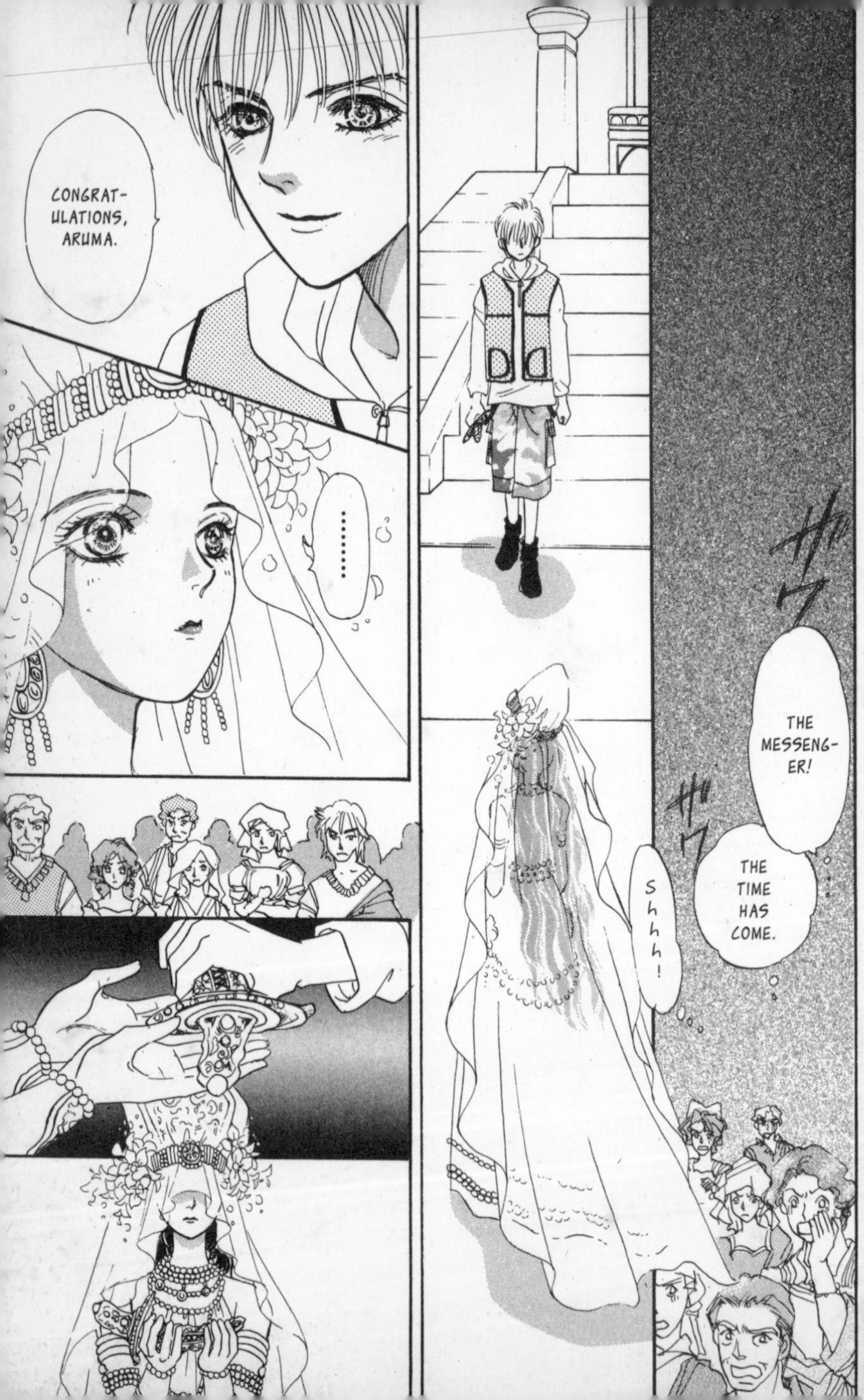

ザワ
THE MESSENG-ER!
ザワ
THE TIME HAS COME.
Shhh!
CONGRAT-ULATIONS, ARUMA.
....

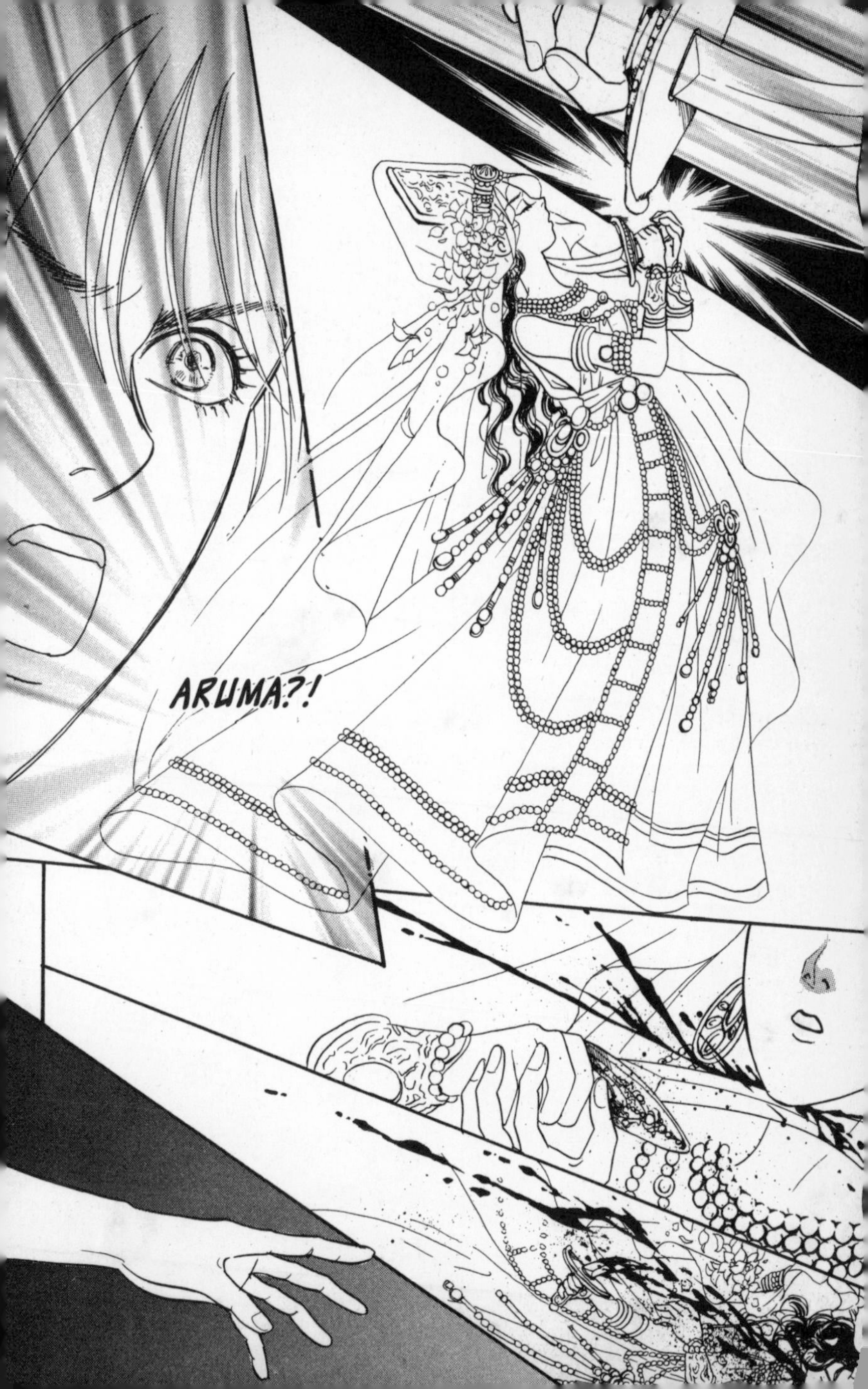
ARUMA?!

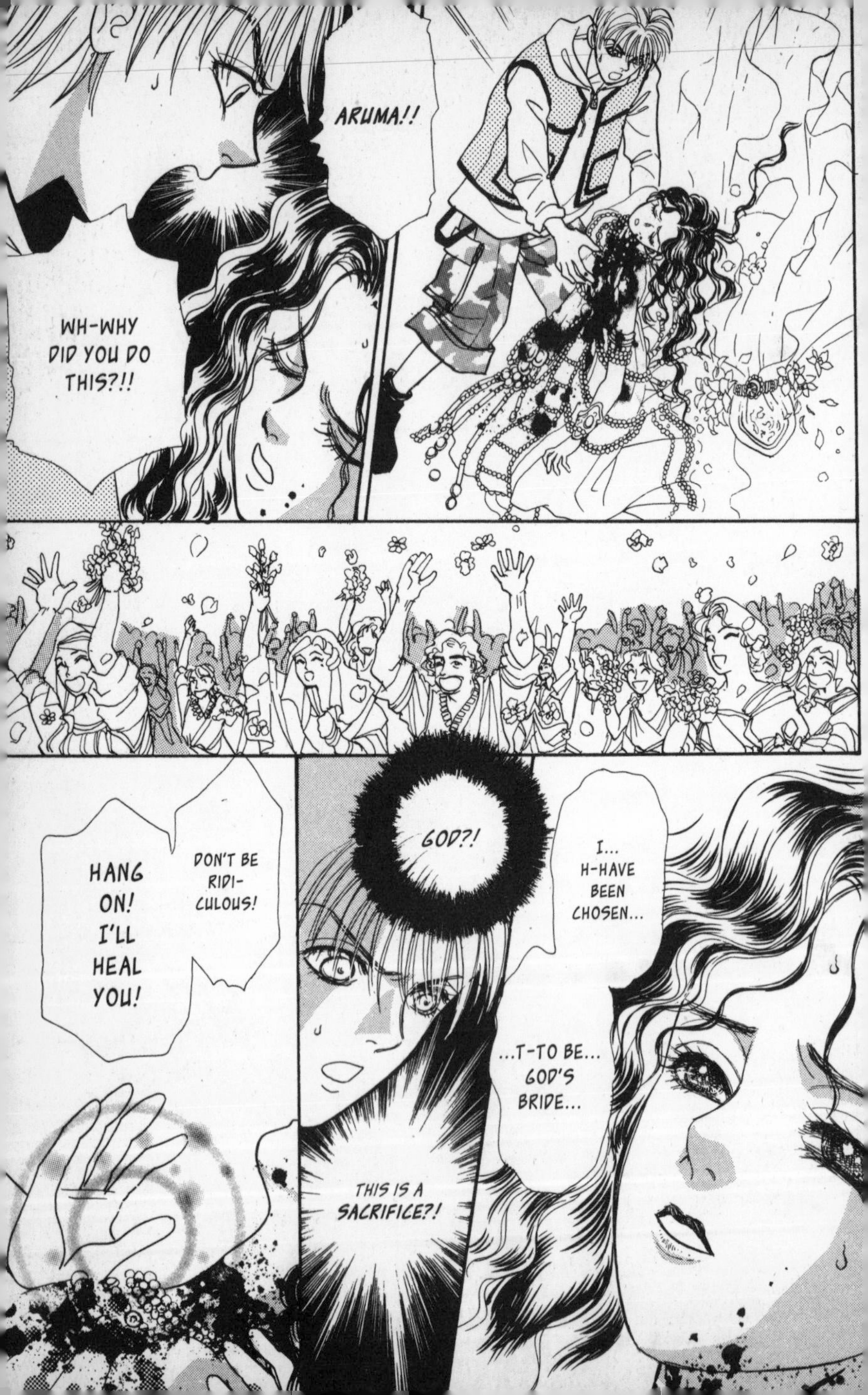
ARUMA!!
WH-WHY DID YOU DO THIS?!!
I... H-HAVE BEEN CHOSEN...
...T-TO BE... GOD'S BRIDE...
GOD?!
THIS IS A SACRIFICE?!
DON'T BE RIDI-CULOUS!
HANG ON! I'LL HEAL YOU!

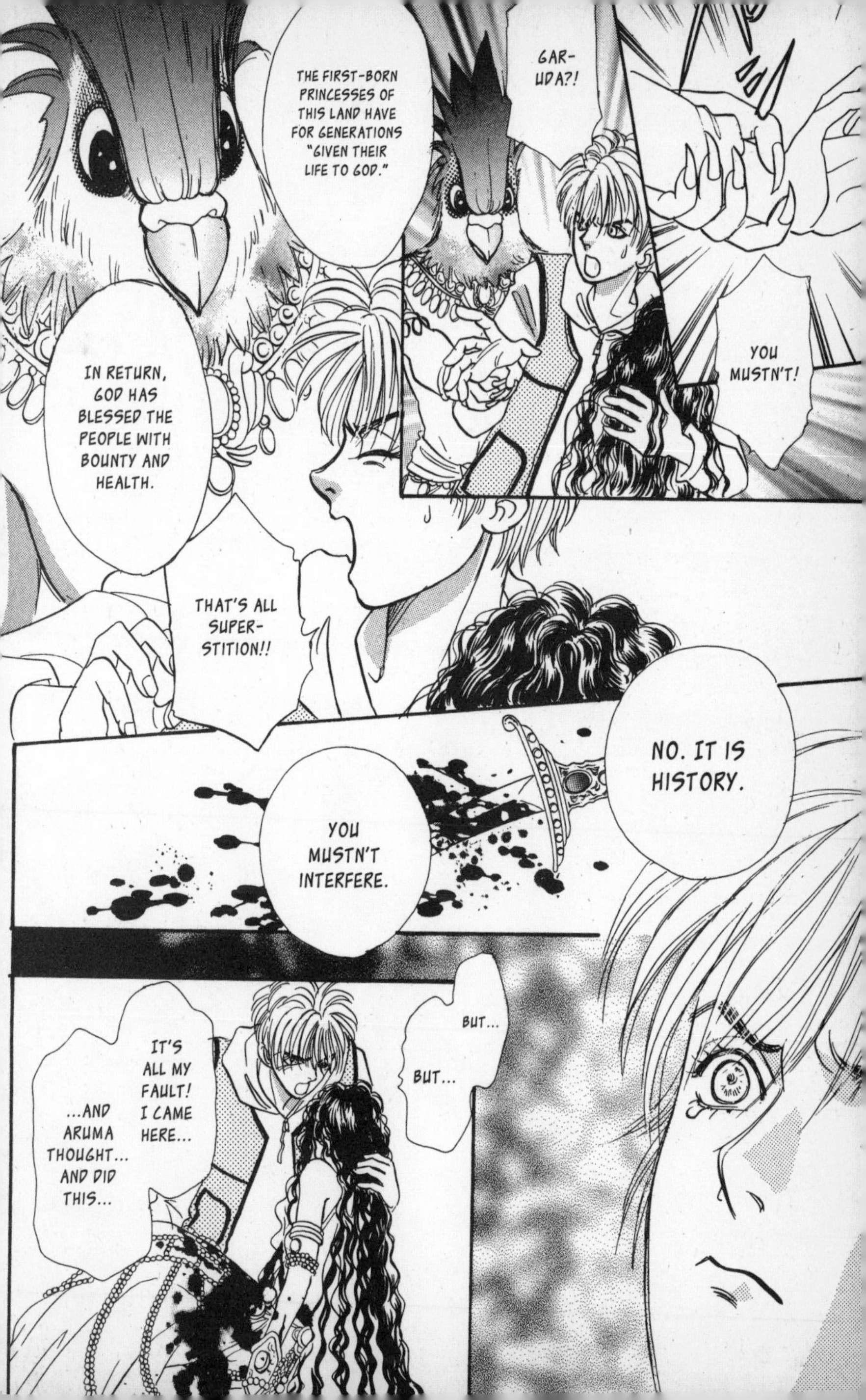
YOU MUSTN'T!
GAR-UDA?!
THE FIRST-BORN PRINCESSES OF THIS LAND HAVE FOR GENERATIONS "GIVEN THEIR LIFE TO GOD."
IN RETURN, GOD HAS BLESSED THE PEOPLE WITH BOUNTY AND HEALTH.
THAT'S ALL SUPER-STITION!!
NO. IT IS HISTORY.
YOU MUSTN'T INTERFERE.
BUT...
BUT...
IT'S ALL MY FAULT! I CAME HERE...
...AND ARUMA THOUGHT... AND DID THIS...

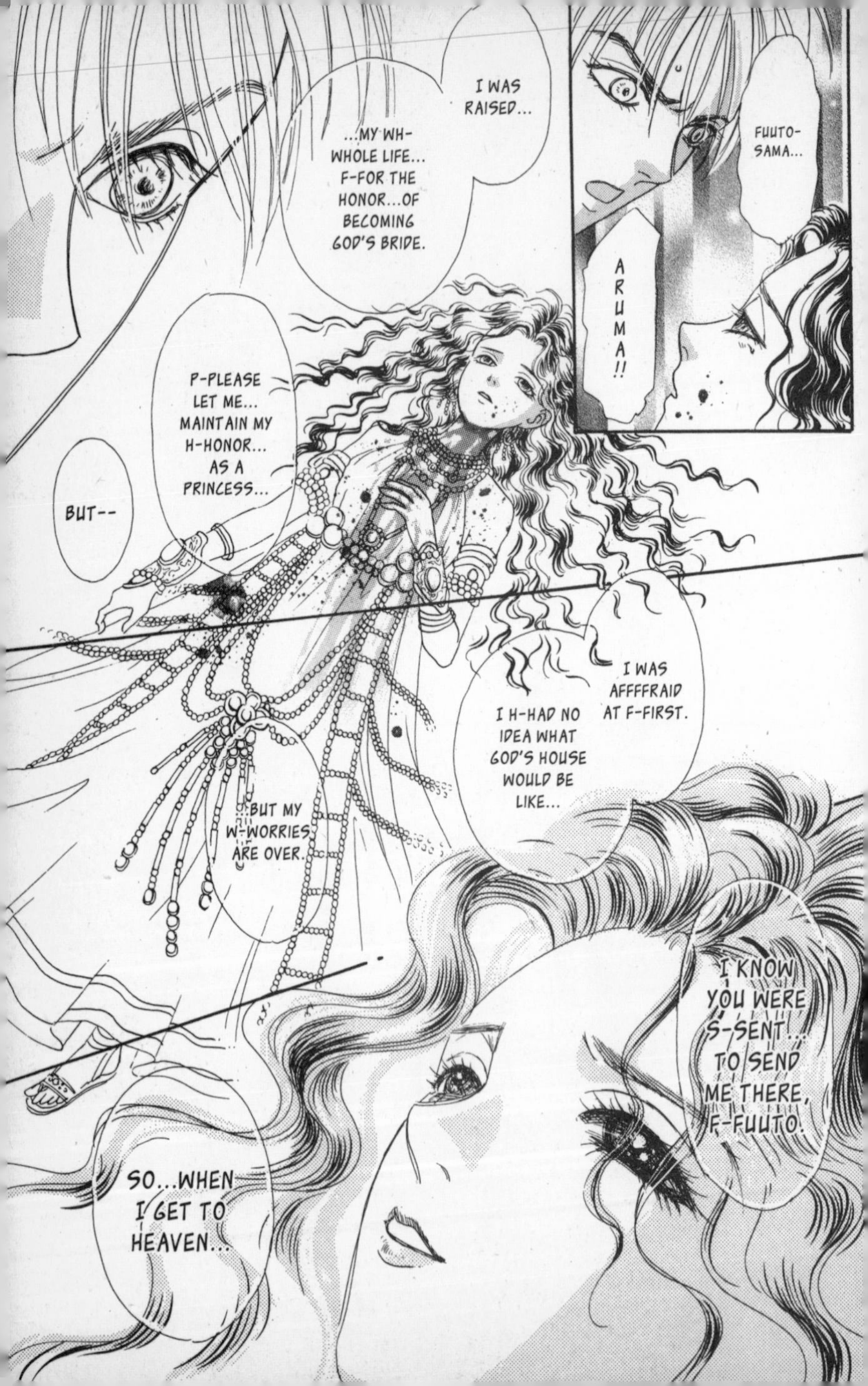
FUUTO-SAMA...
ARUMA!!
I WAS RAISED...
...MY WH-WHOLE LIFE... F-FOR THE HONOR...OF BECOMING GOD'S BRIDE.
P-PLEASE LET ME... MAINTAIN MY H-HONOR... AS A PRINCESS...
BUT--
I WAS AFFFFRAID AT F-FIRST.
I H-HAD NO IDEA WHAT GOD'S HOUSE WOULD BE LIKE...
...BUT MY W-WORRIES ARE OVER.
I KNOW YOU WERE S-SENT... TO SEND ME THERE, F-FUUTO.
SO...WHEN I GET TO HEAVEN...

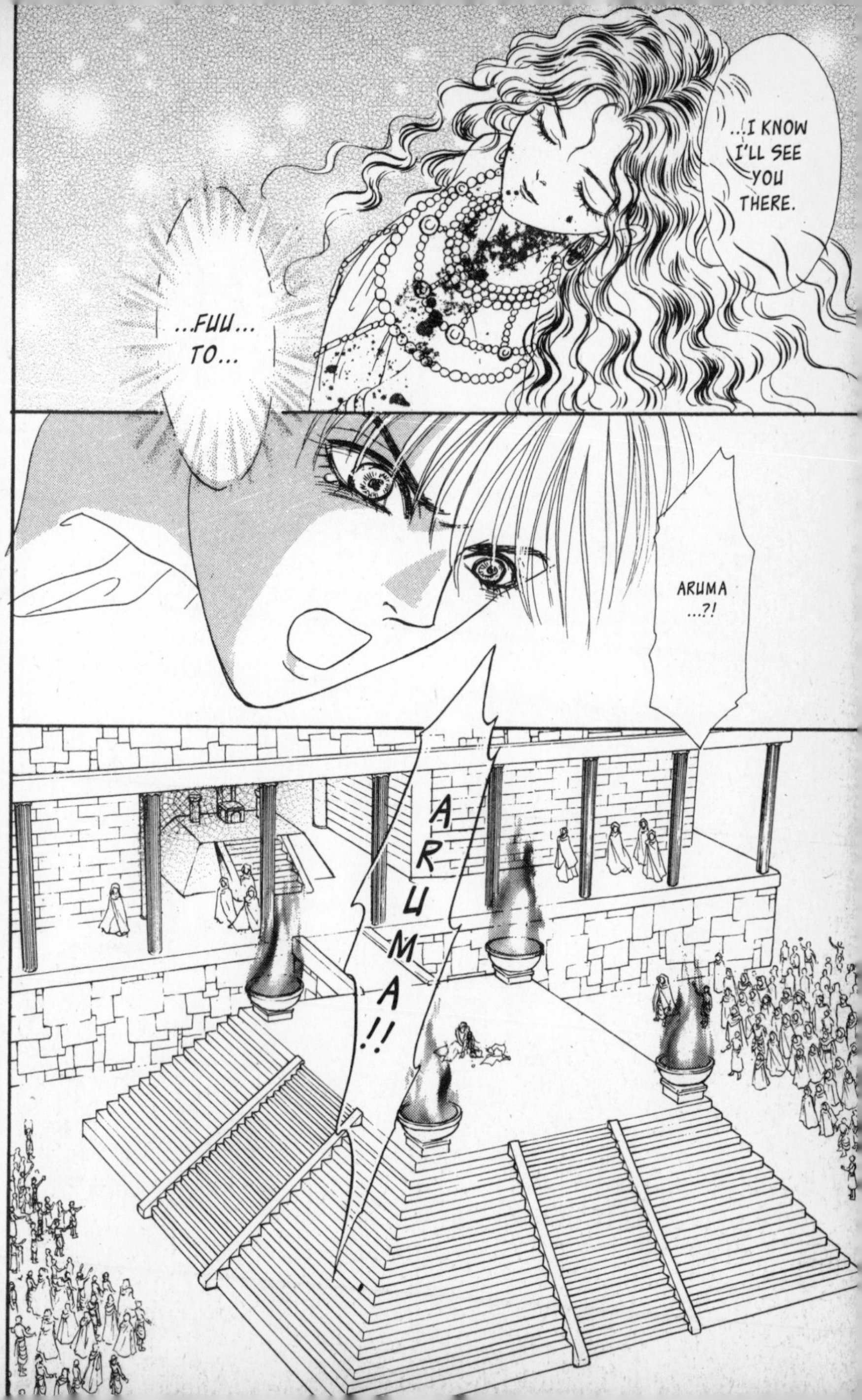
...I KNOW I'LL SEE YOU THERE.
...FUU... TO...
ARUMA ...?!
ARUMA!!

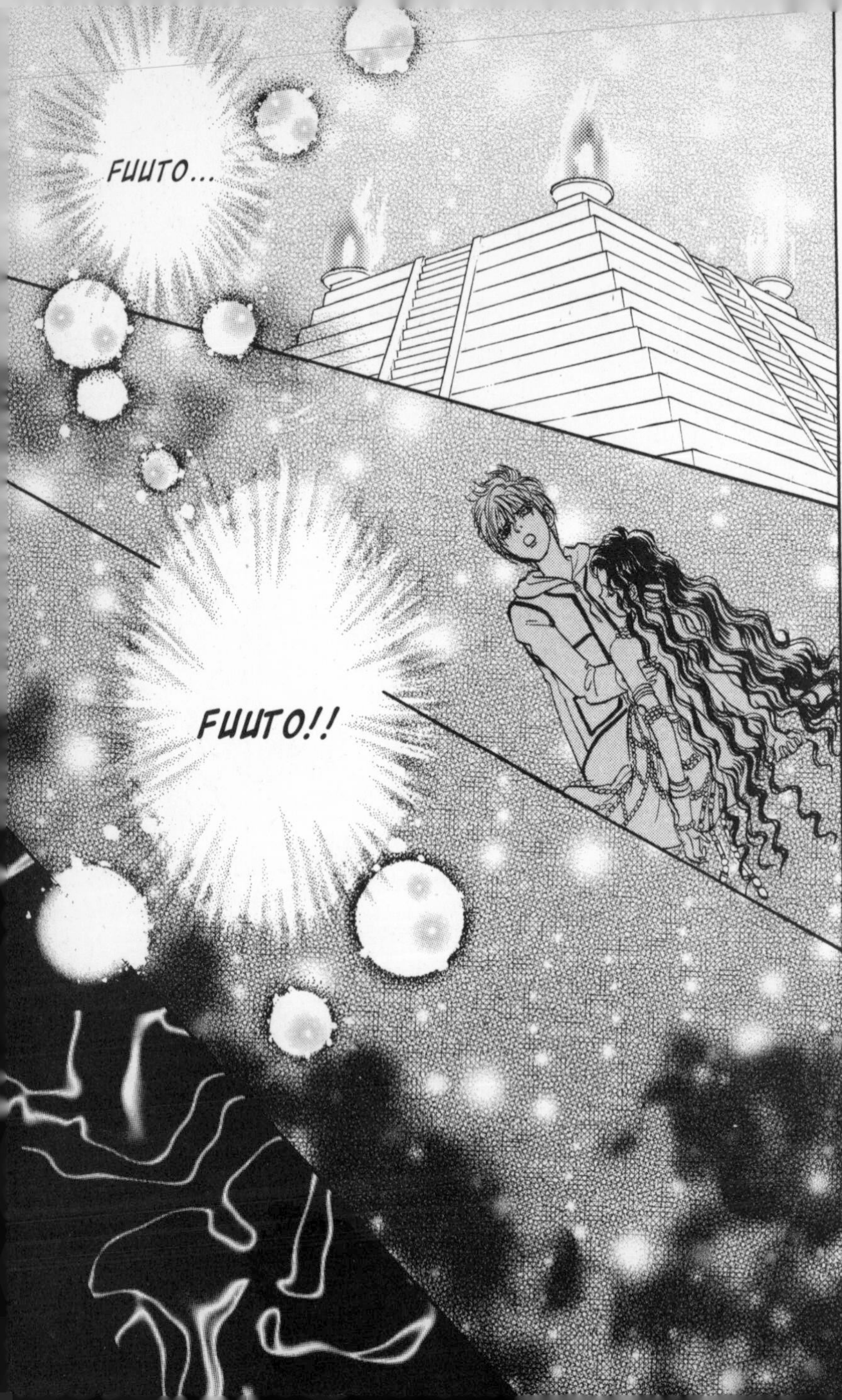
FUUTO...
FUUTO!!

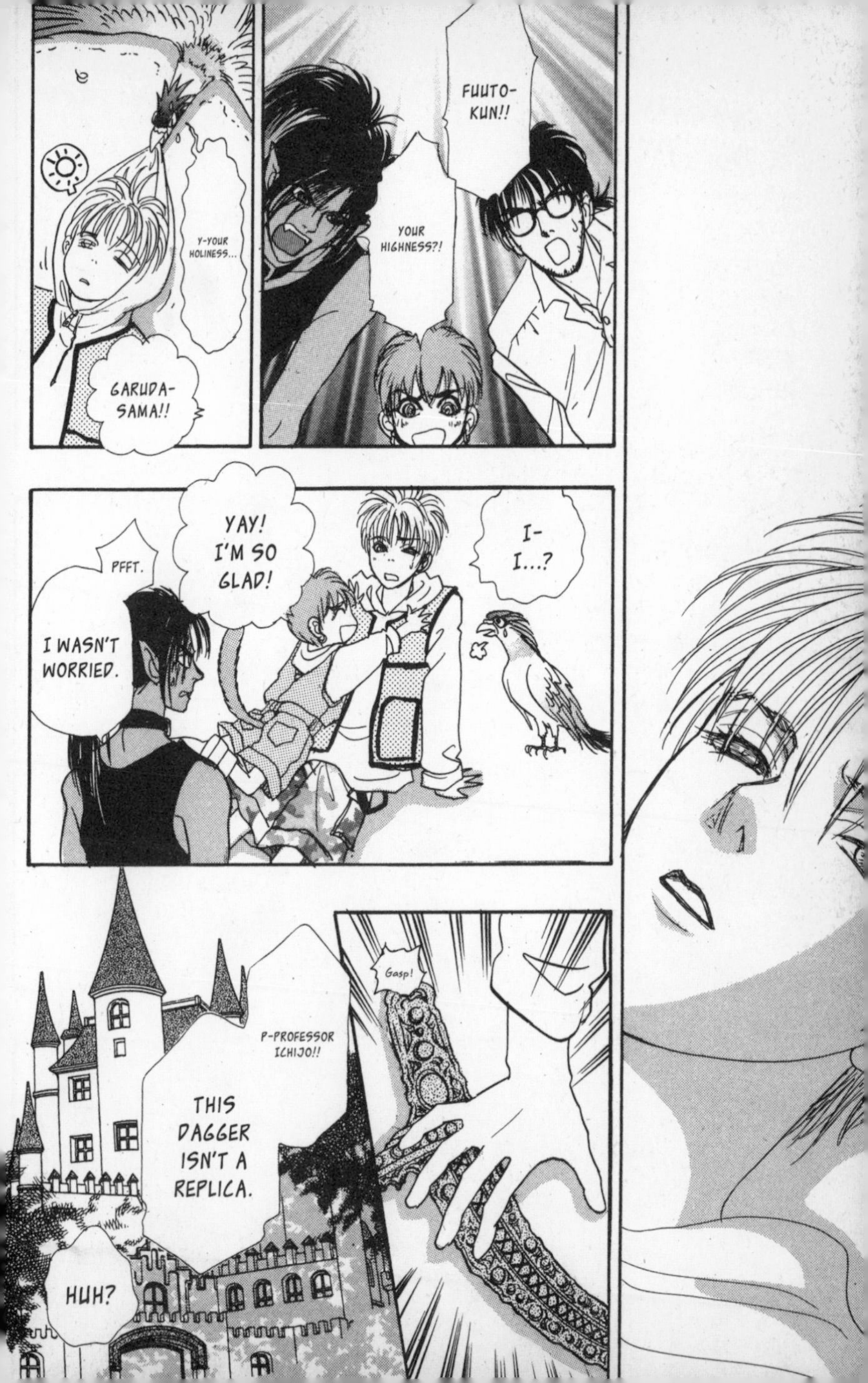
FUUTO-KUN!!
YOUR HIGHNESS?!
Y-YOUR HOLINESS...
GARUDA-SAMA!!
I- I...?
YAY! I'M SO GLAD!
PFFT.
I WASN'T WORRIED.
Gasp!
P-PROFESSOR ICHIJO!!
THIS DAGGER ISN'T A REPLICA.
HUH?

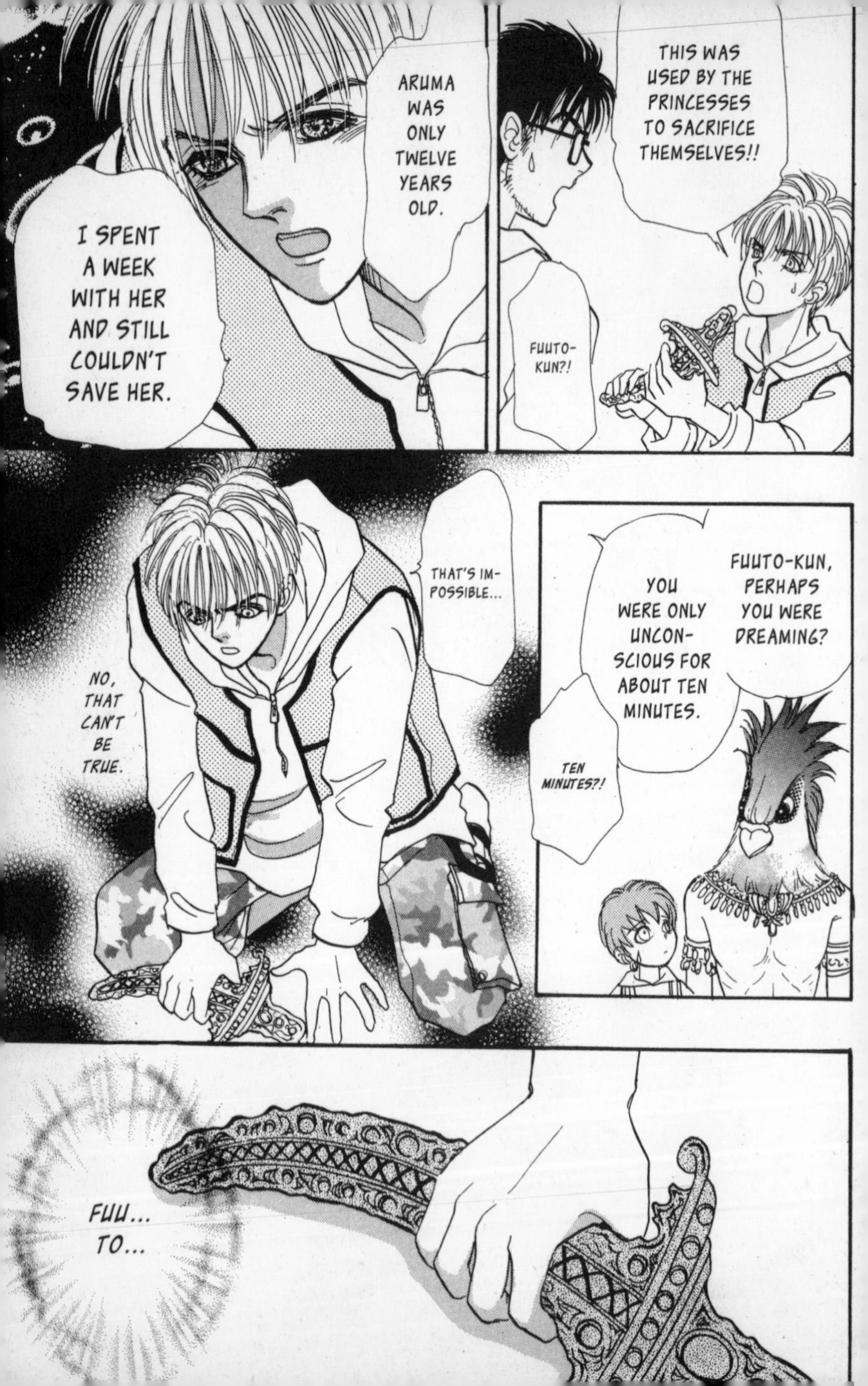
THIS WAS USED BY THE PRINCESSES TO SACRIFICE THEMSELVES!!
FUUTO-KUN?!
ARUMA WAS ONLY TWELVE YEARS OLD.
I SPENT A WEEK WITH HER AND STILL COULDN'T SAVE HER.
FUUTO-KUN, PERHAPS YOU WERE DREAMING?
YOU WERE ONLY UNCONSCIOUS FOR ABOUT TEN MINUTES.
TEN MINUTES?!
THAT'S IMPOSSIBLE...
NO, THAT CAN'T BE TRUE.
FUU... TO...

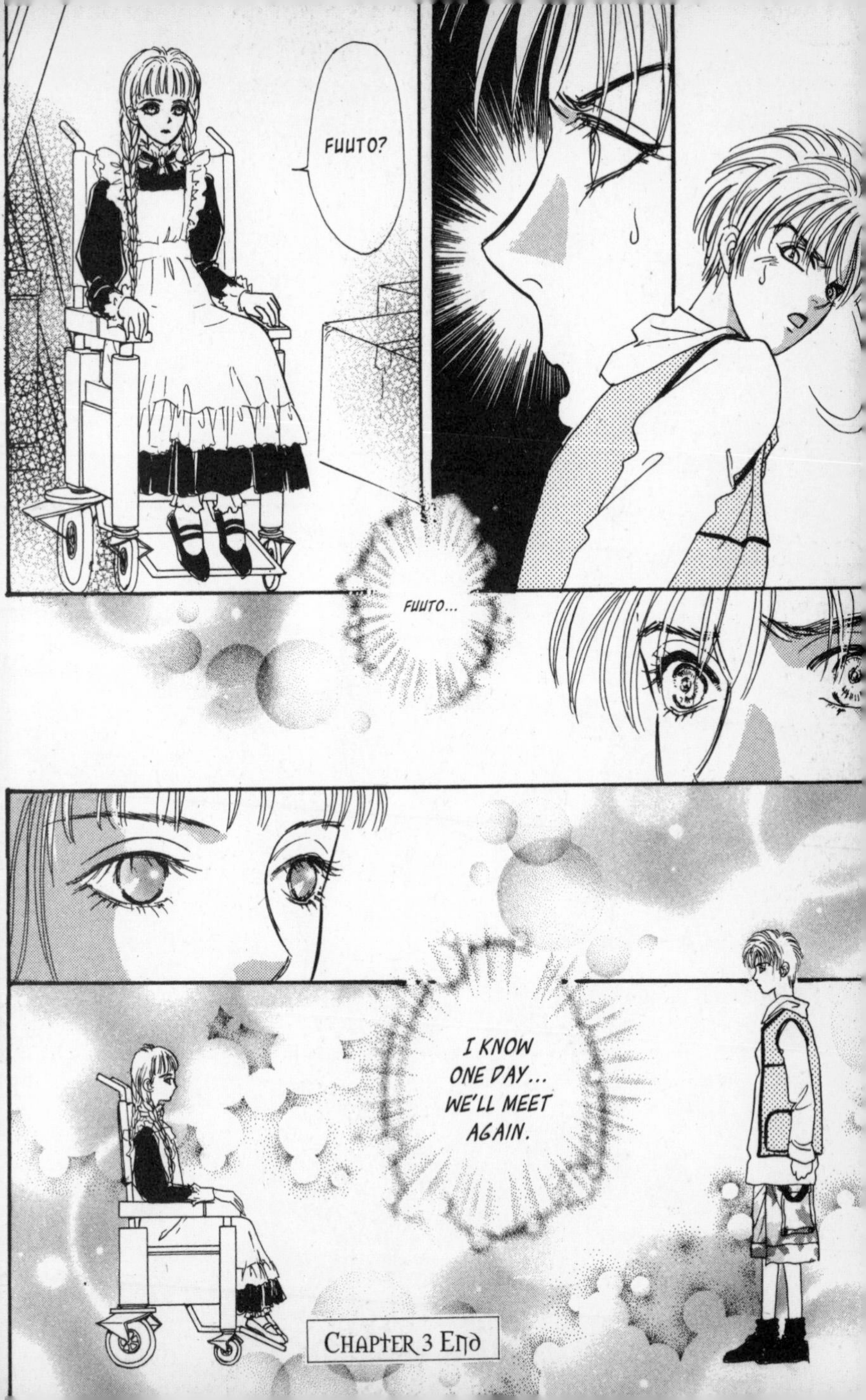
FUUTO?
FUUTO...
I KNOW ONE DAY... WE'LL MEET AGAIN.
Chapter 3 End

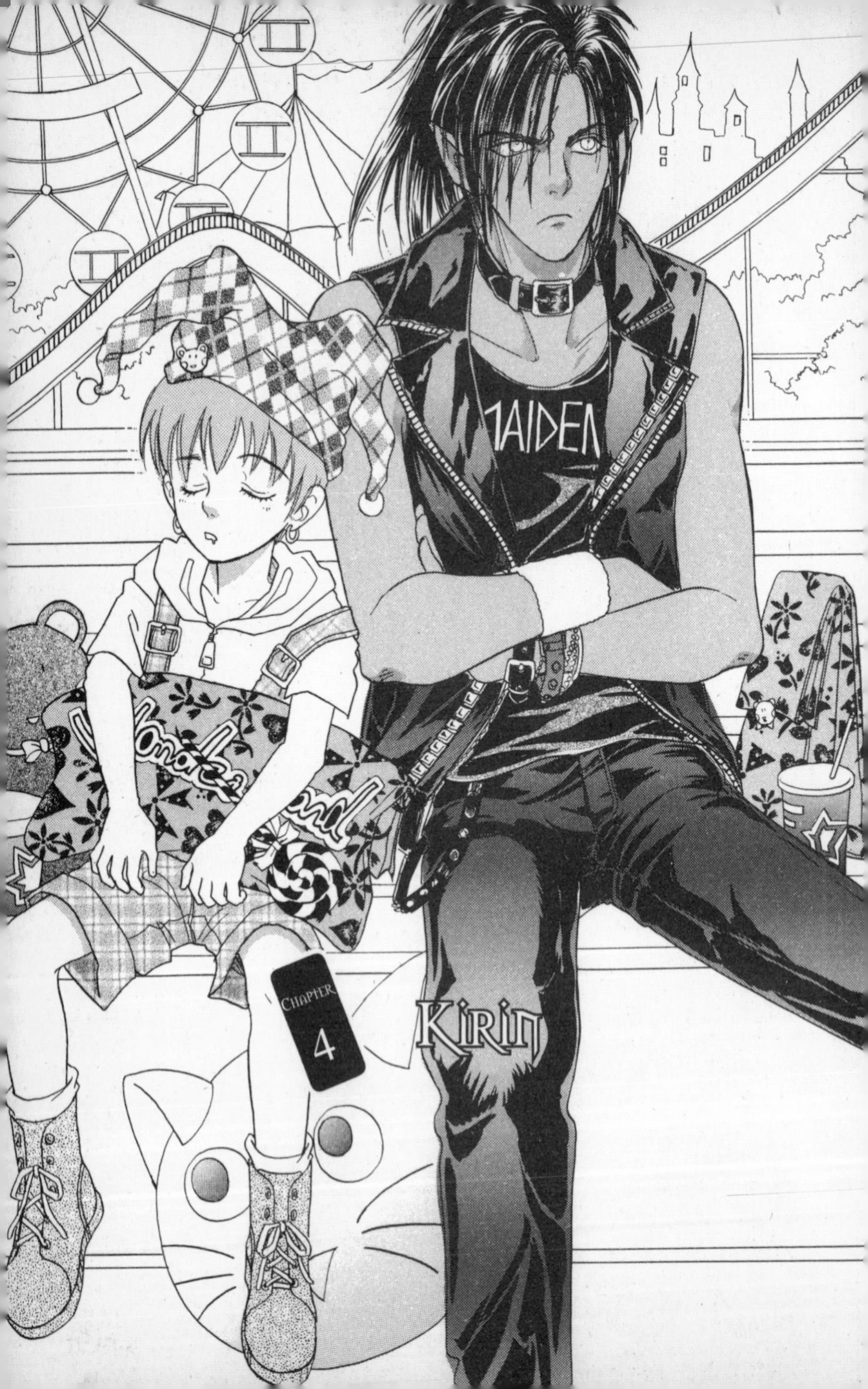

MAIDEN
Chapter
4
Kirin

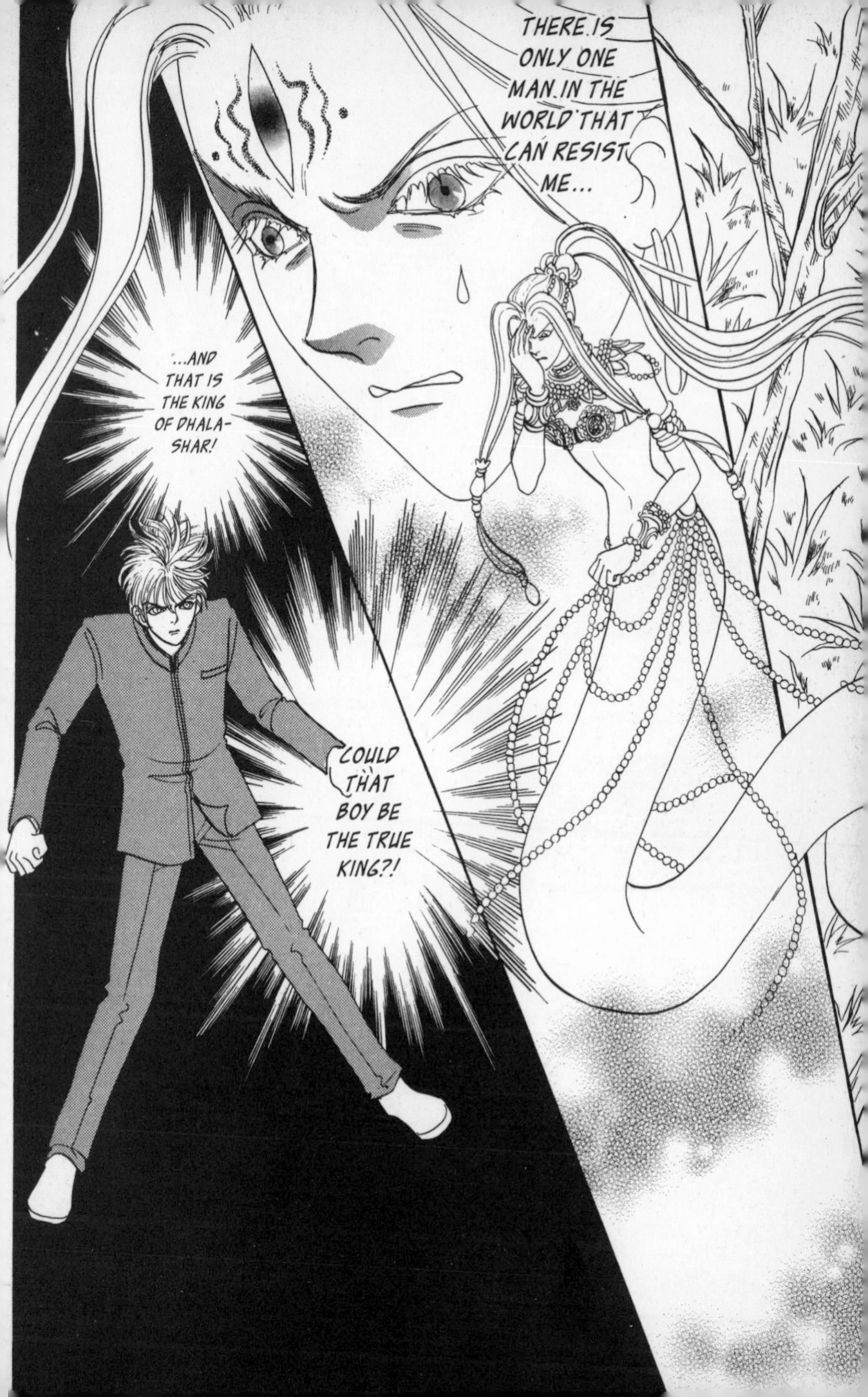
THERE IS ONLY ONE MAN IN THE WORLD THAT CAN RESIST ME...
...AND THAT IS THE KING OF DHALA-SHAR!
COULD THAT BOY BE THE TRUE KING?!

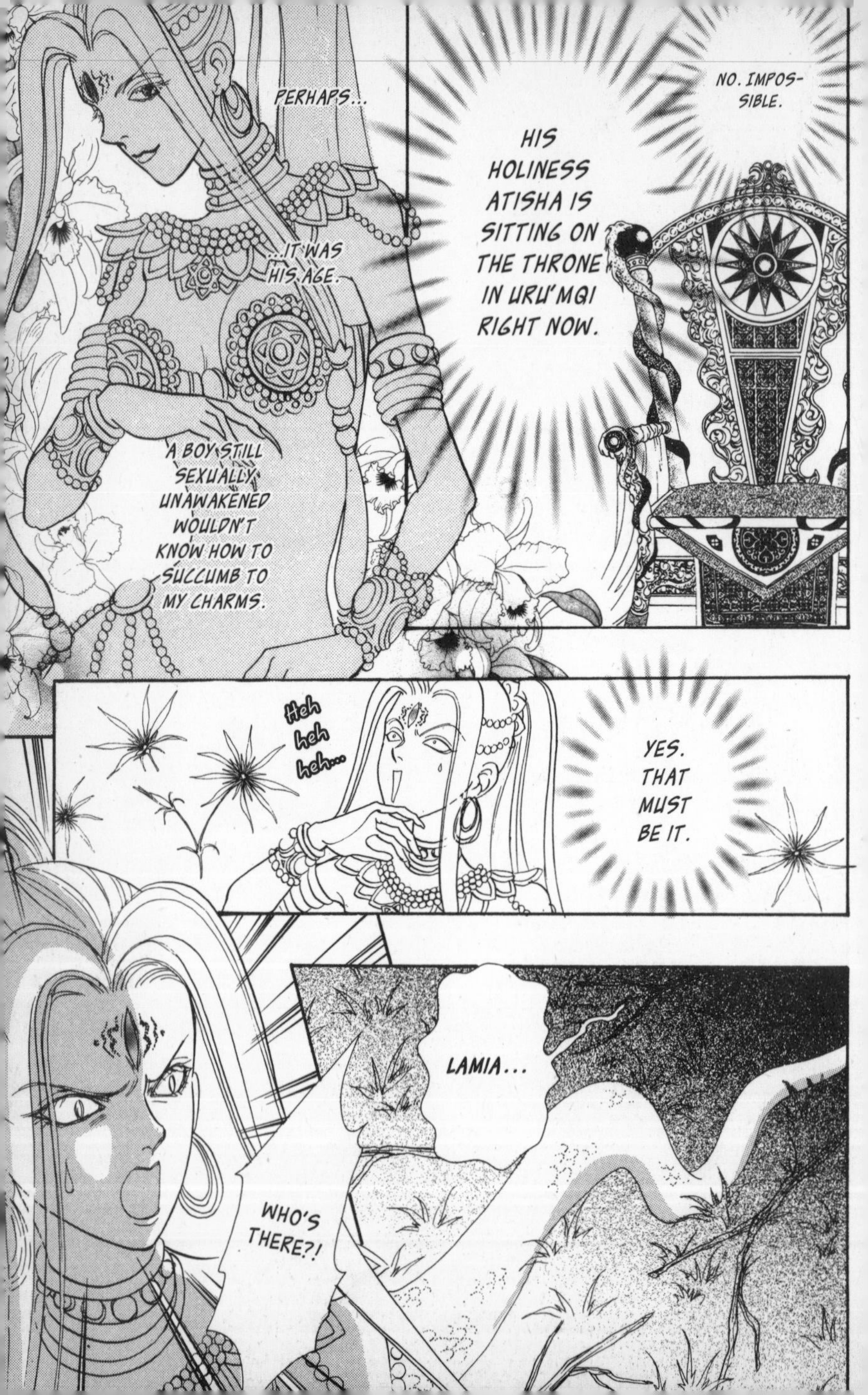
NO. IMPOSSIBLE.
HIS HOLINESS ATISHA IS SITTING ON THE THRONE IN URU'MQI RIGHT NOW.
PERHAPS...
...IT WAS HIS AGE.
A BOY STILL SEXUALLY UNAWAKENED WOULDN'T KNOW HOW TO SUCCUMB TO MY CHARMS.
YES. THAT MUST BE IT.
Heh heh heh...
LAMIA...
WHO'S THERE?!

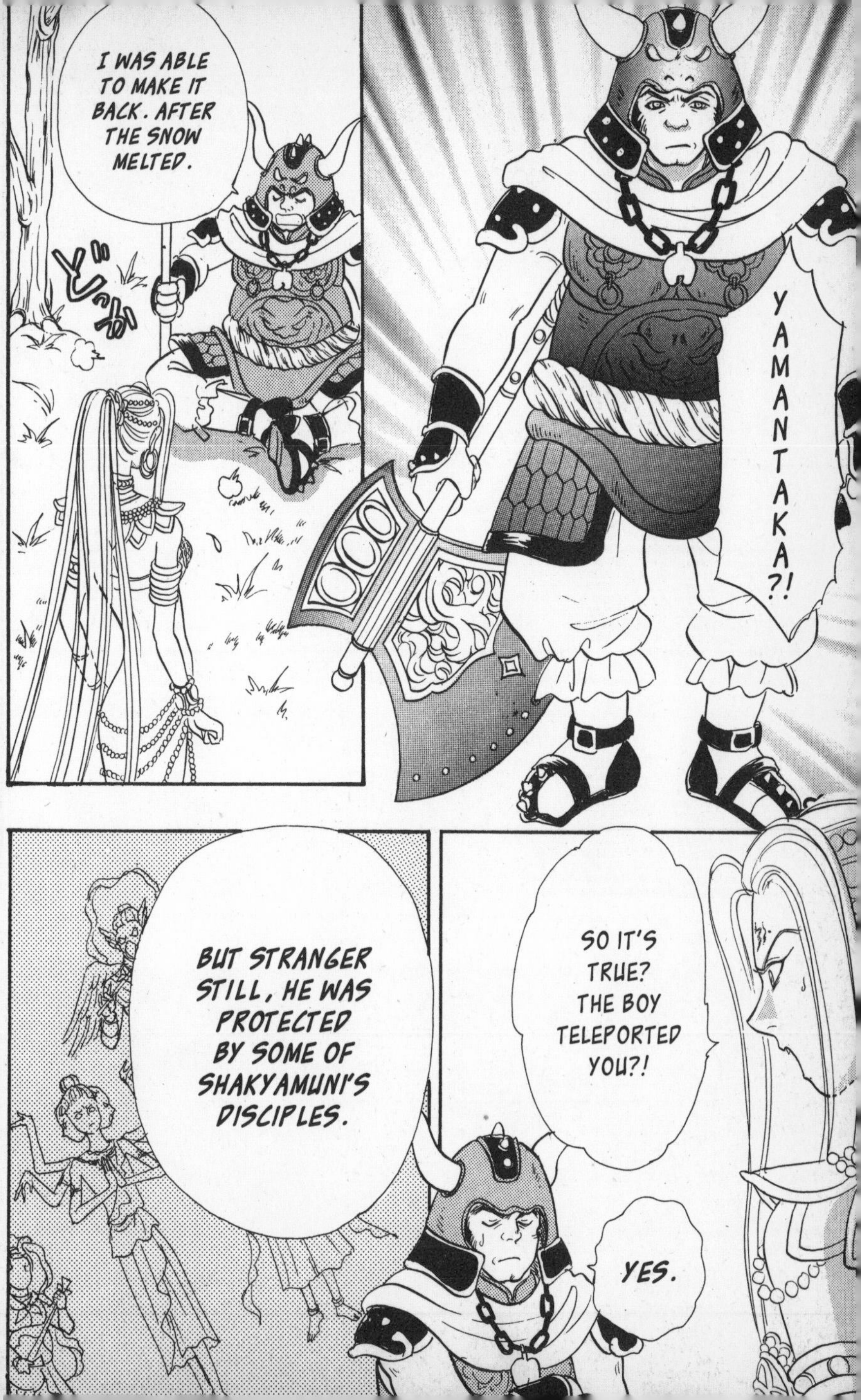

I WAS ABLE TO MAKE IT BACK. AFTER THE SNOW MELTED.
YAMANTAKA?!
SO IT'S TRUE? THE BOY TELEPORTED YOU?!
YES.
BUT STRANGER STILL, HE WAS PROTECTED BY SOME OF SHAKYAMUNI'S DISCIPLES.

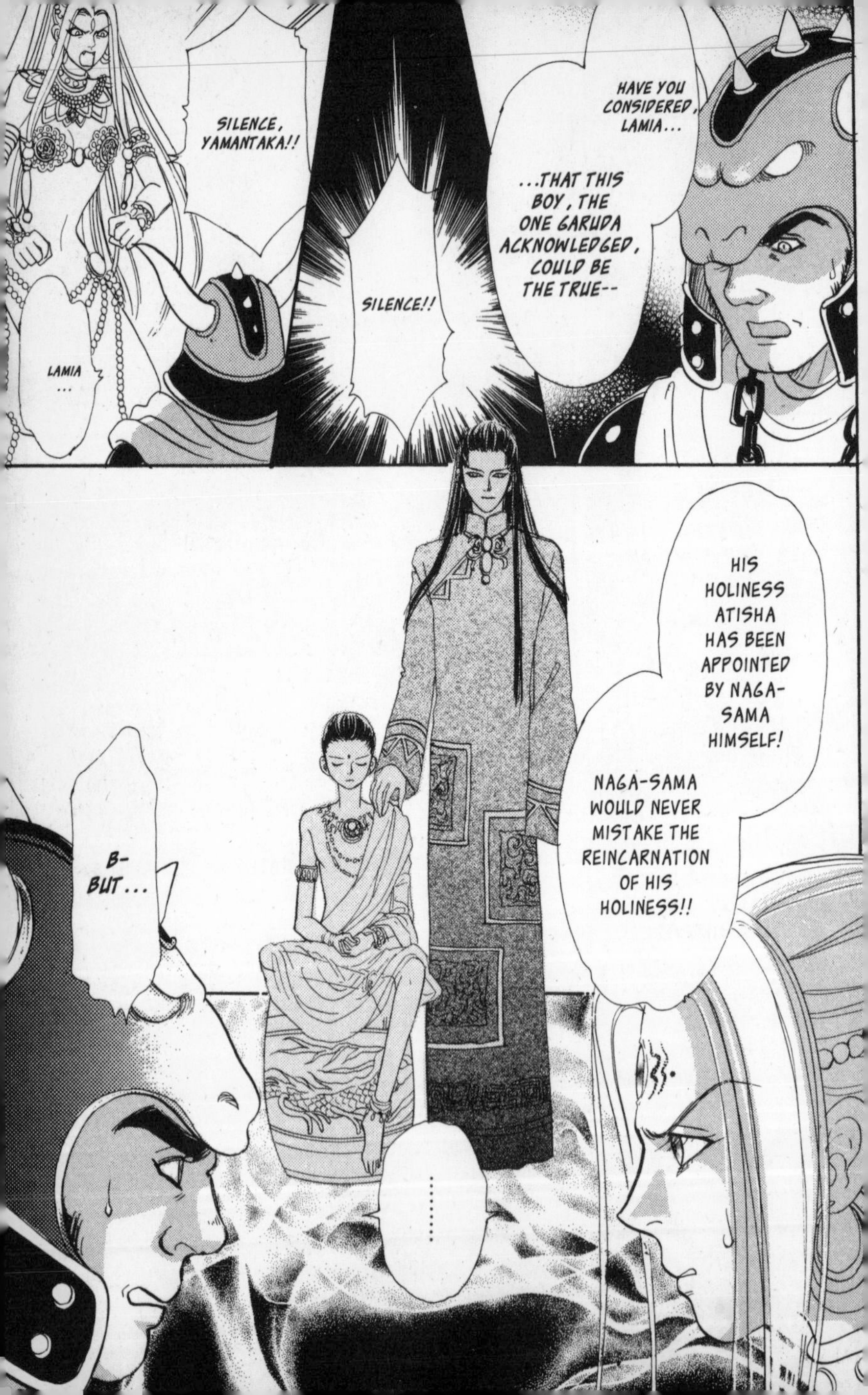
HAVE YOU CONSIDERED, LAMIA...
...THAT THIS BOY, THE ONE GARUDA ACKNOWLEDGED, COULD BE THE TRUE--
SILENCE!!
SILENCE, YAMANTAKA!!
LAMIA ...
HIS HOLINESS ATISHA HAS BEEN APPOINTED BY NAGA-SAMA HIMSELF!
NAGA-SAMA WOULD NEVER MISTAKE THE REINCARNATION OF HIS HOLINESS!!
B-BUT...
......

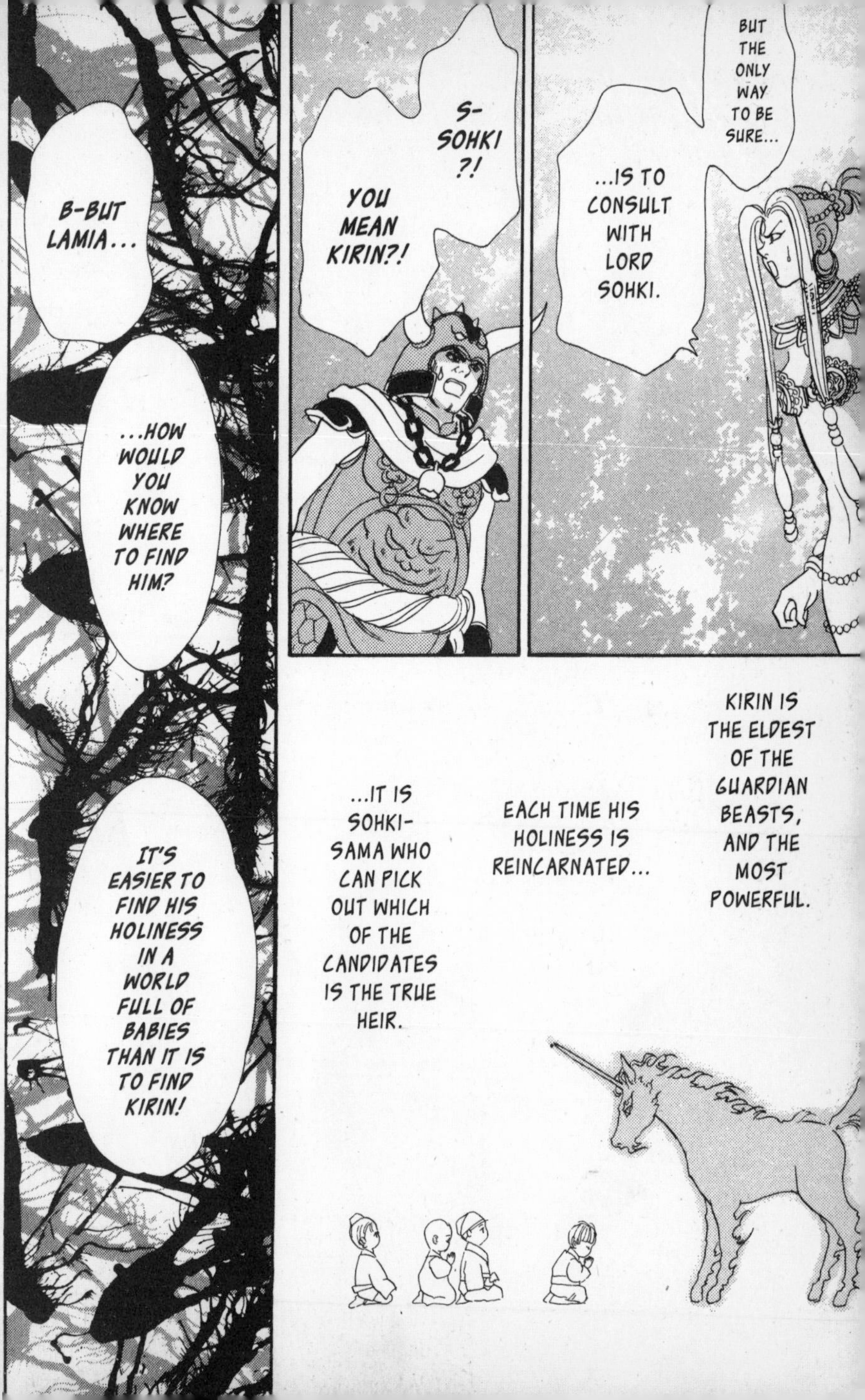
BUT THE ONLY WAY TO BE SURE...
...IS TO CONSULT WITH LORD SOHKI.
S- SOHKI ?!
YOU MEAN KIRIN?!
KIRIN IS THE ELDEST OF THE GUARDIAN BEASTS, AND THE MOST POWERFUL.
EACH TIME HIS HOLINESS IS REINCARNATED...
...IT IS SOHKI-SAMA WHO CAN PICK OUT WHICH OF THE CANDIDATES IS THE TRUE HEIR.
B-BUT LAMIA...
...HOW WOULD YOU KNOW WHERE TO FIND HIM?
IT'S EASIER TO FIND HIS HOLINESS IN A WORLD FULL OF BABIES THAN IT IS TO FIND KIRIN!

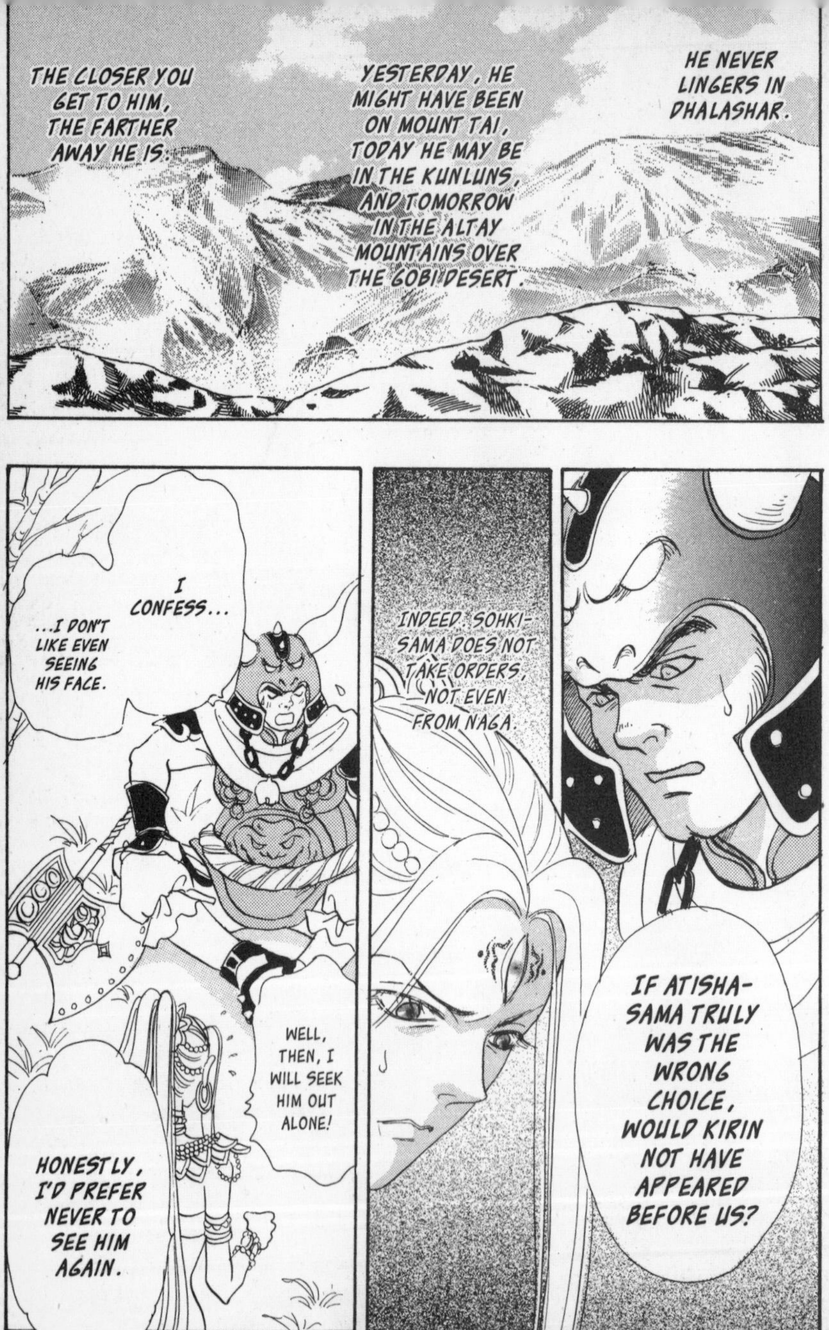
THE CLOSER YOU GET TO HIM, THE FARTHER AWAY HE IS.
YESTERDAY, HE MIGHT HAVE BEEN ON MOUNT TAI, TODAY HE MAY BE IN THE KUNLUNS, AND TOMORROW IN THE ALTAY MOUNTAINS OVER THE GOBI DESERT.
HE NEVER LINGERS IN DHALASHAR.
I CONFESS...
...I DON'T LIKE EVEN SEEING HIS FACE.
WELL, THEN, I WILL SEEK HIM OUT ALONE!
HONESTLY, I'D PREFER NEVER TO SEE HIM AGAIN.
INDEED. SOHKI-SAMA DOES NOT TAKE ORDERS, NOT EVEN FROM NAGA.
IF ATISHA-SAMA TRULY WAS THE WRONG CHOICE, WOULD KIRIN NOT HAVE APPEARED BEFORE US?

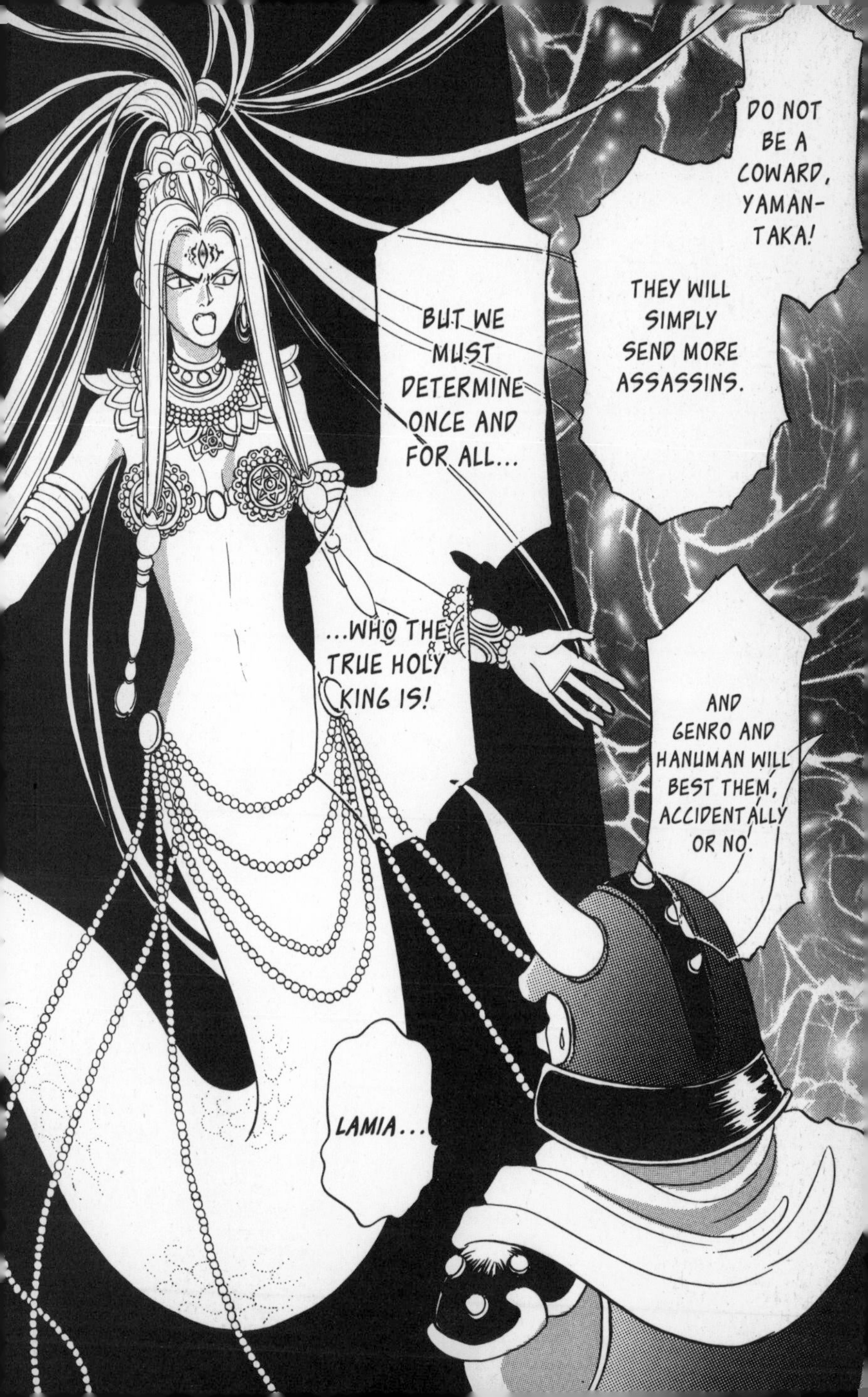
DO NOT BE A COWARD, YAMAN-TAKA!
THEY WILL SIMPLY SEND MORE ASSASSINS.
BUT WE MUST DETERMINE ONCE AND FOR ALL...
...WHO THE TRUE HOLY KING IS!
AND GENRO AND HANUMAN WILL BEST THEM, ACCIDENTALLY OR NO.
LAMIA...

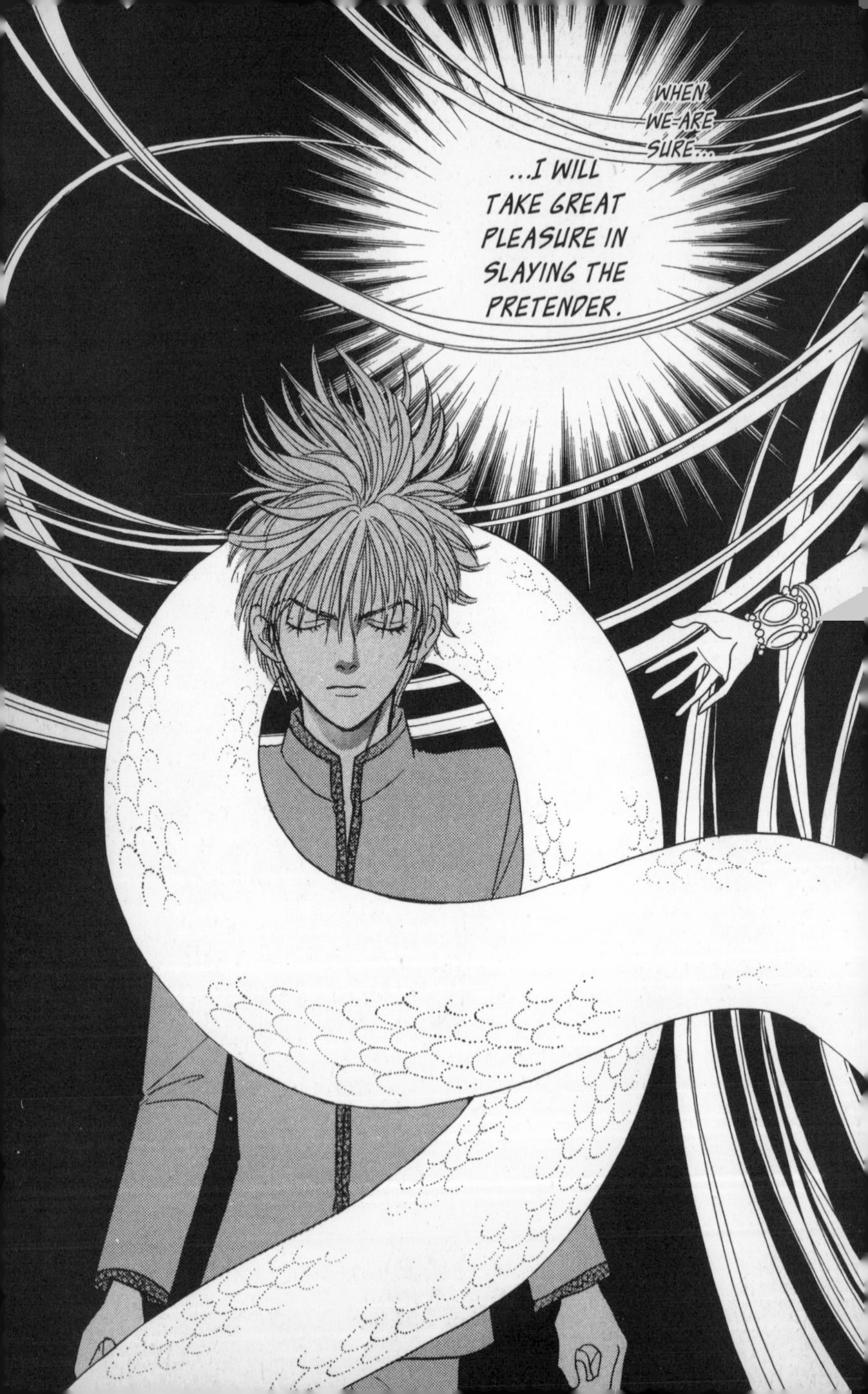
WHEN WE ARE SURE...
...I WILL TAKE GREAT PLEASURE IN SLAYING THE PRETENDER.

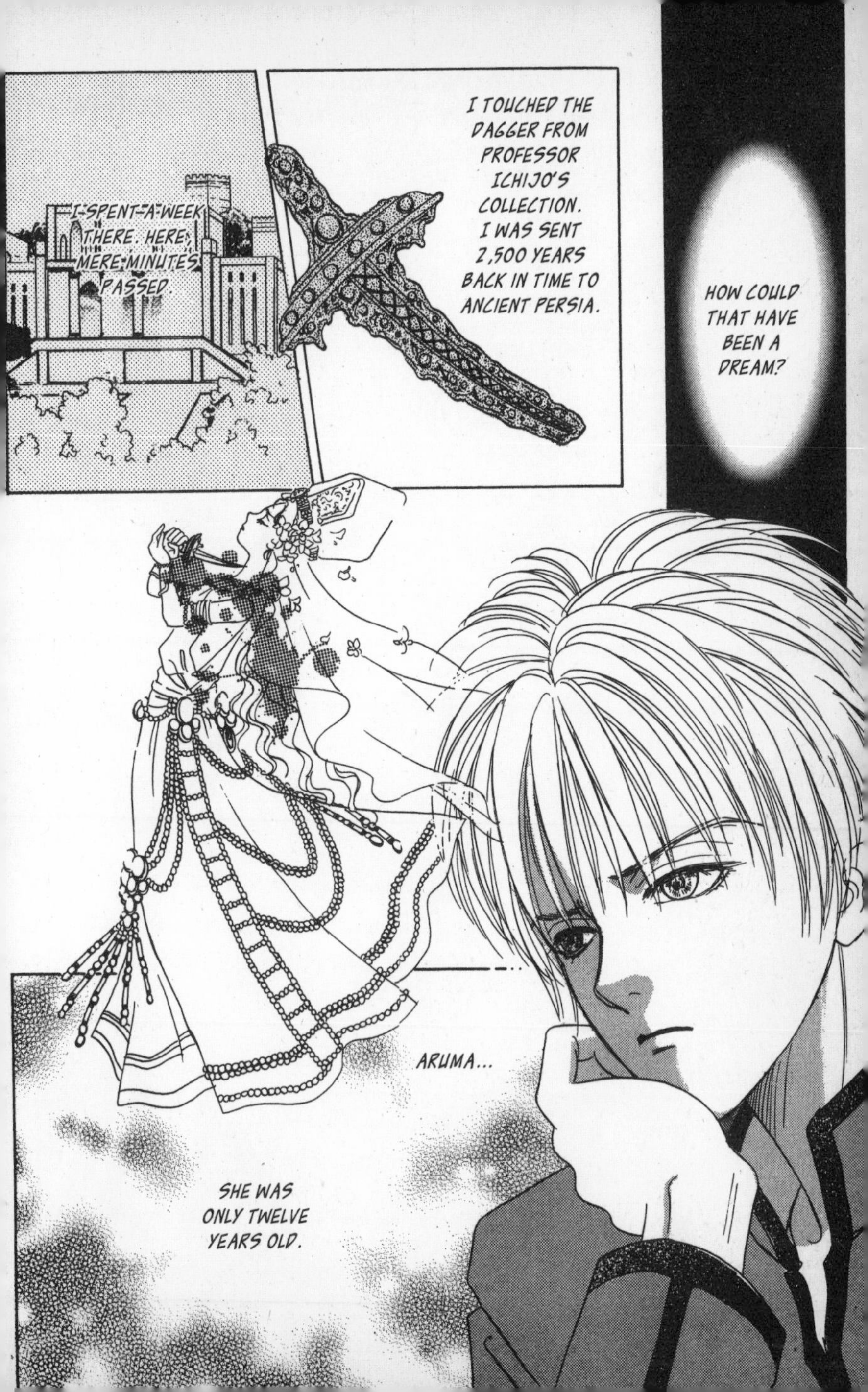

HOW COULD THAT HAVE BEEN A DREAM?
I TOUCHED THE DAGGER FROM PROFESSOR ICHIJO'S COLLECTION. I WAS SENT 2,500 YEARS BACK IN TIME TO ANCIENT PERSIA.
I SPENT A WEEK THERE. HERE, MERE MINUTES PASSED.
ARUMA...
SHE WAS ONLY TWELVE YEARS OLD.

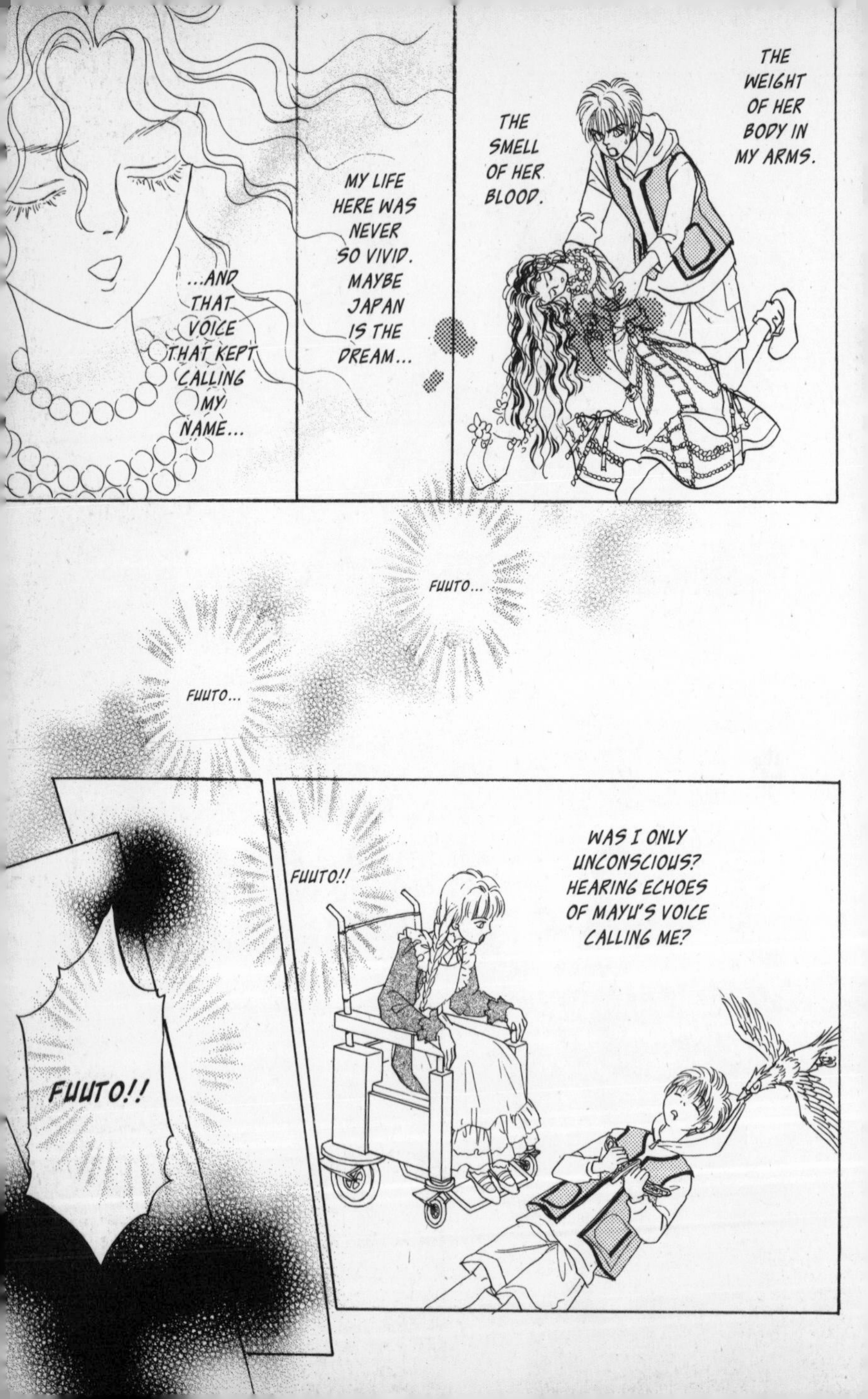
THE WEIGHT OF HER BODY IN MY ARMS.
THE SMELL OF HER BLOOD.
MY LIFE HERE WAS NEVER SO VIVID. MAYBE JAPAN IS THE DREAM...
...AND THAT VOICE THAT KEPT CALLING MY NAME...
FUUTO...
FUUTO...
WAS I ONLY UNCONSCIOUS? HEARING ECHOES OF MAYU'S VOICE CALLING ME?
FUUTO!!
FUUTO!!

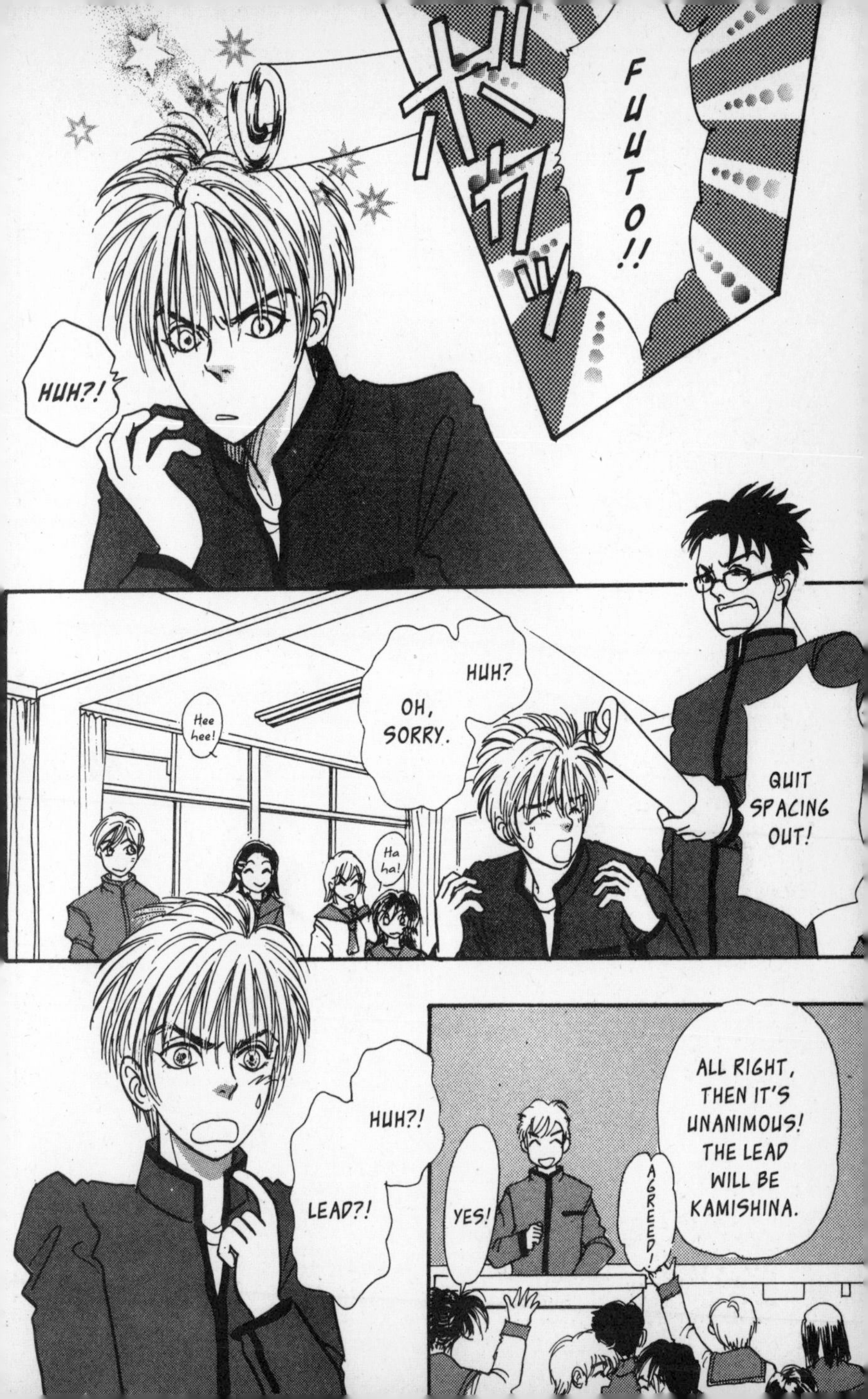
FUUTO!!
HUH?!
QUIT SPACING OUT!
HUH? OH, SORRY.
Hee hee!
Ha ha!
ALL RIGHT, THEN IT'S UNANIMOUS! THE LEAD WILL BE KAMISHINA.
AGREED!
YES!
HUH?! LEAD?!

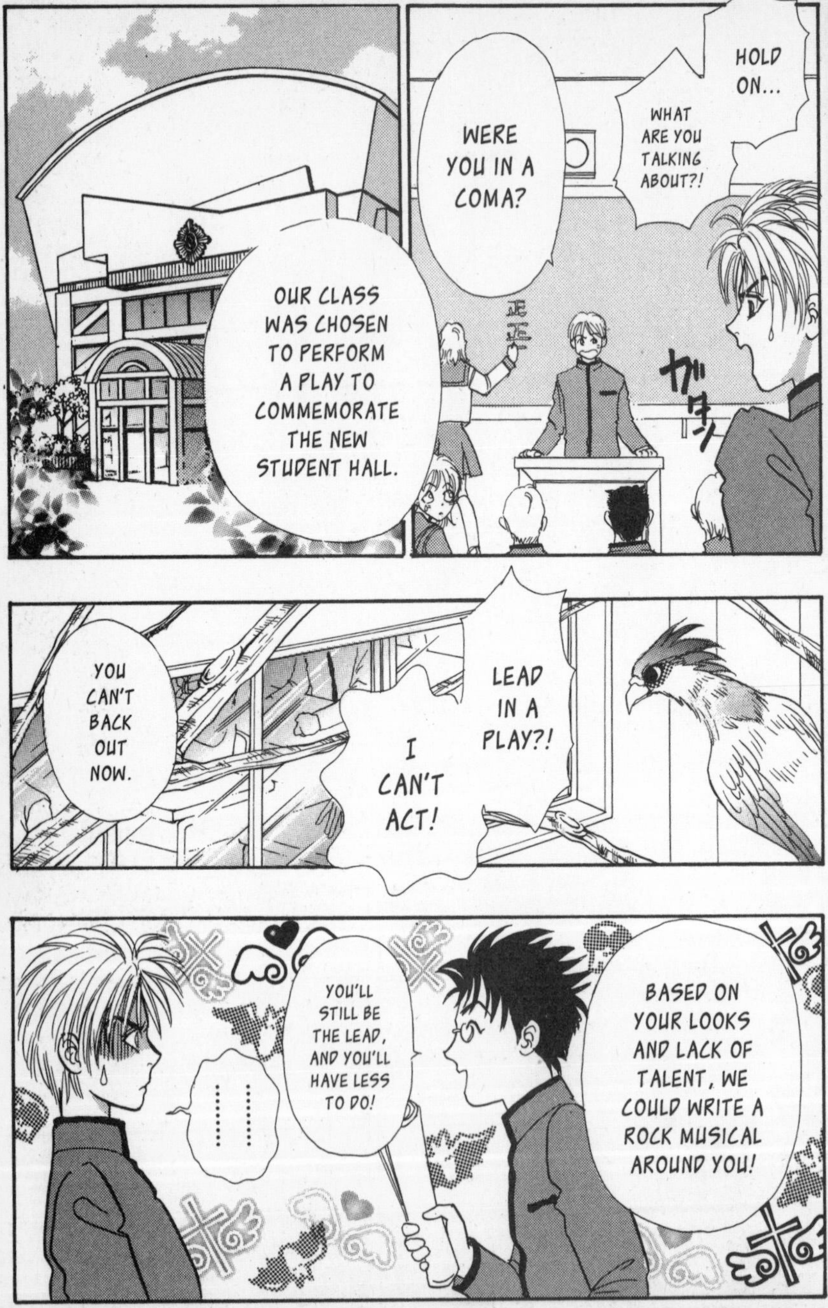
HOLD ON...
WHAT ARE YOU TALKING ABOUT?!
WERE YOU IN A COMA?
OUR CLASS WAS CHOSEN TO PERFORM A PLAY TO COMMEMORATE THE NEW STUDENT HALL.
ガタッ
LEAD IN A PLAY?!
I CAN'T ACT!
YOU CAN'T BACK OUT NOW.
BASED ON YOUR LOOKS AND LACK OF TALENT, WE COULD WRITE A ROCK MUSICAL AROUND YOU!
YOU'LL STILL BE THE LEAD, AND YOU'LL HAVE LESS TO DO!
......

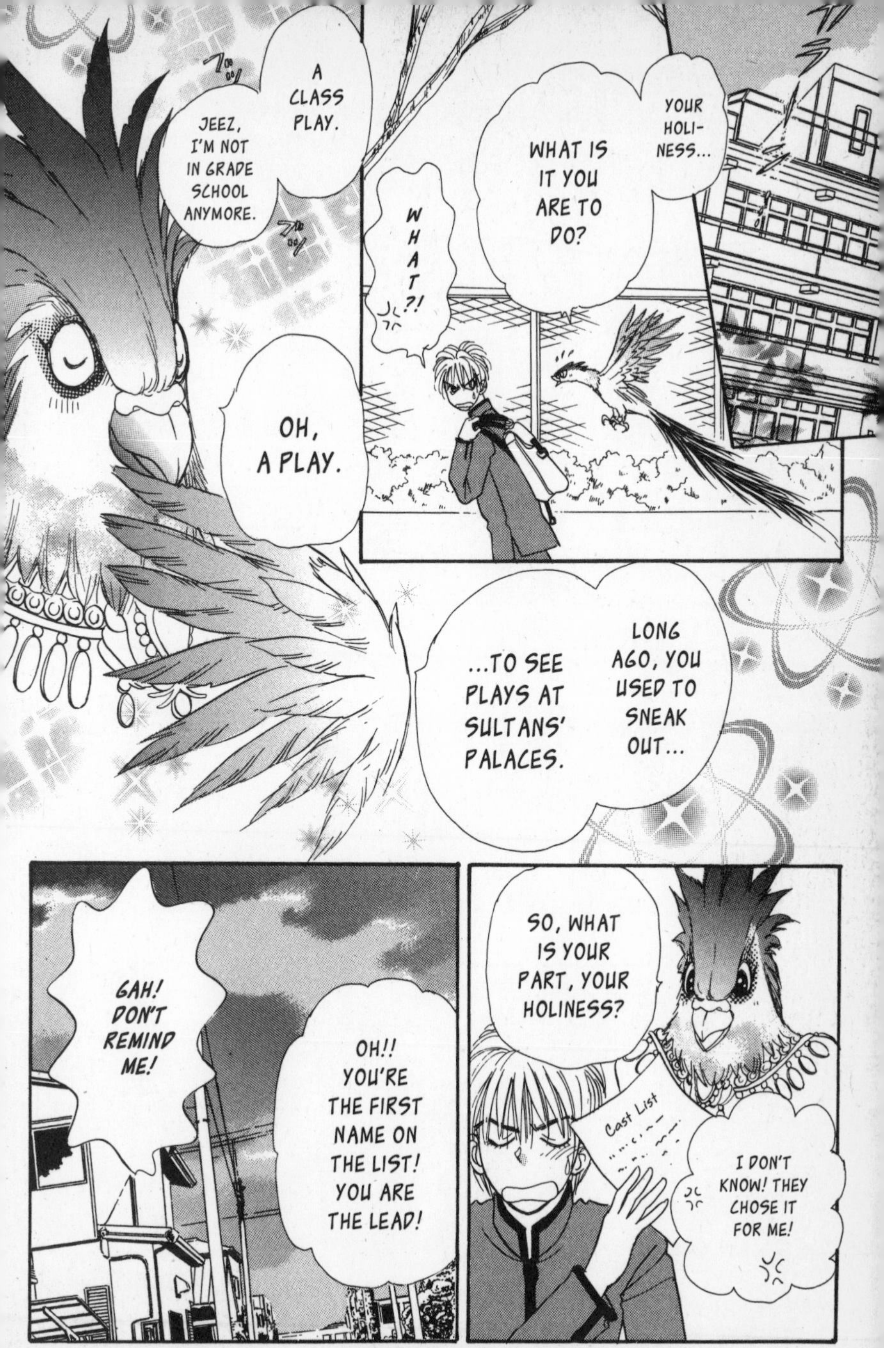
YOUR HOLINESS...
WHAT IS IT YOU ARE TO DO?
WHAT?!
A CLASS PLAY.
JEEZ, I'M NOT IN GRADE SCHOOL ANYMORE.
OH, A PLAY.
LONG AGO, YOU USED TO SNEAK OUT...
...TO SEE PLAYS AT SULTANS' PALACES.
SO, WHAT IS YOUR PART, YOUR HOLINESS?
Cast List
I DON'T KNOW! THEY CHOSE IT FOR ME!
OH!! YOU'RE THE FIRST NAME ON THE LIST! YOU ARE THE LEAD!
GAH! DON'T REMIND ME!

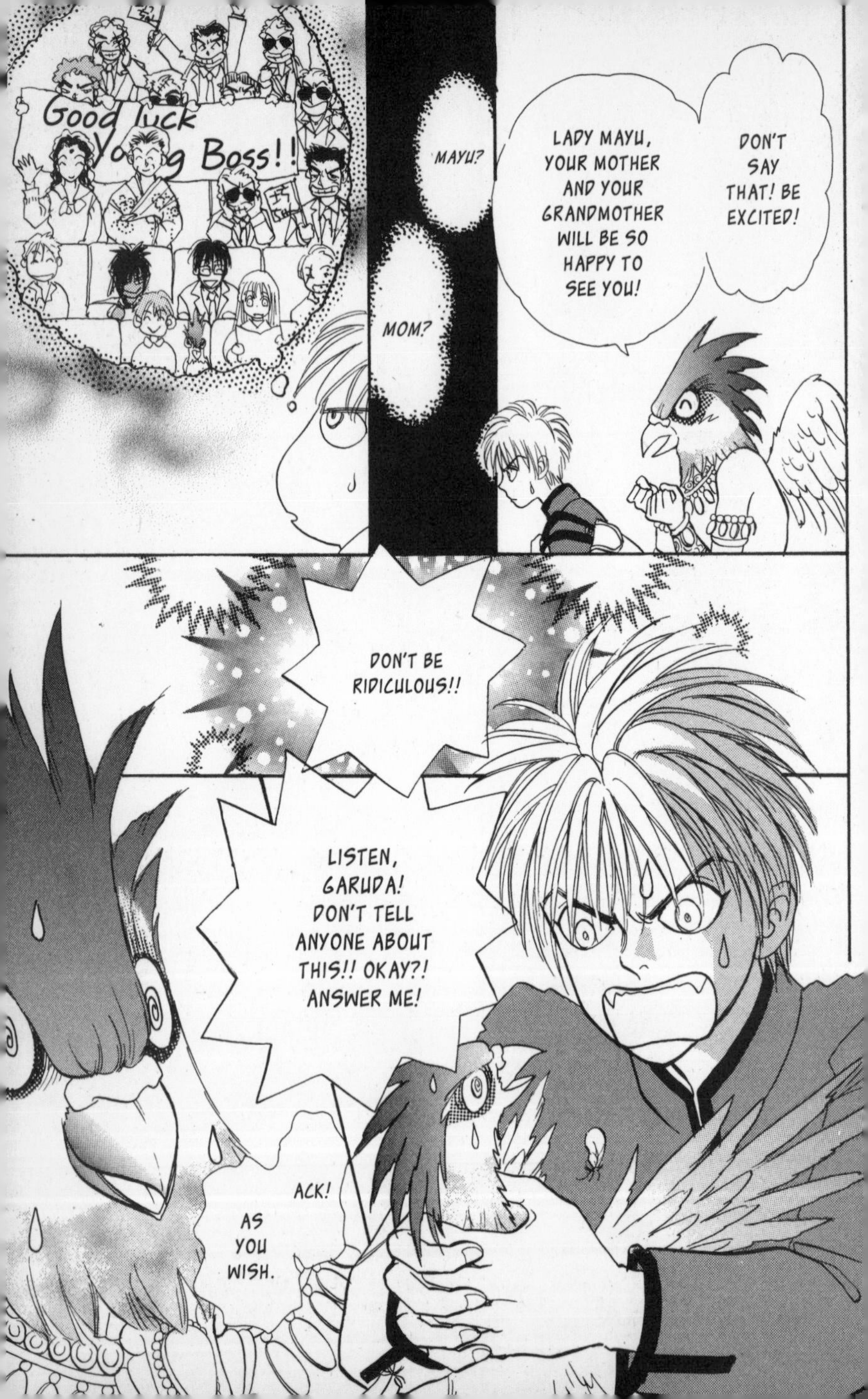

DON'T SAY THAT! BE EXCITED!
LADY MAYU, YOUR MOTHER AND YOUR GRANDMOTHER WILL BE SO HAPPY TO SEE YOU!
MAYU?
MOM?
Good luck
Boss!!
DON'T BE RIDICULOUS!!
LISTEN, GARUDA! DON'T TELL ANYONE ABOUT THIS!! OKAY?! ANSWER ME!
ACK!
AS YOU WISH.

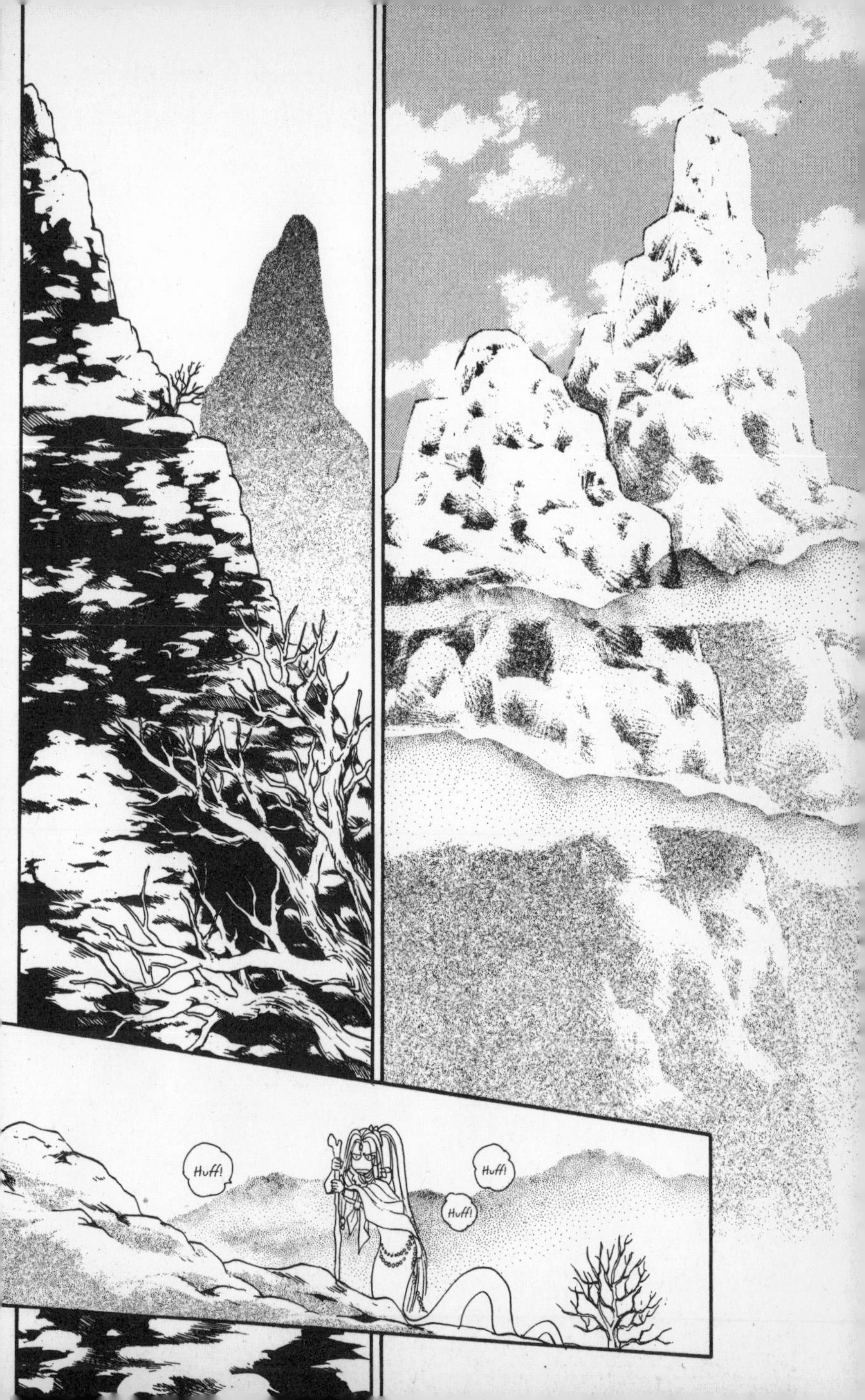
Huff!
Huff!
Huff!

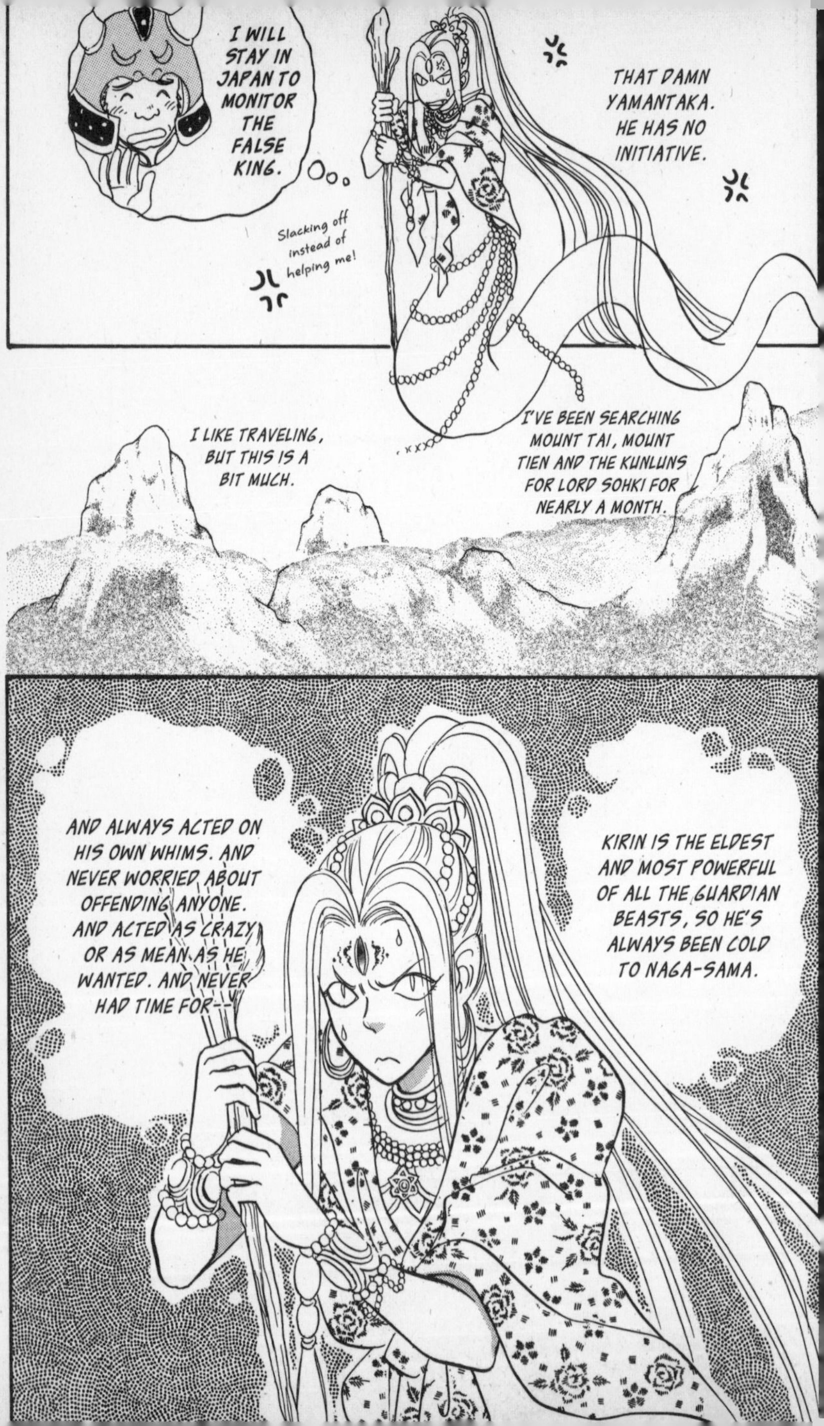
THAT DAMN YAMANTAKA. HE HAS NO INITIATIVE.
I WILL STAY IN JAPAN TO MONITOR THE FALSE KING.
Slacking off instead of helping me!
I'VE BEEN SEARCHING MOUNT TAI, MOUNT TIEN AND THE KUNLUNS FOR LORD SOHKI FOR NEARLY A MONTH.
I LIKE TRAVELING, BUT THIS IS A BIT MUCH.
KIRIN IS THE ELDEST AND MOST POWERFUL OF ALL THE GUARDIAN BEASTS, SO HE'S ALWAYS BEEN COLD TO NAGA-SAMA.
AND ALWAYS ACTED ON HIS OWN WHIMS. AND NEVER WORRIED ABOUT OFFENDING ANYONE. AND ACTED AS CRAZY OR AS MEAN AS HE WANTED. AND NEVER HAD TIME FOR--

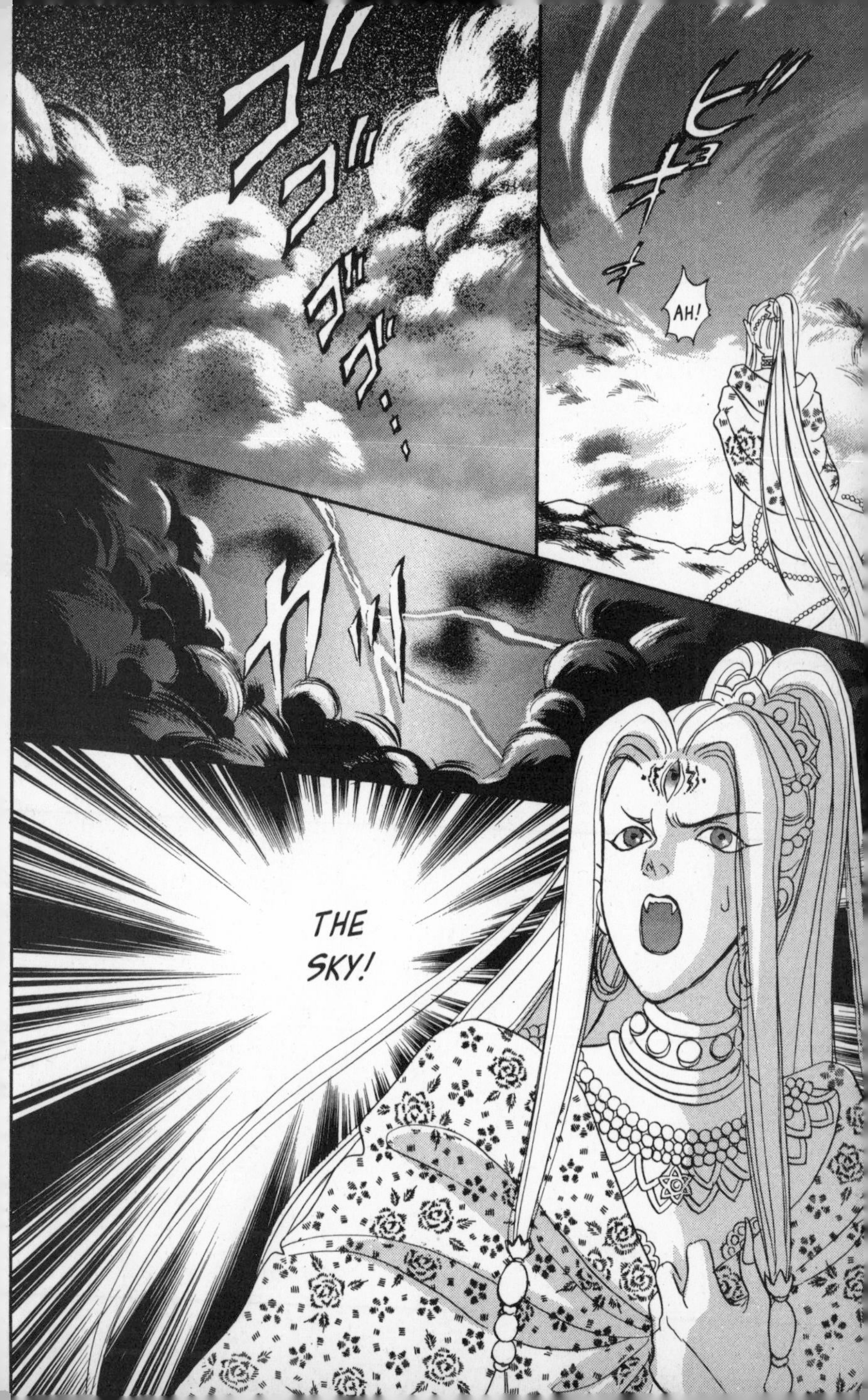
AH!
THE SKY!

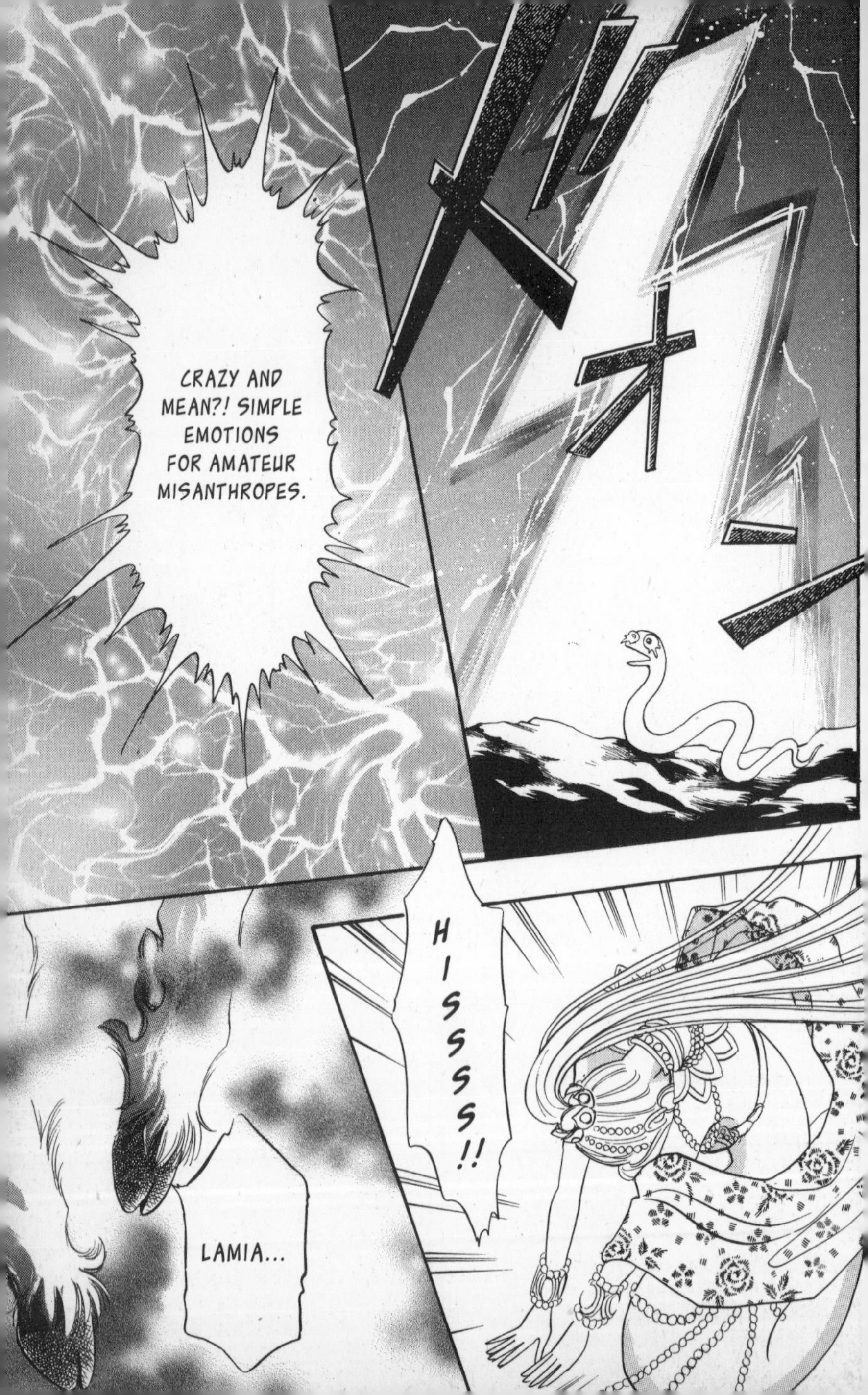

CRAZY AND MEAN?! SIMPLE EMOTIONS FOR AMATEUR MISANTHROPES.
HISSSS!!
LAMIA...

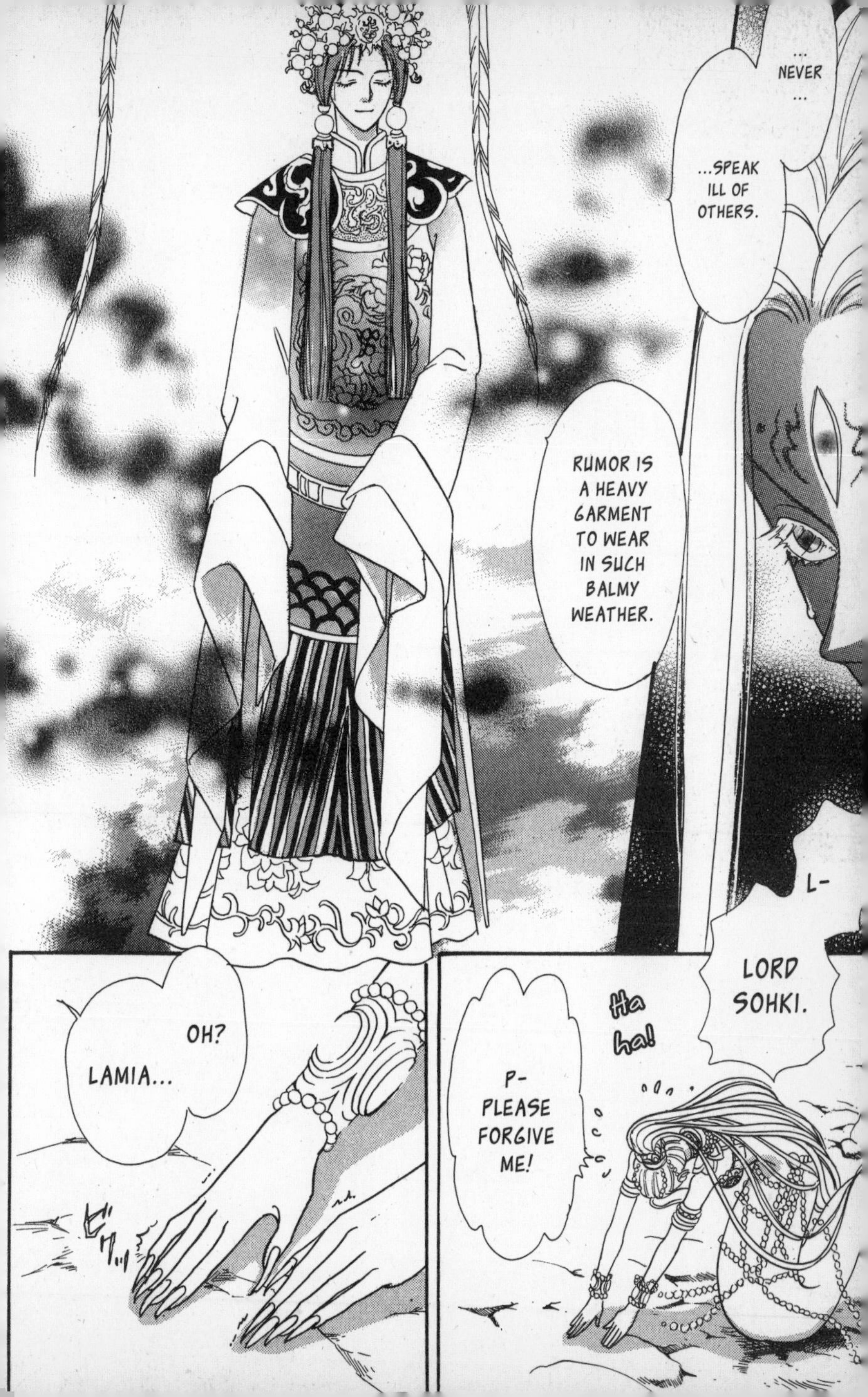
... NEVER ...
...SPEAK ILL OF OTHERS.
RUMOR IS A HEAVY GARMENT TO WEAR IN SUCH BALMY WEATHER.
L-
LORD SOHKI.
Ha ha!
P- PLEASE FORGIVE ME!
OH? LAMIA...

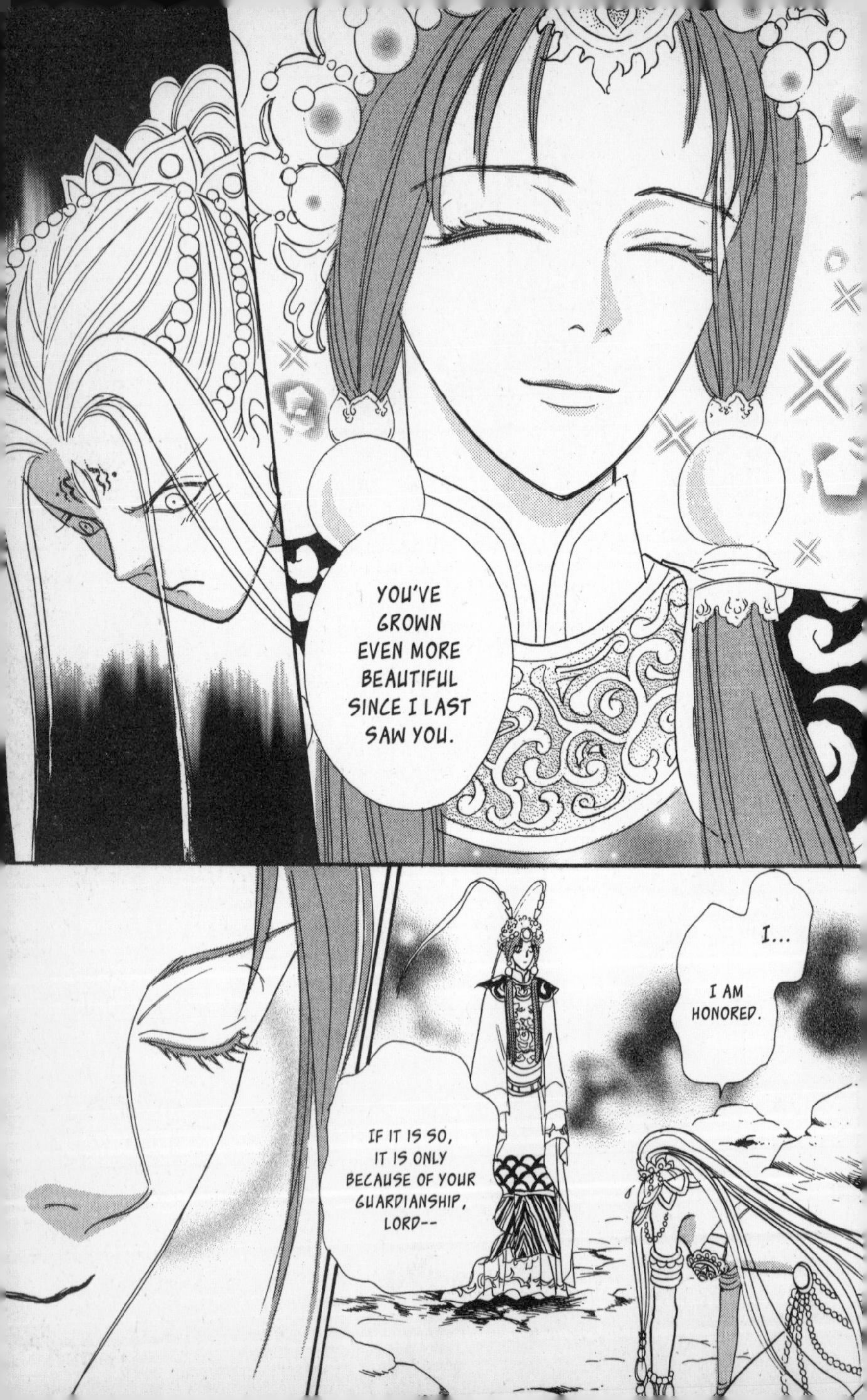
YOU'VE GROWN EVEN MORE BEAUTIFUL SINCE I LAST SAW YOU.
I...
I AM HONORED.
IF IT IS SO, IT IS ONLY BECAUSE OF YOUR GUARDIANSHIP, LORD--

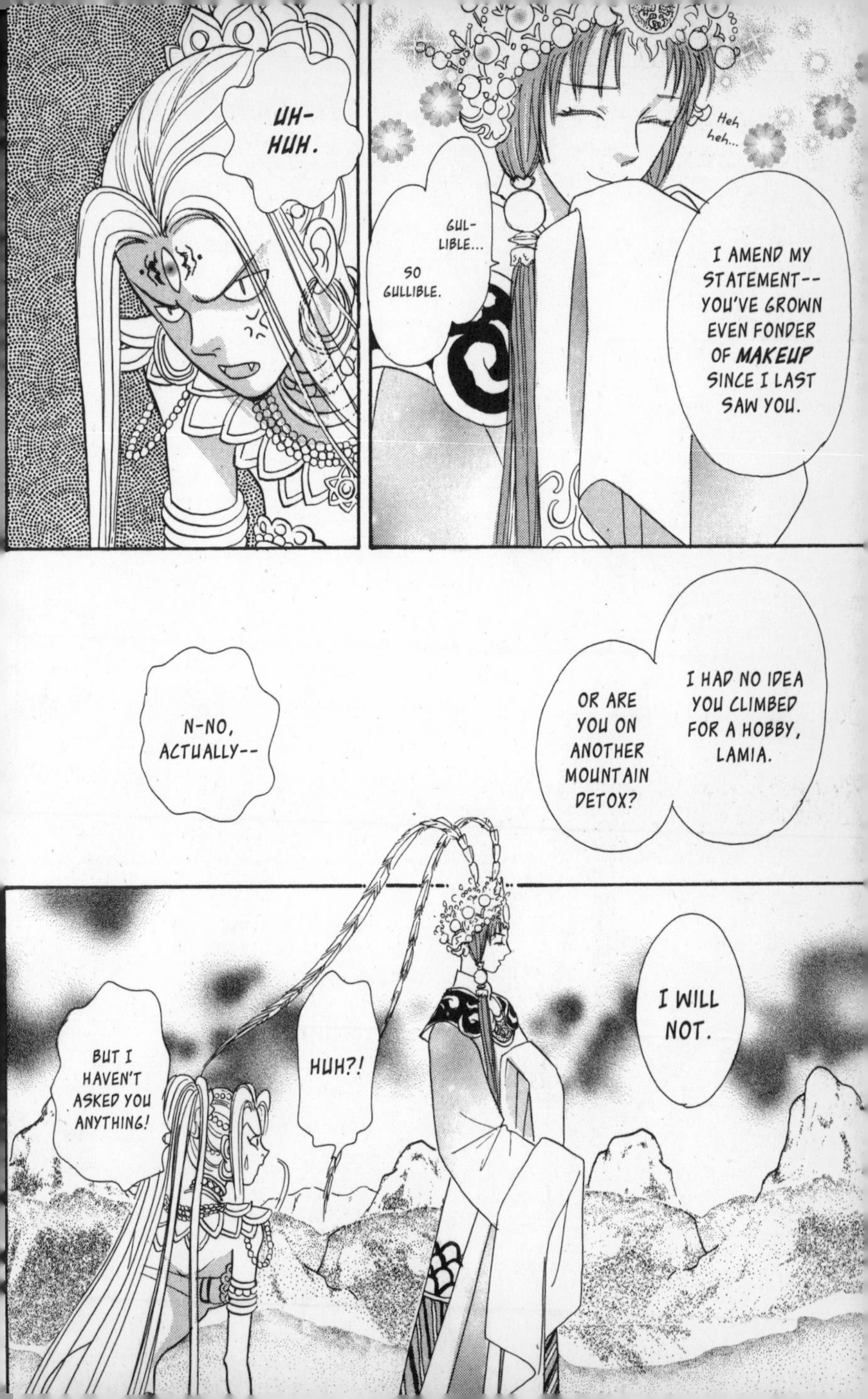
UH-HUH.
GUL-LIBLE...
SO GULLIBLE.
Heh heh...
I AMEND MY STATEMENT-- YOU'VE GROWN EVEN FONDER OF MAKEUP SINCE I LAST SAW YOU.
N-NO, ACTUALLY--
I HAD NO IDEA YOU CLIMBED FOR A HOBBY, LAMIA.
OR ARE YOU ON ANOTHER MOUNTAIN DETOX?
BUT I HAVEN'T ASKED YOU ANYTHING!
HUH?!
I WILL NOT.

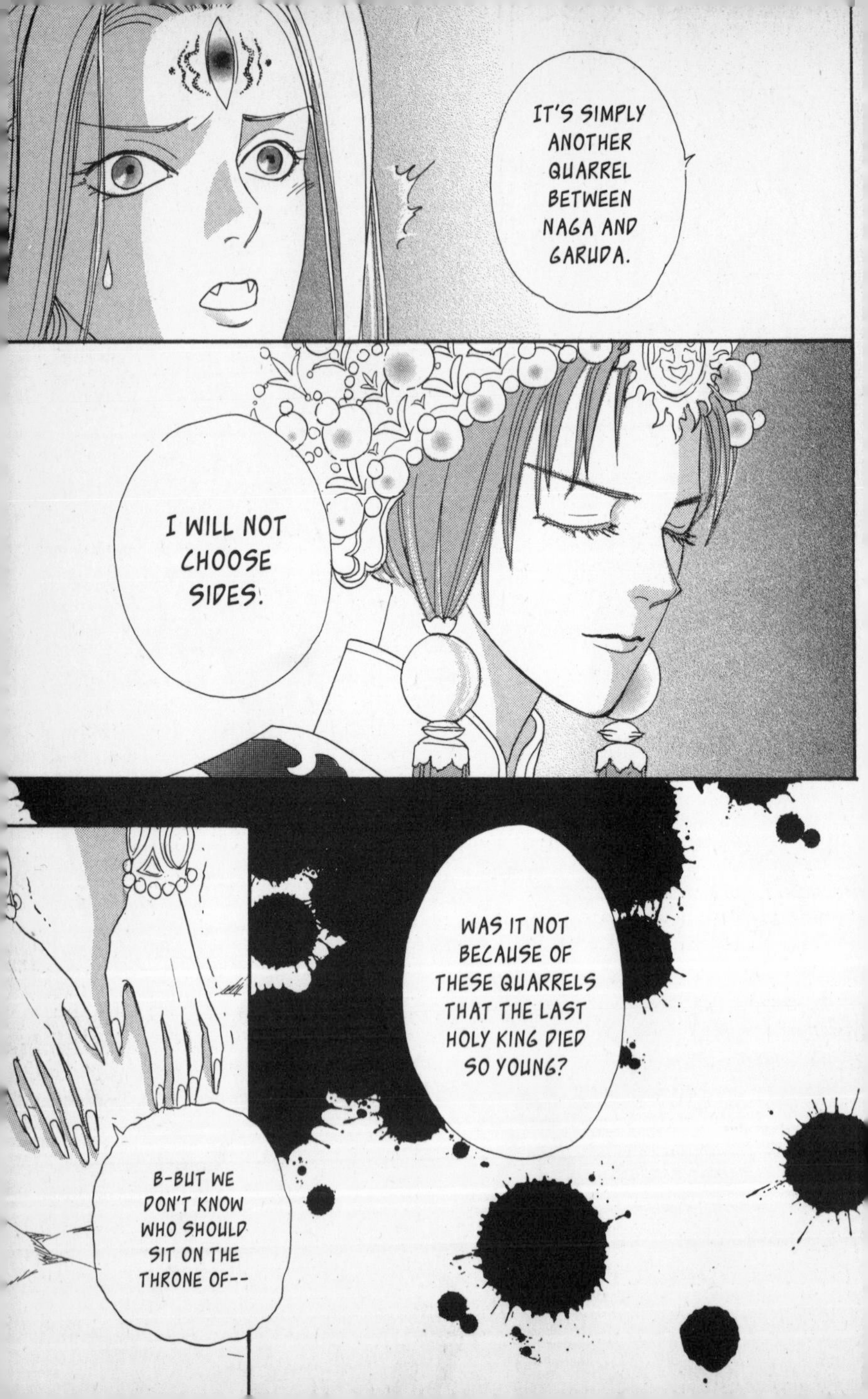
IT'S SIMPLY ANOTHER QUARREL BETWEEN NAGA AND GARUDA.
I WILL NOT CHOOSE SIDES.
WAS IT NOT BECAUSE OF THESE QUARRELS THAT THE LAST HOLY KING DIED SO YOUNG?
B-BUT WE DON'T KNOW WHO SHOULD SIT ON THE THRONE OF--

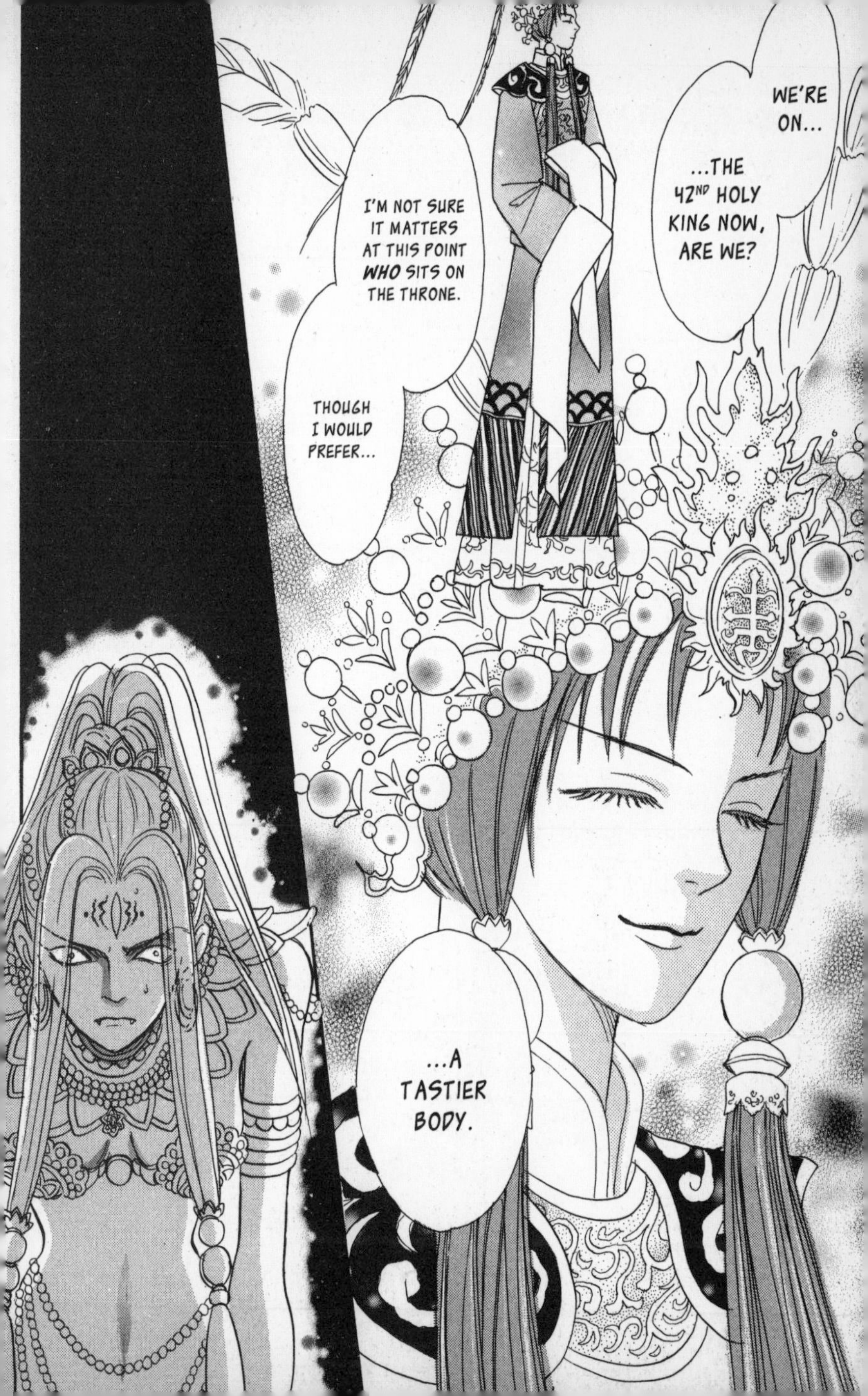
WE'RE ON...
...THE 42ND HOLY KING NOW, ARE WE?
I'M NOT SURE IT MATTERS AT THIS POINT WHO SITS ON THE THRONE.
THOUGH I WOULD PREFER...
...A TASTIER BODY.

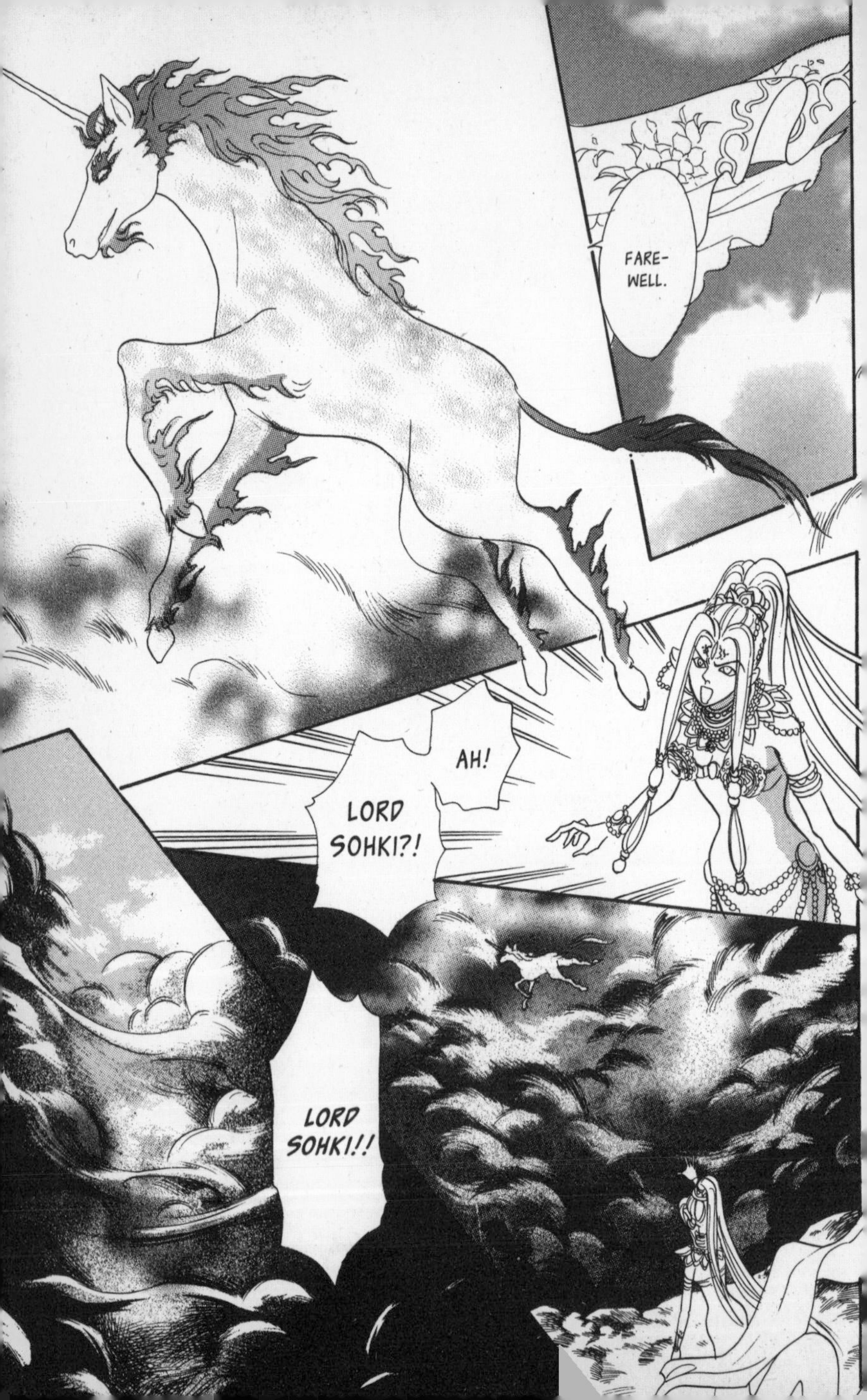
FARE-
WELL.
AH!
LORD
SOHKI?!
LORD
SOHKI!!

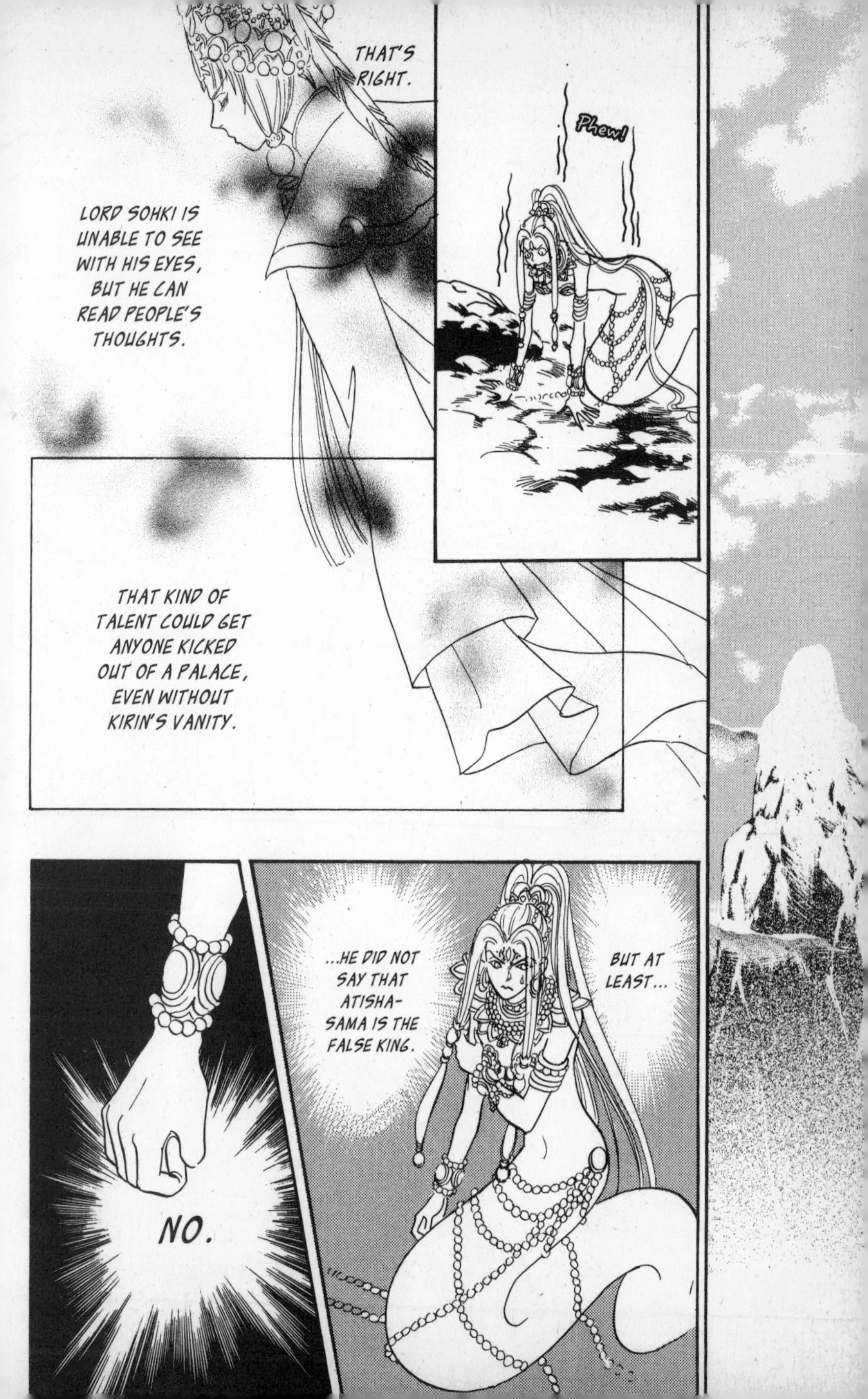
Phew!
THAT'S RIGHT.
LORD SOHKI IS UNABLE TO SEE WITH HIS EYES, BUT HE CAN READ PEOPLE'S THOUGHTS.
THAT KIND OF TALENT COULD GET ANYONE KICKED OUT OF A PALACE, EVEN WITHOUT KIRIN'S VANITY.
BUT AT LEAST...
...HE DID NOT SAY THAT ATISHA-SAMA IS THE FALSE KING.
NO.

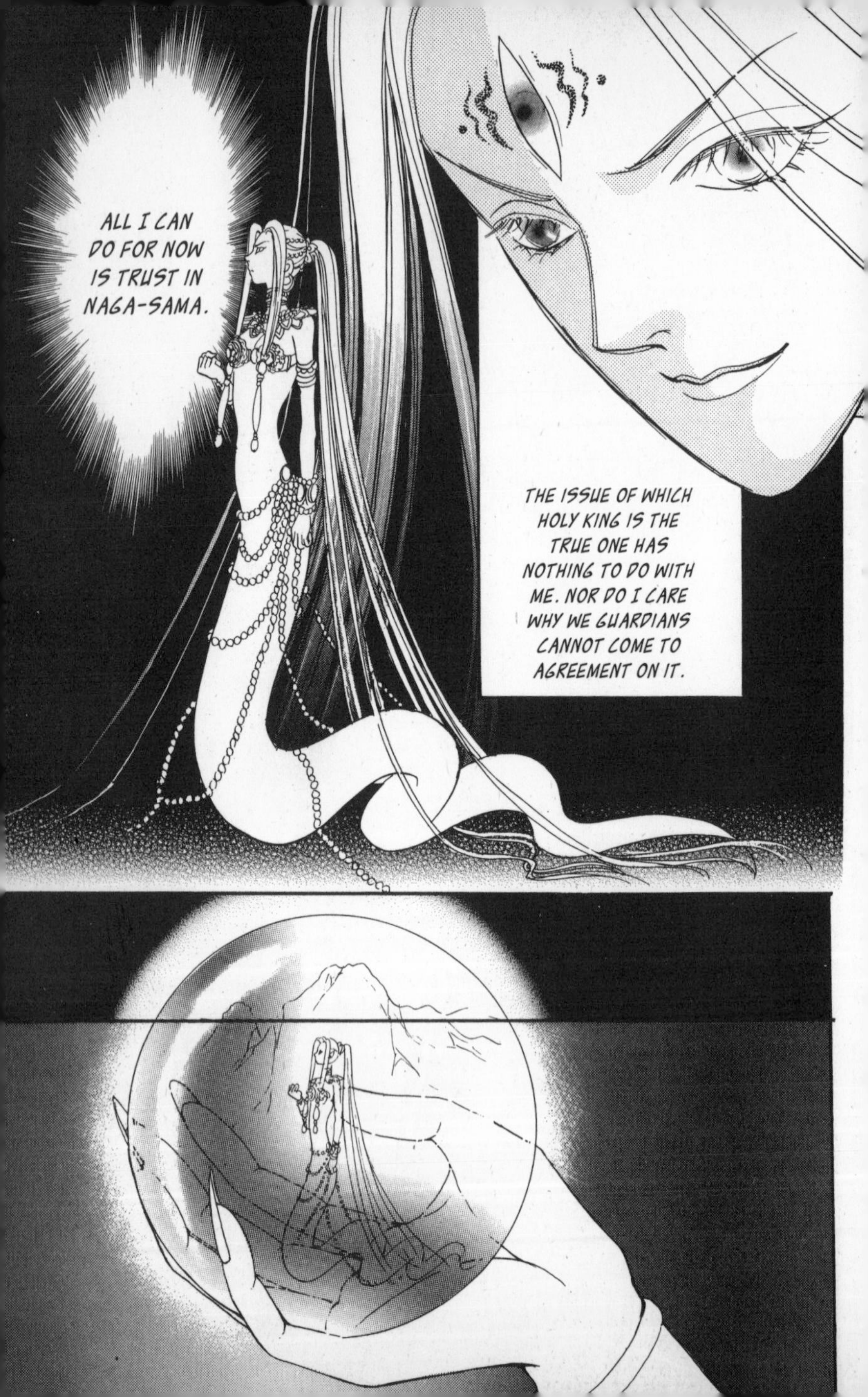
THE ISSUE OF WHICH HOLY KING IS THE TRUE ONE HAS NOTHING TO DO WITH ME. NOR DO I CARE WHY WE GUARDIANS CANNOT COME TO AGREEMENT ON IT.
ALL I CAN DO FOR NOW IS TRUST IN NAGA-SAMA.

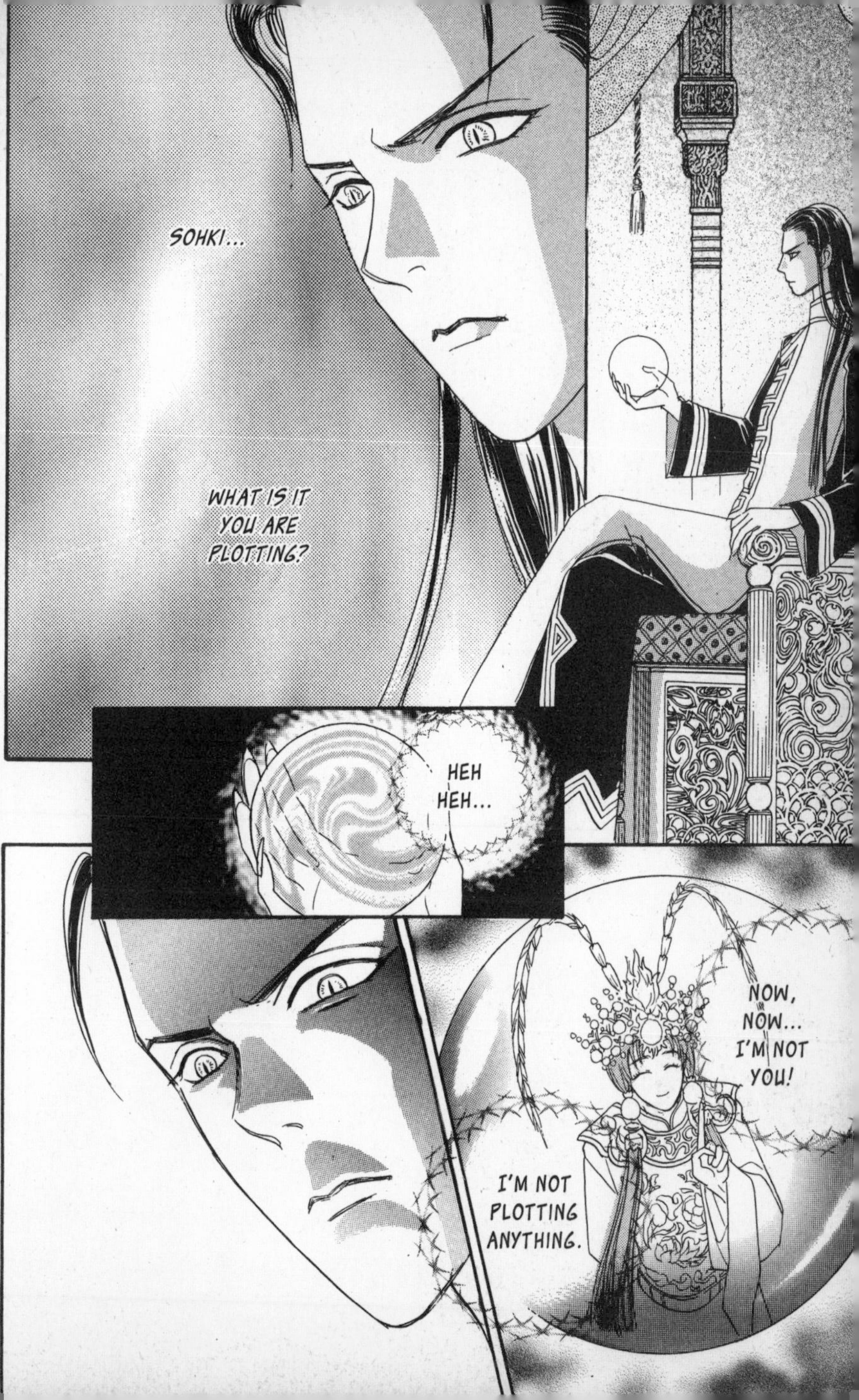
SOHKI...
WHAT IS IT YOU ARE PLOTTING?
HEH HEH...
NOW, NOW... I'M NOT YOU!
I'M NOT PLOTTING ANYTHING.

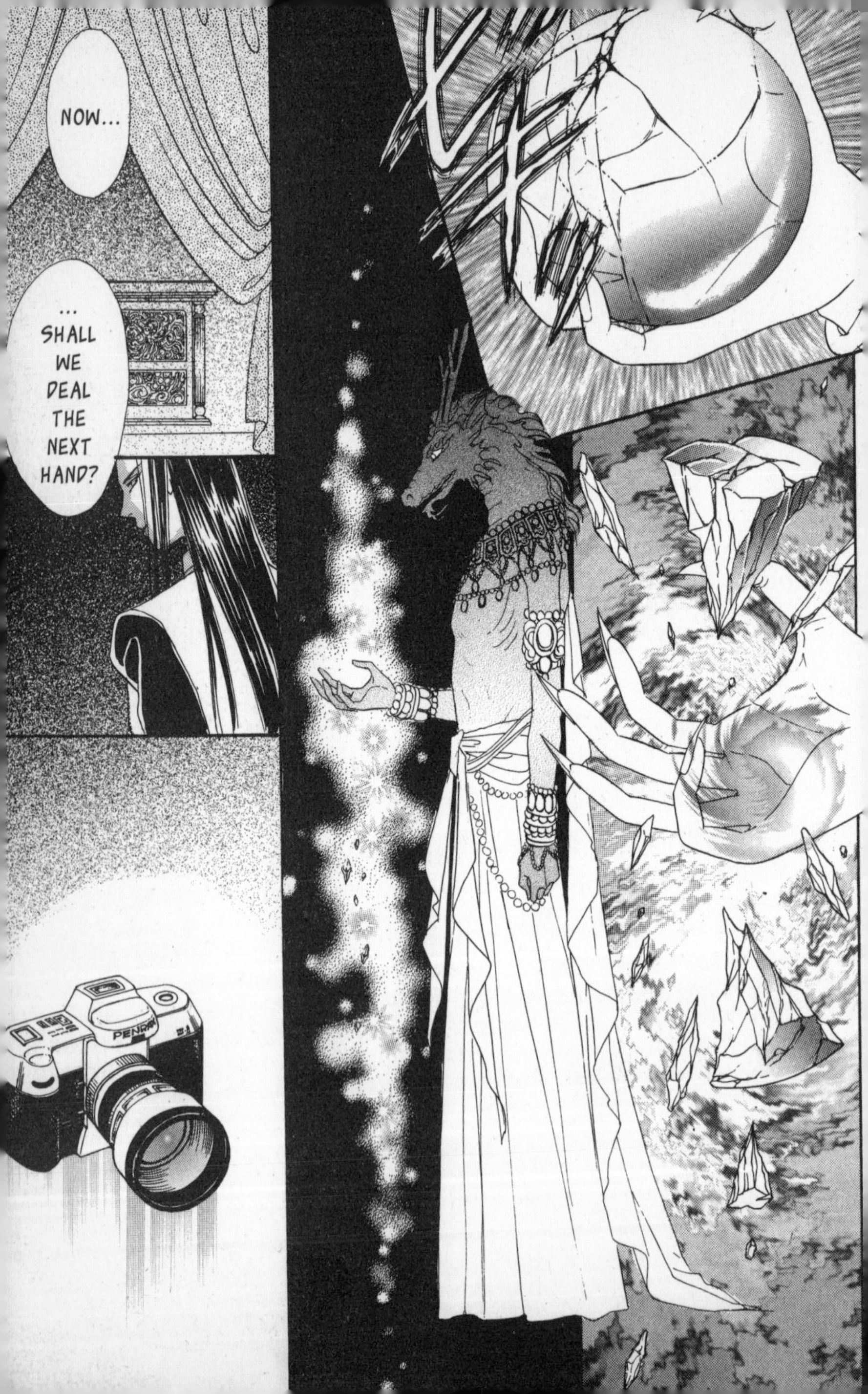
NOW...
... SHALL WE DEAL THE NEXT HAND?

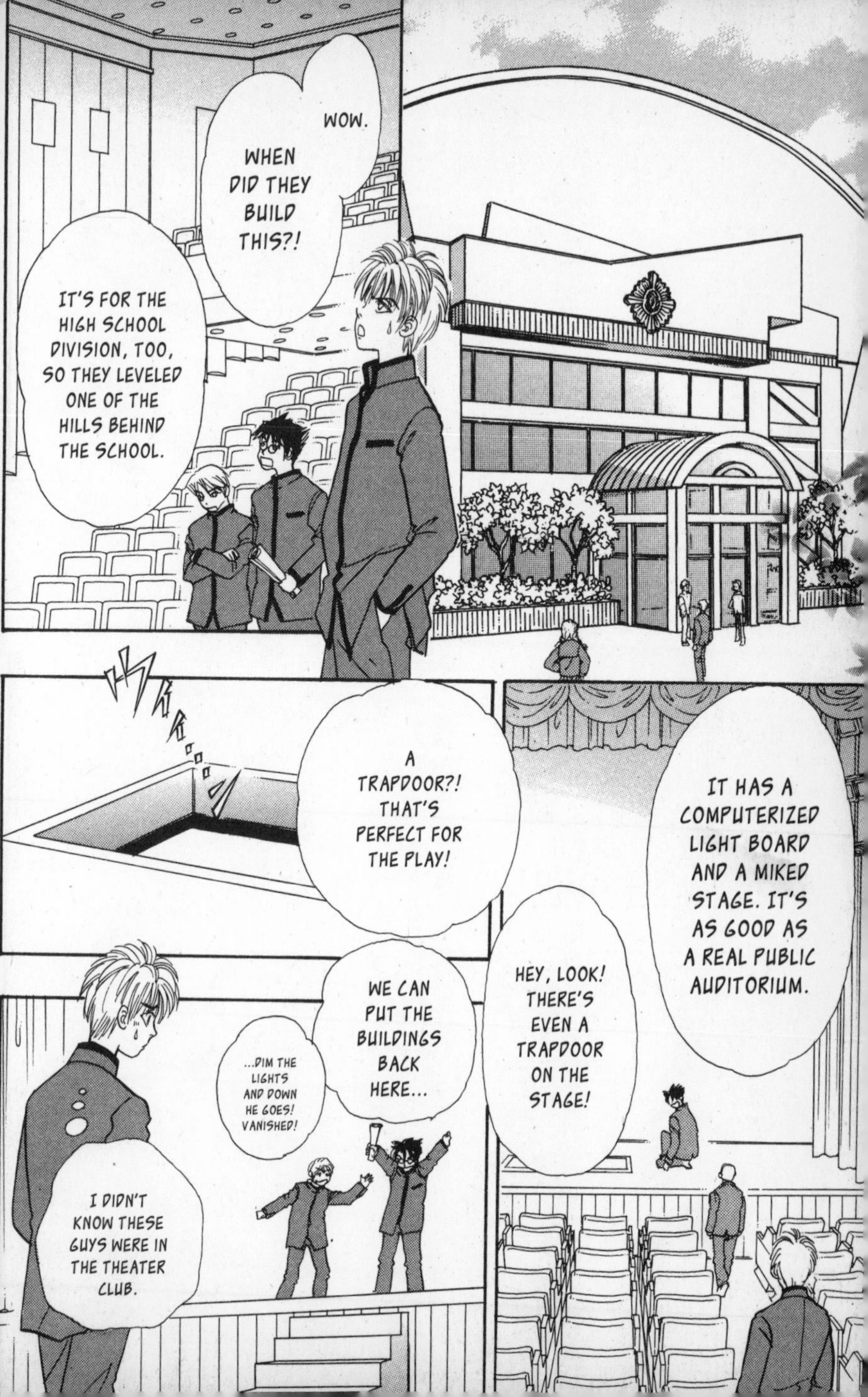
WOW.
WHEN DID THEY BUILD THIS?!
IT'S FOR THE HIGH SCHOOL DIVISION, TOO, SO THEY LEVELED ONE OF THE HILLS BEHIND THE SCHOOL.
IT HAS A COMPUTERIZED LIGHT BOARD AND A MIKED STAGE. IT'S AS GOOD AS A REAL PUBLIC AUDITORIUM.
A TRAPDOOR?! THAT'S PERFECT FOR THE PLAY!
HEY, LOOK! THERE'S EVEN A TRAPDOOR ON THE STAGE!
WE CAN PUT THE BUILDINGS BACK HERE...
...DIM THE LIGHTS AND DOWN HE GOES! VANISHED!
I DIDN'T KNOW THESE GUYS WERE IN THE THEATER CLUB.

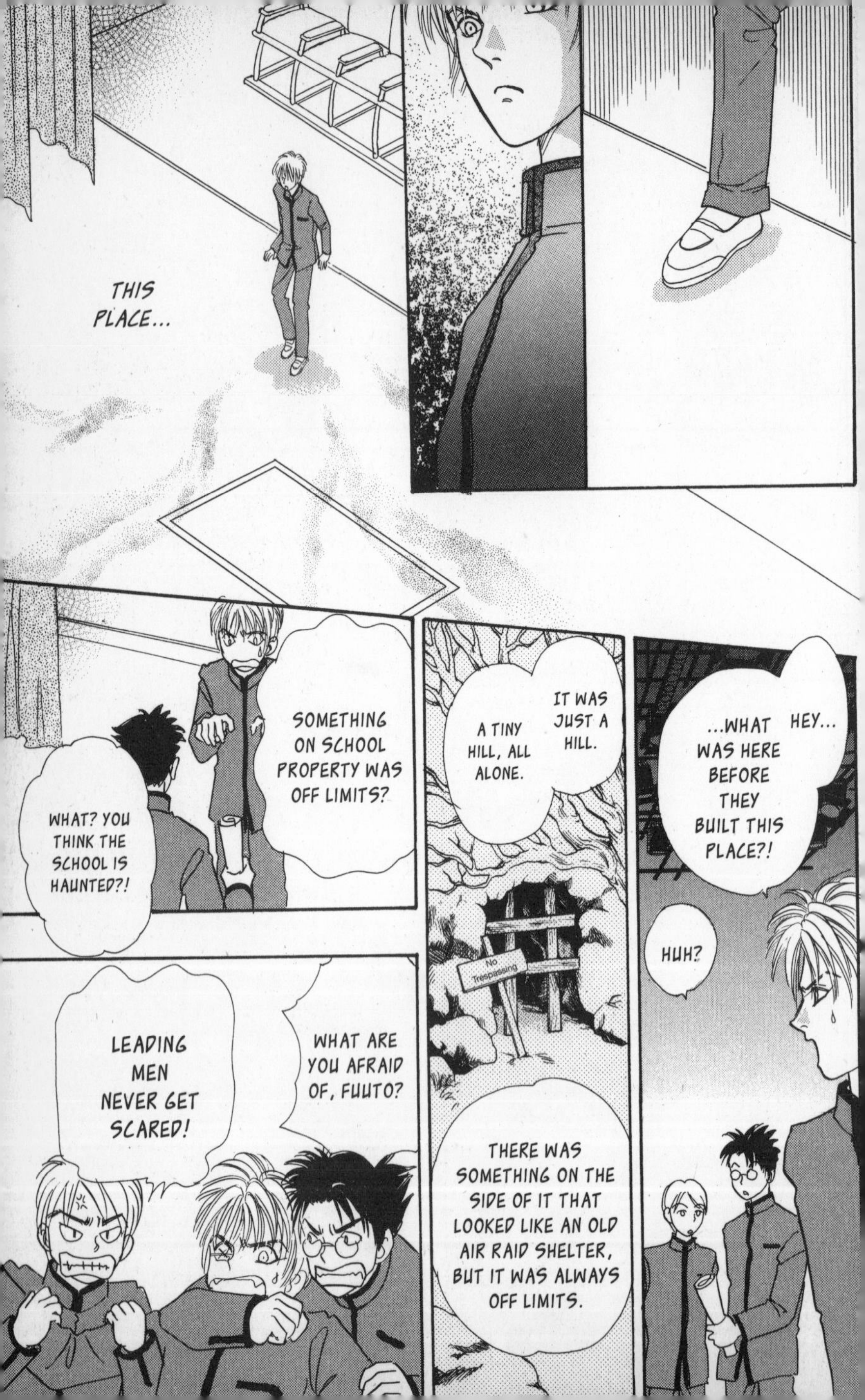
THIS PLACE...
HEY...
...WHAT WAS HERE BEFORE THEY BUILT THIS PLACE?!
HUH?
IT WAS JUST A HILL.
A TINY HILL, ALL ALONE.
No Trespassing
THERE WAS SOMETHING ON THE SIDE OF IT THAT LOOKED LIKE AN OLD AIR RAID SHELTER, BUT IT WAS ALWAYS OFF LIMITS.
SOMETHING ON SCHOOL PROPERTY WAS OFF LIMITS?
WHAT? YOU THINK THE SCHOOL IS HAUNTED?!
WHAT ARE YOU AFRAID OF, FUUTO?
LEADING MEN NEVER GET SCARED!

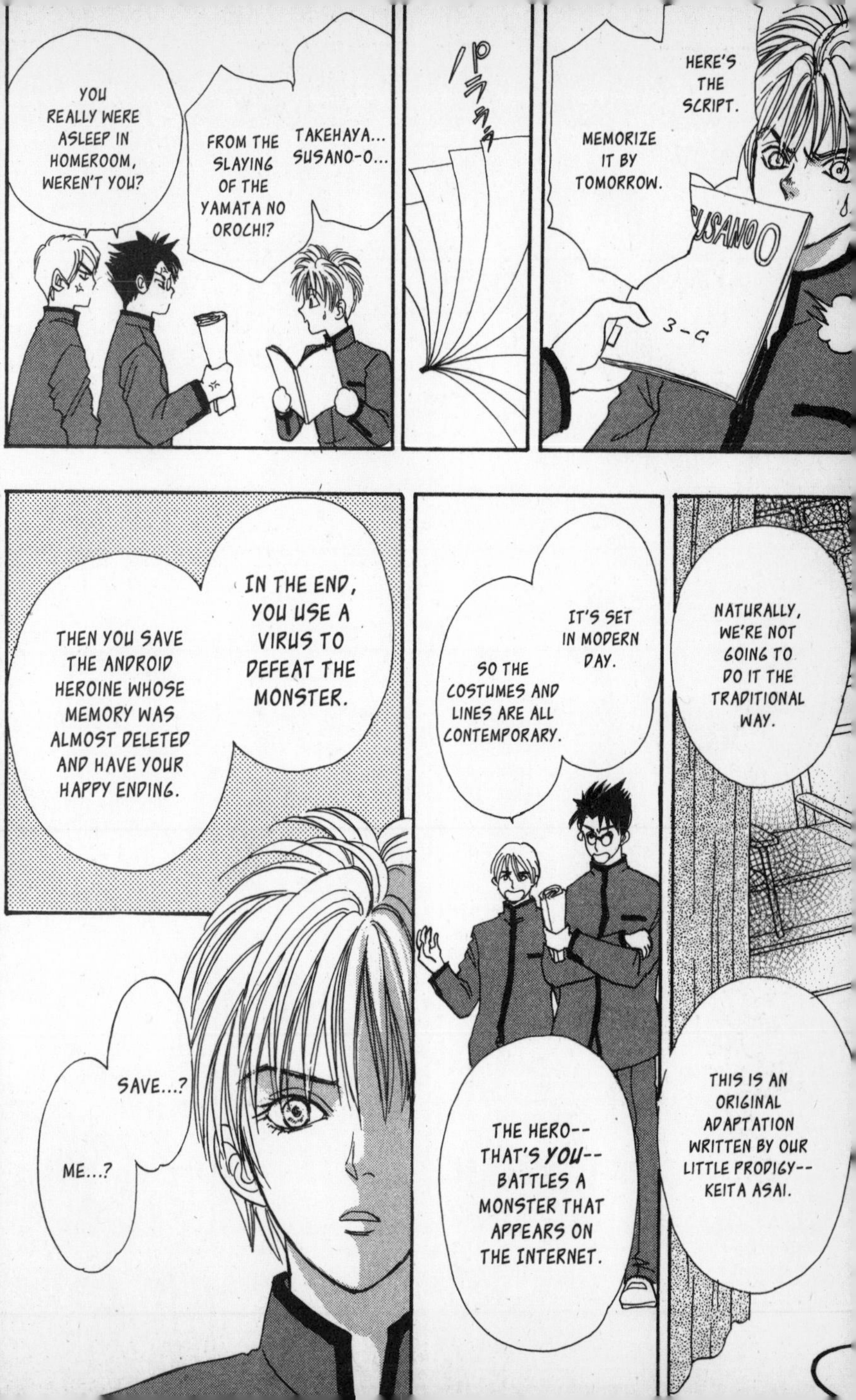
HERE'S THE SCRIPT.
MEMORIZE IT BY TOMORROW.
SUSANO O
3-G
TAKEHAYA... SUSANO-O...
FROM THE SLAYING OF THE YAMATA NO OROCHI?
YOU REALLY WERE ASLEEP IN HOMEROOM, WEREN'T YOU?
NATURALLY, WE'RE NOT GOING TO DO IT THE TRADITIONAL WAY.
THIS IS AN ORIGINAL ADAPTATION WRITTEN BY OUR LITTLE PRODIGY-- KEITA ASAI.
IT'S SET IN MODERN DAY.
SO THE COSTUMES AND LINES ARE ALL CONTEMPORARY.
THE HERO-- THAT'S *YOU*-- BATTLES A MONSTER THAT APPEARS ON THE INTERNET.
IN THE END, YOU USE A VIRUS TO DEFEAT THE MONSTER.
THEN YOU SAVE THE ANDROID HEROINE WHOSE MEMORY WAS ALMOST DELETED AND HAVE YOUR HAPPY ENDING.
SAVE...?
ME...?

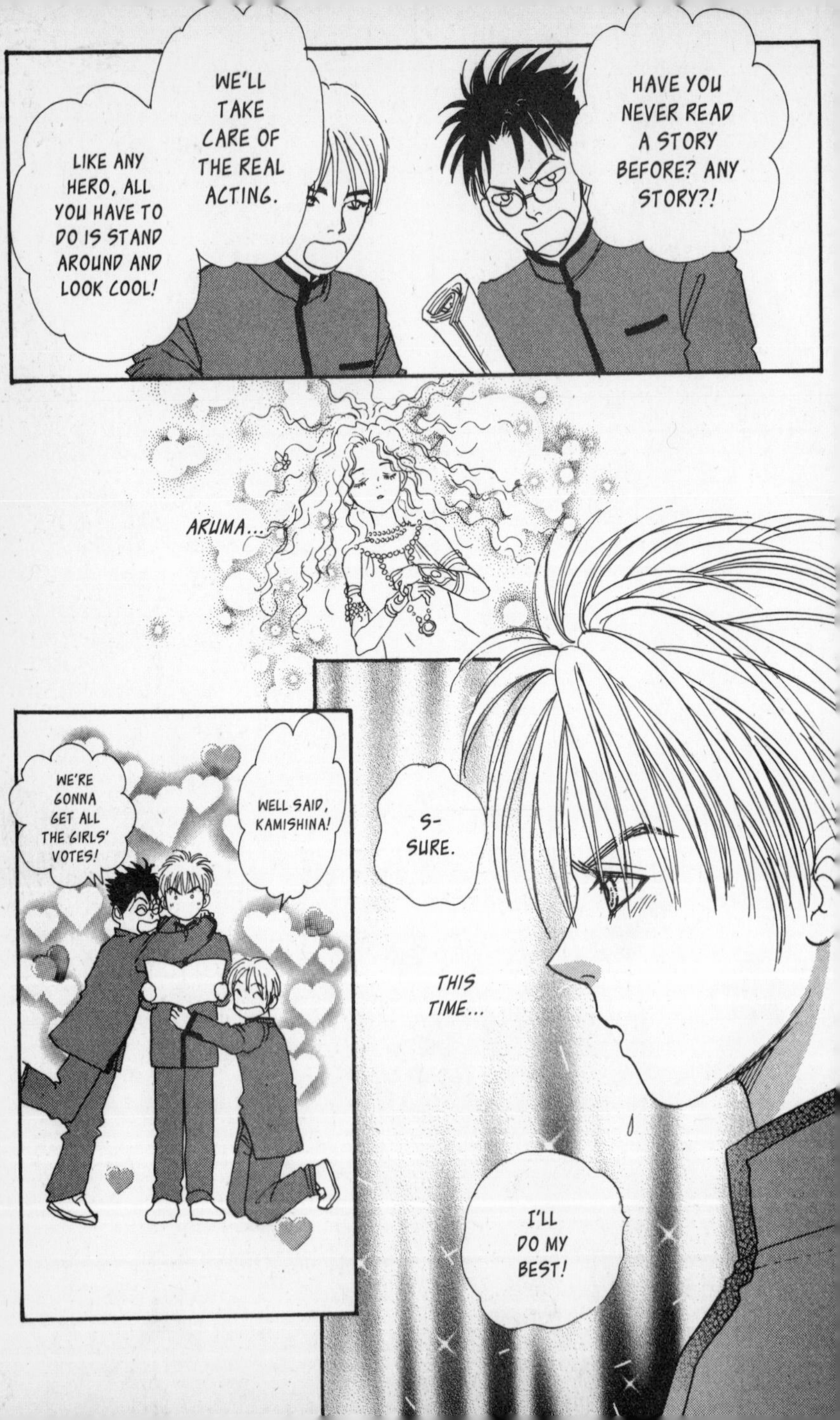
HAVE YOU NEVER READ A STORY BEFORE? ANY STORY?!
WE'LL TAKE CARE OF THE REAL ACTING.
LIKE ANY HERO, ALL YOU HAVE TO DO IS STAND AROUND AND LOOK COOL!
ARUMA...
S- SURE.
THIS TIME...
I'LL DO MY BEST!
WELL SAID, KAMISHINA!
WE'RE GONNA GET ALL THE GIRLS' VOTES!

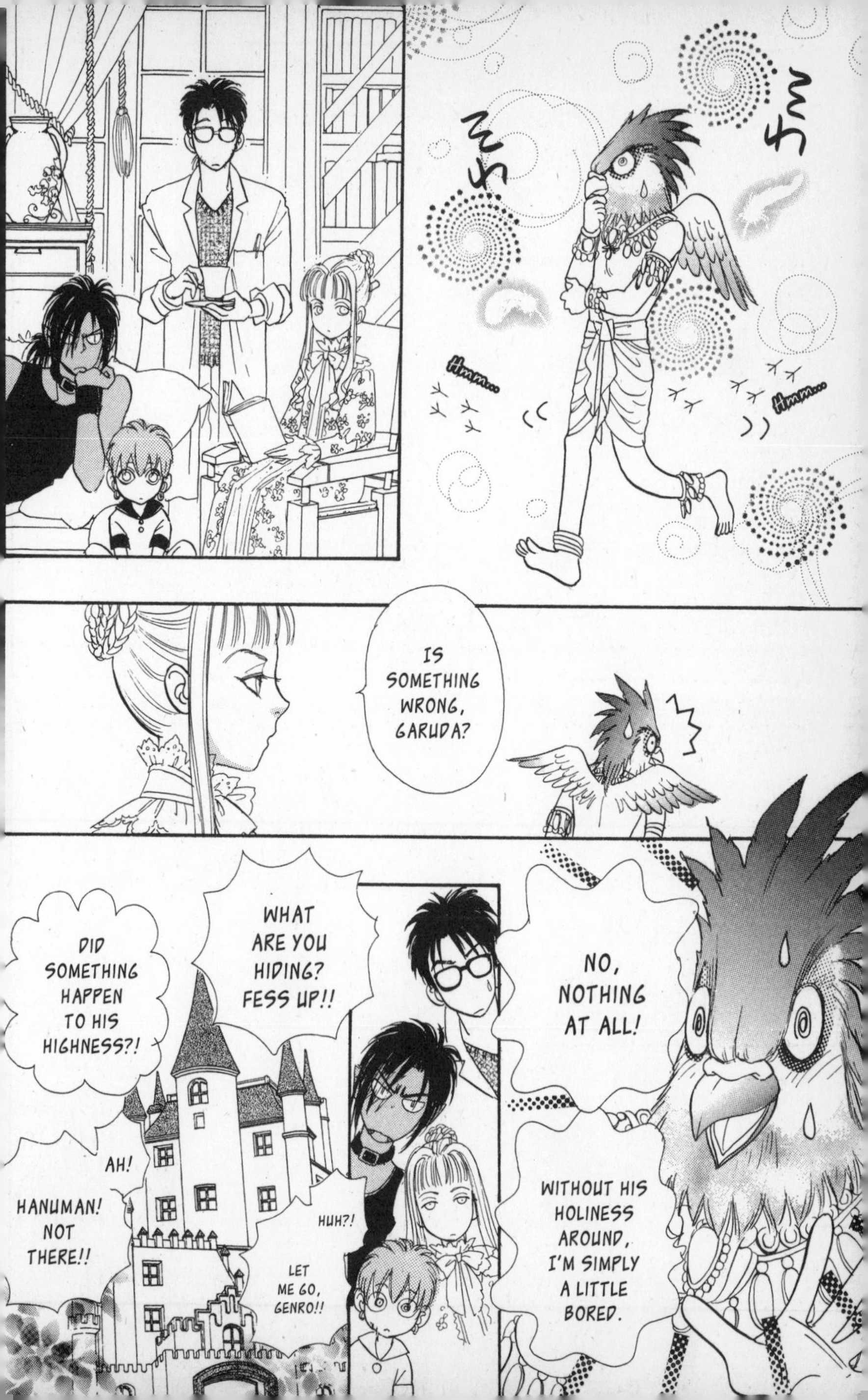
Hmm...
Hmm...
IS SOMETHING WRONG, GARUDA?
NO, NOTHING AT ALL!
WITHOUT HIS HOLINESS AROUND, I'M SIMPLY A LITTLE BORED.
WHAT ARE YOU HIDING? FESS UP!!
DID SOMETHING HAPPEN TO HIS HIGHNESS?!
HUH?!
LET ME GO, GENRO!!
AH!
HANUMAN! NOT THERE!!

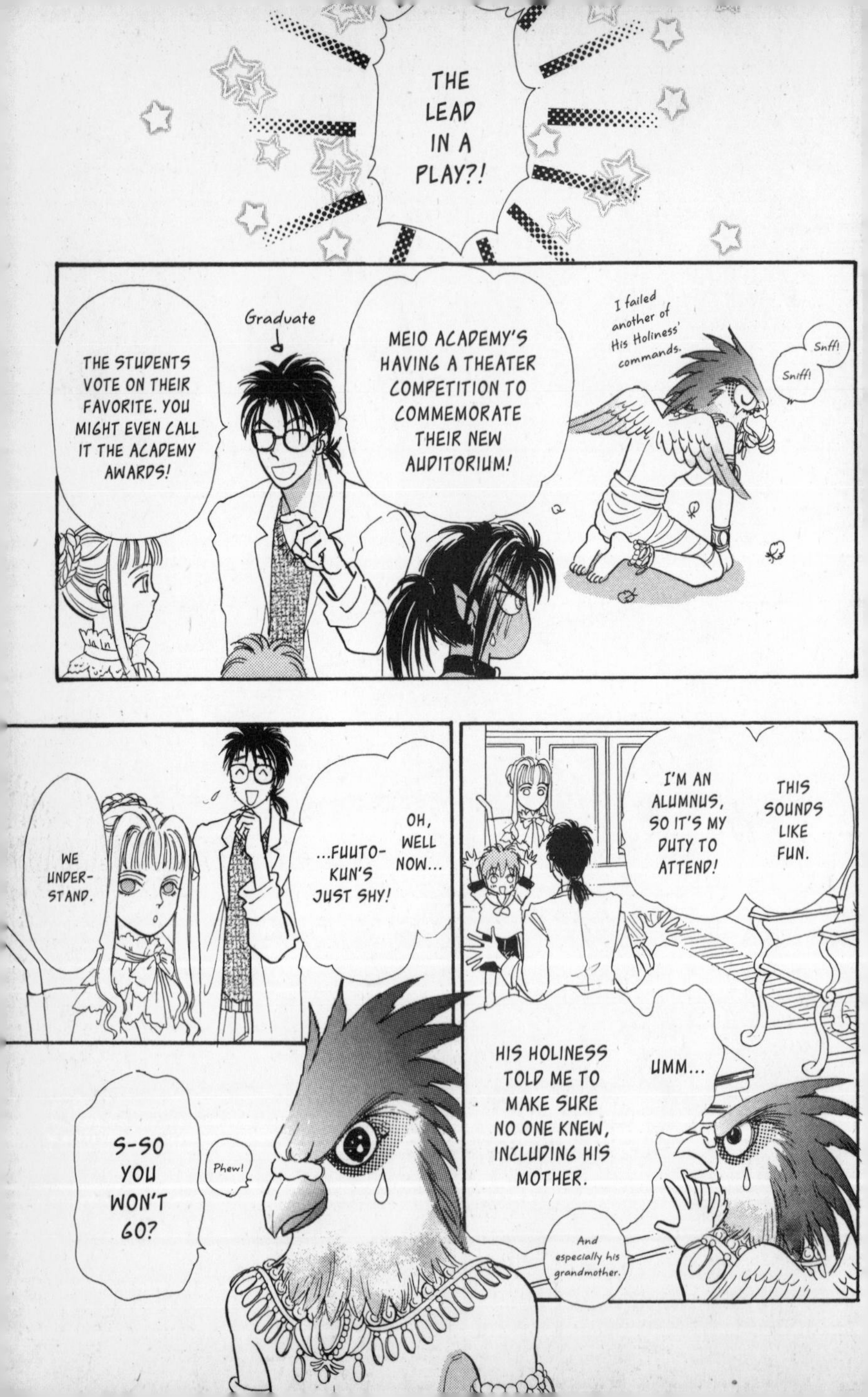
THE LEAD IN A PLAY?!
I failed another of His Holiness' commands.
Snff!
Sniff!
MEIO ACADEMY'S HAVING A THEATER COMPETITION TO COMMEMORATE THEIR NEW AUDITORIUM!
Graduate
THE STUDENTS VOTE ON THEIR FAVORITE. YOU MIGHT EVEN CALL IT THE ACADEMY AWARDS!
THIS SOUNDS LIKE FUN.
I'M AN ALUMNUS, SO IT'S MY DUTY TO ATTEND!
OH, WELL NOW...
...FUUTO-KUN'S JUST SHY!
WE UNDER-STAND.
UMM...
HIS HOLINESS TOLD ME TO MAKE SURE NO ONE KNEW, INCLUDING HIS MOTHER.
And especially his grandmother.
Phew!
S-SO YOU WON'T GO?

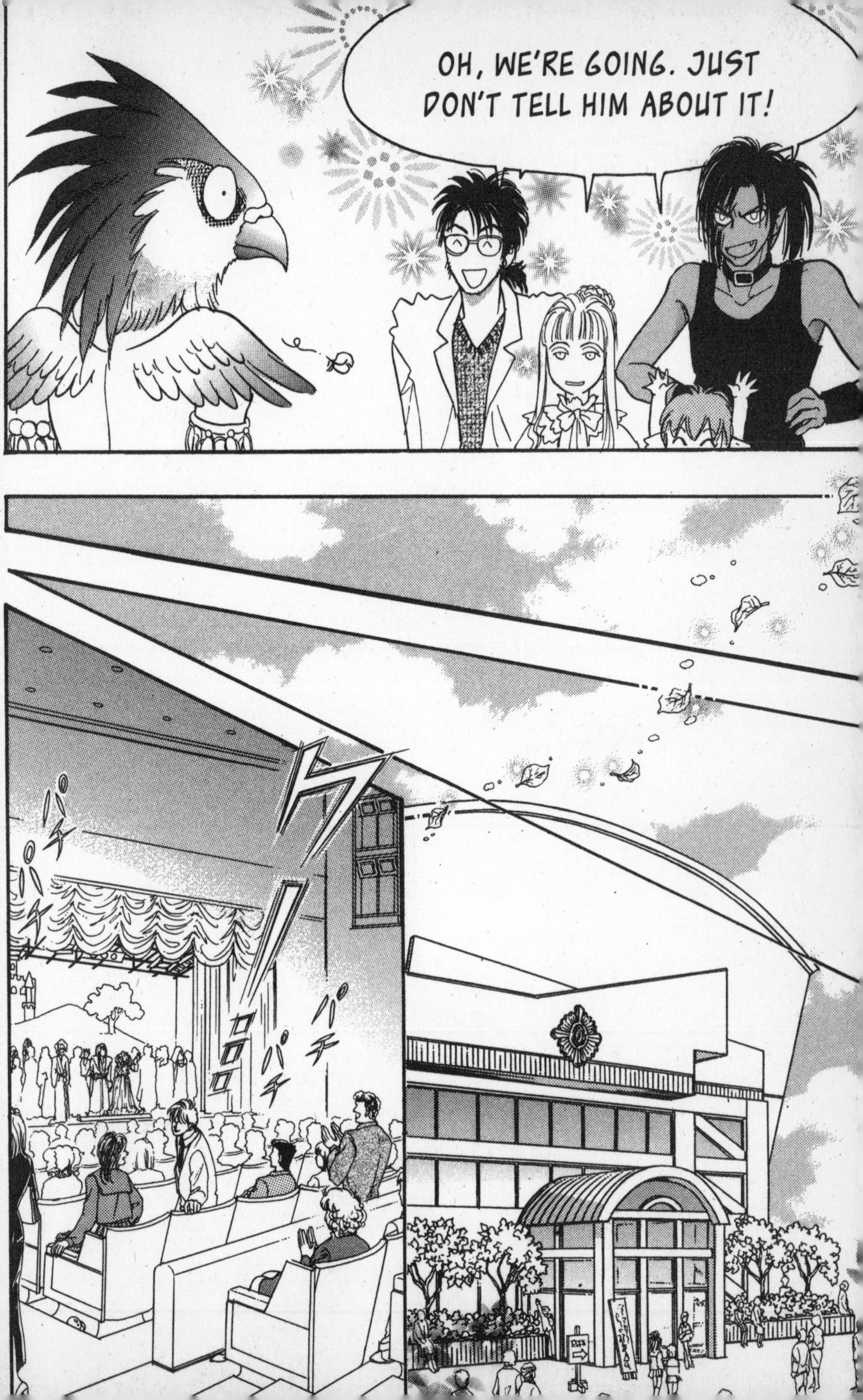
OH, WE'RE GOING. JUST DON'T TELL HIM ABOUT IT!

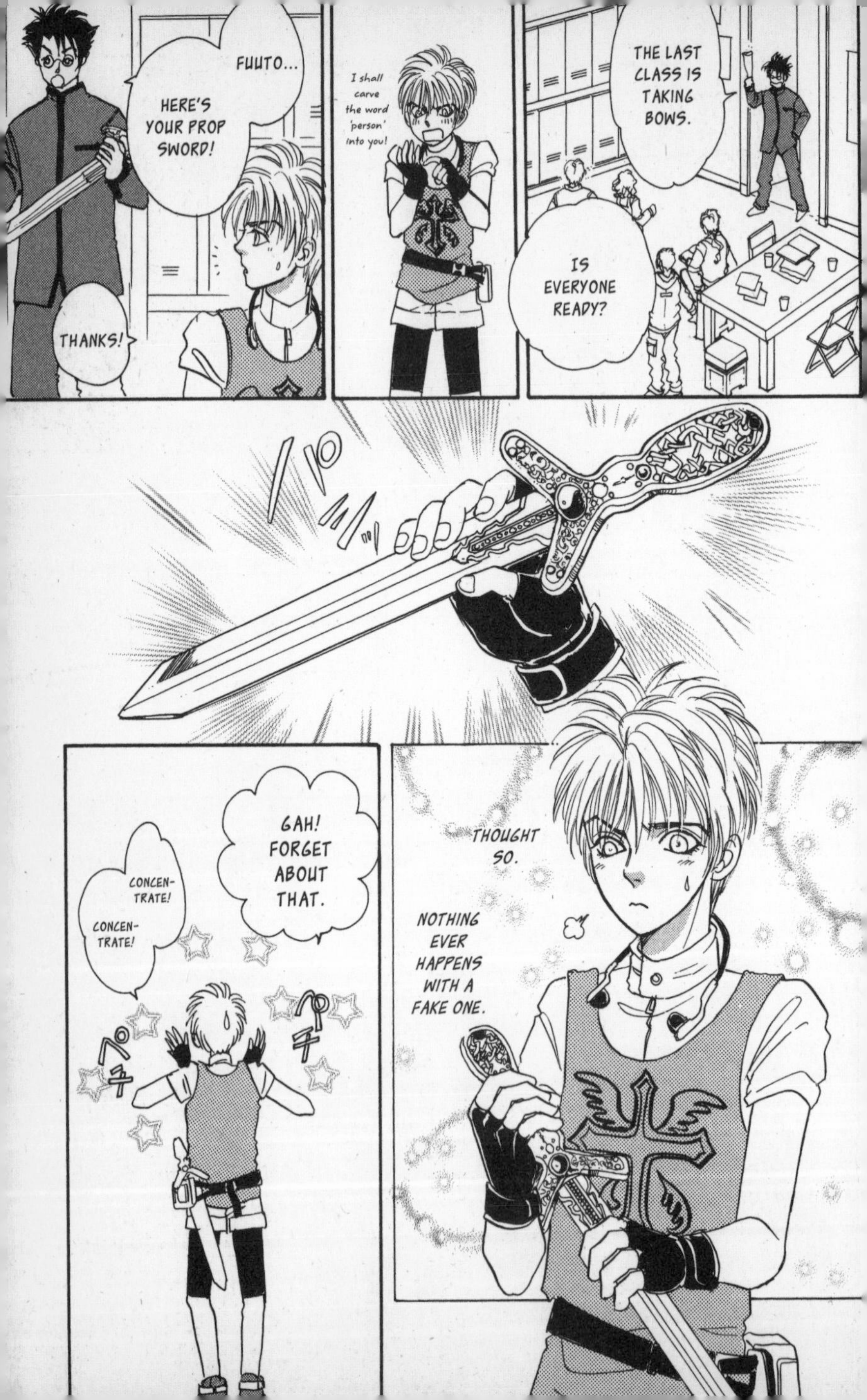

THE LAST CLASS IS TAKING BOWS.
IS EVERYONE READY?
I shall carve the word 'person' into you!
FUUTO...
HERE'S YOUR PROP SWORD!
THANKS!
THOUGHT SO.
NOTHING EVER HAPPENS WITH A FAKE ONE.
GAH! FORGET ABOUT THAT.
CONCEN-TRATE!
CONCEN-TRATE!

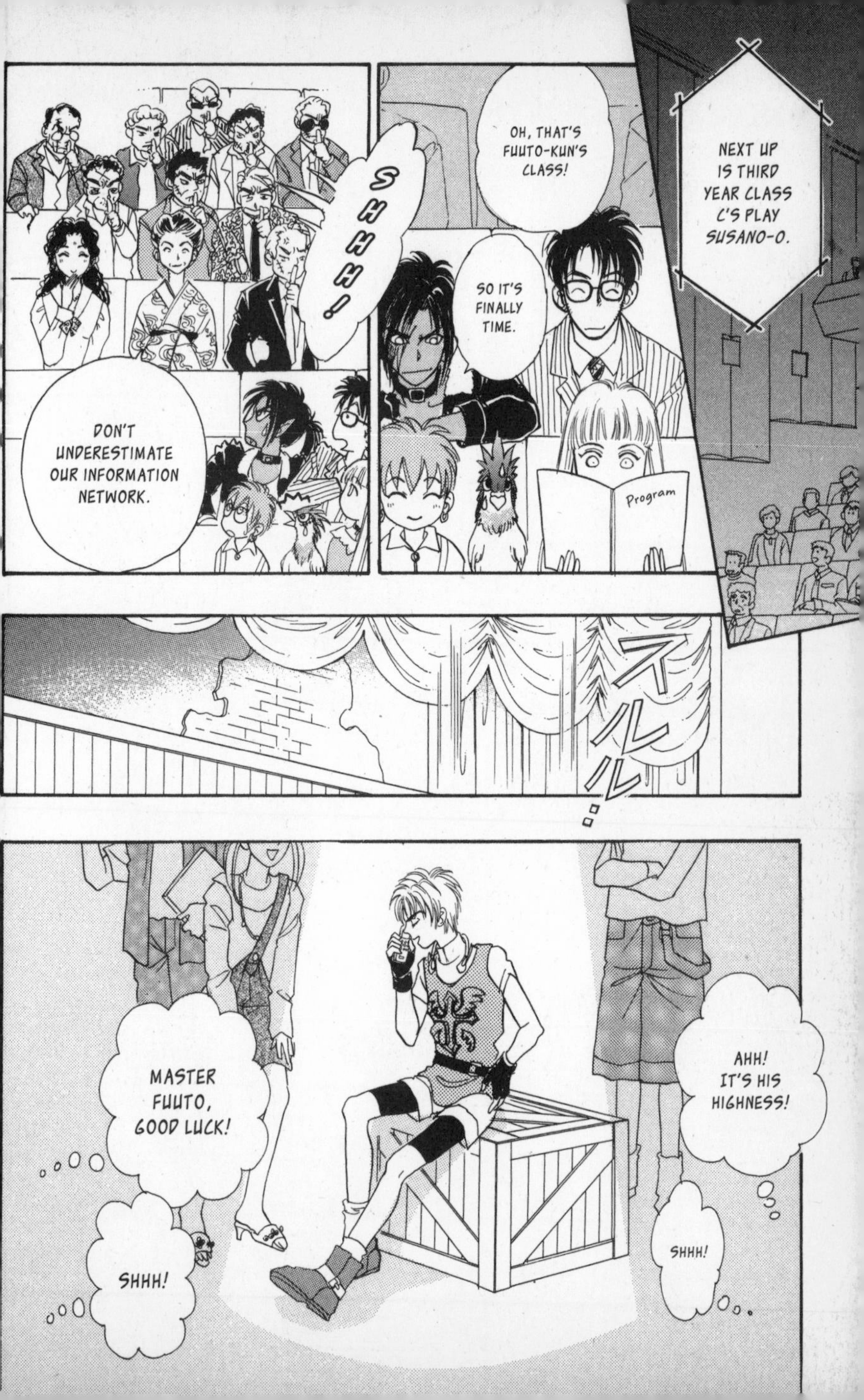
NEXT UP IS THIRD YEAR CLASS C'S PLAY SUSANO-O.
OH, THAT'S FUUTO-KUN'S CLASS!
SO IT'S FINALLY TIME.
SHHHH!
DON'T UNDERESTIMATE OUR INFORMATION NETWORK.
スルル…
AHH! IT'S HIS HIGHNESS!
SHHH!
MASTER FUUTO, GOOD LUCK!
SHHH!

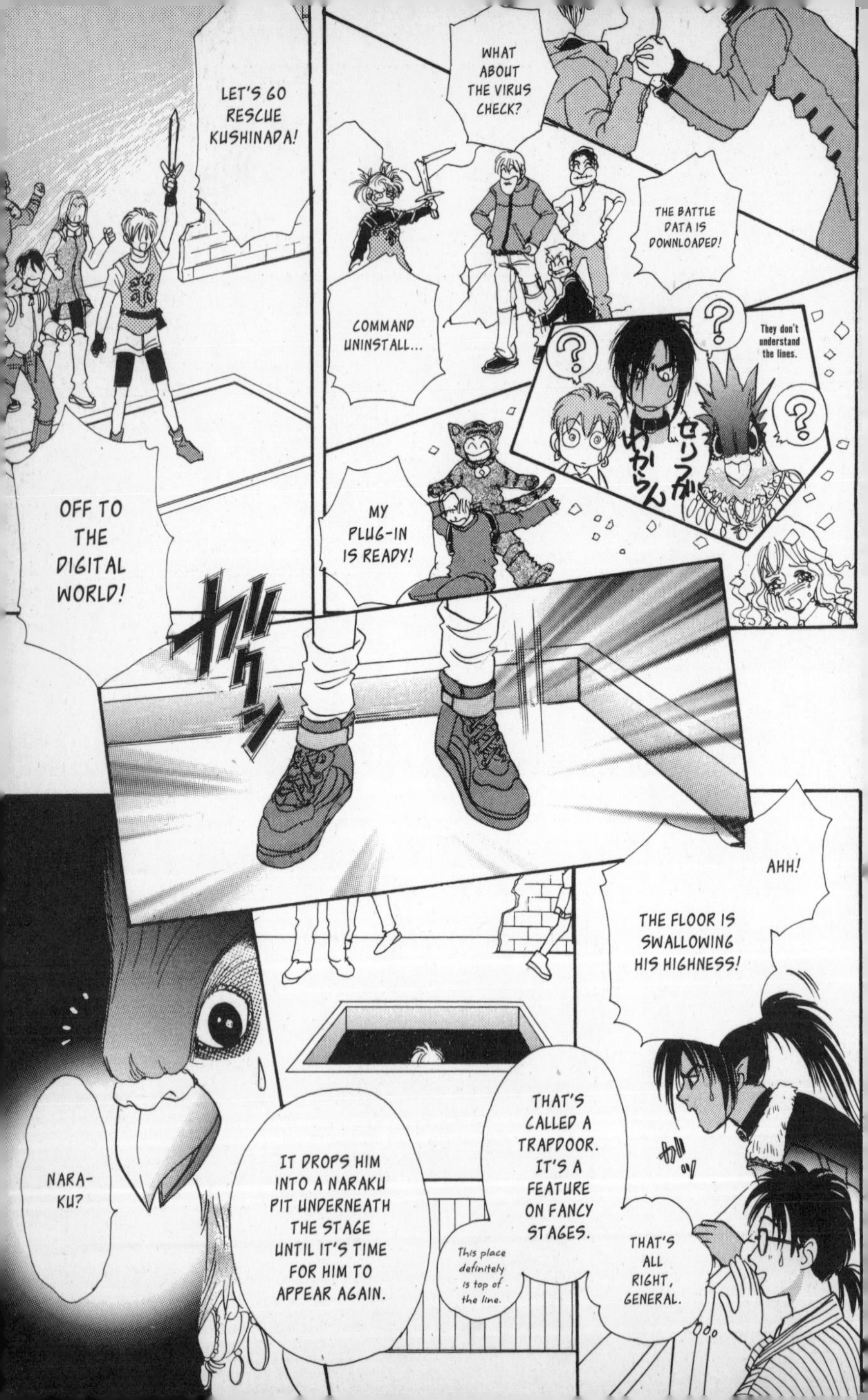

WHAT ABOUT THE VIRUS CHECK?
THE BATTLE DATA IS DOWNLOADED!
COMMAND UNINSTALL...
They don't understand the lines.
セリフがわからん
MY PLUG-IN IS READY!
LET'S GO RESCUE KUSHINADA!
OFF TO THE DIGITAL WORLD!
ガクン
AHH!
THE FLOOR IS SWALLOWING HIS HIGHNESS!
ガッ
THAT'S ALL RIGHT, GENERAL.
THAT'S CALLED A TRAPDOOR. IT'S A FEATURE ON FANCY STAGES.
This place definitely is top of the line.
IT DROPS HIM INTO A NARAKU PIT UNDERNEATH THE STAGE UNTIL IT'S TIME FOR HIM TO APPEAR AGAIN.
NARA-KU?

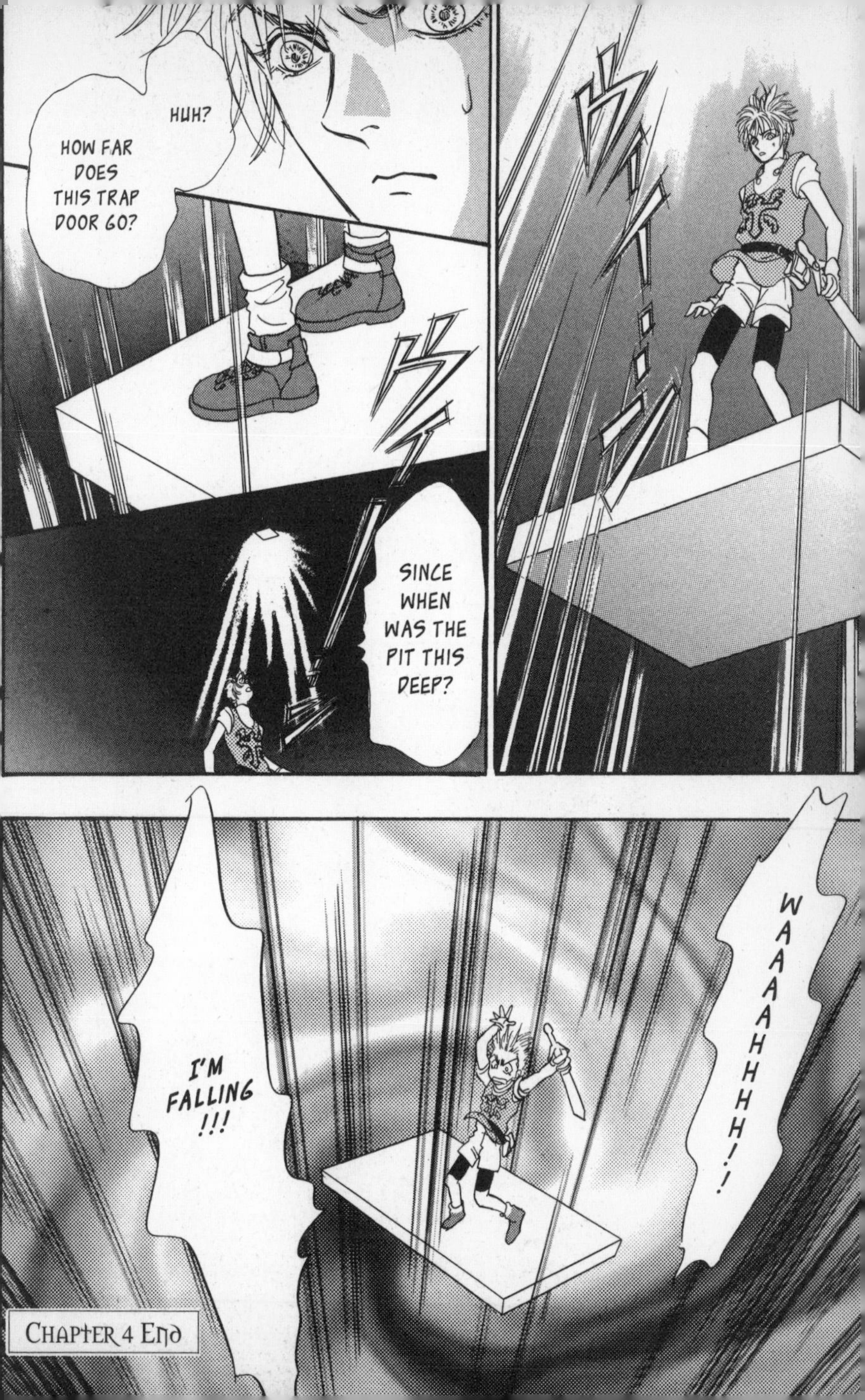
HUH?
HOW FAR DOES THIS TRAP DOOR GO?
SINCE WHEN WAS THE PIT THIS DEEP?
WAAAAHHHH!!!
I'M FALLING!!!
Chapter 4 End

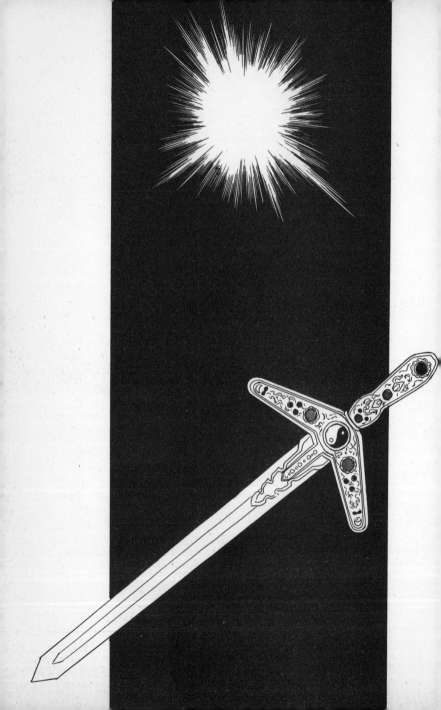

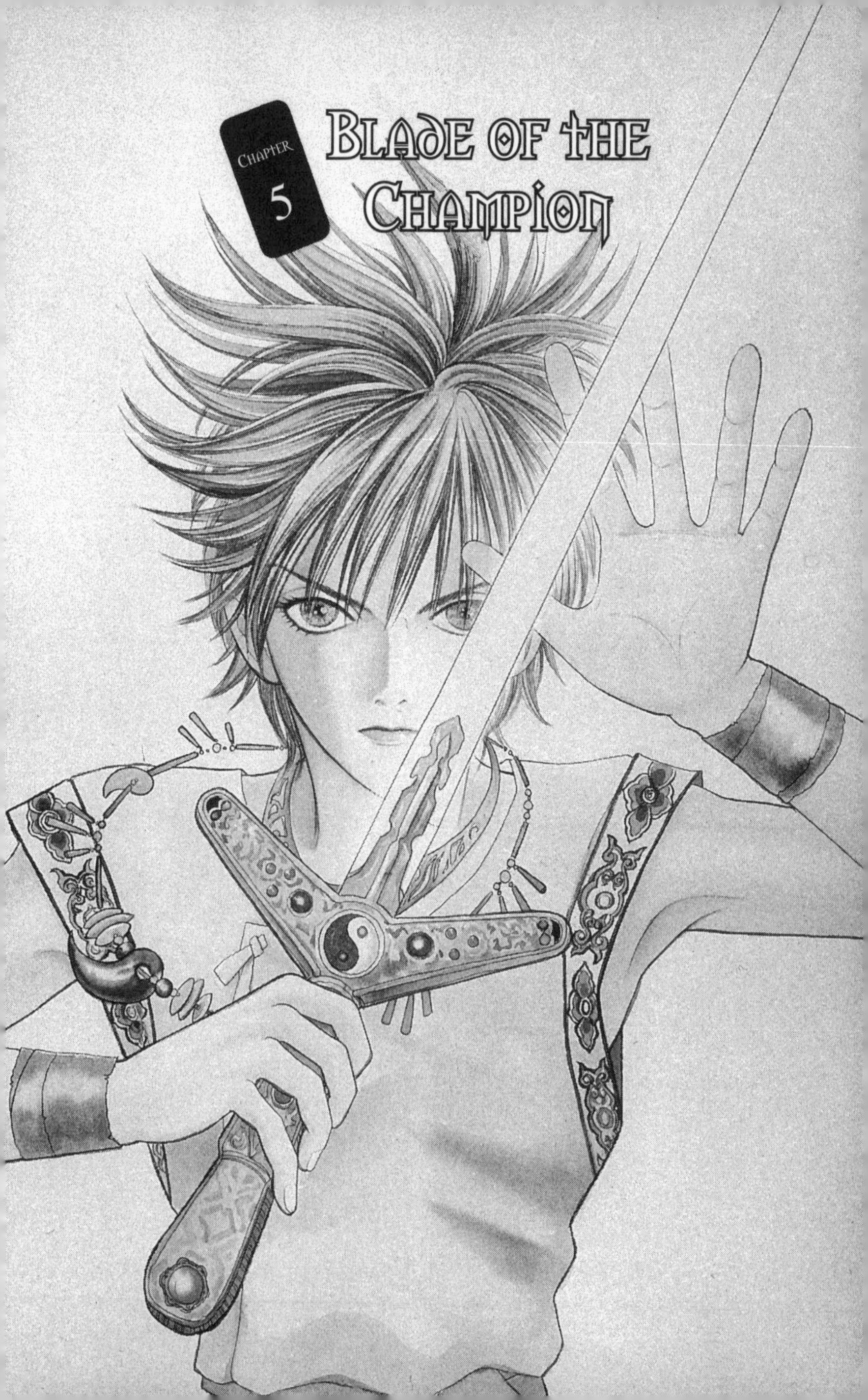
Chapter
5
Blade of the Champion

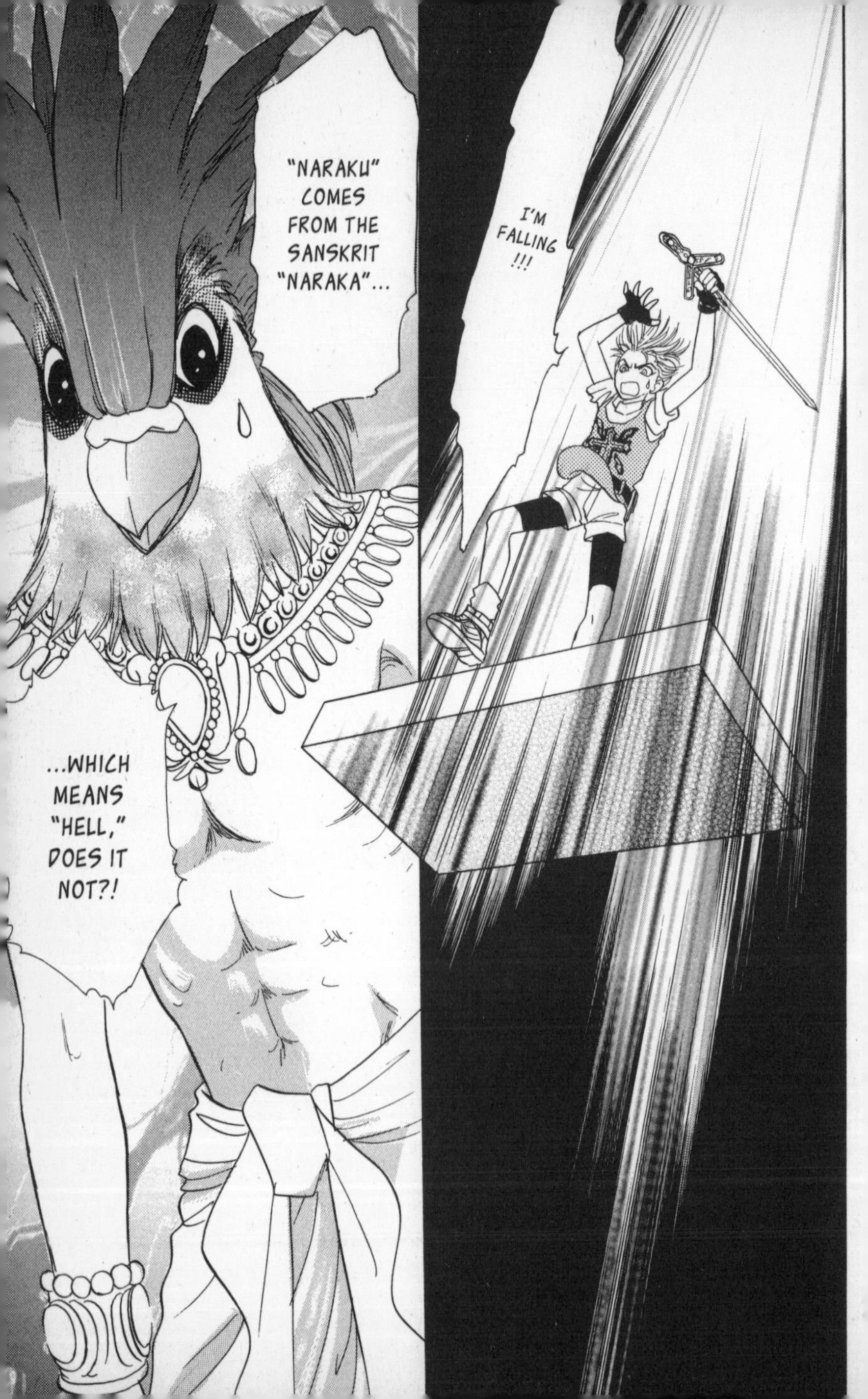
I'M FALLING !!!
"NARAKU" COMES FROM THE SANSKRIT "NARAKA"...
...WHICH MEANS "HELL," DOES IT NOT?!

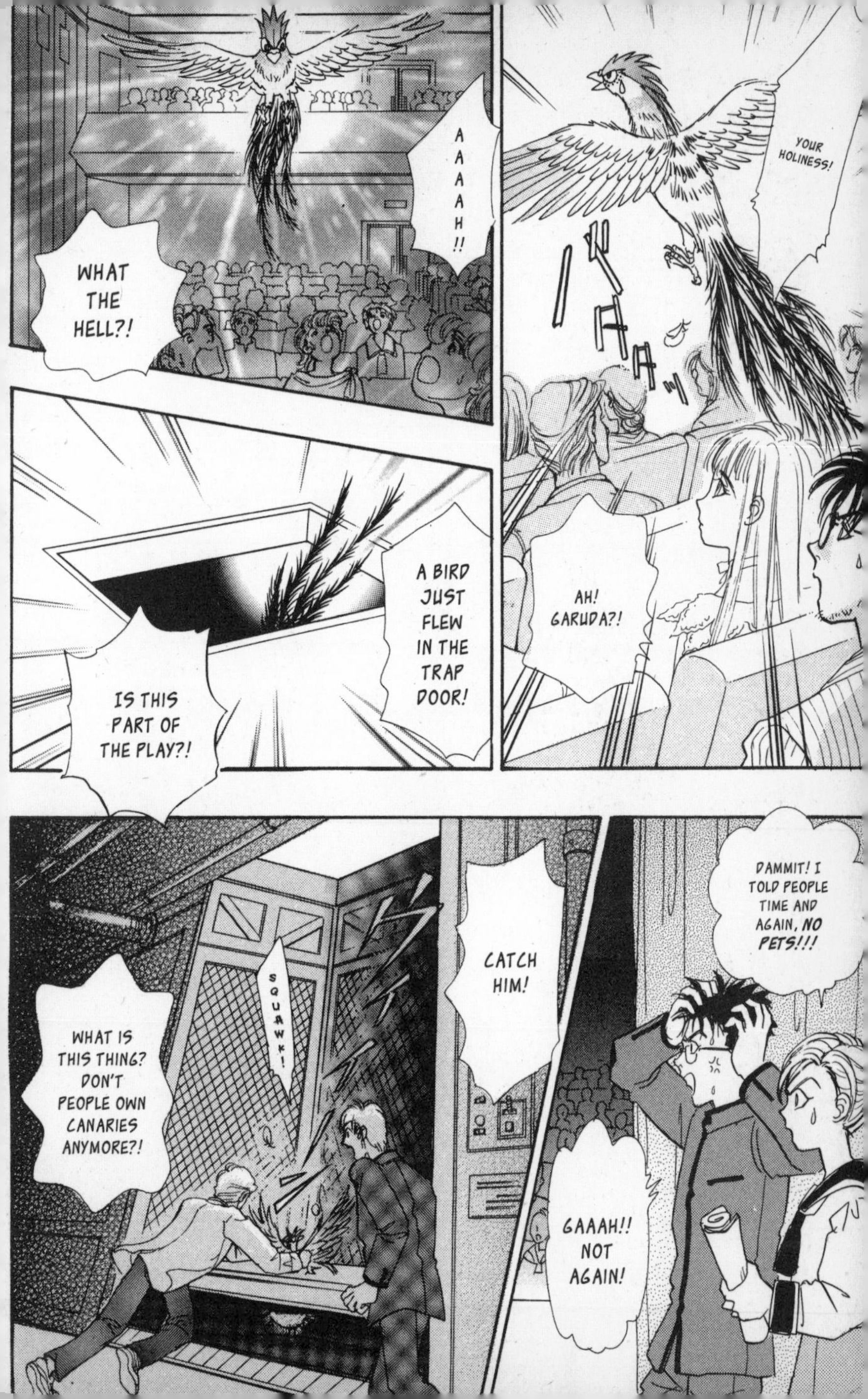
YOUR HOLINESS!
AH! GARUDA?!
AAAAAH!!
WHAT THE HELL?!
A BIRD JUST FLEW IN THE TRAP DOOR!
IS THIS PART OF THE PLAY?!
DAMMIT! I TOLD PEOPLE TIME AND AGAIN, **NO PETS!!!**
GAAAH!! NOT AGAIN!
CATCH HIM!
SQUAWK!
WHAT IS THIS THING? DON'T PEOPLE OWN CANARIES ANYMORE?!

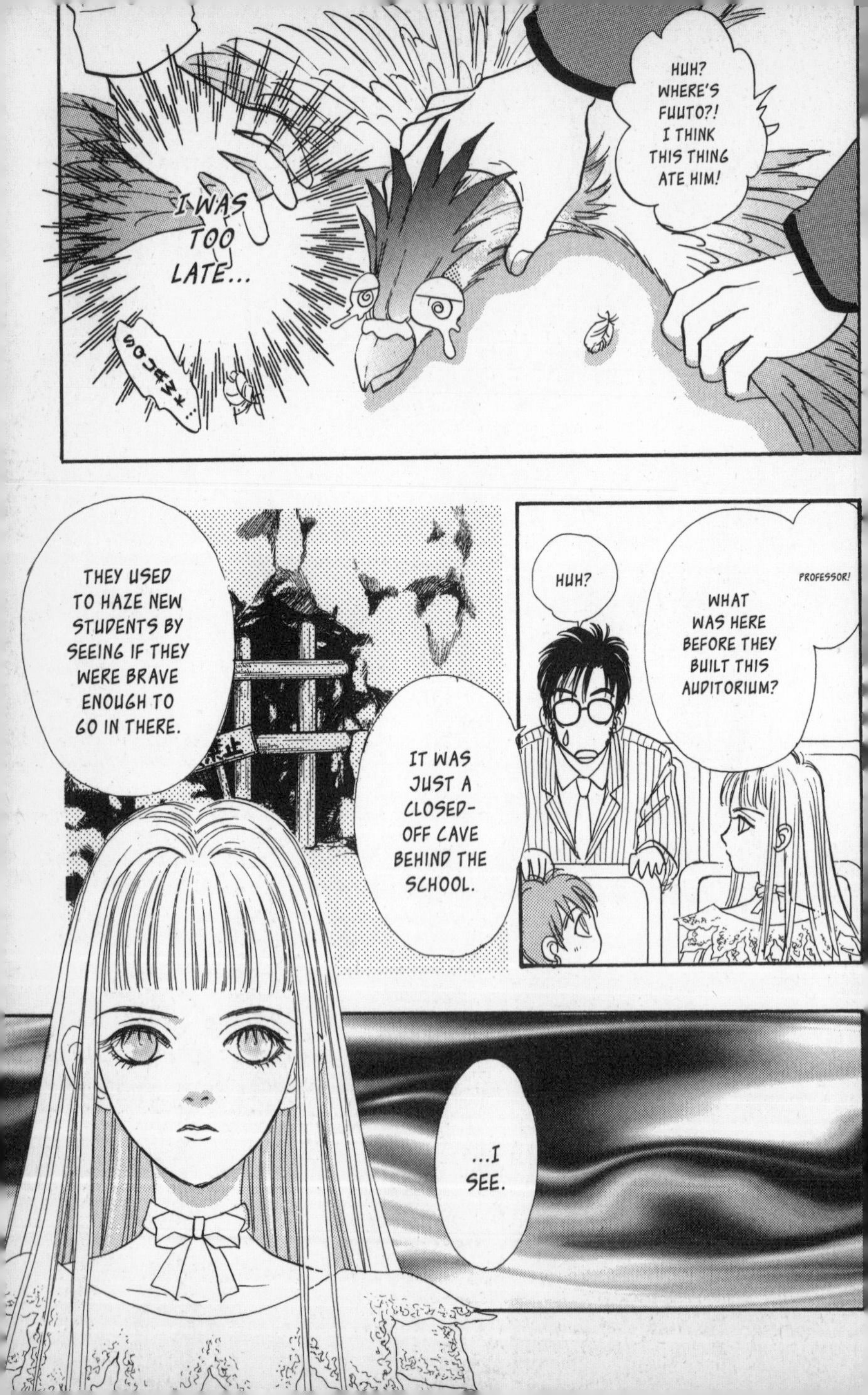
HUH? WHERE'S FUUTO?! I THINK THIS THING ATE HIM!
I WAS TOO LATE...
PROFESSOR!
WHAT WAS HERE BEFORE THEY BUILT THIS AUDITORIUM?
HUH?
IT WAS JUST A CLOSED-OFF CAVE BEHIND THE SCHOOL.
THEY USED TO HAZE NEW STUDENTS BY SEEING IF THEY WERE BRAVE ENOUGH TO GO IN THERE.
...I SEE.

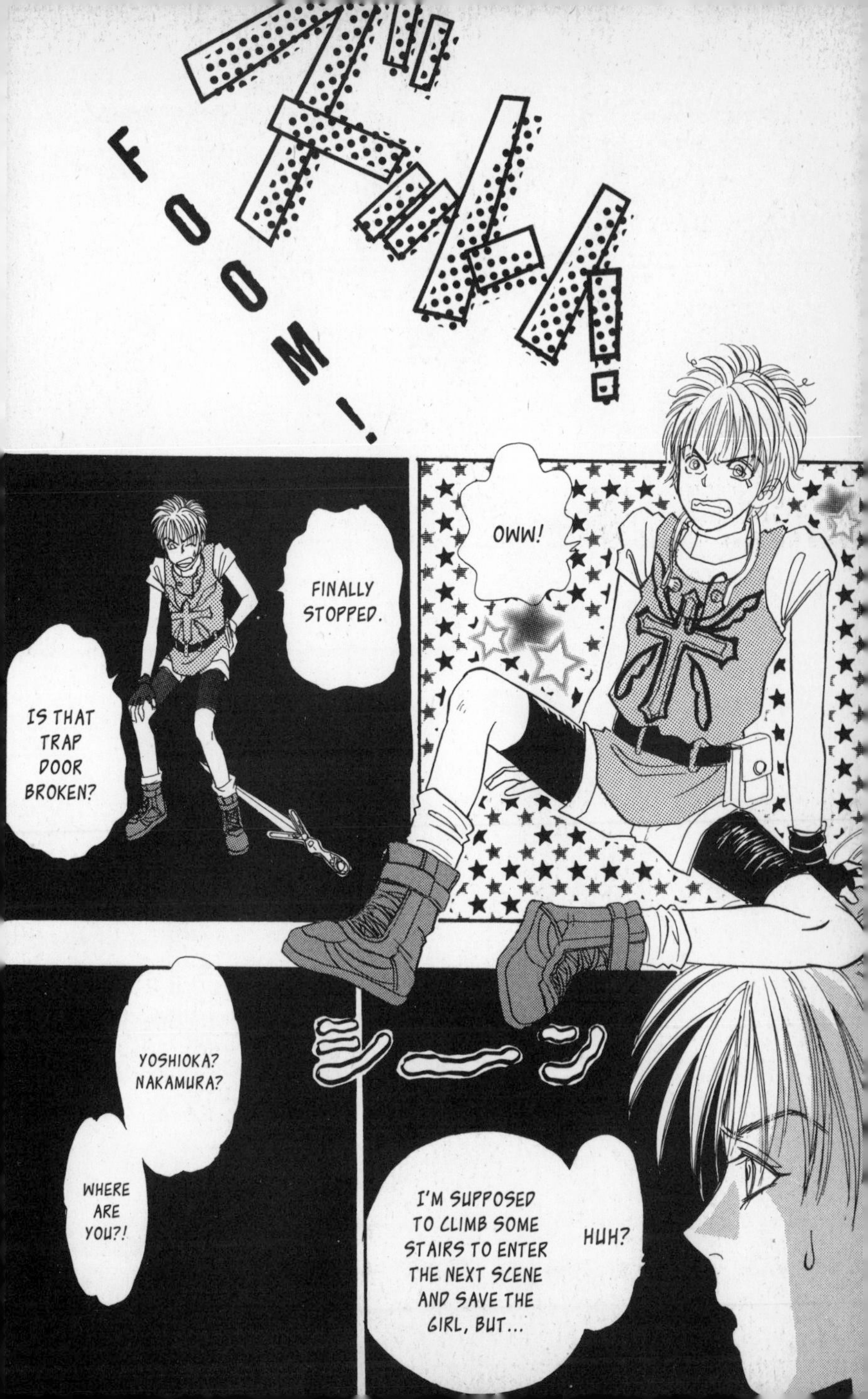
FOOM!
OWW!
FINALLY STOPPED.
IS THAT TRAP DOOR BROKEN?
HUH?
I'M SUPPOSED TO CLIMB SOME STAIRS TO ENTER THE NEXT SCENE AND SAVE THE GIRL, BUT...
YOSHIOKA? NAKAMURA?
WHERE ARE YOU?!

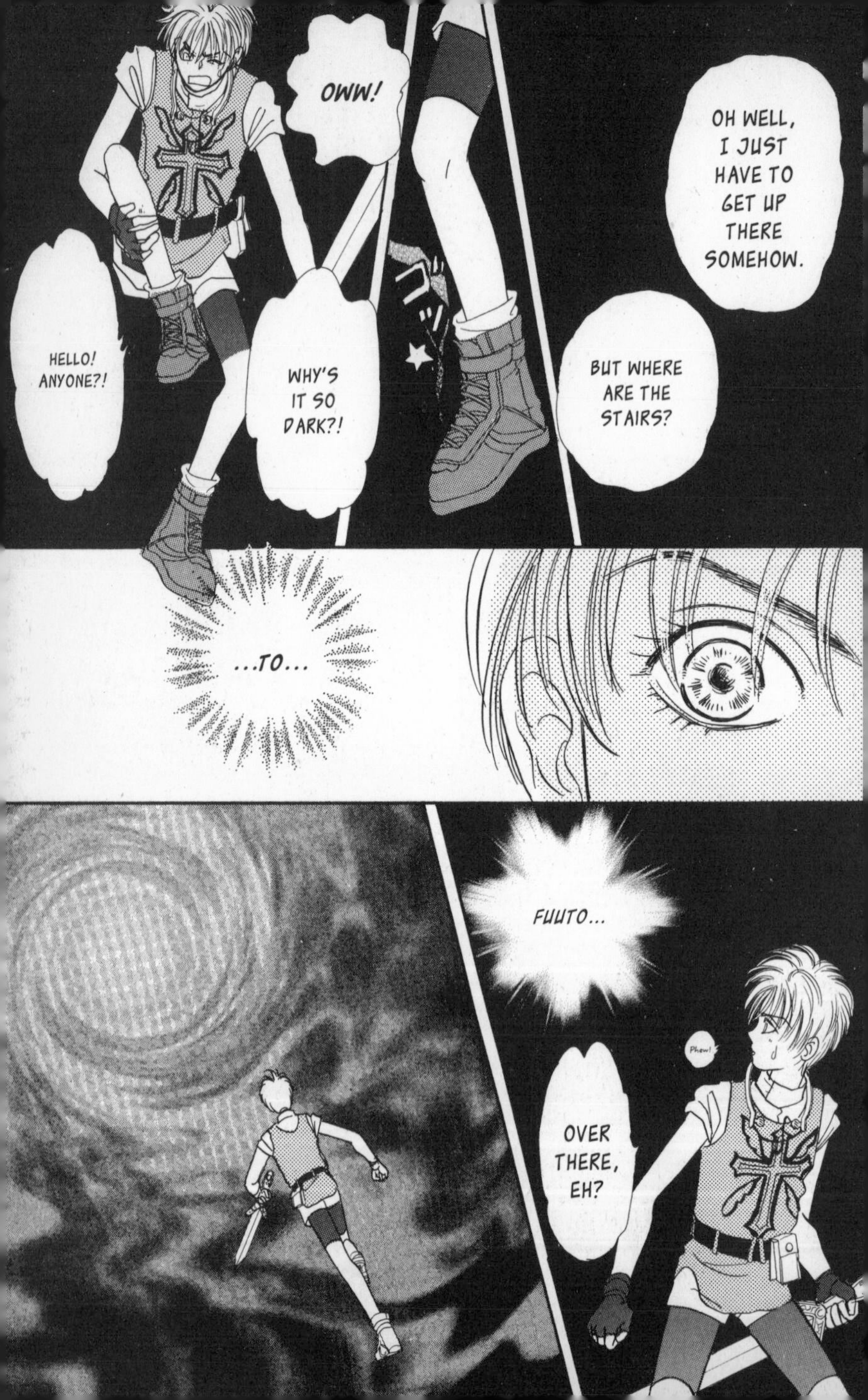
OH WELL, I JUST HAVE TO GET UP THERE SOMEHOW.
BUT WHERE ARE THE STAIRS?
WHY'S IT SO DARK?!
OWW!
HELLO! ANYONE?!
...TO...
FUUTO...
Phew!
OVER THERE, EH?

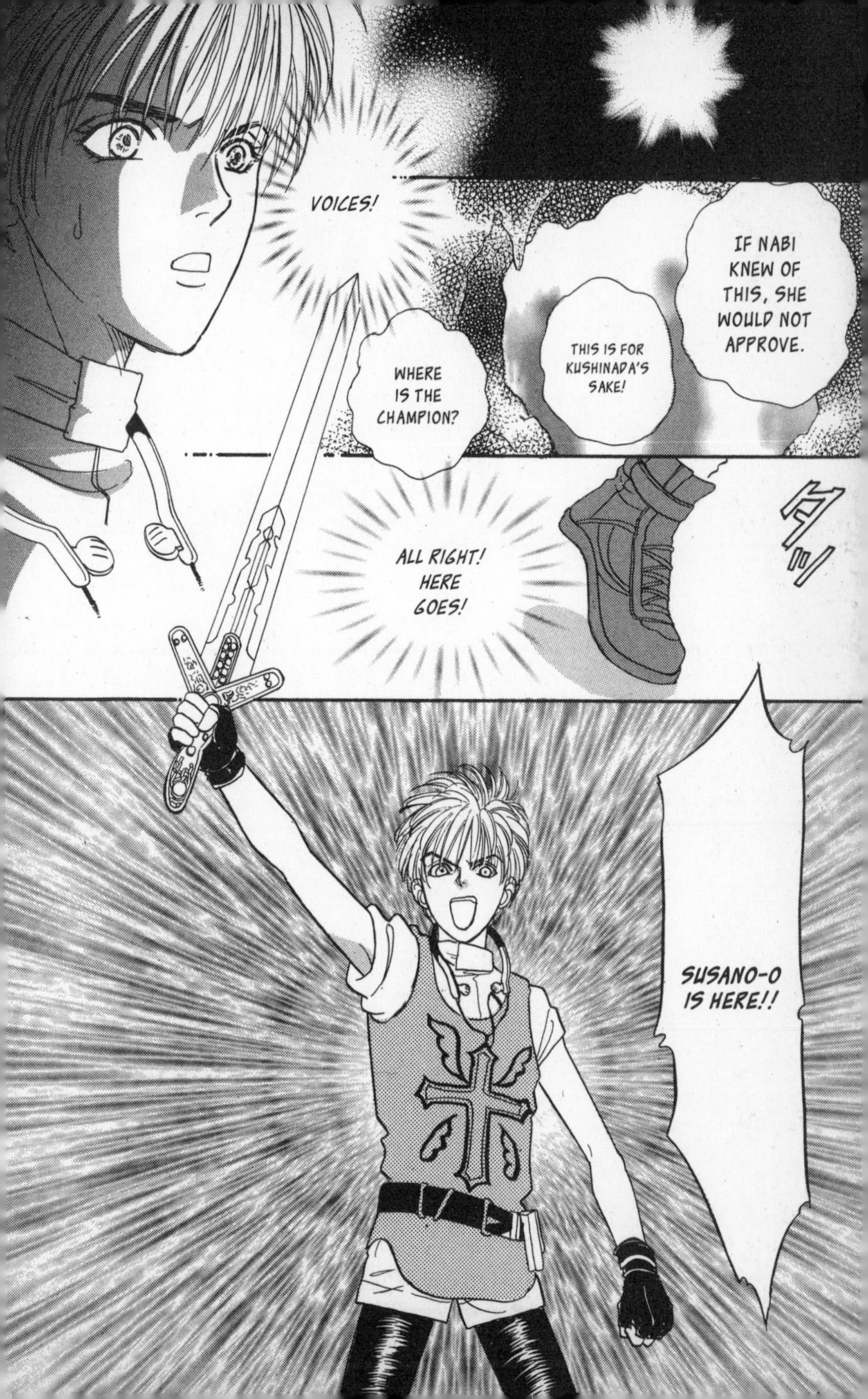
VOICES!
IF NABI KNEW OF THIS, SHE WOULD NOT APPROVE.
THIS IS FOR KUSHINADA'S SAKE!
WHERE IS THE CHAMPION?
ダッ
ALL RIGHT! HERE GOES!
SUSANO-O IS HERE!!

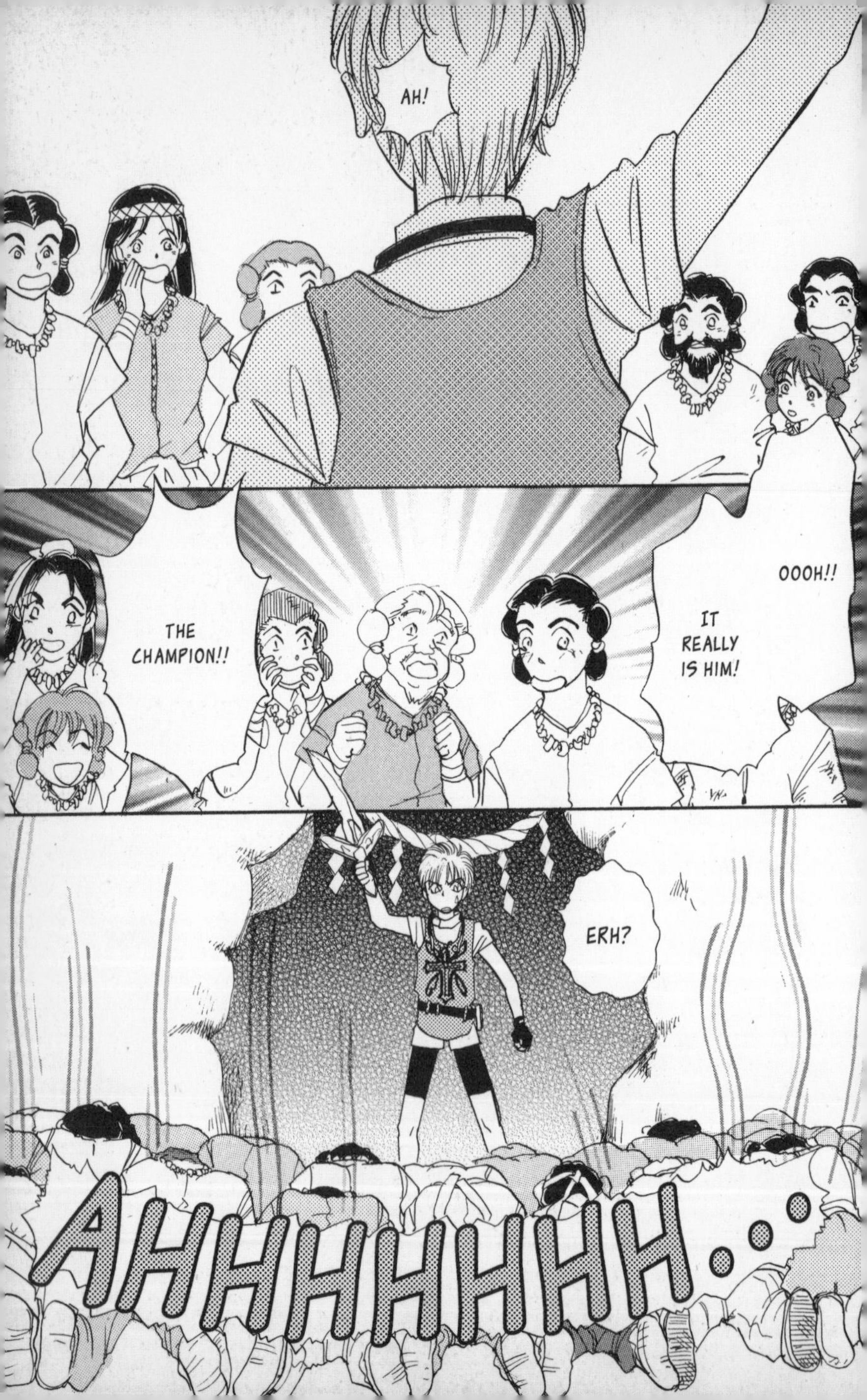
AH!
OOOH!!
IT REALLY IS HIM!
THE CHAMPION!!
ERH?
AHHHHHHHH..:

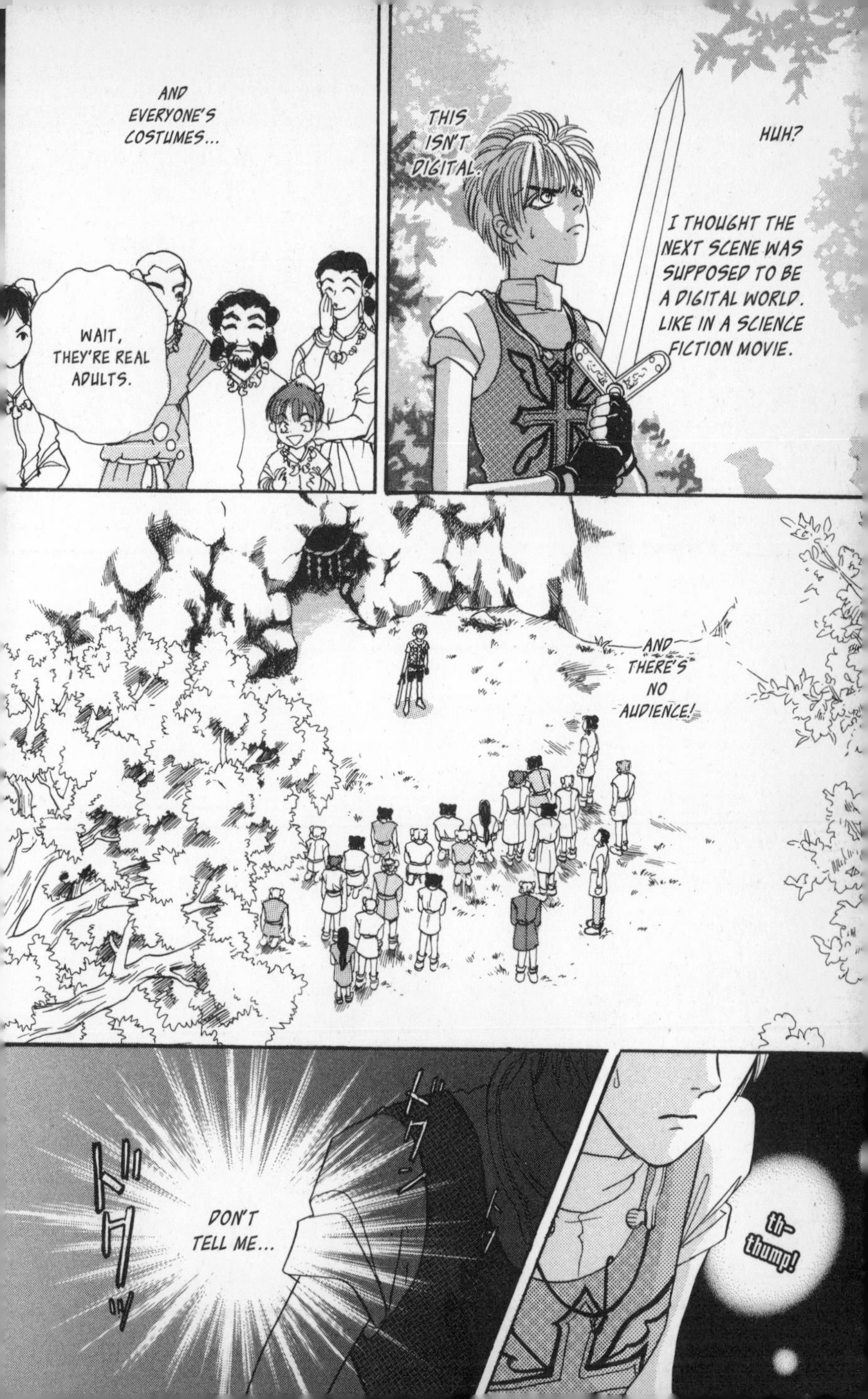
HUH?
I THOUGHT THE NEXT SCENE WAS SUPPOSED TO BE A DIGITAL WORLD. LIKE IN A SCIENCE FICTION MOVIE.
THIS ISN'T DIGITAL.
AND EVERYONE'S COSTUMES...
WAIT, THEY'RE REAL ADULTS.
AND THERE'S NO AUDIENCE!
th-thump!
DON'T TELL ME...

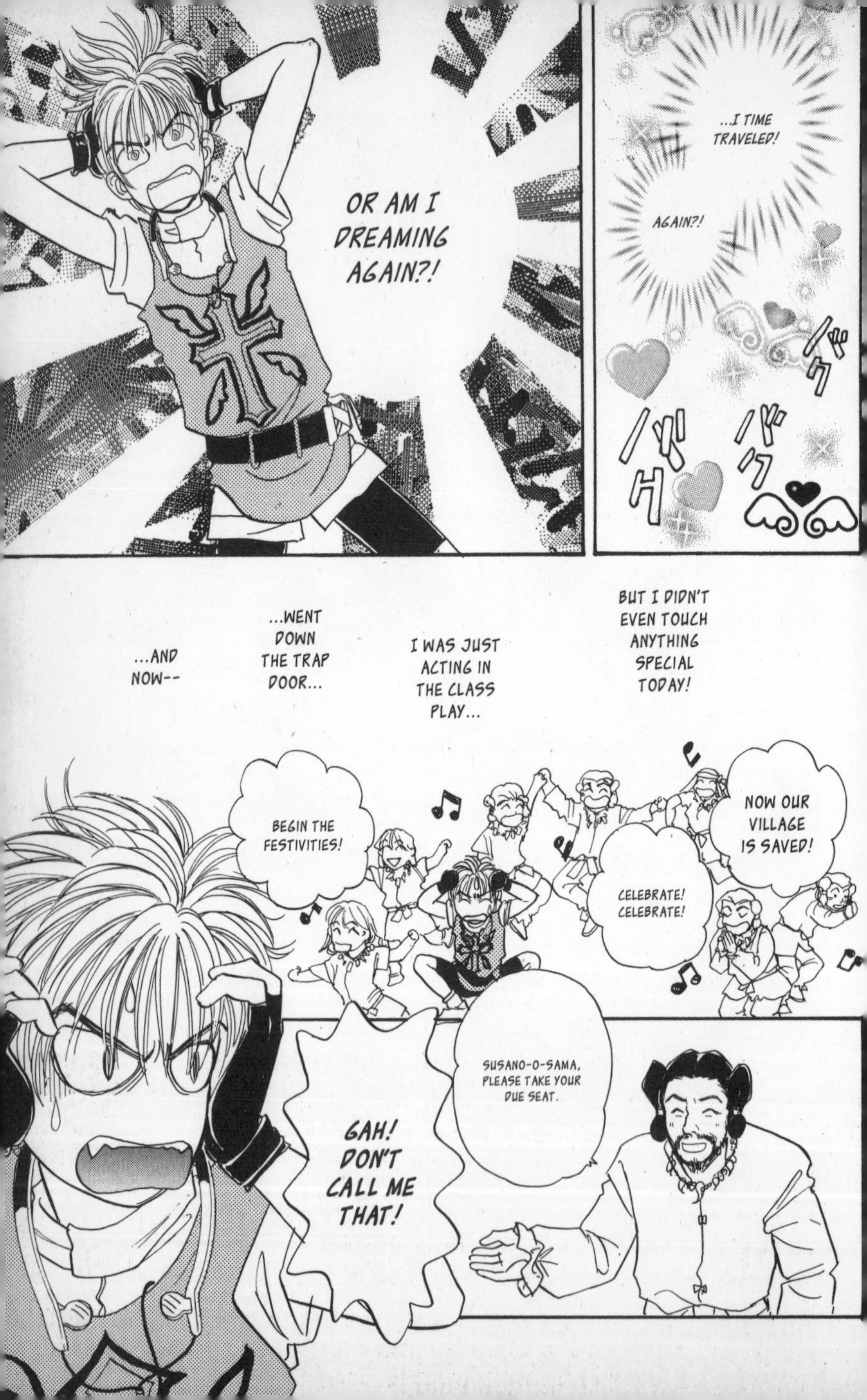
...I TIME TRAVELED!
AGAIN?!
OR AM I DREAMING AGAIN?!
BUT I DIDN'T EVEN TOUCH ANYTHING SPECIAL TODAY!
I WAS JUST ACTING IN THE CLASS PLAY...
...WENT DOWN THE TRAP DOOR...
...AND NOW--
NOW OUR VILLAGE IS SAVED!
CELEBRATE! CELEBRATE!
BEGIN THE FESTIVITIES!
SUSANO-O-SAMA, PLEASE TAKE YOUR DUE SEAT.
GAH! DON'T CALL ME THAT!

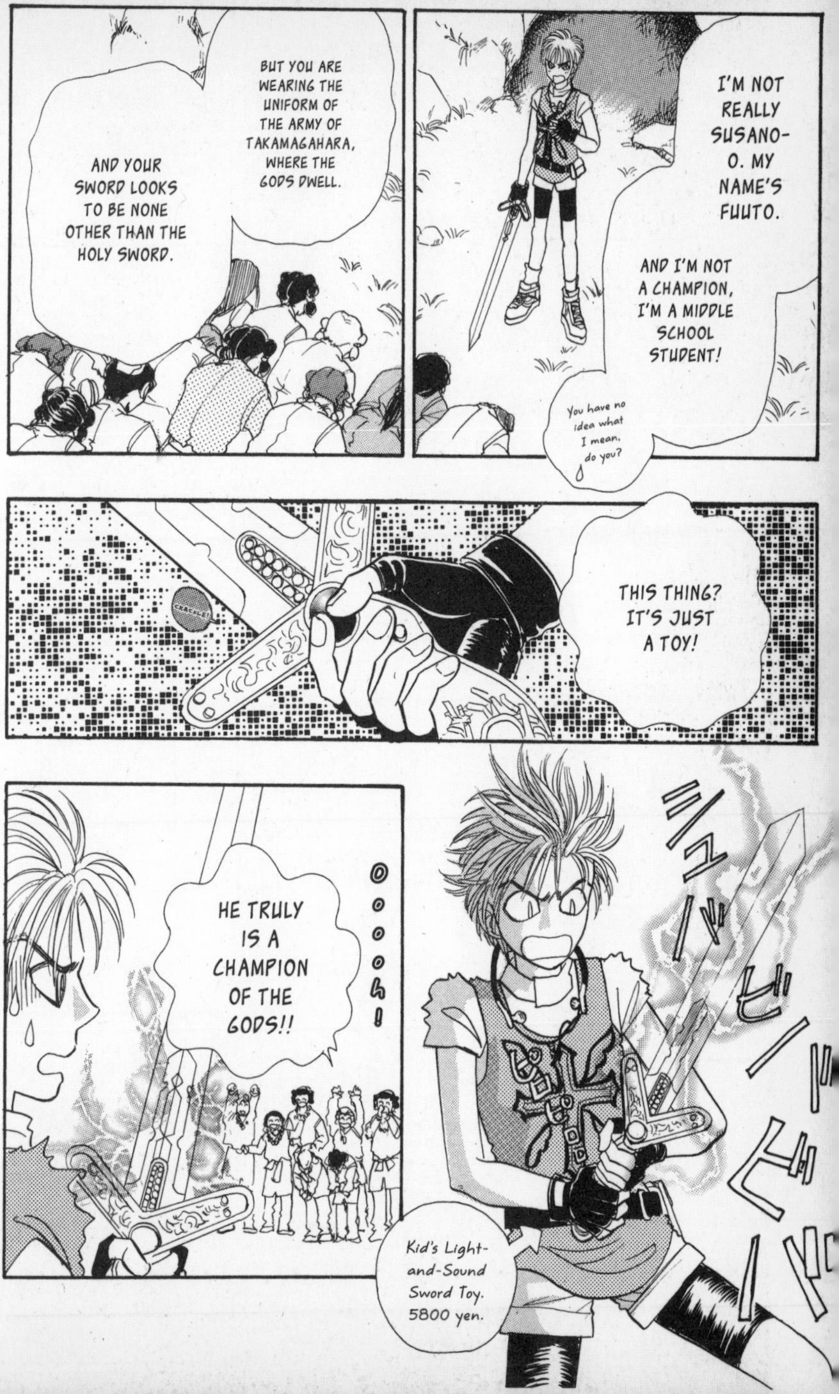

BUT YOU ARE WEARING THE UNIFORM OF THE ARMY OF TAKAMAGAHARA, WHERE THE GODS DWELL.
AND YOUR SWORD LOOKS TO BE NONE OTHER THAN THE HOLY SWORD.
I'M NOT REALLY SUSANO-O. MY NAME'S FUUTO.
AND I'M NOT A CHAMPION, I'M A MIDDLE SCHOOL STUDENT!
You have no idea what I mean, do you?
CRACKLE!
THIS THING? IT'S JUST A TOY!
HE TRULY IS A CHAMPION OF THE GODS!!
Ooooooh!
Kid's Light-and-Sound Sword Toy. 5800 yen.

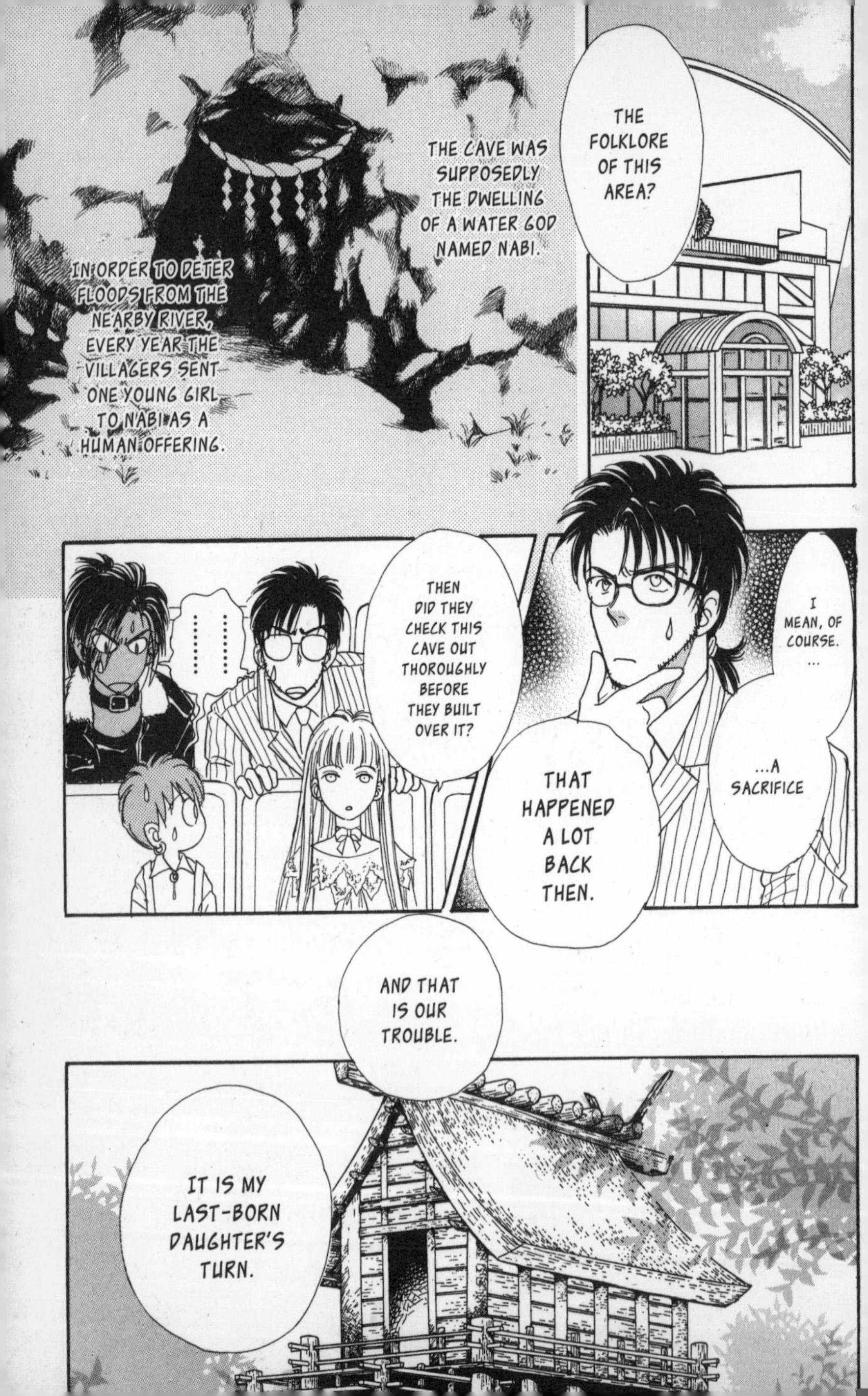
THE FOLKLORE OF THIS AREA?
THE CAVE WAS SUPPOSEDLY THE DWELLING OF A WATER GOD NAMED NABI.
IN ORDER TO DETER FLOODS FROM THE NEARBY RIVER, EVERY YEAR THE VILLAGERS SENT ONE YOUNG GIRL TO NABI AS A HUMAN OFFERING.
I MEAN, OF COURSE. ...
...A SACRIFICE
THAT HAPPENED A LOT BACK THEN.
THEN DID THEY CHECK THIS CAVE OUT THOROUGHLY BEFORE THEY BUILT OVER IT?
......
AND THAT IS OUR TROUBLE.
IT IS MY LAST-BORN DAUGHTER'S TURN.

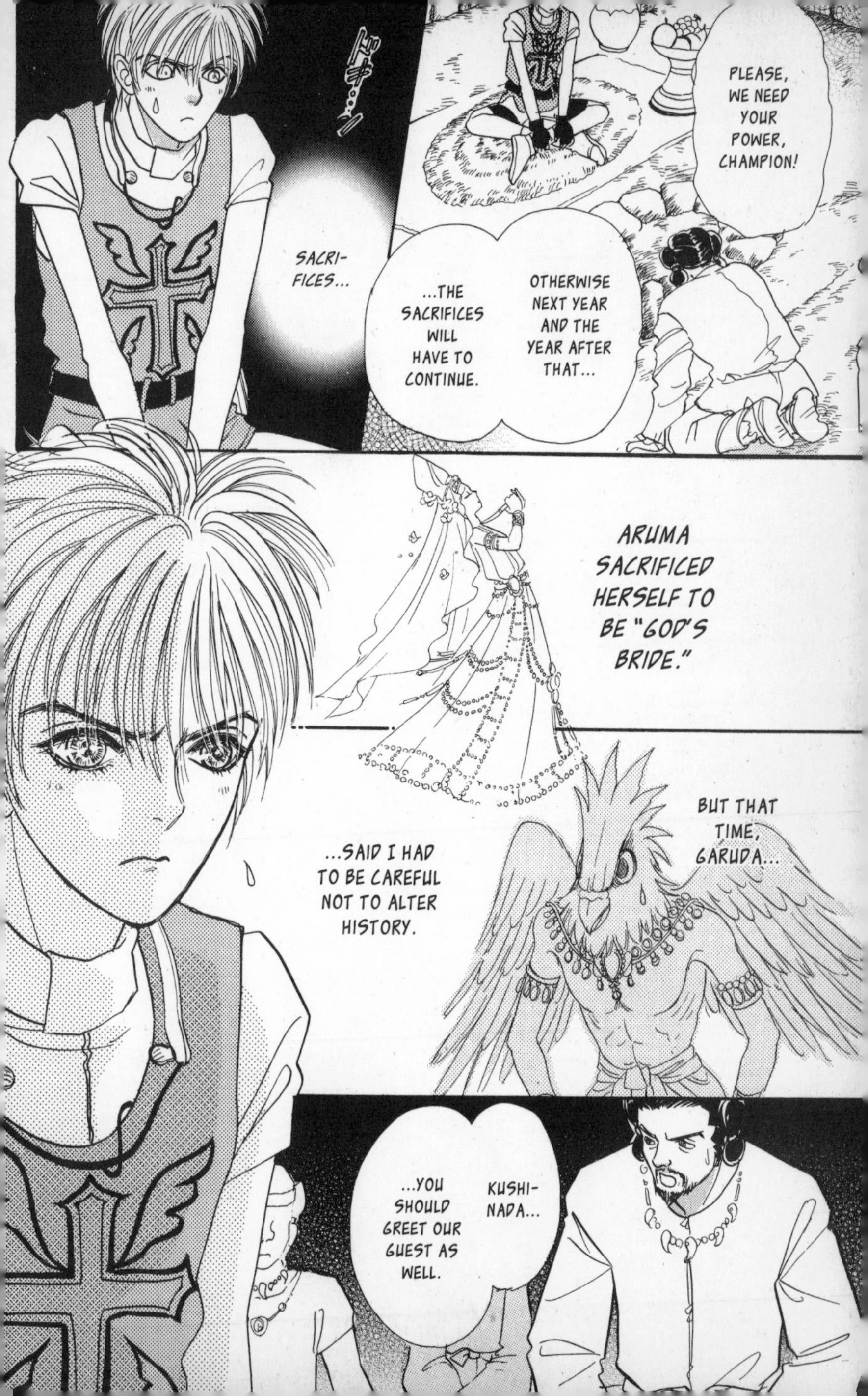
PLEASE, WE NEED YOUR POWER, CHAMPION!
OTHERWISE NEXT YEAR AND THE YEAR AFTER THAT...
...THE SACRIFICES WILL HAVE TO CONTINUE.
SACRI-FICES...
ARUMA SACRIFICED HERSELF TO BE "GOD'S BRIDE."
BUT THAT TIME, GARUDA...
...SAID I HAD TO BE CAREFUL NOT TO ALTER HISTORY.
KUSHI-NADA...
...YOU SHOULD GREET OUR GUEST AS WELL.

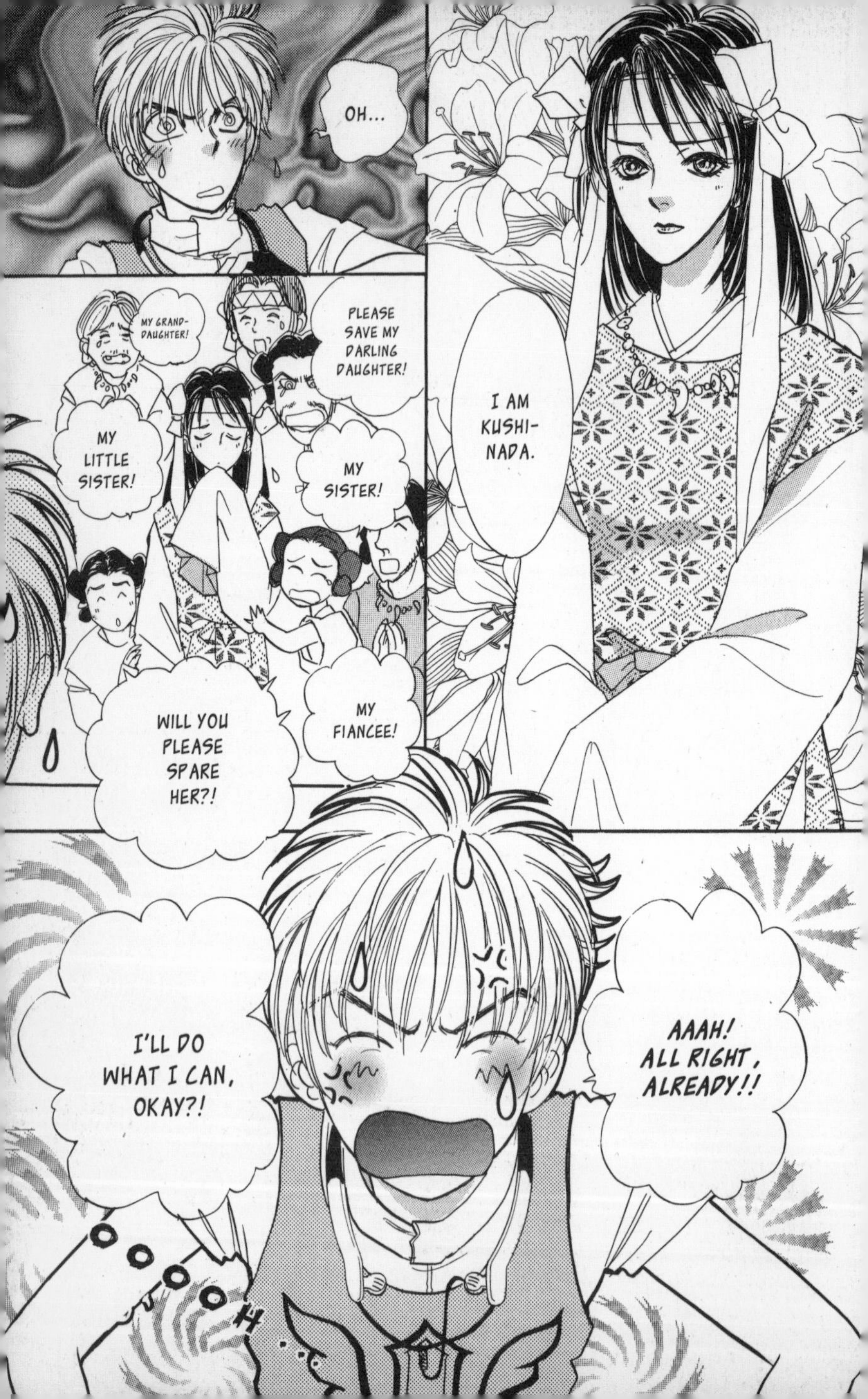
I AM KUSHINADA.
OH...
PLEASE SAVE MY DARLING DAUGHTER!
MY GRAND-DAUGHTER!
MY LITTLE SISTER!
MY SISTER!
MY FIANCEE!
WILL YOU PLEASE SPARE HER?!
AAAH! ALL RIGHT, ALREADY!!
I'LL DO WHAT I CAN, OKAY?!
OOOOH

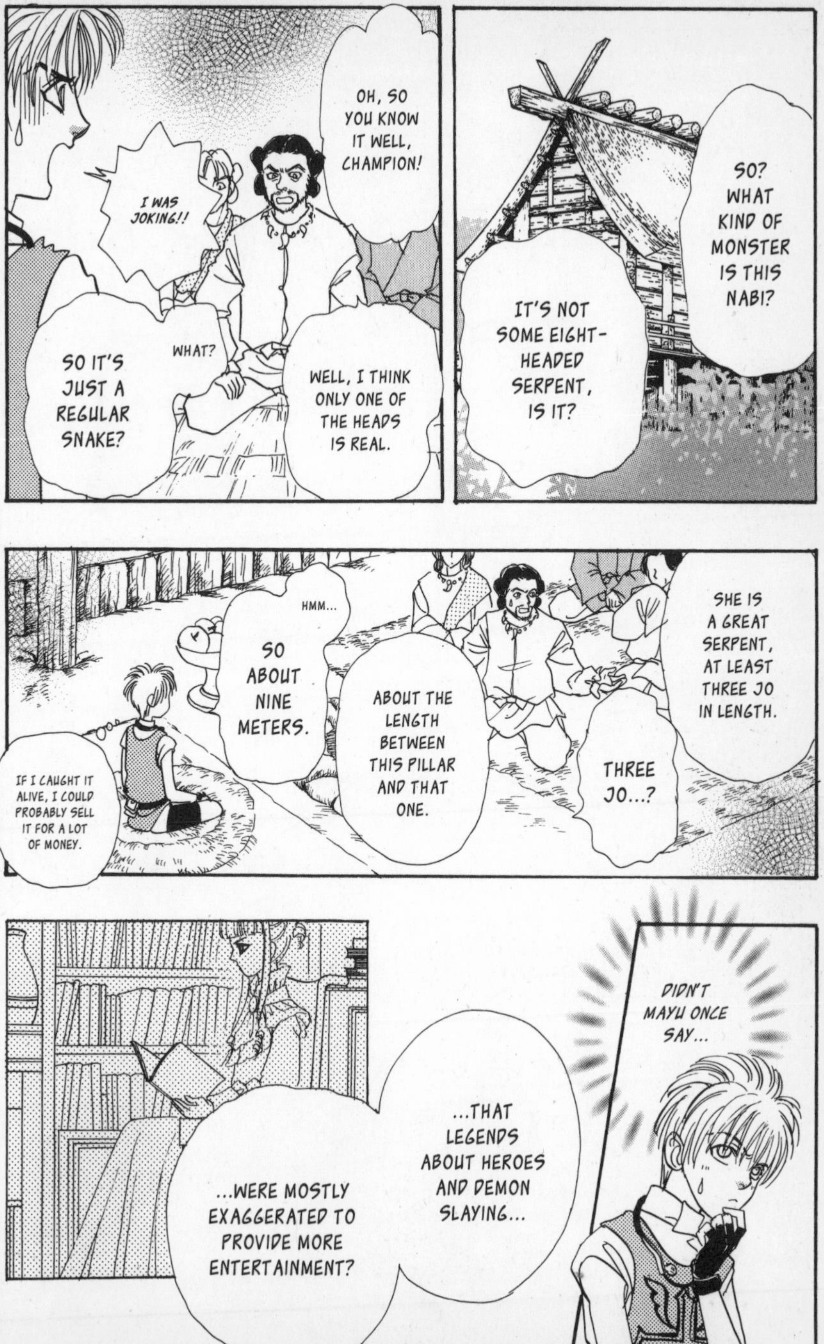
SO? WHAT KIND OF MONSTER IS THIS NABI?
IT'S NOT SOME EIGHT-HEADED SERPENT, IS IT?
OH, SO YOU KNOW IT WELL, CHAMPION!
I WAS JOKING!!
WELL, I THINK ONLY ONE OF THE HEADS IS REAL.
WHAT?
SO IT'S JUST A REGULAR SNAKE?
SHE IS A GREAT SERPENT, AT LEAST THREE JO IN LENGTH.
THREE JO...?
ABOUT THE LENGTH BETWEEN THIS PILLAR AND THAT ONE.
HMM...
SO ABOUT NINE METERS.
IF I CAUGHT IT ALIVE, I COULD PROBABLY SELL IT FOR A LOT OF MONEY.
DIDN'T MAYU ONCE SAY...
...THAT LEGENDS ABOUT HEROES AND DEMON SLAYING...
...WERE MOSTLY EXAGGERATED TO PROVIDE MORE ENTERTAINMENT?

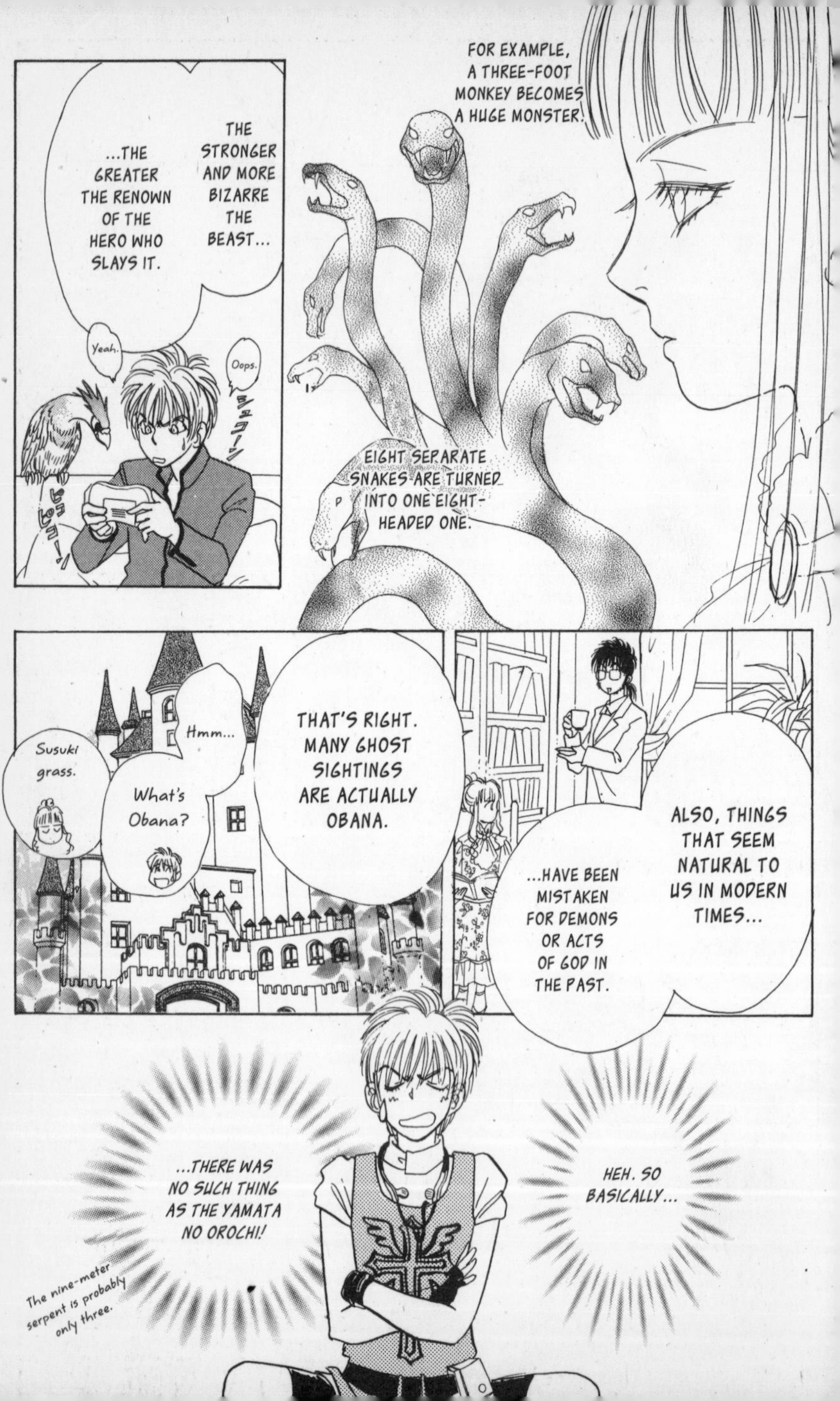
FOR EXAMPLE, A THREE-FOOT MONKEY BECOMES A HUGE MONSTER.
EIGHT SEPARATE SNAKES ARE TURNED INTO ONE EIGHT-HEADED ONE.
THE STRONGER AND MORE BIZARRE THE BEAST...
...THE GREATER THE RENOWN OF THE HERO WHO SLAYS IT.
Oops.
Yeah.
ALSO, THINGS THAT SEEM NATURAL TO US IN MODERN TIMES...
...HAVE BEEN MISTAKEN FOR DEMONS OR ACTS OF GOD IN THE PAST.
THAT'S RIGHT. MANY GHOST SIGHTINGS ARE ACTUALLY OBANA.
Hmm...
What's Obana?
Susuki grass.
HEH. SO BASICALLY...
...THERE WAS NO SUCH THING AS THE YAMATA NO OROCHI!
The nine-meter serpent is probably only three.

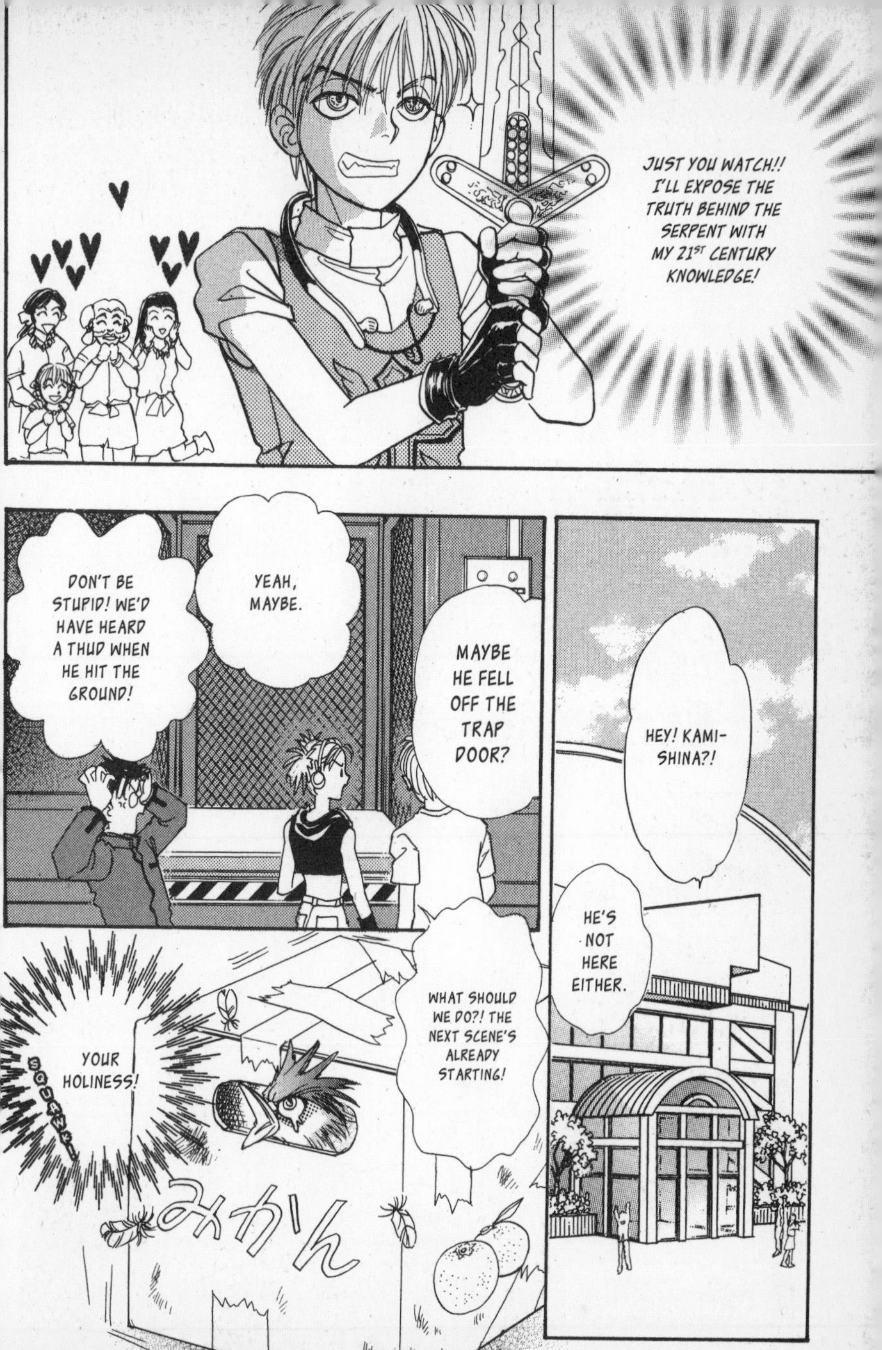
JUST YOU WATCH!! I'LL EXPOSE THE TRUTH BEHIND THE SERPENT WITH MY 21ST CENTURY KNOWLEDGE!
HEY! KAMI-SHINA?!
HE'S NOT HERE EITHER.
MAYBE HE FELL OFF THE TRAP DOOR?
YEAH, MAYBE.
DON'T BE STUPID! WE'D HAVE HEARD A THUD WHEN HE HIT THE GROUND!
WHAT SHOULD WE DO?! THE NEXT SCENE'S ALREADY STARTING!
YOUR HOLINESS!
SQUAWK!
みかん

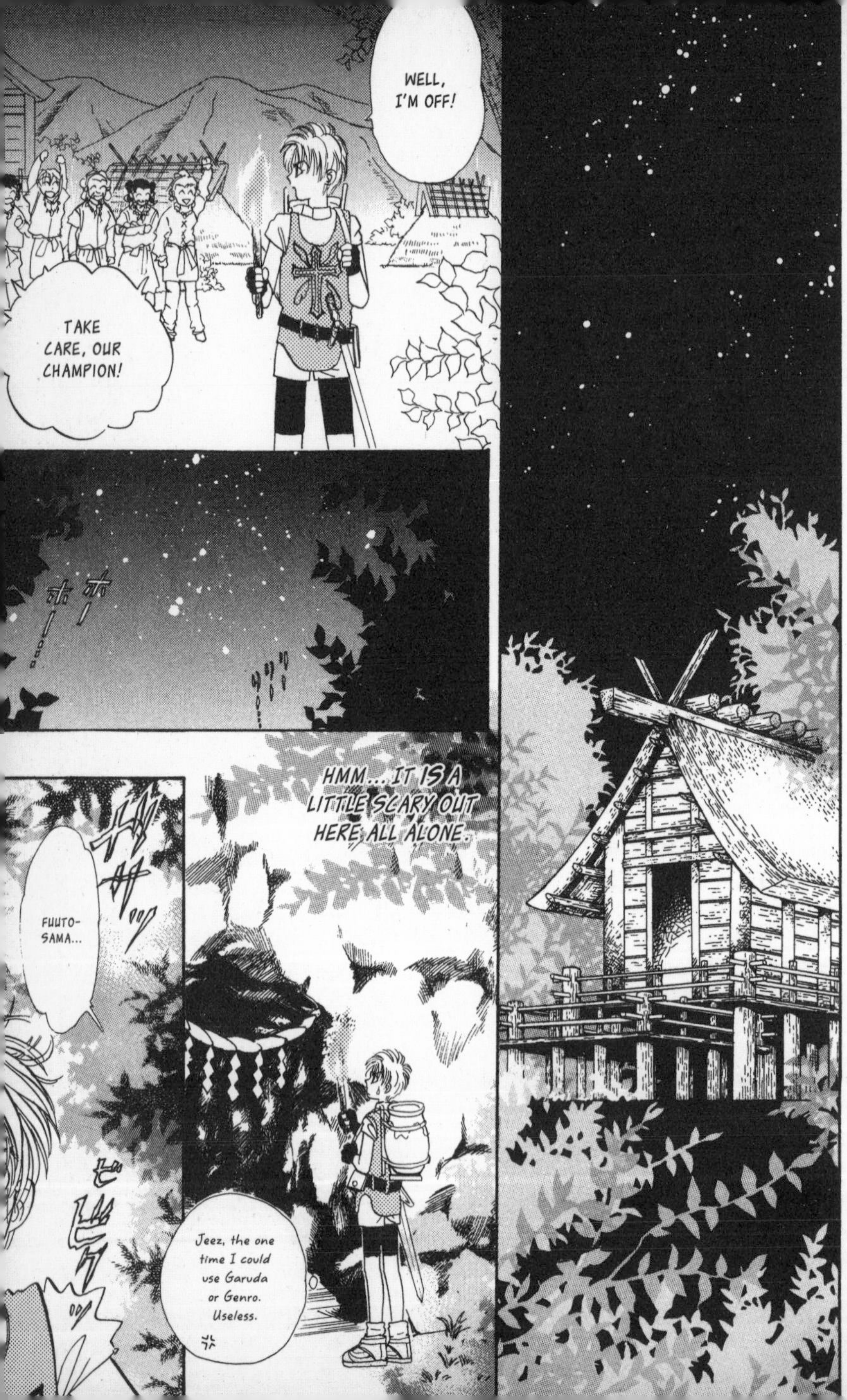
WELL, I'M OFF!
TAKE CARE, OUR CHAMPION!
HMM... IT IS A LITTLE SCARY OUT HERE ALL ALONE.
Jeez, the one time I could use Garuda or Genro. Useless.
FUUTO-SAMA...

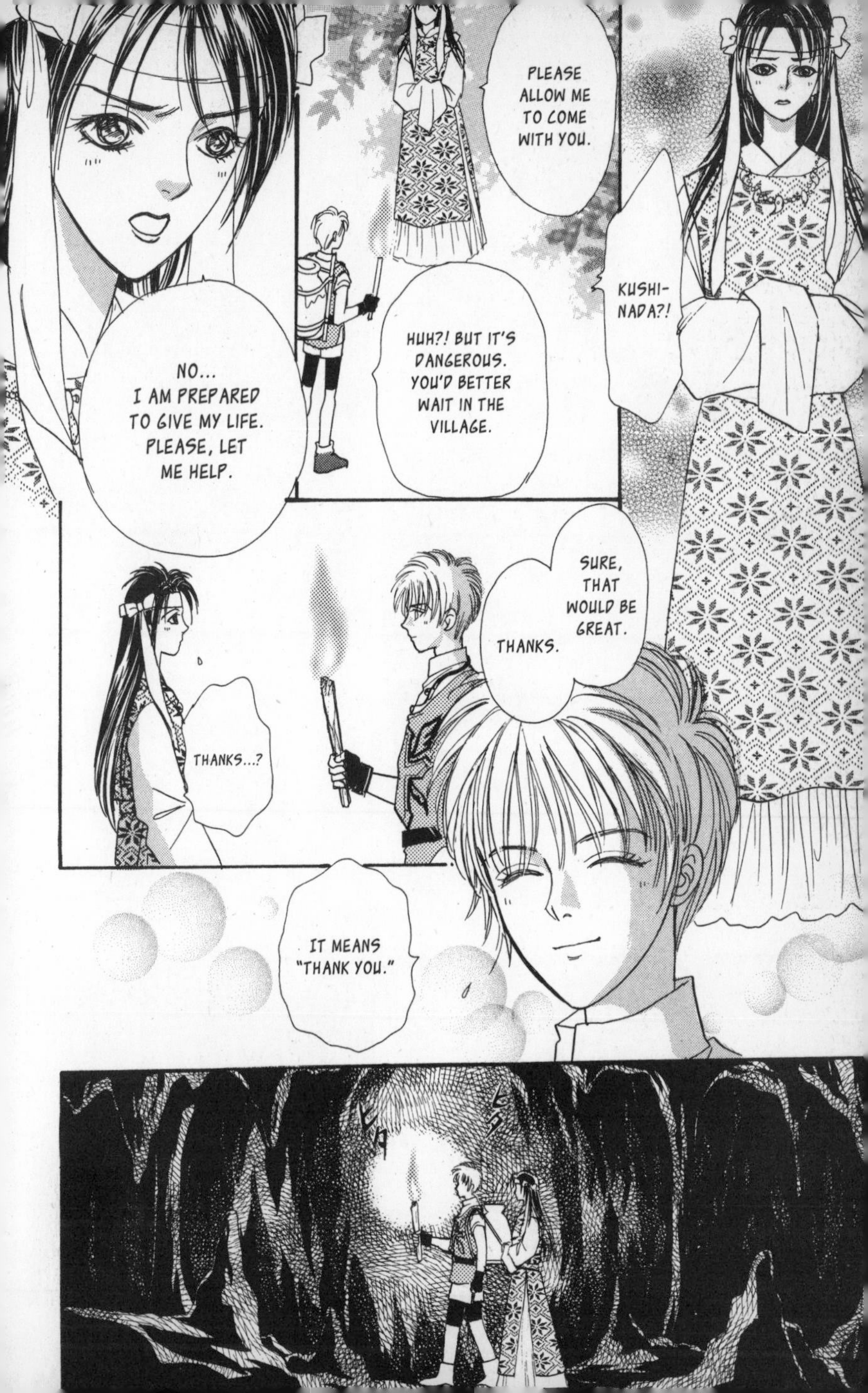
KUSHI-NADA?!
PLEASE ALLOW ME TO COME WITH YOU.
HUH?! BUT IT'S DANGEROUS. YOU'D BETTER WAIT IN THE VILLAGE.
NO... I AM PREPARED TO GIVE MY LIFE. PLEASE, LET ME HELP.
SURE, THAT WOULD BE GREAT.
THANKS.
THANKS...?
IT MEANS "THANK YOU."

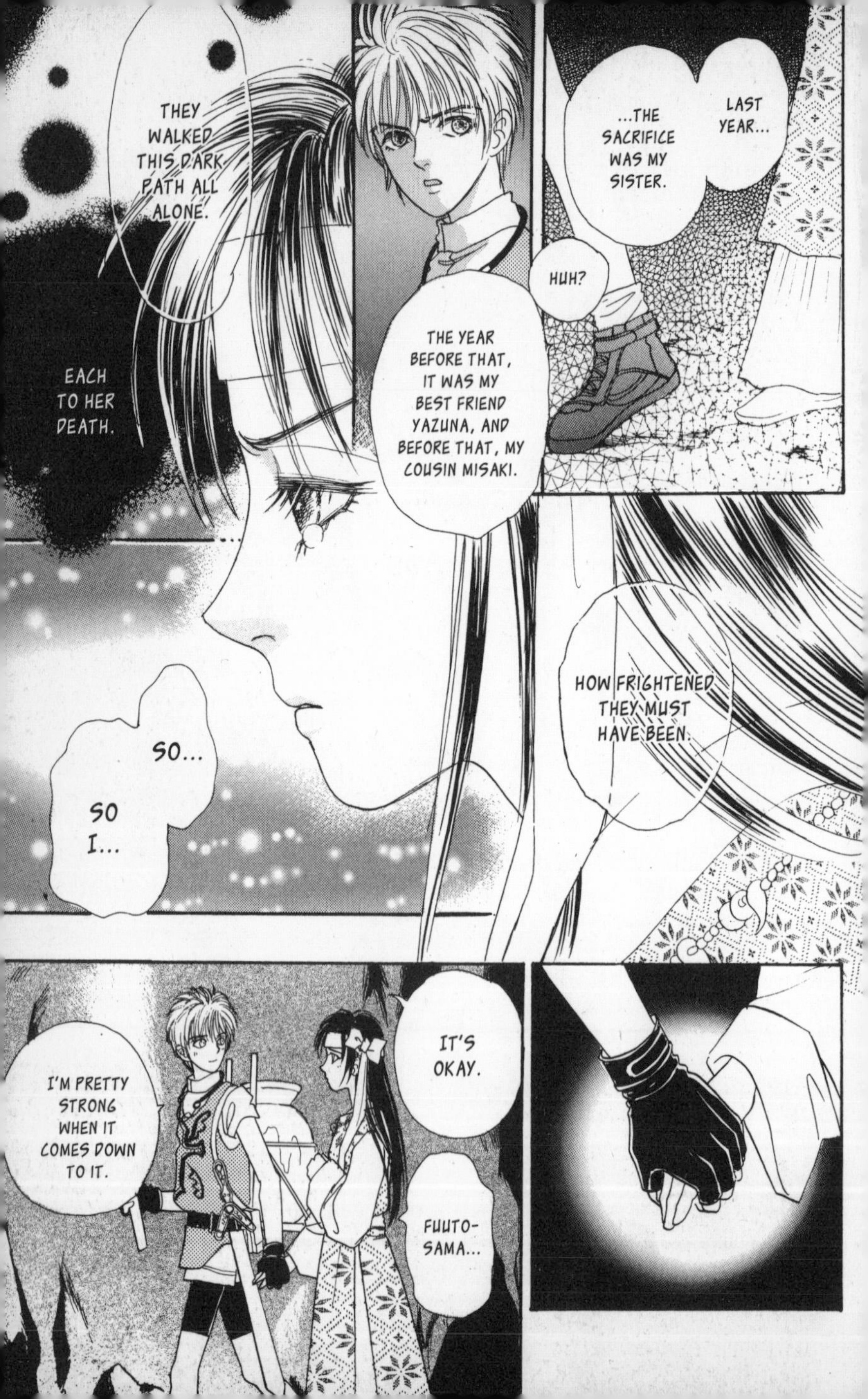
LAST YEAR...
...THE SACRIFICE WAS MY SISTER.
HUH?
THE YEAR BEFORE THAT, IT WAS MY BEST FRIEND YAZUNA, AND BEFORE THAT, MY COUSIN MISAKI.
THEY WALKED THIS DARK PATH ALL ALONE.
EACH TO HER DEATH.
HOW FRIGHTENED THEY MUST HAVE BEEN.
SO...
SO I...
IT'S OKAY.
FUUTO-SAMA...
I'M PRETTY STRONG WHEN IT COMES DOWN TO IT.

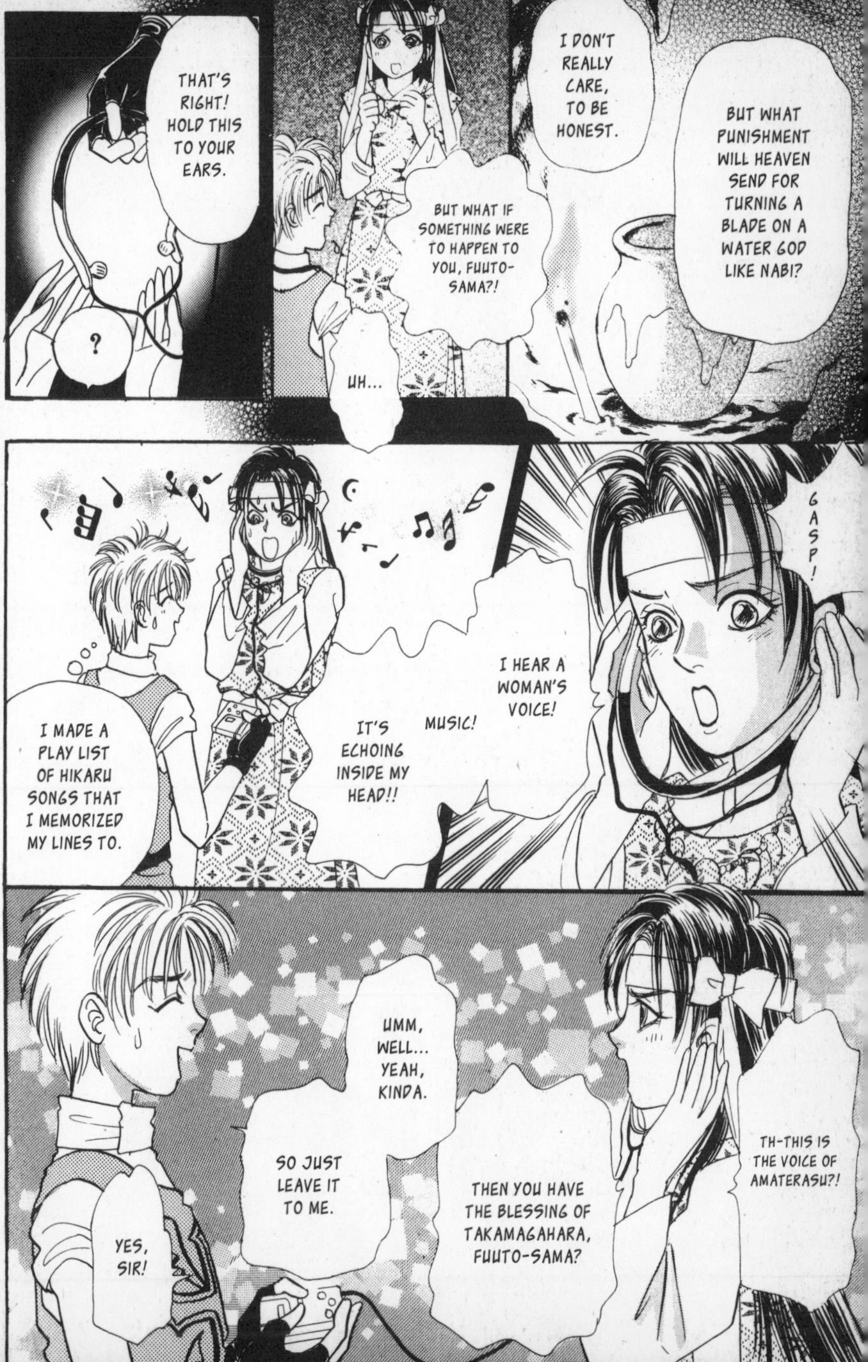
BUT WHAT PUNISHMENT WILL HEAVEN SEND FOR TURNING A BLADE ON A WATER GOD LIKE NABI?
I DON'T REALLY CARE, TO BE HONEST.
BUT WHAT IF SOMETHING WERE TO HAPPEN TO YOU, FUUTO-SAMA?!
UH...
THAT'S RIGHT! HOLD THIS TO YOUR EARS.
?
GASP!
I HEAR A WOMAN'S VOICE!
MUSIC!
IT'S ECHOING INSIDE MY HEAD!!
I MADE A PLAY LIST OF HIKARU SONGS THAT I MEMORIZED MY LINES TO.
TH-THIS IS THE VOICE OF AMATERASU?!
THEN YOU HAVE THE BLESSING OF TAKAMAGAHARA, FUUTO-SAMA?
UMM, WELL... YEAH, KINDA.
SO JUST LEAVE IT TO ME.
YES, SIR!

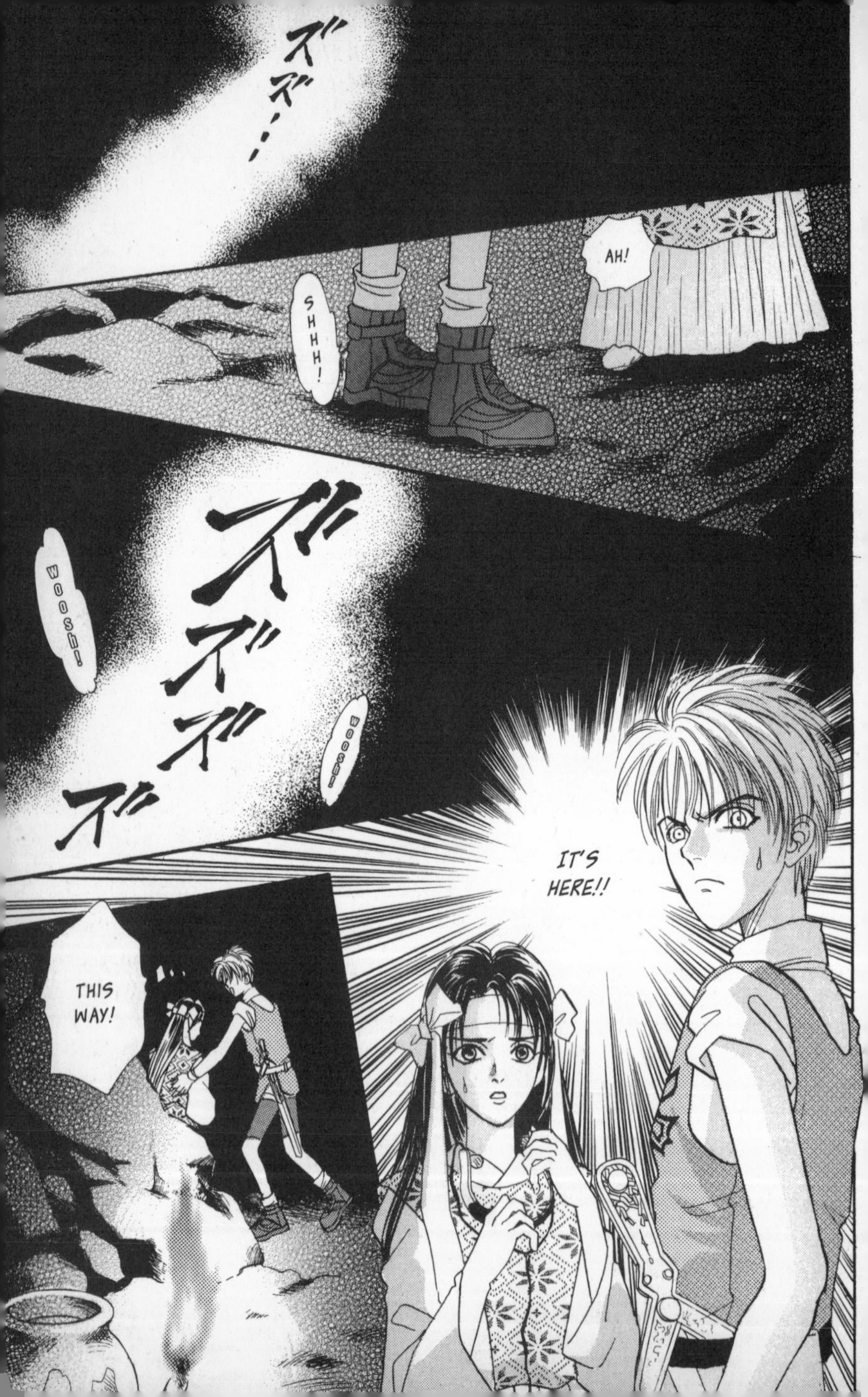
AH!
SHHH!
ズズ・・・
ズズズズ
WOOSH!
WOOSH!
IT'S HERE!!
THIS WAY!

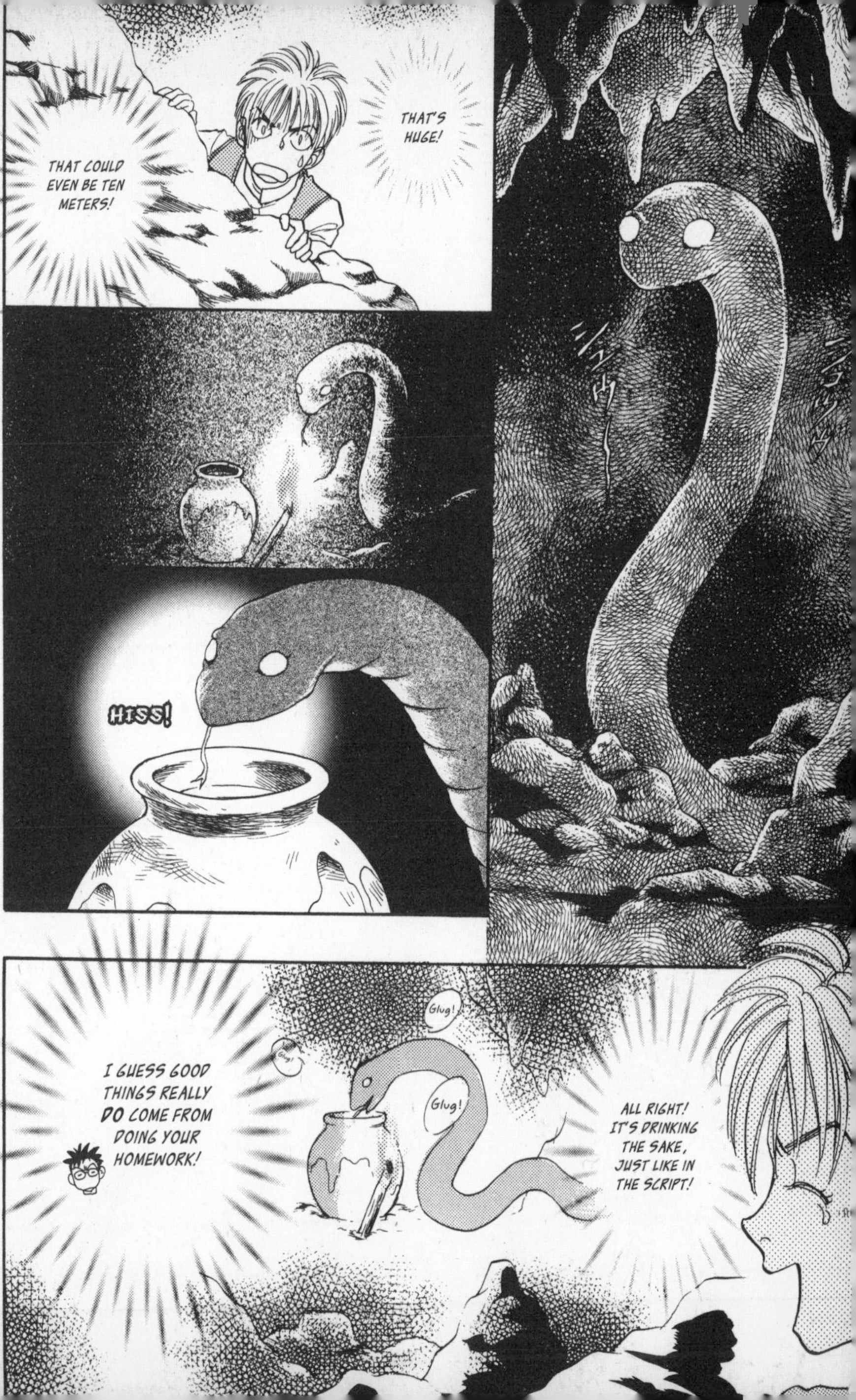
THAT'S HUGE!
THAT COULD EVEN BE TEN METERS!
HISS!
ALL RIGHT! IT'S DRINKING THE SAKE, JUST LIKE IN THE SCRIPT!
Glug!
Glug!
Glug!
I GUESS GOOD THINGS REALLY DO COME FROM DOING YOUR HOMEWORK!

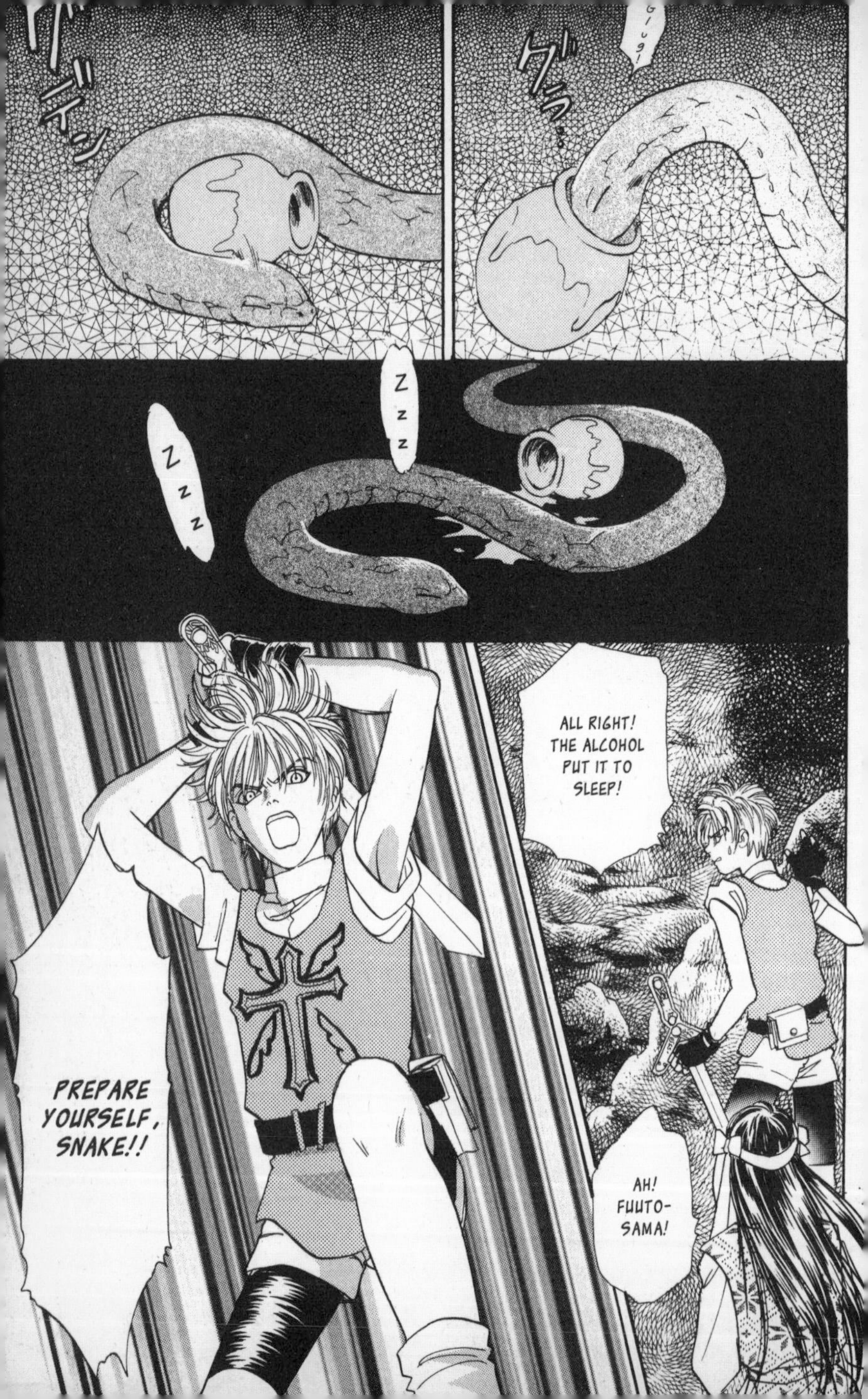

Glug!
Z z z
Z z z
ALL RIGHT! THE ALCOHOL PUT IT TO SLEEP!
AH! FUUTO-SAMA!
PREPARE YOURSELF, SNAKE!!

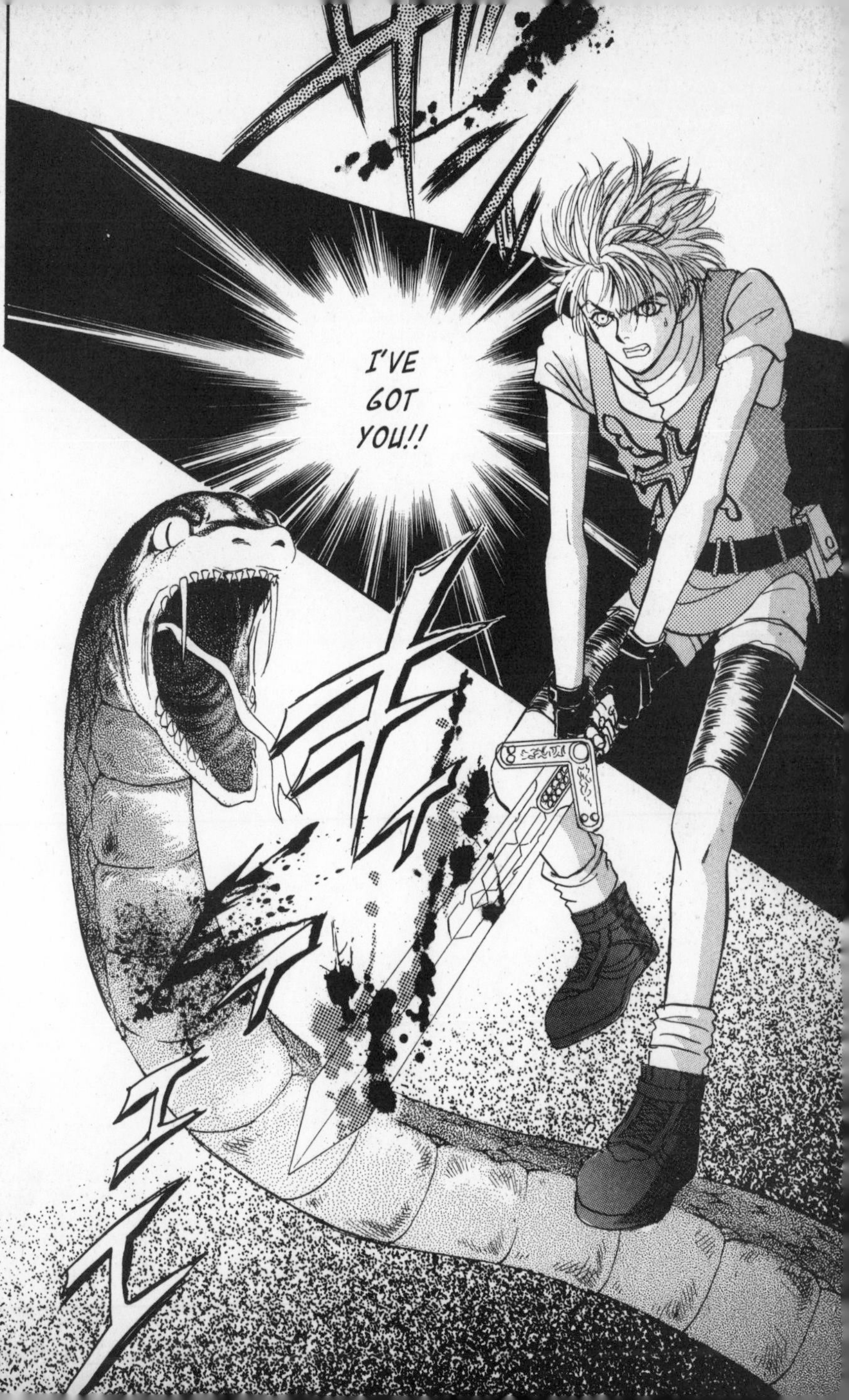
I'VE GOT YOU!!

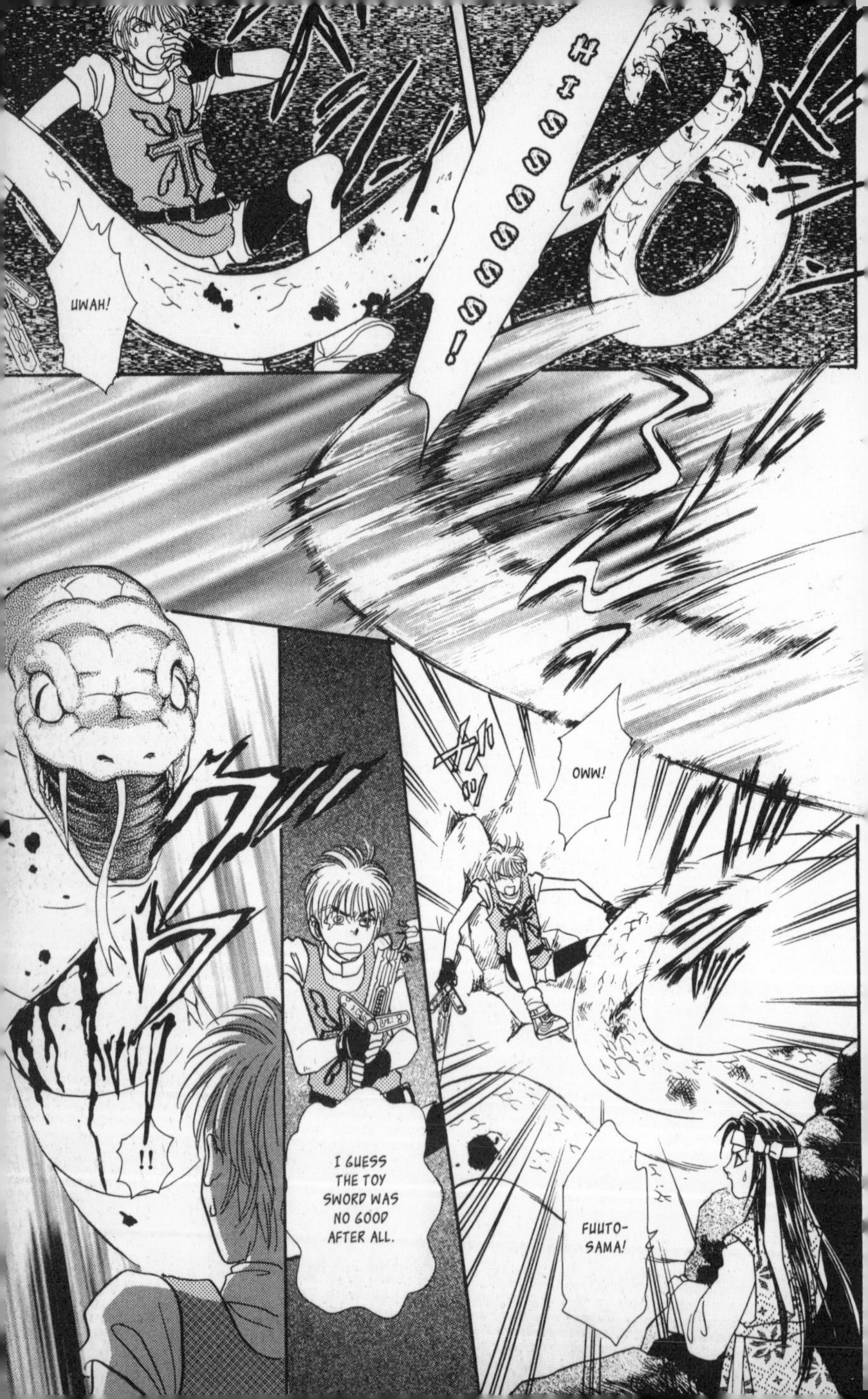
HISSSSSSSSS!
UWAH!
OWW!
FUUTO-SAMA!
I GUESS THE TOY SWORD WAS NO GOOD AFTER ALL.
!!

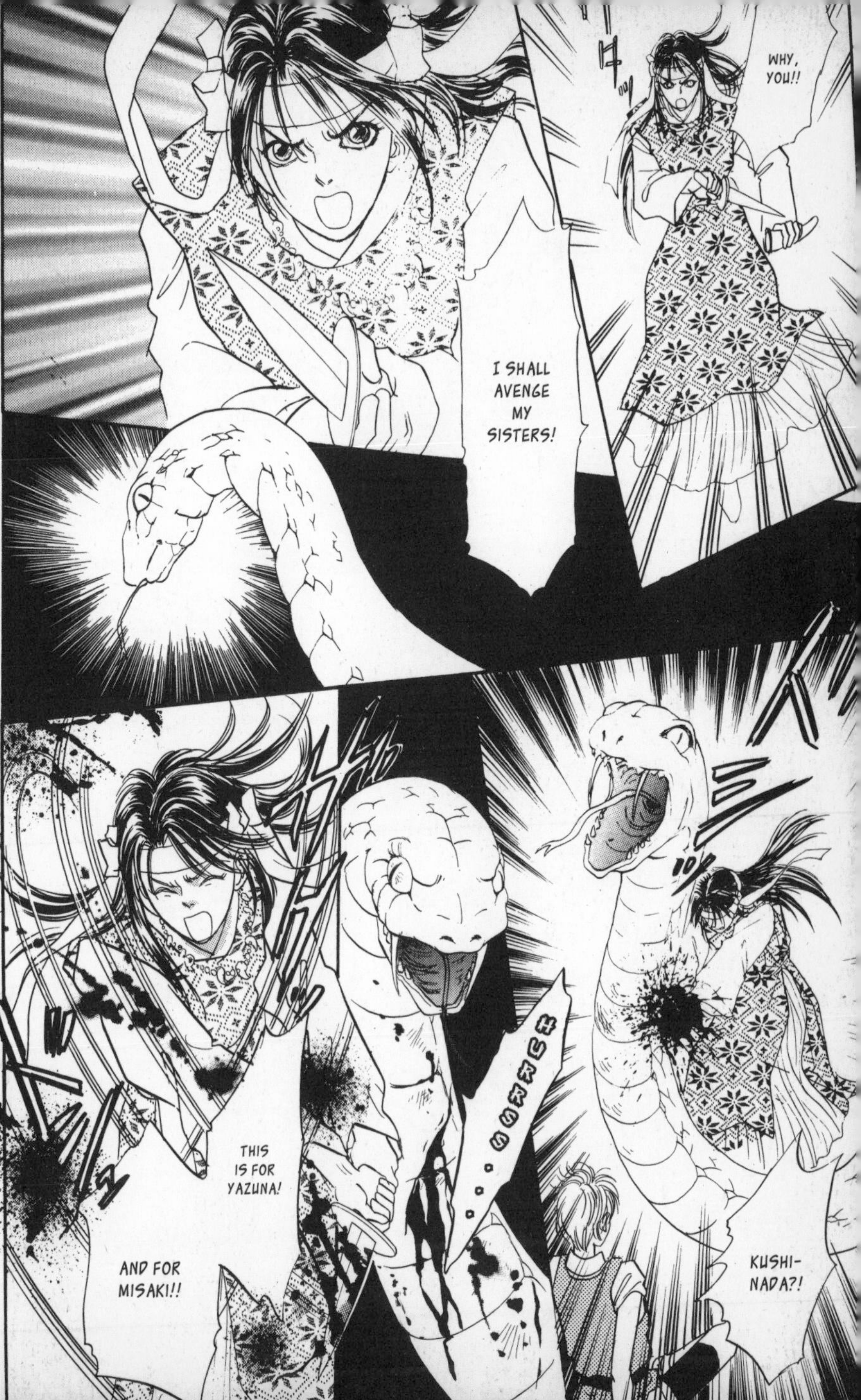
WHY, YOU!!
I SHALL AVENGE MY SISTERS!
KUSHI-NADA?!
SHRRGH
THIS IS FOR YAZUNA!
AND FOR MISAKI!!

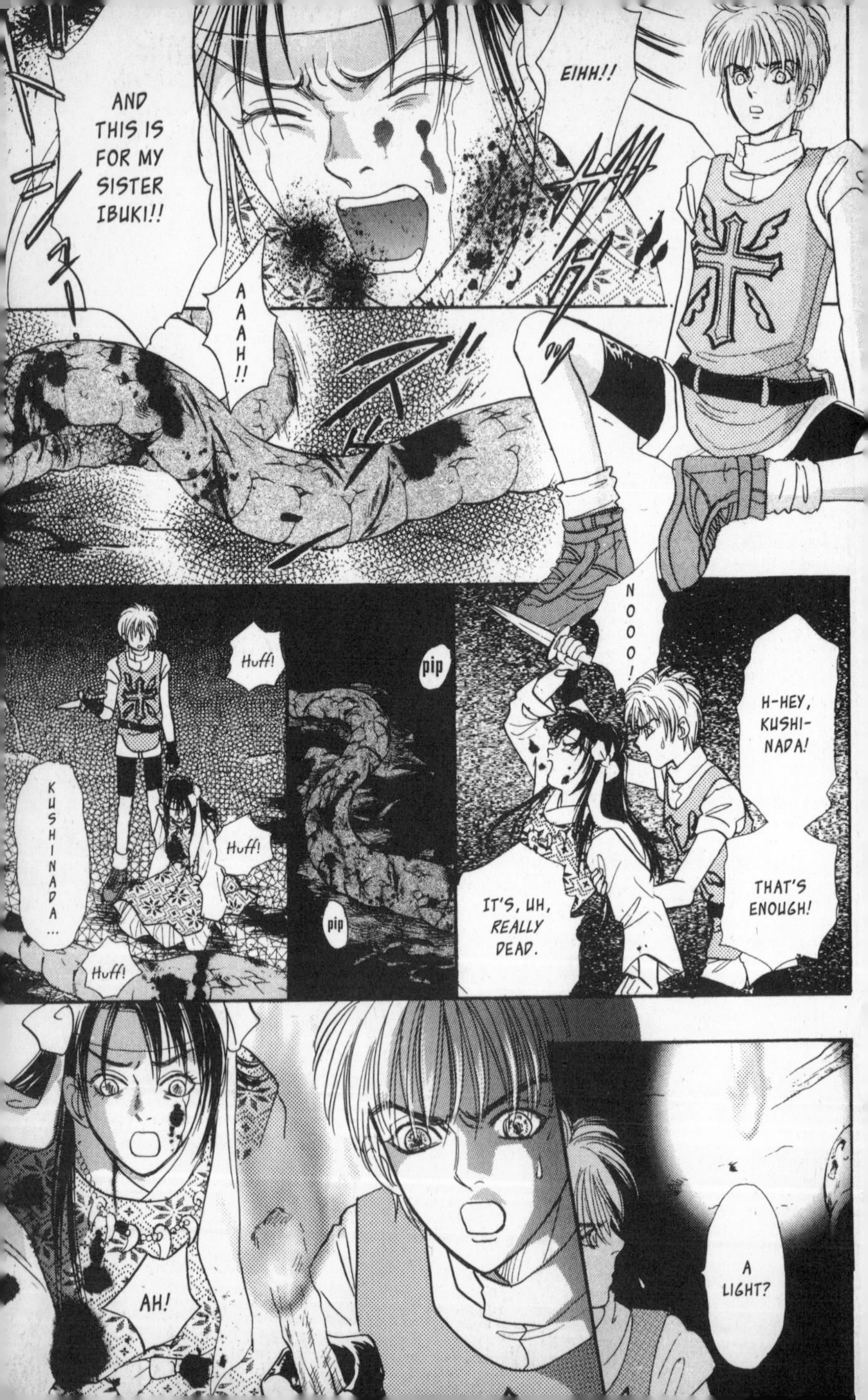
EIHH!!
AND THIS IS FOR MY SISTER IBUKI!!
AAAAH!!
NOOOO!
H-HEY, KUSHINADA!
THAT'S ENOUGH!
IT'S, UH, REALLY DEAD.
pip
pip
Huff!
Huff!
Huff!
KUSHINADA...
A LIGHT?
AH!

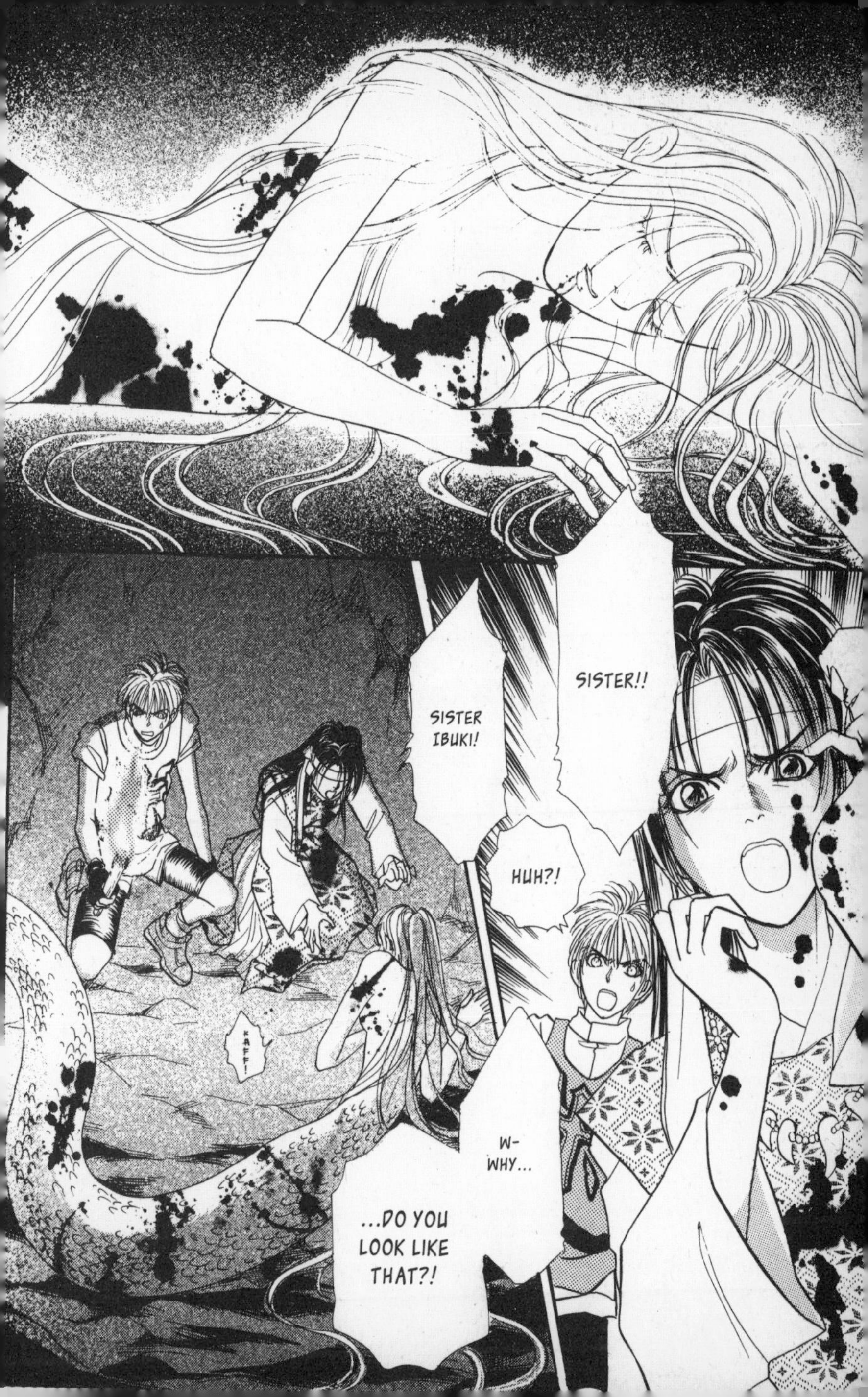
SISTER!!
SISTER IBUKI!
HUH?!
KAFF!
W- WHY...
...DO YOU LOOK LIKE THAT?!

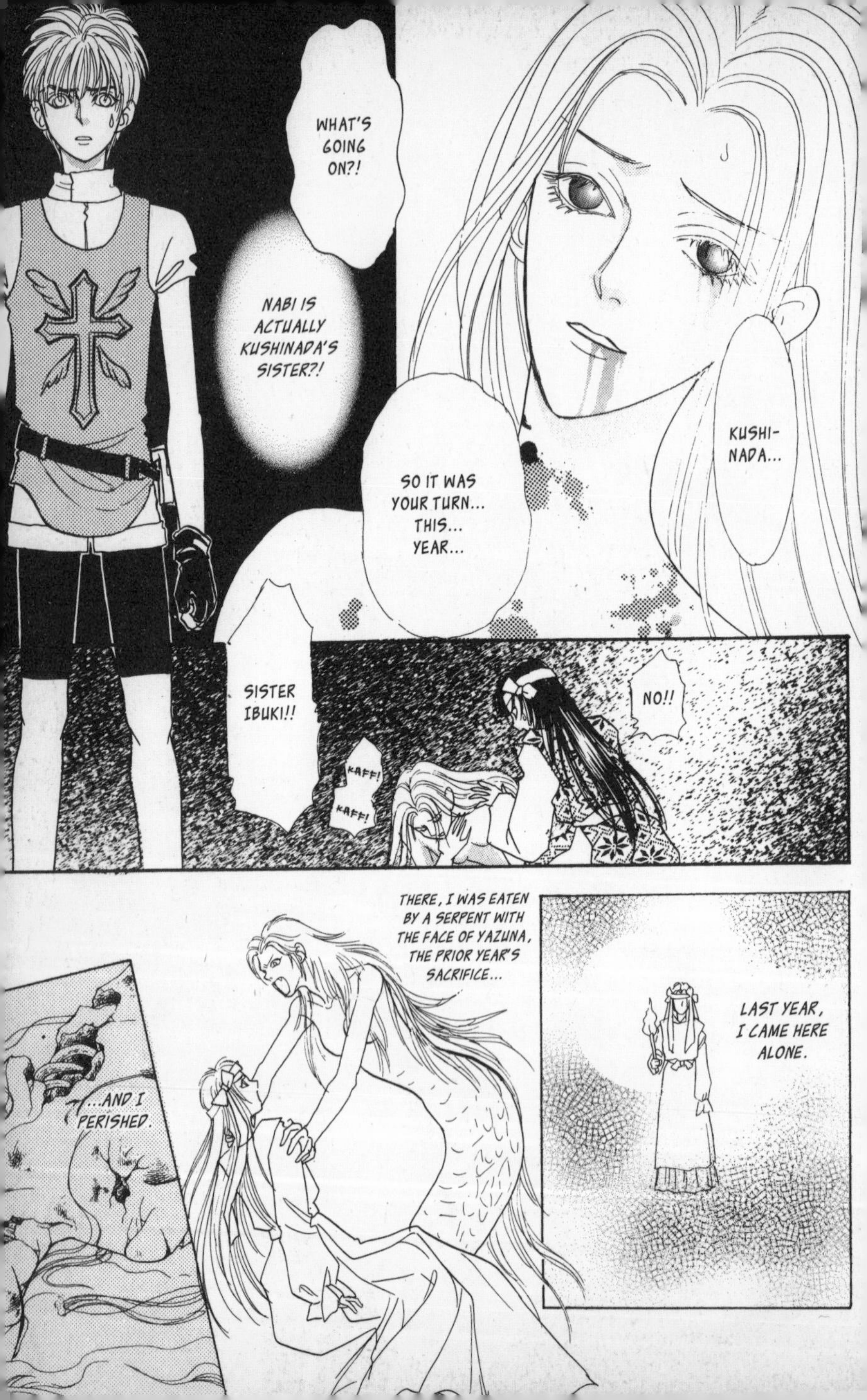
KUSHI-
NADA...
SO IT WAS
YOUR TURN...
THIS...
YEAR...
WHAT'S
GOING
ON?!
NABI IS
ACTUALLY
KUSHINADA'S
SISTER?!
NO!!
KAFF!
KAFF!
SISTER
IBUKI!!
LAST YEAR,
I CAME HERE
ALONE.
THERE, I WAS EATEN
BY A SERPENT WITH
THE FACE OF YAZUNA,
THE PRIOR YEAR'S
SACRIFICE...
...AND I
PERISHED.

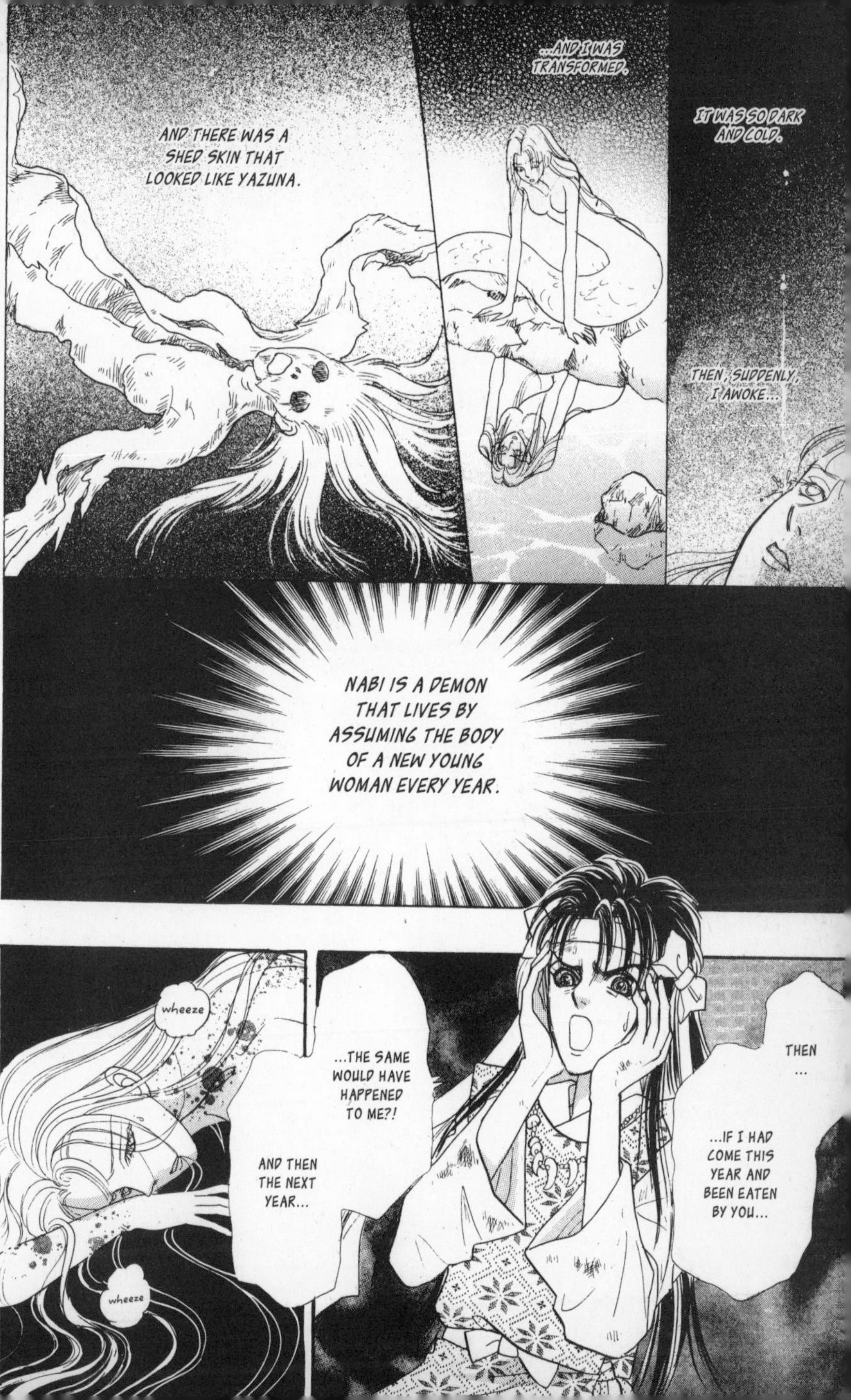
...AND I WAS TRANSFORMED.
IT WAS SO DARK AND COLD.
THEN, SUDDENLY, I AWOKE...
AND THERE WAS A SHED SKIN THAT LOOKED LIKE YAZUNA.
NABI IS A DEMON THAT LIVES BY ASSUMING THE BODY OF A NEW YOUNG WOMAN EVERY YEAR.
THEN ...
...IF I HAD COME THIS YEAR AND BEEN EATEN BY YOU...
...THE SAME WOULD HAVE HAPPENED TO ME?!
AND THEN THE NEXT YEAR...
wheeze
wheeze

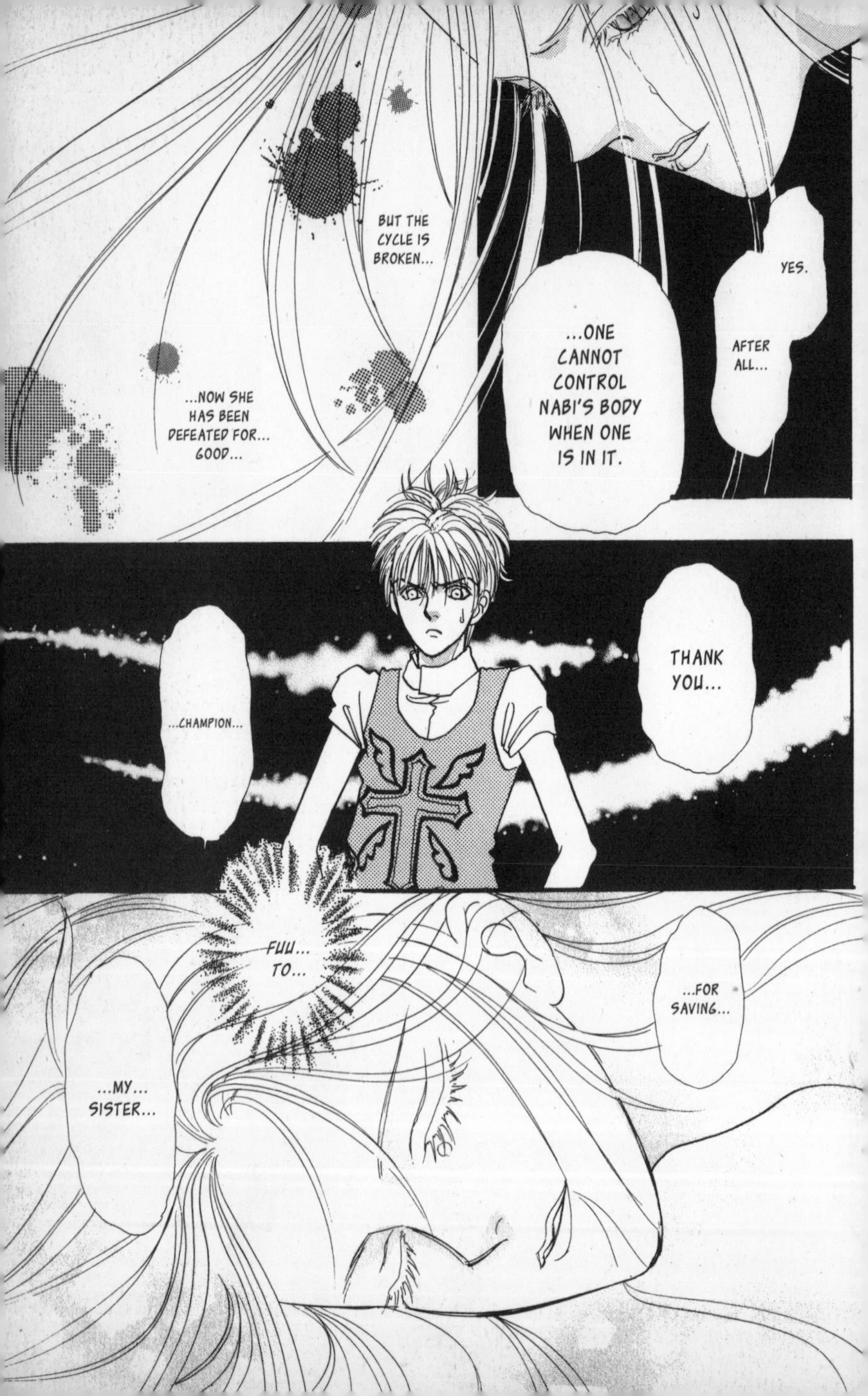
YES.
AFTER ALL...
...ONE CANNOT CONTROL NABI'S BODY WHEN ONE IS IN IT.
BUT THE CYCLE IS BROKEN...
...NOW SHE HAS BEEN DEFEATED FOR... GOOD...
THANK YOU...
...CHAMPION...
FUU... TO...
...FOR SAVING...
...MY... SISTER...

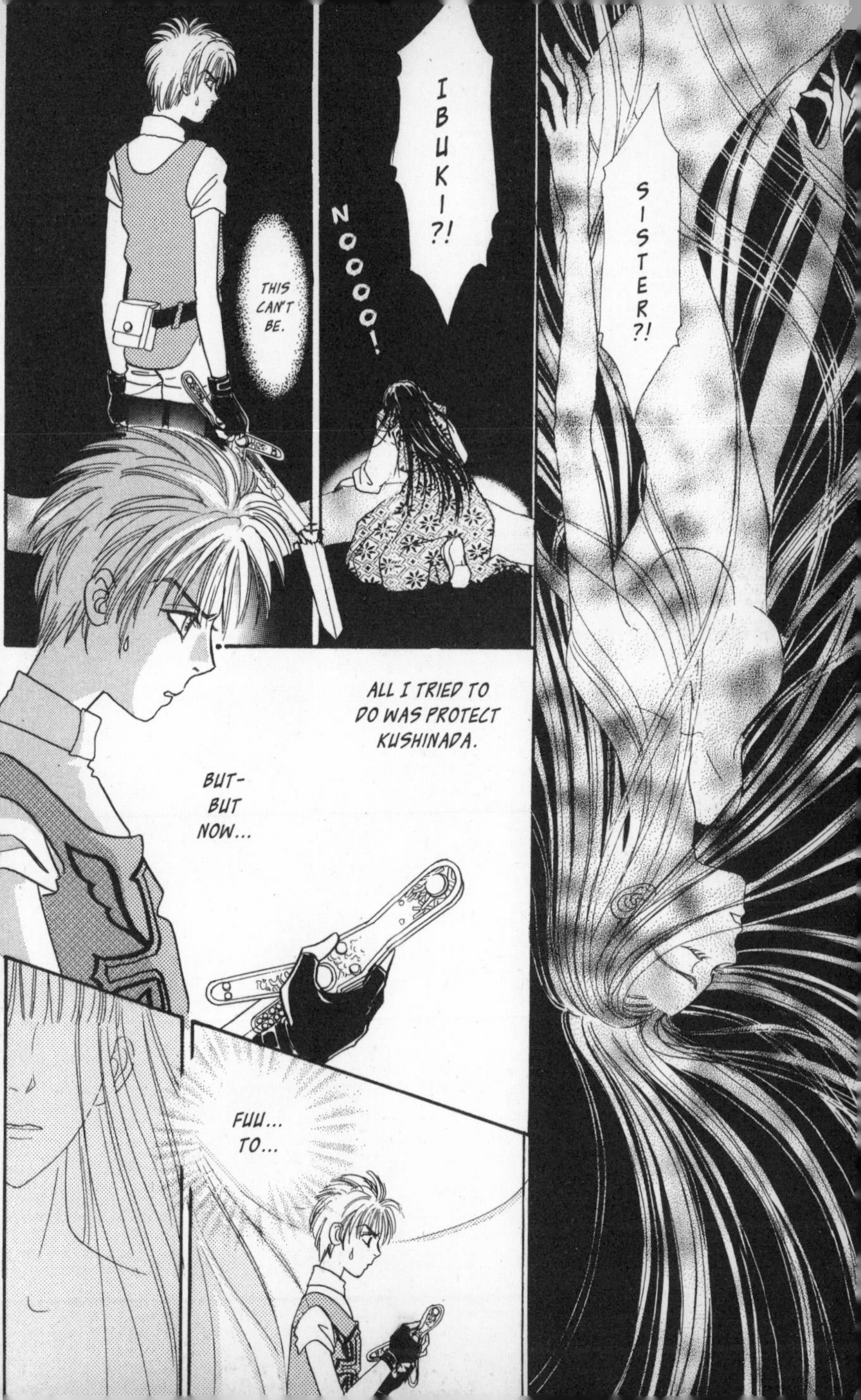
SISTER?!
IBUKI?!
NOOOOO!
THIS CAN'T BE.
ALL I TRIED TO DO WAS PROTECT KUSHINADA.
BUT- BUT NOW...
FUU... TO...

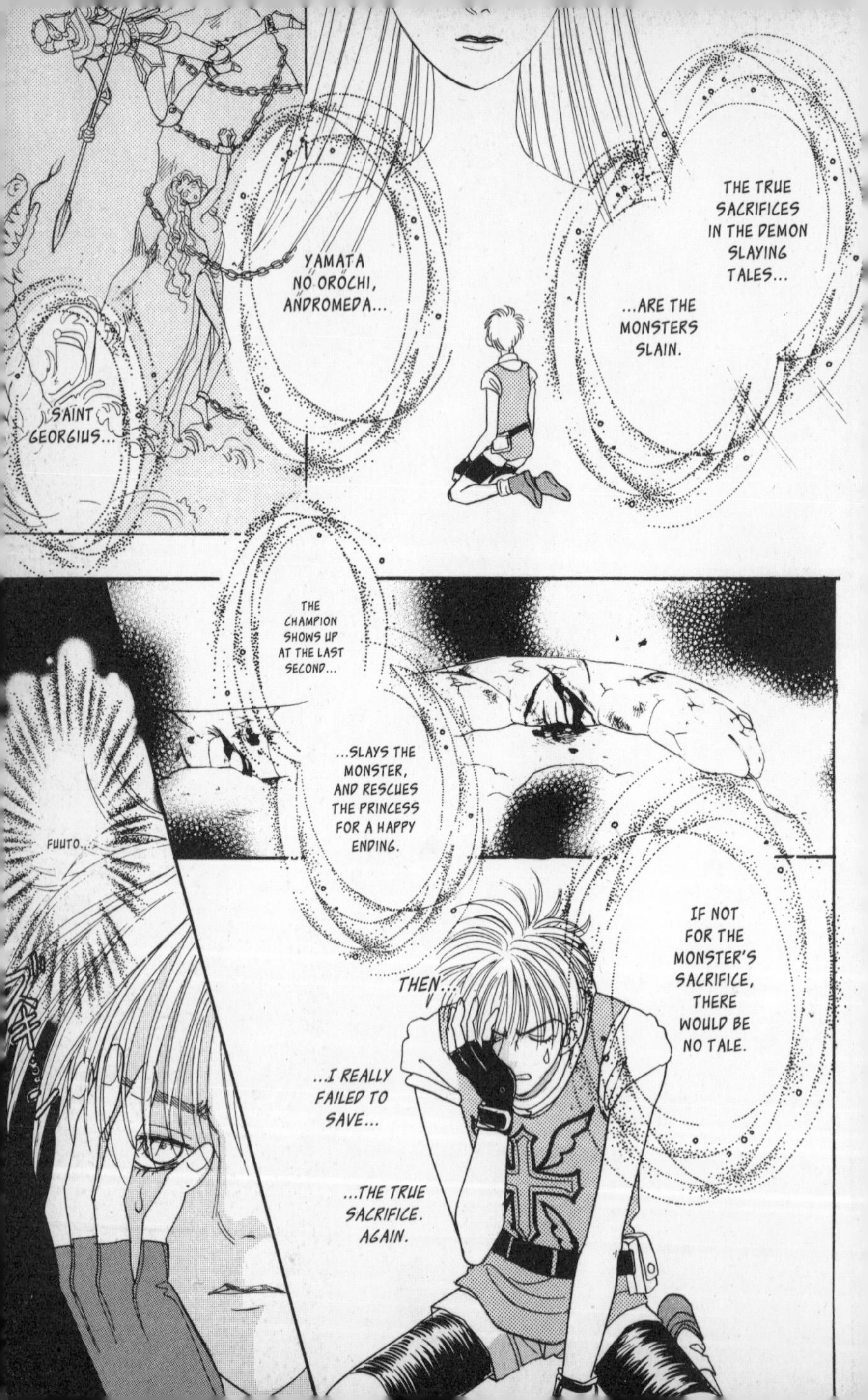
THE TRUE SACRIFICES IN THE DEMON SLAYING TALES...
...ARE THE MONSTERS SLAIN.
YAMATA NO OROCHI, ANDROMEDA...
SAINT GEORGIUS...
THE CHAMPION SHOWS UP AT THE LAST SECOND...
...SLAYS THE MONSTER, AND RESCUES THE PRINCESS FOR A HAPPY ENDING.
IF NOT FOR THE MONSTER'S SACRIFICE, THERE WOULD BE NO TALE.
THEN...
...I REALLY FAILED TO SAVE...
...THE TRUE SACRIFICE. AGAIN.
FUUTO...

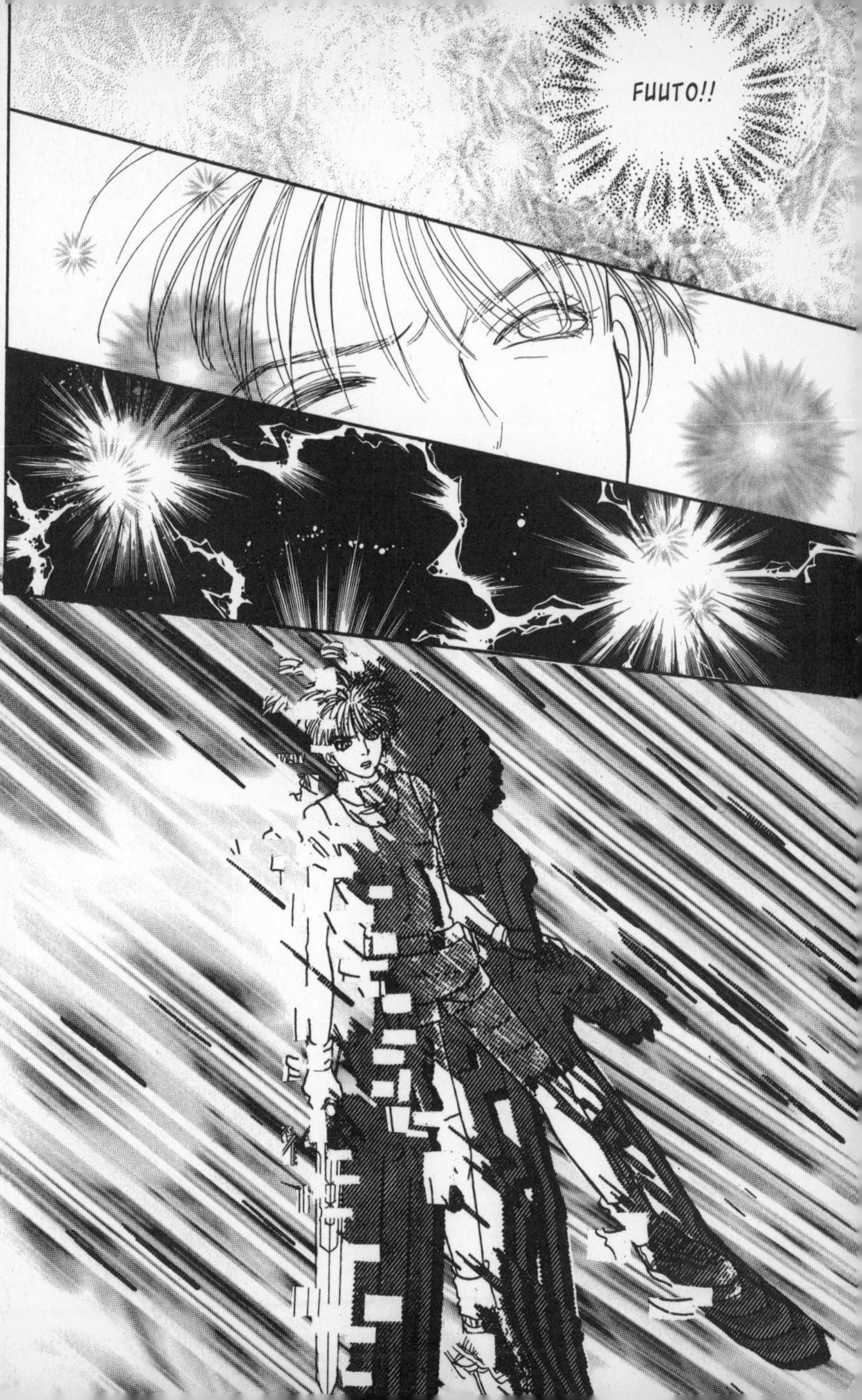
FUUTO!!

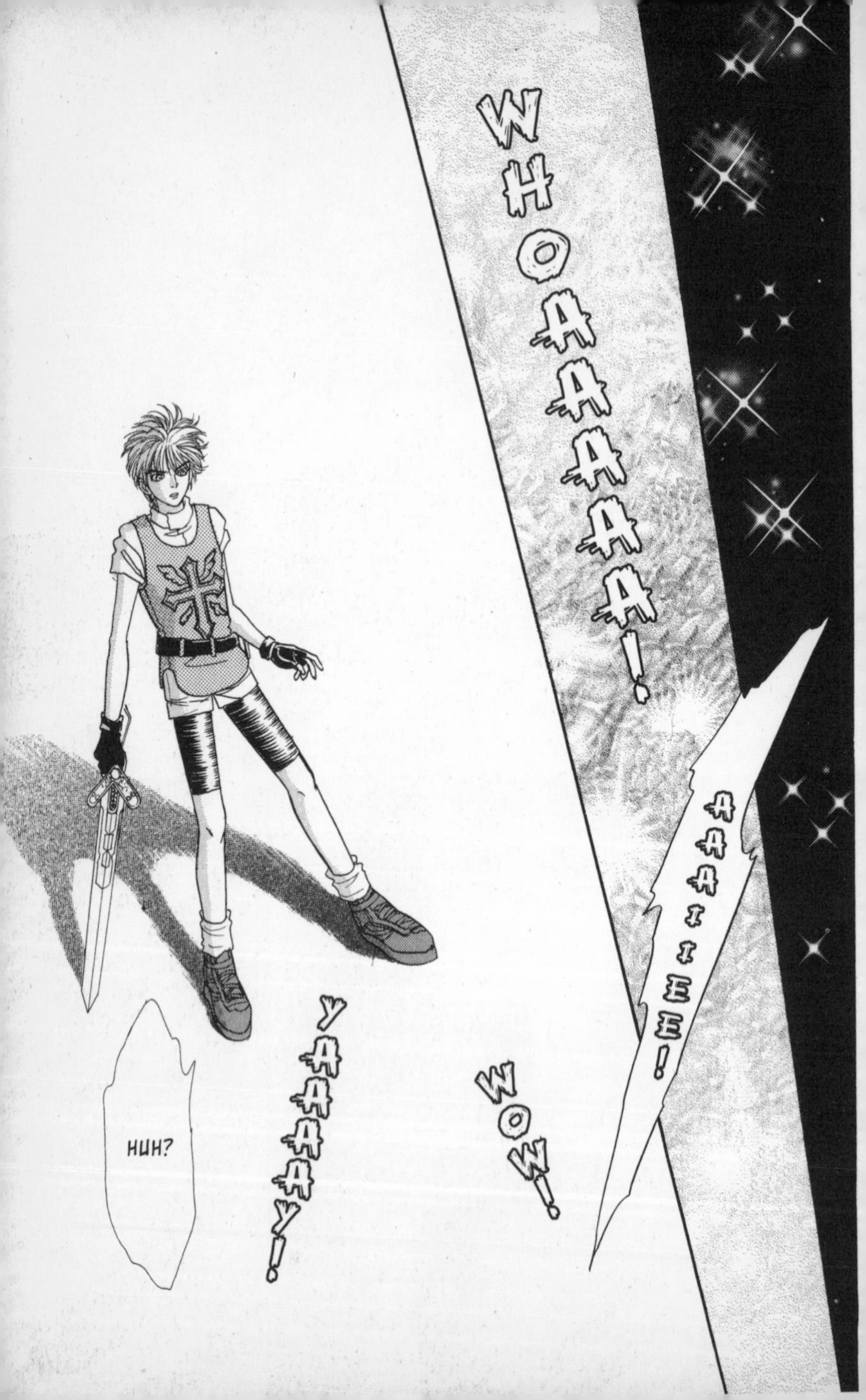

WHOAAAAA!
AAAIIEEE!
WOW!
YAAAAY!
HUH?

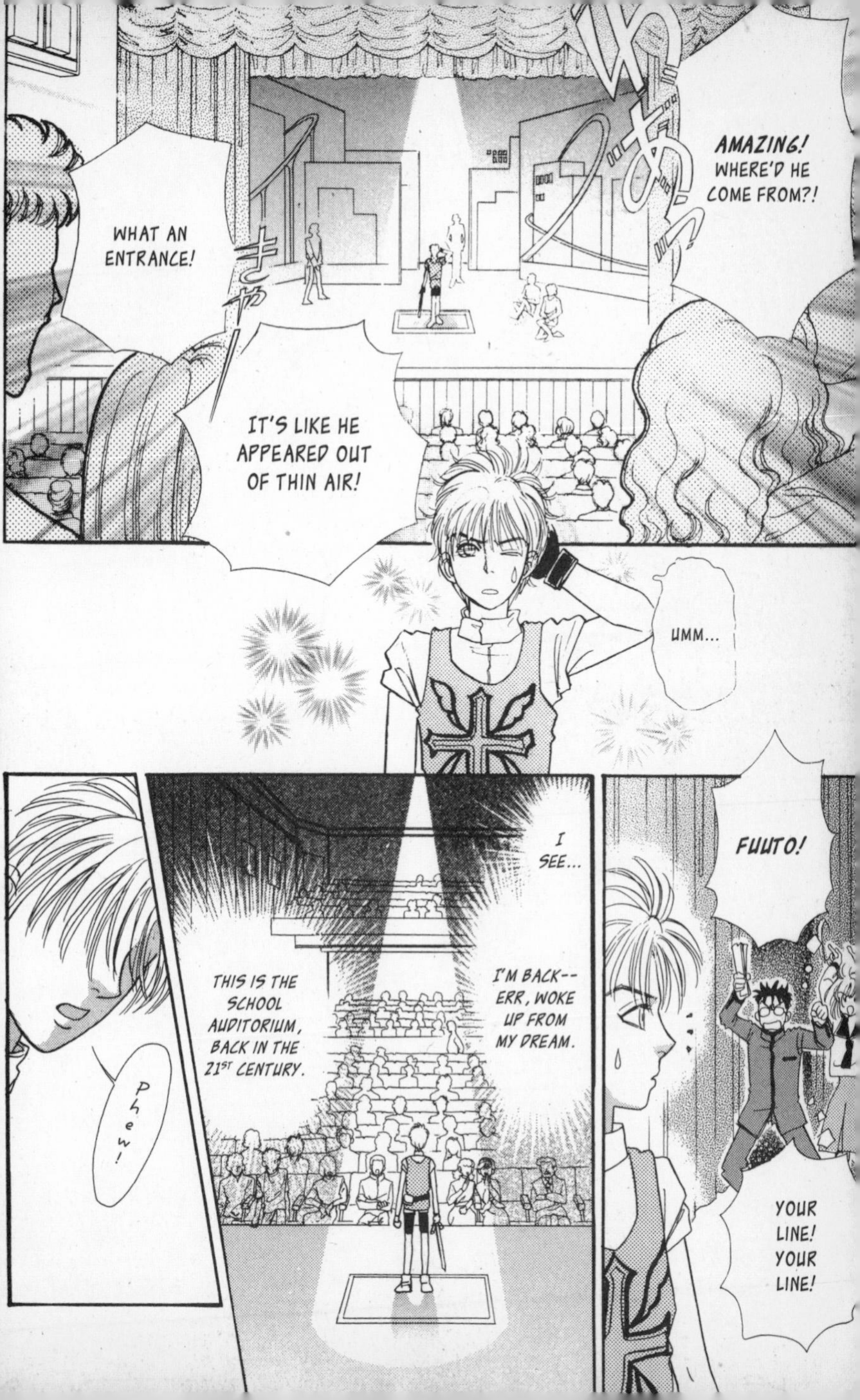
AMAZING! WHERE'D HE COME FROM?!
WHAT AN ENTRANCE!
IT'S LIKE HE APPEARED OUT OF THIN AIR!
UMM...
FUUTO!
YOUR LINE! YOUR LINE!
I SEE...
I'M BACK-- ERR, WOKE UP FROM MY DREAM.
THIS IS THE SCHOOL AUDITORIUM, BACK IN THE 21ST CENTURY.
Phew!

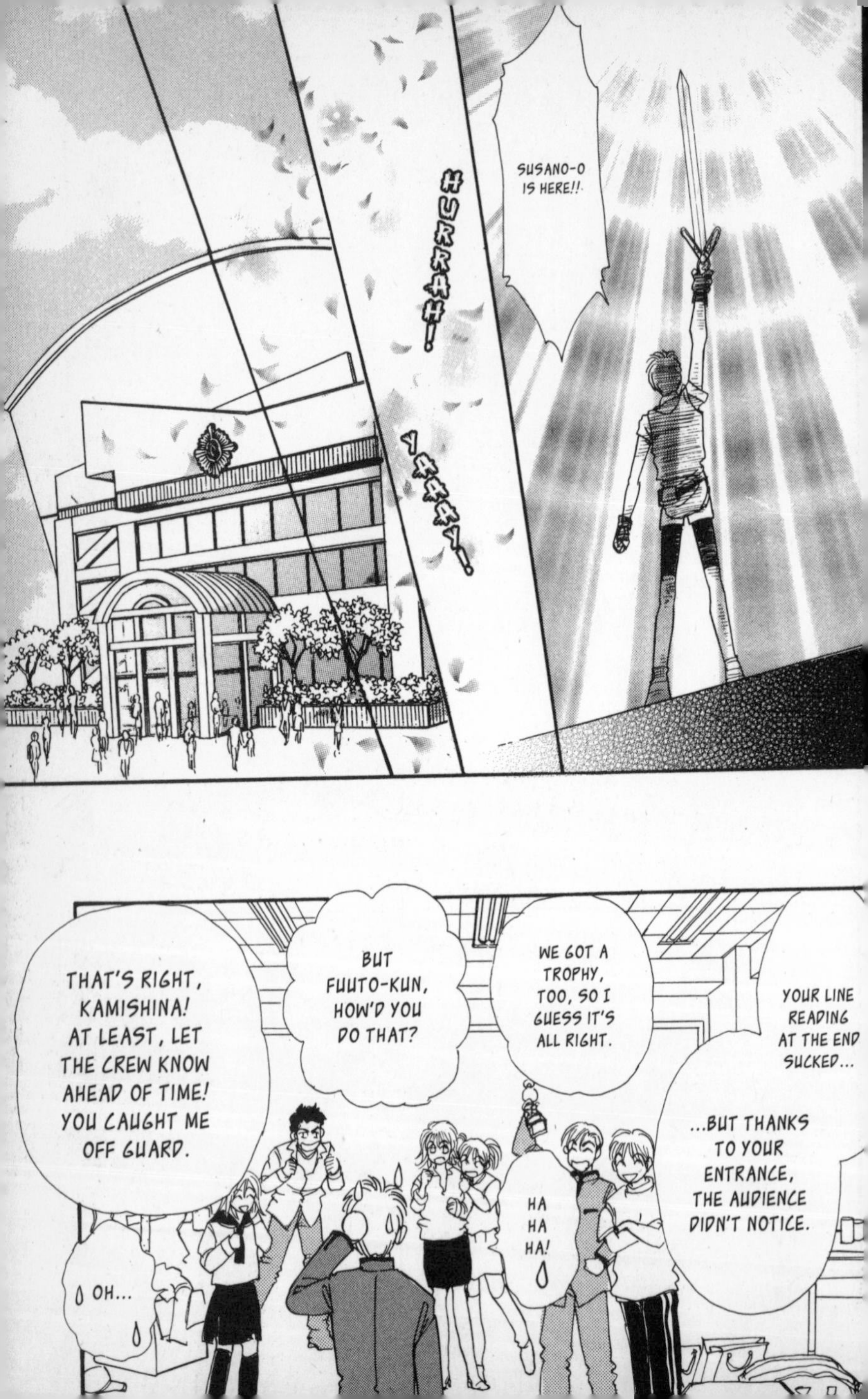
SUSANO-O IS HERE!!
HURRAH!
YAAAY!
YOUR LINE READING AT THE END SUCKED...
...BUT THANKS TO YOUR ENTRANCE, THE AUDIENCE DIDN'T NOTICE.
WE GOT A TROPHY, TOO, SO I GUESS IT'S ALL RIGHT.
HA HA HA!
BUT FUUTO-KUN, HOW'D YOU DO THAT?
THAT'S RIGHT, KAMISHINA! AT LEAST, LET THE CREW KNOW AHEAD OF TIME! YOU CAUGHT ME OFF GUARD.
OH...

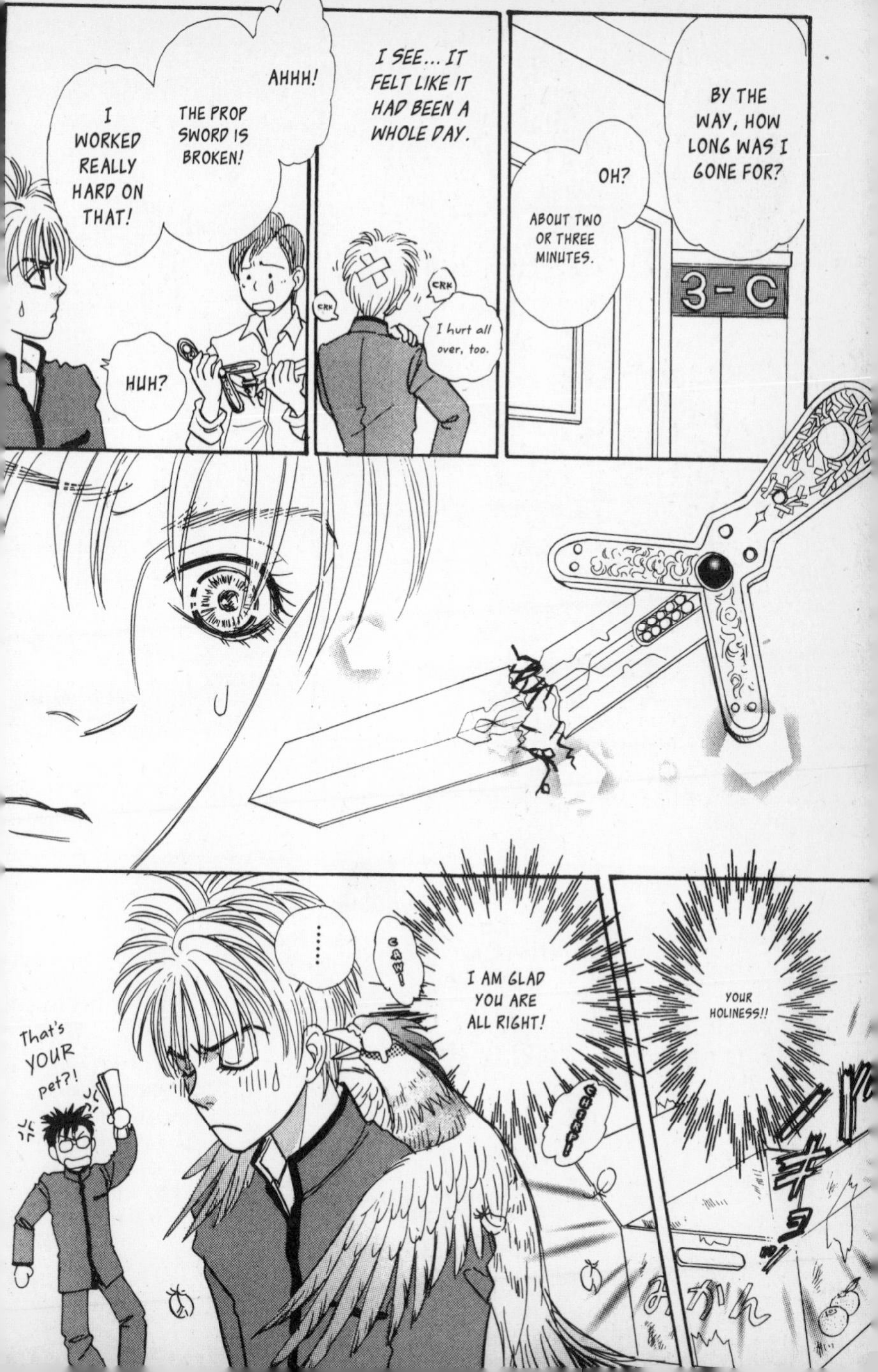

BY THE WAY, HOW LONG WAS I GONE FOR?
OH?
ABOUT TWO OR THREE MINUTES.
3-C
I SEE... IT FELT LIKE IT HAD BEEN A WHOLE DAY.
CRK
CRK
I hurt all over, too.
AHHH!
THE PROP SWORD IS BROKEN!
I WORKED REALLY HARD ON THAT!
HUH?
YOUR HOLINESS!!
みかん
I AM GLAD YOU ARE ALL RIGHT!
CAW!
......
That's YOUR pet?!

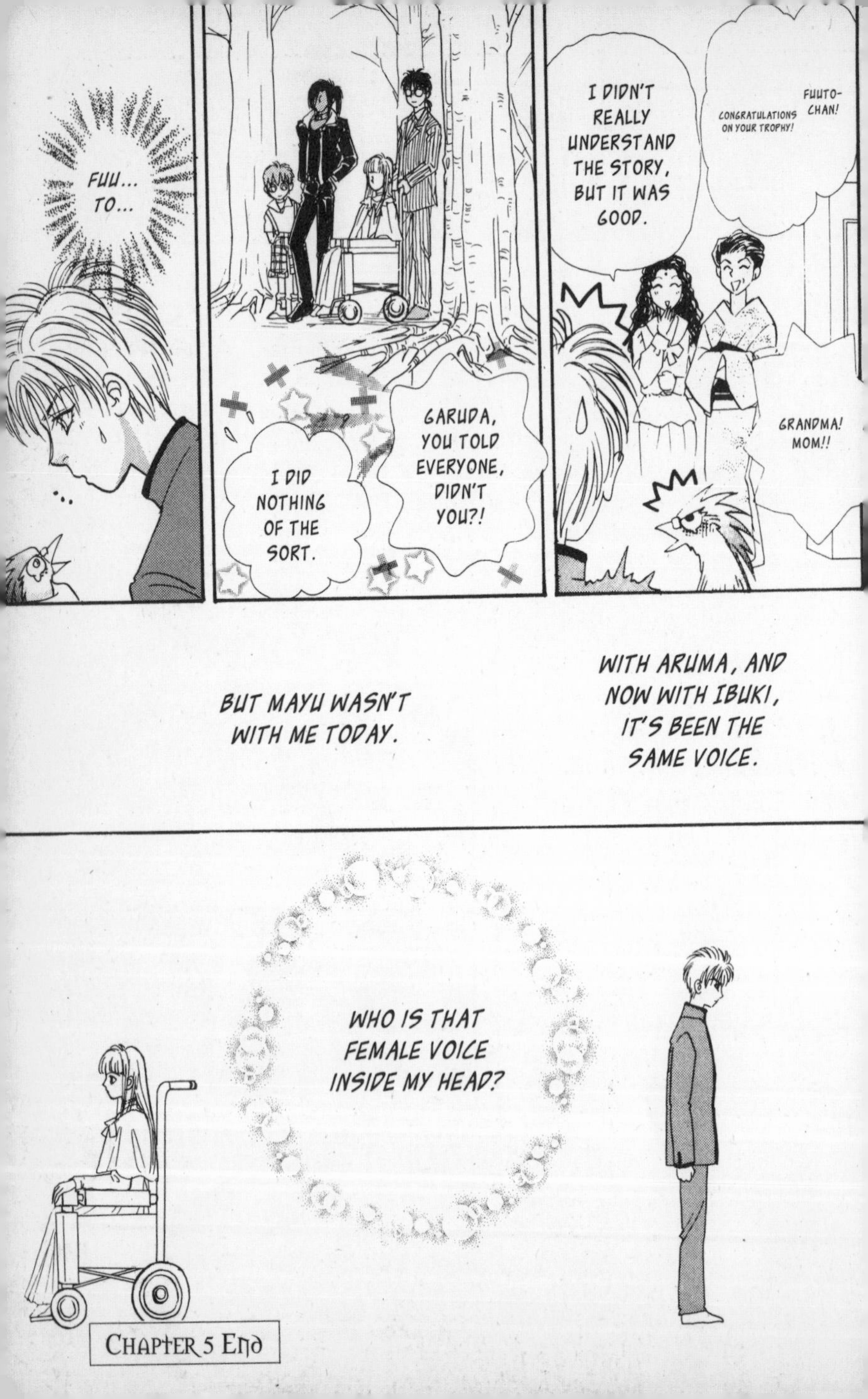
FUU... TO...
...
GARUDA, YOU TOLD EVERYONE, DIDN'T YOU?!
I DID NOTHING OF THE SORT.
I DIDN'T REALLY UNDERSTAND THE STORY, BUT IT WAS GOOD.
FUUTO-CHAN!
CONGRATULATIONS ON YOUR TROPHY!
GRANDMA! MOM!!
BUT MAYU WASN'T WITH ME TODAY.
WITH ARUMA, AND NOW WITH IBUKI, IT'S BEEN THE SAME VOICE.
WHO IS THAT FEMALE VOICE INSIDE MY HEAD?
Chapter 5 End

THE GENJU FILES #1

Extra #0: Kappa
A purely
Japanese beast

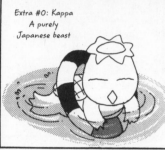

THANK YOU ALL FOR READING *GENJU NO SEIZA* VOLUME 3. GREETINGS TO ANY FIRST TIME READERS, AND WELCOME BACK TO THE REST. MY NAME IS MATSURI AKINO. NOT MARI. *MATSURI*. I'D LIKE TO INTRODUCE YOU TO THE CHARACTERS THAT HAVE APPEARED SO FAR.

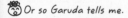

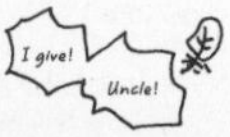

FUUTO KAMISHINA

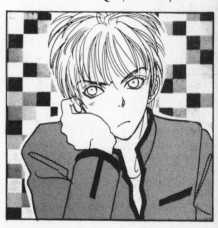

THE 42ND HOLY KING OF DHALASHAR (POSSIBLY). THIRD YEAR AT MEIO ACADEMY MIDDLE SCHOOL, AGE 15.
HEIGHT: ("I'M STILL GROWING!" HE CLAIMS.)
WEIGHT: 110 LBS. ("I'M STILL GETTING BIGGER!" HE PROTESTS.)

ON THE OUTSIDE, HE JUST LOOKS LIKE A REGULAR MIDDLE SCHOOLER, THOUGH GRUMPIER. HE'S A LITTLE BIT CHEEKY AT TIMES, BUT HE ALSO HAS A GOOD HEART. HE HAS NO CONCENTRATION AND NO MOTIVATION. HE'S EASILY BOTHERED AND GETS UPSET EASILY, TOO.

Or so Garuda tells me.

(Ga) Huh? What?! Hold on!

I give!
Uncle!

No. 1 GARUDA

鳥

A BEAST FROM ANCIENT INDIA'S RELIGIOUS TEXTS. IN THE WEST, HE'S KNOWN AS THE PHOENIX. BETWEEN A BIRD AND A BIRD-HEADED MAN, THERE ARE FIVE STAGES TO HIS APPEARANCE. HE IS A HARD WORKER AND ALWAYS DEPENDABLE.

FUUTO LIVES IN AN APARTMENT (TWO BEDROOMS, LIVING ROOM, KITCHEN, NO PETS ALLOWED) SO HIS "MOMOTARO TRIO" STAYS AT PROFESSOR ICHIJO'S ESTATE.

IN HUMAN FORM, HANUMAN AND GENRO ORIGINALLY WORE ANCIENT CHINESE MILITARY UNIFORMS, BUT THOSE STOOD OUT TOO MUCH, SO LATELY THEY'VE CHANGED INTO MORE MODERN CLOTHES.

No. 3 GENERAL GENRO

狼

HIS CHARACTER HAS ROOTS ALL OVER EURASIA. GENRO LOVES BATTLES AND WAR PLAY, AND HIS CANINE NATURE MAKES HIM LOYAL TO HIS MASTER.

No. 2 HANUMAN

猿

ANOTHER BEAST FROM ANCIENT INDIAN TEXTS. YOU COULD SAY HE'S THE MODEL FOR SUN WU'KONG, OR SON GOKU FROM *SAIYUKI*. THERE'S RUMORS THAT HE IS SMALLER NOW THAN WHEN HE WAS FIRST INTRODUCED, BUT DON'T PAY ANY ATTENTION TO THEM.

DHALASHAR IS A MYSTERIOUS KINGDOM RULED FOR GENERATIONS BY REINCARNATIONS OF ITS HOLY KING. THE DHALASHAR PALACE IN THE MIDDLE OF THE CENTRAL ASIAN DESERT STILL HOLDS MANY MORE GUARDIAN BEASTS. PERHAPS THE SOHKI (KIRIN) WE SAW THIS TIME AND OTHERS WILL APPEAR AGAIN...

No. 4 Naga

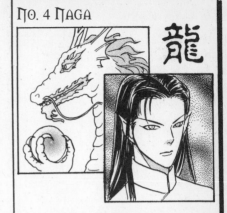

龍

A WATER BEAST IN LEGENDS FROM ALL THROUGHOUT THE WORLD. HIS DRAGON CLAN SEEMS TO BE AT ODDS WITH GARUDA'S BIRD CLAN.

No. 5 Yamantaka

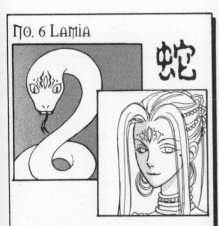

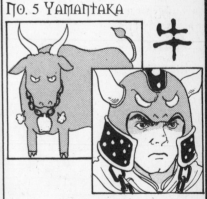

牛

THE STRONGEST MYTHICAL BEAST IN TIBETAN TRADITIONS. HE IS REGARDED AS A GOD OF DEATH WHO RULES OVER THE AFTERWORLD. IN JAPAN, HE IS THE SAME AS KING ENMA. DID YOU KNOW THAT?

No. 6 Lamia

蛇

A SNAKE-BEAST UNDER NAGA. IN ANCIENT GREECE AND THE ORIENT, SHE WAS FEARED AS A SUCCUBUS, AND IS VERY CLEVER AND TENACIOUS.

Mayu

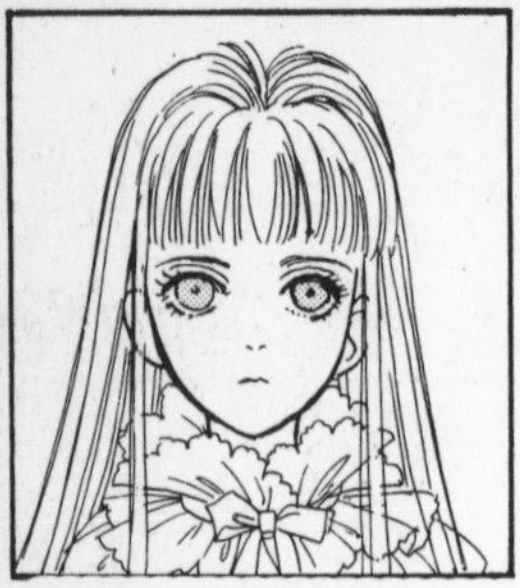

AGE: 14 (?)
HEIGHT: ?
WEIGHT: ?
BUST: ?
WAIST: ?
HIPS: ?

A MYSTERIOUS GENIUS WHO LIVES AT THE ICHIJO ESTATE. SHE DOES HAVE SOMEWHAT OF A SIXTH SENSE AND USES IT TO HELP FUUTO OUT. SHE LOOKS VERY GIRLY AND DOLL-LIKE, THOUGH HER PERSONALITY IS UNEMOTIONAL.

Kimihiko Ichijo

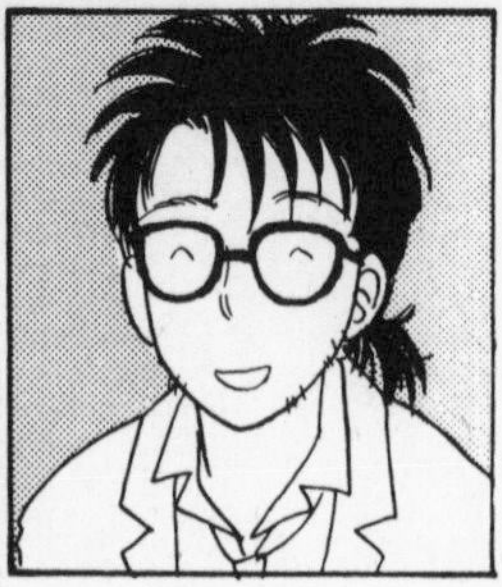

AGE: 32
HEIGHT: 5 FT 9 IN.
WEIGHT: 139 LBS.

GRADUATE OF MEIO ACADEMY, AND A MULTI-FIELD SCHOLAR FROM AN ANCIENT KYOTO FAMILY. HE'S VERY INTERESTED IN THE SUPERNATURAL, EVEN THOUGH HE HAS NO SIXTH SENSE HIMSELF. FOR A WORLD-RENOWNED INDIVIDUAL, HE IS ACTUALLY VERY EASY-GOING. HE HAS NO FASHION SENSE.

Tserin (Fuuto's Mom)

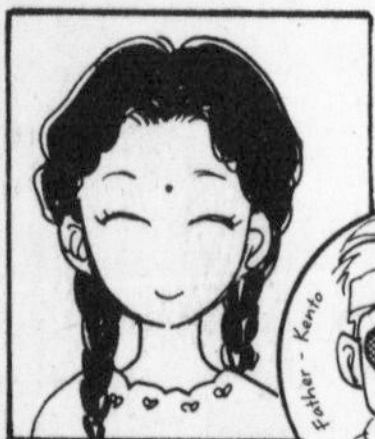

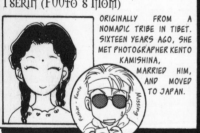

ORIGINALLY FROM A NOMADIC TRIBE IN TIBET. SIXTEEN YEARS AGO, SHE MET PHOTOGRAPHER KENTO KAMISHINA, MARRIED HIM, AND MOVED TO JAPAN.

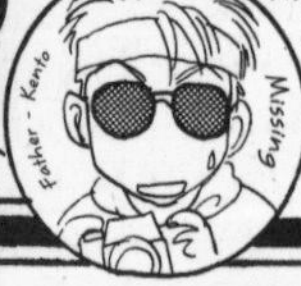
Father - Kento
Missing

Takako Kamishina

IT APPEARS THAT KENTO COMES FROM A YAKUZA FAMILY. FUUTO'S GRANDMOTHER TAKAKO IS THE GODMOTHER.

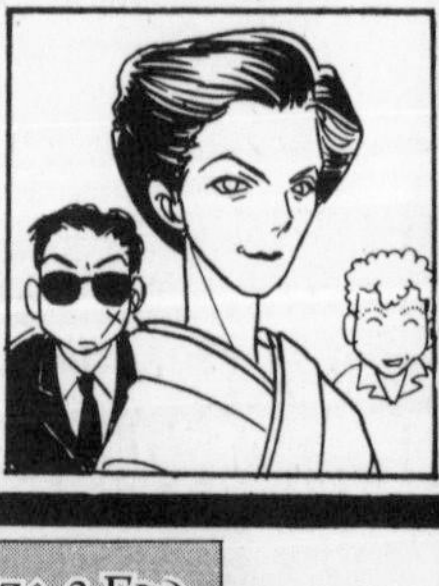

FUUTO LIVES IN A BEDROOM TOWN ON THE OUTSKIRTS OF TOKYO. HIS SCHOOL, MEIO ACADEMY, IS A PRIVATE SCHOOL WITH MIDDLE AND HIGH SCHOOL UNDER ONE ROOF. BUT IN THE HILLS NEARBY IS A MISMATCHED, LOVE HOTEL-LIKE EUROPEAN PALACE. THAT IS PROFESSOR ICHIJO'S ESTATE. WITHIN IT ARE EVEN MORE MYSTERIOUS ARTIFACTS AND PIECES OF ART. AND EVEN MORE MYSTERIOUS THAN THAT IS THE GIRL, MAYU, THAT LIVES THERE...

Genju no Seiza 3 End

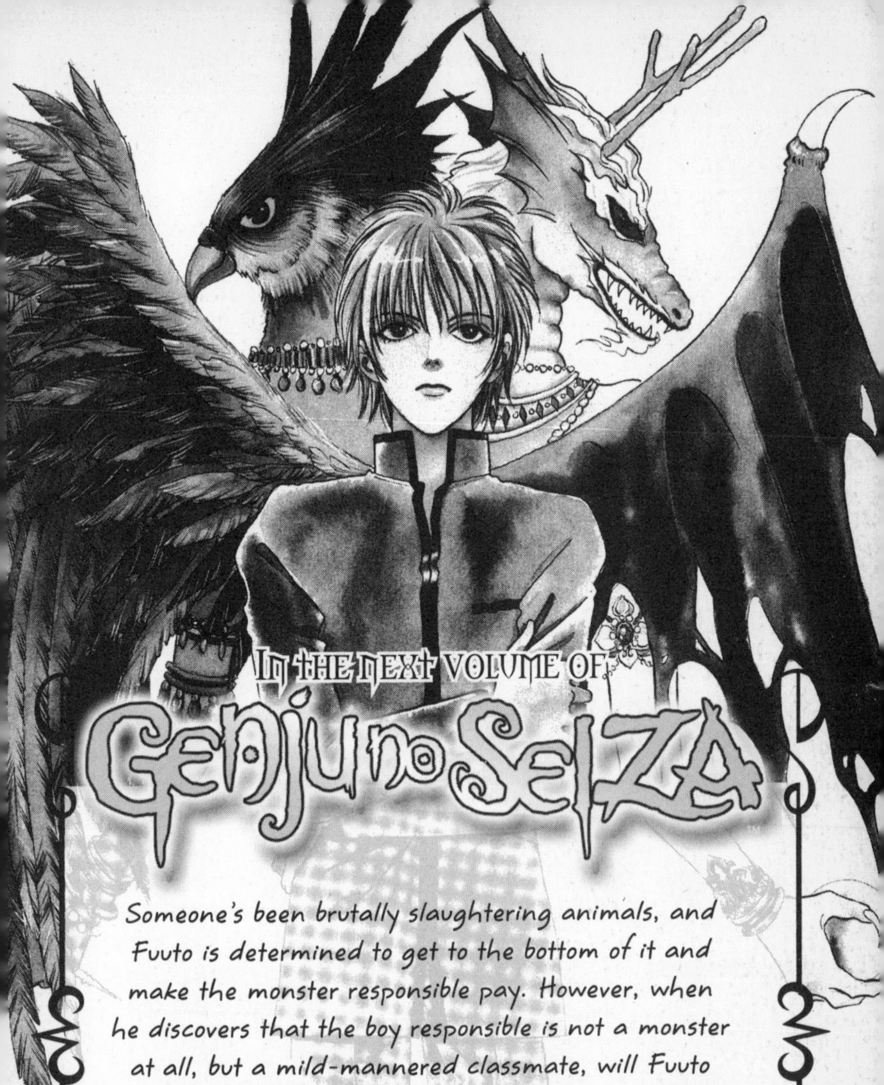

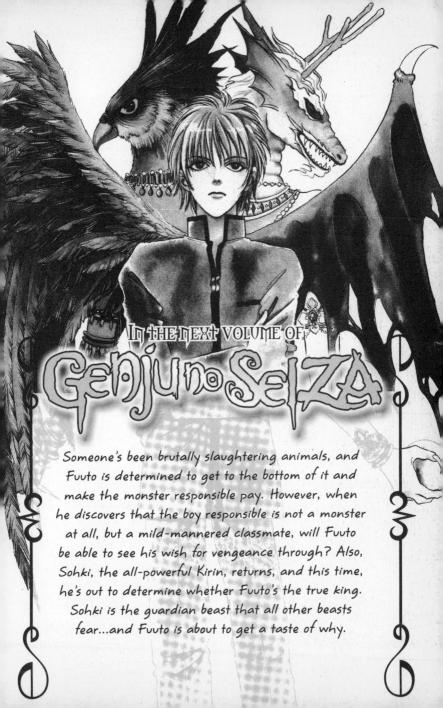

In the next volume of Genju no Seiza

Someone's been brutally slaughtering animals, and Fuuto is determined to get to the bottom of it and make the monster responsible pay. However, when he discovers that the boy responsible is not a monster at all, but a mild-mannered classmate, will Fuuto be able to see his wish for vengeance through? Also, Sohki, the all-powerful Kirin, returns, and this time, he's out to determine whether Fuuto's the true king. Sohki is the guardian beast that all other beasts fear...and Fuuto is about to get a taste of why.